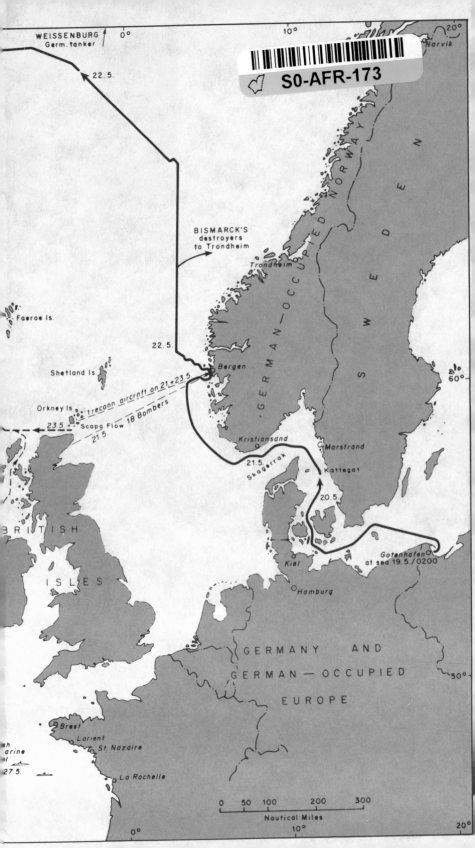

WEISSENBURG
Germ. tanker

0°

10°

20°

Narvik

22.5.

G E R M A N - O C C U P I E D   N O R W A Y

S W E D E N

BISMARCK'S
destroyers
to Trondheim

Trondheim

Faeroe Is.

22.5.

Bergen

60°

Shetland Is.

1 reconn. aircraft on 21.+23.5.

Orkney Is.

Scapa Flow 18 Bombers

23.5.

21.5.

Kristiansand

Marstrand

B R I T I S H

21.5.

Skagerrak

Kattegat

20.5.

I S L E S

Gotenhafen
at sea 19.5./0200

Kiel

Hamburg

G E R M A N Y   A N D

G E R M A N — O C C U P I E D

E U R O P E

50°

Brest

sh
arine
al

27.5.

Lorient   St. Nazaire

La Rochelle

0   50   100   200   300

Nautical Miles

0°

10°

20°

BATTLESHIP
BISMARCK

Jon Ethier

Kapitän zur See Ernst Lindemann

New and Expanded Edition

BATTLESHIP BISMARCK

A Survivor's Story

By Burkard Baron von Müllenheim-Rechberg

Translated by Jack Sweetman

NAVAL INSTITUTE PRESS   ANNAPOLIS, MARYLAND

This book was originally published in German by Verlag Ullstein.
The English translation of the first edition was published
in 1980 by the Naval Institute Press. This 1990
edition is a translation of a new and
expanded edition first published in German
in 1987 by Verlag Ullstein.

Library of Congress Cataloging-in-Publication Data

Müllenheim-Rechberg, Burkard, Freiherr von, 1910–
    [Schlachtschiff Bismarck. English]
    Battleship Bismarck : a survivor's story / by Burkard Baron von
Müllenheim-Rechberg ; translated by Jack Sweetman. — New & expanded
ed.
        p.   cm.
    Translation of: Schlachtschiff Bismarck.
    Includes bibliographical references (p.   ) and index.
    ISBN 0-87021-027-0
    1. Müllenheim-Rechberg, Burkard, Freiherr von, 1910–   2. Bismarck
(Battleship) 3. World War, 1939–1945—Personal narratives, German.
  4. World War, 1939–45—Naval operations, German.   5. Germany.
Kriegsmarine—Biography.   6. Seamen—Germany—Biography.   I. Title.
D772.B5M83   1990
940.54'5943—dc20
                                                                90-6448
                                                                CIP

Printed in the United States of America on acid-free paper ∞

2   4   6   8   9   7   5   3

First Printing

In honored memory
of the
German Resistance
1933–1945

Contents

CONTENTS

CONTENTS

Foreword

When I lived through the opening days of September 1939, the war that was so suddenly at hand and would later limit the operational life of the battleship *Bismarck* to only nine days, appeared to me as nothing less than a natural catastrophe, a fateful, somehow "outbroken" war. And yet much less than one which had been forced upon us from without, as the Reich's propaganda loved to pretend. I immediately regarded it as Hitler's war—his very own, coddled creation, something he had long planned and pursued in a skillful deception of German and world opinion from January 1933 to August 1939.

If and when the individual German understood Hitler's lust for war, whether sooner or later, naturally varied from person to person. A tiny, politically insignificant minority had seen through Hitler even before he took power; yet there are those who until today have not and will not see this unscrupulous warmonger for what he was.

But for those who took a critical perspective and from the beginning understood the war as one cynically unleashed by Hitler out of racial fanaticism and megalomania to enslave the continent of Europe, the very first German projectile would appear as having been fired in the service of a politically reprehensible and nationally ruinous goal. To feel this way was purely a question of individual perception that on its part became the impetus of the wish to see the "Führer" disappear in the best interests of the nation, and the sooner the better. Because of the impossibility of escape from the wartime situation, the growing doubts I had felt soon after Hitler's emergence, which during the thirties increased to a passionate rejection, gave rise to a more painful inner conflict than ever before, a deadly dilemma. I was torn between the spoiler of the Reich, who demanded my loyalty, and my country, to which I owed it. How else could this inner conflict find an end than with the destruction of the Brown dictatorship?*

The first edition of the life and death of the battleship *Bismarck* and the majority of her crew appeared in 1980. In accordance with the interests of my publisher, the United States Naval Institute, it was limited to the maritime aspects of these themes. I dedicated it to the memory of those who—presumably without exception—had risked their lives in naive faith in Hitler, who seemed to them to be the incarnation, the living spirit of Germany. The book was published in ten languages, sometimes in several printings, and provoked a friendly, almost worldwide response. Among the numerous letters received from readers were many from Germans and others who from their own knowledge or experiences provided interesting additions to the contents in my story. Among the foreigners I must mention by name is first of all the Briton Donald C. Campbell. During the final phase of the battle on 27 May 1941 Campbell was a senior lieutenant and air defense officer on HMS *Rodney*. His personal narrative makes fascinating reading. Others furnished details regarding various phases of the *Bismarck*'s operations, such as, for example, our meeting with the Swedish aircraft carrier *Gotland* in the Kattegat on 20 May 1941, the voyage up the Norwegian coast, the dummy ships intended to deceive us in Scapa Flow, the location of the *Bismarck* by British direction finding after the loss of contact on 25 May, and the British destroyer attacks on the *Bismarck* the night before the last battle. As for Germans, there appeared for the first time the only survivor from the forepart of the ship, whose battle station was in the damage-control center adjacent to the First Officer's command center: Maschinengast Josef Statz. Towards the end of the battle Statz succeeded in reaching the platform of the devastated forward conning tower through a communications shaft and, in the last phase of the ship's life, gathered sensational impressions. Thanks are due to all these correspondents for allowing me to work their valuable contributions into the present narrative. It is my final account as a participant in the operation.

*"Brown" refers to the brown shirted uniforms worn by members of the Nazi *Sturmabteilung* or SA (storm troopers).

Above all, however, the new version of the work delves into politics. I have included events and ideas that affected me as a citizen, which I was in addition to being a professional naval officer. But to keep political content within bounds, I have proceeded along strictly autobiographical lines, sketching only those events and ideas that actually touched my life. And I describe them according to my knowledge and perception at the time; all subsequent reflections are expressly identified as such. This expansion of the scope of the book has allowed me to utilize politically oriented entries in the personal diary of Captain R. N. T. Troubridge, British naval attaché in Berlin, 1936–39. The family of the late Captain Troubridge kindly granted me permission to use this record following the appearance of the English-language edition of the first edition of my book. His comments show Troubridge to have been an unusually sharpsighted observer of the German political scene in the years immediately before the war.

Altogether, the present work will expand my previous, purely naval narrative into a general historical record. Here I have tried to show something of the inner tension felt by those Germans to whom doubts about the Hitler state came early. In the course of years the conformity of our views revealed in an ever clearer light the women and men who, sooner than others, identified the stranglehold from which it was imperative to free our fatherland, and fought in the German Resistance. Their clear vision, their suffering as patriots, their courage, and their sacrifice of life and liberty determined the dedication of the second edition of this book.

Burkard Baron von Müllenheim-Rechberg

January 1987

Preface to the
First Edition

It is somewhat unusual to write a personal account of something that happened nearly forty years after the event. However, the idea of writing this book was born while I was still standing on the upper deck of the sinking *Bismarck* on 27 May 1941: since there is no vantage point from which the whole of this giant ship is visible, I thought, will it ever be possible for anyone, even an eyewitness, to assemble the countless details of the battle now ending into a complete and coherent account? If so, who would do it and when? Given the uncertainty of my own fate and against the background of the war, it was an absurd thought and it left my mind as quickly as it had entered it. But it did not die.

I had to resist the temptation to spend the endless time I had on my hands as a prisoner of war in England and Canada in making notes about the ship's operations while they were still fresh in my mind, because, in that status, I had no way of safeguarding secret, or even confidential, papers. The only thing I could do was keep my recollections as intact as possible and rely on written records to fill in at least some of the gaps later.

In May 1949 I received a letter from Dr. Kurt Hesse, a writer on military affairs. He wrote to me at the suggestion of Admiral Walter Gladisch, one of our former Fleet Commanders, urging me to publish my unique story. He thereby encouraged me to do what I had first thought about doing years earlier. But at that time there were several reasons why I had to push it into the back of my mind again: so much of Germany was still lying in ruins that it did not seem an appropriate time to write on a military subject; not enough time had elapsed for me to be able to write about something that touched me so deeply; I was studying law at Johann Wolfgang Goethe University; I had to finance not only my schooling but my subsistence, no easy task in the immediate postwar years, and at the same time engage in the urgent and time-consuming business of seeking a new profession.

During my years of service overseas as consul general and ambassador of the Federal Republic of Germany, many people, particularly foreigners, told me, "you *must* write about the *Bismarck* someday." But not until 1975, when I retired, did I have the time and other prerequisites to deal responsibly with the subject; by that time the British had returned the official records of the German Navy to the Federal German Archives.

Much had already been written, both at home and abroad, on the operations and sinking of the *Bismarck*. Naturally, none of the writers was able to provide the reasoning behind the crucial tactical decisions that the Fleet Commander, Admiral Günther Lütjens, made during the ship's Atlantic sortie. Nor, of course, can I, but in the pages that follow I have tried to put myself in Lütjens's place and frame of mind and I believe that, having been an officer in the ship, I can make a contribution to the history of the *Bismarck* and Exercise Rhine.

This book is dedicated to the memory of all who died as a result of the sinking of the *Bismarck* but especially to the memory of her commanding officer, Kapitän zur See Ernst Lindemann. As captain of a flagship, he served in the shadow of his Fleet Commander, and did not have the opportunity to demonstrate the outstanding leadership of which he was capable.

Burkard Baron von Müllenheim-Rechberg

Herrsching am Ammersee
November 1979

Acknowledgments

I would like to thank Dr. Jürgen Rohwer and Vice Admiral B. B. Schofield for permission to use their charts of Exercise Rhine; Fregattenkapitän Paul Schmalenbach, second gunnery officer in the *Prinz Eugen* during Exercise Rhine, for photographs of the battle off Iceland; Kapitänleutnant Herbert Wohlfarth, captain of the *U-556* in May 1941, for permission to use the certificate proclaiming the *U-556* the guardian of the *Bismarck*; and Herr Rolf Schindler, for preparing the track charts for publication.

I would also like to thank the following people and institutions for their advice and deeds: Captain Robert L. Bridges, USN (Ret.), Castle Creek, New York, U.S.A.; Herr Joachim Fensch, Weingarten, Federal Republic of Germany; Mr. Daniel Gibson Harris, Ottawa, Canada, who was assistant to the British naval attaché in Stockholm in May 1941; Herr Franz Hahn of the Military Historical Training Center, Mürwik Naval School, Federal Republic of Germany; Dr. Mathias Haupt of the Bundesarchiv, Koblenz, Federal Republic of Germany; Herr Bodo Herzog, Oberhausen, Federal Republic of Germany; Herr Hans H. Hildebrand, Hamburg, Federal Republic of Germany; Konteradmiral Günther Horstmann, German Navy (Ret.), Basel, Switzerland; the Department of Photographs of the Imperial War Museum, London, England; Mr. Esmond Knight, London, England; who was a lieutenant in the Royal Naval Volunteer Reserve aboard the *Prince of Wales* in May 1941; Dr. Karl Lautenschlager; Dr. Hansjoseph Maierhöfer of the Bundesarchiv-Militärarchiv-Freiburg, Federal Republic of Germany; Mr. Philip Mathias, Toronto, Canada; Mrs. Mary

Z. Pain, London, England; Fregattenkapitän Dr. Werner Rahn, Mürwik, Federal Republic of Germany; Dr. Hans Ulrich Sareyko, Aüswärtigen Amt, Bonn, Federal Republic of Germany; Kapitän zur See Hans-Henning von Schultz, German Navy (Ret.), Ramsau, Federal Republic of Germany, who was the intelligence officer aboard the *Prinz Eugen* during Exercise Rhine; Herr Torsten Spiller of the *Deutsche Dienststelle (WASt)*, Berlin, Federal Republic of Germany; and Mr. Tom Wharam, Cardiff, Wales.

I want to convey my special thanks to those who have helped to prepare this new and expanded English-language edition. I am grateful to my translator, Dr. Jack Sweetman, who has succeeded admirably in retaining the flavor and spirit of my story; to Mr. William H. Garzke, Jr., and Mr. Robert O. Dulin, Jr., who provided me unselfishly with technical and editorial assistance; and to my editor, Ms. Naomi Grady, who demonstrated rare skill in making my story appear as if it were written originally in English. Others at the Naval Institute Press to whom I would like to express my gratitude include Dagmar Stock, Mary Lou Kenney, and R. Dawn Sollars.

B.v.M-R.

Translator's Note

For assistance in the preparation of the translations of both editions, it is a pleasure to record my thanks to: Commander George L. Breeden II, USN (Ret.), Mr. Fred H. Rainbow, and Commander Paul Stillwell, USNR, whose expert advise was invaluable in dealing with technical matters; the author, Burkard Baron von Müllenheim-Rechberg, who kindly read and commented on the translation of his book; Naomi Grady, who eliminated many infelicities of expression; and, last but never least, my wife, Gisela, who helped in countless ways.

Table of Equivalent Ranks

Kriegsmarine	United States Navy	Royal Navy
Grossadmiral	Fleet Admiral	Admiral of the Fleet
Generaladmiral	—	—
Admiral	Admiral	Admiral
Vizeadmiral	Vice Admiral	Vice-Admiral
Konteradmiral	Rear Admiral	Rear-Admiral
Kommodore	Commodore	Commodore
Kapitän zur See	Captain	Captain
Fregattenkapitän	—	—
Korvettenkapitän	Commander	Commander
Kapitänleutnant	Lieutenant Commander	Lieutenant Commander
Oberleutnant zur See	Lieutenant	Lieutenant
Leutnant zur See	Ensign	Sub-Lieutenant
Oberfähnrich zur See	—	—
Fähnrich zur See	Midshipman	Midshipman
—	—	Cadet
Stabsoberbootsmann*	Chief Warrant Officer	—
Oberbootsmann*	Warrant Officer (W-3)	Warrant Officer
Stabsbootsmann*	Warrant Officer (W-2)	—
Bootsmann*	Warrant Officer (W-1)	—
—	Master Chief Petty Officer	—
—	Senior Chief Petty Officer	—
Oberbootsmannsmaat*	Chief Petty Officer	Chief Petty Officer
Bootsmannsmatt*	Petty Officer 1st Class	Petty Officer
Matrosenstabsobergefreiter	Petty Officer 2nd Class	—
Matrosenstabsgefreiter	Petty Officer 3rd Class	Leading Seaman
Matrosenhauptgefreiter	Seaman	Able Seaman
Matrosenobergefreiter	—	—
Matrosengefreiter	Seaman Apprentice	Ordinary Seaman
Matrose	Seaman Recruit	—

*Bootsmann designates the rating or specialty of petty officers and warrant officers. The suffix maat designates a senior petty officer. A title without a suffix designates a warrant officer. Other ratings are substituted as appropriate. For example: Maschinenmaat, Obersignalmaat, Oberartilleriemechaniker, Stabsoberbootsmann.

Table of Equivalent Deck Designations

Kriegsmarine	United States Navy	Royal Navy
Stauung	Tank Top	Tank Top
Unteres Platformdeck	3rd Platform	
Mittleres, Platformdeck	2nd Platform	Lower Platform
Oberes Platformdeck	1st Platform	Upper Platform
Panterdeck	Fourth Deck	Lower Deck
Zwischendeck	Third Deck	Middle Deck
Batteriedeck	Second Deck	Main Deck
Oberdeck	Main Deck	Upper Deck
Aufbandeck	01 Level	Shelter Deck
Unteres Bruckendeck	02 Level	Boat Deck
Unteres Mastdeck	03 Level	No. 2 Platform
Oberes Mastdeck	04 Level	Signal Deck
Admiralbrucke	05 Level	Lower Bridge
	06 Level	Upper Bridge

BATTLESHIP
BISMARCK

 **1**

The *Bismarck*
and Her Captain

*Sea Battle Between the English and French! Churchill
Bombards the French Fleet!* So read the giant headlines
in the daily newspapers on Hamburg kiosks. This sensational display
told the German public of the bloody attack by a British naval force
on French warships lying in the harbor at Oran, Algeria, at the beginning
of July 1940. The attack was part of a determined British attempt
to prevent the Germans from seizing the French Navy, a threat
raised by the French surrender late in June. Nominally, the fleet was
under the control of the Pétain government, but most of it had taken
refuge in ports outside of France. On the morning of 3 July, a British
naval force, consisting of two battleships, a battle cruiser, an aircraft
carrier, two cruisers, and eleven destroyers, appeared off the coast of
Algeria. Its commander immediately presented the French admiral
with an ultimatum to surrender his ships. When the allotted time
had expired and the French had taken no action, the British opened
fire. Thirteen hundred French seamen were killed that afternoon, and
three French battleships were destroyed or damaged. Only the battleship
Strasbourg and five destroyers managed to escape to Toulon.

As I read the news accounts of this amazing event, I was reminded
of the British seizure of the Danish fleet at Copenhagen in the midst
of peace in the year 1807. But this attack, taking place in my day and
between two states that had been allies until then, impressed me so
deeply that I made note of the commander of the task force and ships
involved: Vice Admiral Sir James Somerville, the battle cruiser *Hood*,
and the aircraft carrier *Ark Royal.* Still, I had no inkling of the role

that within a year this admiral and these ships would play in the fate of the battleship *Bismarck*, to which I, a thirty-year-old Kapitän-leutnant,* had just been assigned.

In June 1940, when I first saw the *Bismarck*, she was in the Hamburg yard of her builders, Blohm & Voss, awaiting completion and acceptance by the German Navy. Therefore, what I saw was a dusty steel giant, made fast to a wharf and littered with tools, welding equipment, and cables. An army of workmen was hustling to complete the job, while the crew already on board were familiarizing themselves with the ship and conducting whatever training was possible under the circumstances.

But under this disguise, the distinctive features, both traditional and novel, of the future battleship were already apparent. There it was again—that elegant curve of the ship's silhouette fore and aft from the tip of the tower mast—then a characteristic of German warship design that sometimes led the enemy to confuse our ship types at long range. Other things about her were familiar to me because I had served in the battleship *Scharnhorst*, but everything about the *Bismarck* was bigger and more powerful: her dimensions, especially her enormous beam, her high superstructure, her 38-centimeter main-battery guns (the first of that caliber installed in the Kriegsmarine), the great number of guns she had in her secondary and antiaircraft batteries, and the heavy armor-plating of her hull, gun turrets, and forward command- and fire-control station. She had a double-ended aircraft catapult athwartships, another first for the Kriegsmarine, and, as did the *Scharnhorst* and her sister the *Gneisenau*, the new, spherical splinter shields on her antiaircraft stations on both sides of her tower mast.

At first sight of this gigantic ship, so heavily armed and armored, I felt sure that she would be able to rise to any challenge, and that it would be a long time before she met her match. A long life was very obviously in store for her. Still, I thought, the British fleet had numerical superiority, and the outcome of any action would depend on the combination of forces engaged. But questions like that seemed to lie far in the future, as I began my service in the *Bismarck*. I had supreme confidence in this ship. How could it be otherwise?

When my assignment to the battleship *Bismarck* reached me in May 1940, eleven years of naval service lay behind me. I was born in Spandau in 1910, into a family that originated in Baden but some of

*Lieutenant Commander

Looking aft over the *Bismarck* on the slipway at Blohm & Voss. She is complete up to her armored deck, where an octagonal hole awaits the installation of the armored barbette for 38-centimeter turret Bruno. The barbettes for turret Caesar and for all six 15-centimeter turrets are in place. (Photograph courtesy of Württembergische Landesbibliothek, Stuttgart.)

The *Bismarck* is shown almost complete to her upper-deck level. Barbettes for the main and secondary batteries have been installed. (Photograph courtesy of Württembergische Landesbibliotek, Stuttgart.)

whom migrated to the east. The profession of arms was a family tradition. My father was killed in action as a major in command of the 5th Jäger Battalion in the Argonne in April 1916; my only brother, who was younger than I and a captain in the Luftwaffe, was killed on 2 September 1939 while serving as a squadron commander in the Richthofen Wing during the Polish campaign.

In April 1929, I graduated "with excellence" from a classical high school and entered the Weimar Republic's 15,000-man Reischsmarine. By the time the several thousand applicants had been subjected to rigorous examination, the class of 1929, to which I belonged, numbered about eighty men. A year-long cruise in a light cruiser to Africa, the West Indies, and the United States in 1930 got us accustomed to life aboard ship, and at the same time assuaged our yearning to see the big, wide world, which naturally had played a role in our choice of profession. We then went through the Naval School and took the standard courses on weapons before, towards the end of 1932, we were dispersed among the various ships of the Reichsmarine as Fähnrich zur See.*

A year later, together with my classmates, I became a Leutnant zur See† and then served as a junior officer in a deck division and as range-finder officer in the light cruisers *Königsberg* and *Karlsruhe*. Following my promotion to Oberleutnant zur See‡ in 1935, I spent a year as a group officer at the Mürwik Naval School, training midshipmen. Early in 1936, I took a course at the Naval Gunnery School in Kiel in fire control, which began my specialization in naval ordnance. There followed two years in our then-very-modern destroyers, first as adjutant to the commander of the 1st Destroyer Division, then as a division and gunnery officer. At the end of these tours, I was promoted to Kapitänleutnant.

In the autumn of 1938 the Oberkommando der Kriegsmarines§ first sent assistants to the naval attachés in the most important countries. There were very few of these posts and when I was offered one of them, and moreover the important one in London, not only did I feel honored but I felt that an inner longing was being satisfied. I accepted it and took up my post with great pleasure.

The outbreak of the Second World War brought this assignment to

*Midshipmen
†Ensign
‡Lieutenant
§Naval High Command

The author as a Leutnant zur See aboard the light cruiser *Königsberg* in 1934. He served as a range-finder officer in the *Königsberg* and in her sister, the *Karlsruhe*, thus beginning a career in gunnery. (Photograph from the author's collection).

an abrupt end and, in October 1939, I began two months' service as fourth gunnery officer of the battleship *Scharnhorst*. The following month, I took part in the sweep into the Faeroes-Shetland passage, which was led by the Fleet Commander, Admiral Wilhelm Marschall, in his flagship *Gneisenau*, and which culminated in the sinking of the British auxiliary cruiser *Rawalpindi*. Afterwards, the *Scharnhorst* had to go into the yard for an extensive overhaul and I was appointed First

Officer of the destroyer *Erich Giese*. As such, I participated in mine-laying operations off the east coast of Britain in the winter of 1939–40 and in the occupation of Narvik during the Norwegian campaign of April 1940. All ten of the German destroyers engaged in this operation were lost, half of Germany's destroyer force. I had to be given a new assignment and, because of my weapons training, I was appointed fourth gunnery officer, my action station being the after fire-control station, in the *Bismarck*, which was soon to be commissioned. I looked forward with keen anticipation to serving in this wonderful, new ship.

Before going to my new duty, however, I took a short leave. In the quiet of an Upper Bavarian health resort, where visitors were few in wartime, my thoughts continually wandered back, whether I wanted them to or not, to the moving months I had spent in London, only a year earlier. What changes had taken place in Anglo-German relations since then, so completely at variance with my hopes and wishes! Very early in life, actually during my school days, I acquired a special interest in Great Britain, her people, language, history, and political system. My own family history influenced me in this direction. In the eighteenth century, Sir George Browne, son of John, Count of Altamont, of the house of Neale O'Connor, an Anglo-Norman family that settled in Ireland and later spread to England, entered French service. Subsequently, he transferred to the Prussian Army, in which he fought in the Seven Years' War. Made a privy councillor after the war, he became a chamberlain and treasurer in Lower Silesia. His daughter, Franziska, married one of my direct forebears. Visits to Britain over the years had deepened my interest in that country. In 1936 I accepted an invitation to the home of English friends in Colchester, and now I could not forget the long discussions we held over the burning necessity to preserve peace between our two peoples.

Unfortunately, the time I had spent as assistant naval attaché in London, personally very enjoyable, was tragically overshadowed from the outset by the continued deterioration of Anglo-German relations. A relentless succession of international events was responsible. I remembered it with a heavy heart.

By the time I arrived in London in November 1938, the British public had all but given up hope that the ceding of the German-populated Sudetenland to the Reich, which had been forced upon the Czech government with British and French consent at Munich the previous September, would produce the hoped-for relaxation of international tensions. Aggressive speeches by Hitler in Saarbrücken, Weimar, and Munich within two months of the Munich Conference had contributed to Britain's anxiety.

I had listened to the Saarbrücken speech over the radio. Hitler began by comparing the incorporation of the Sudetenland into the Reich with the return of the Saar in 1935.* Then he denounced the "Spirit of Versailles" that was still at large in the world and directed against Germany,† and emphasized the necessity of our rearmament, for which he had "fanatically exerted" himself for almost six years now. Germany had only one real, true friend in the outside world: Benito Mussolini. But in the western democracies, which might still want peace today, one could never be sure that tomorrow there wouldn't be a change that would bring warmongers into the government. In order to guard against such dangers, he had now ordered the construction of our western fortifications to go forward with increased energy. The remainder of his speech he devoted to relations with England, which he indirectly threatened—nine days after signing his agreement with Chamberlain to hold mutual consultations on questions concerning both countries, nine days after an agreement that the world had held to be a great success.

I had hoped for a more conciliatory speech. But, as it was, it had angered and disturbed me. Can't the fellow ever get enough? I thought. As yet I knew nothing of the agonized aversion with which Hitler had gone to the Munich Conference. And even that was only under last-minute pressure from Mussolini, who was not ready for war. For the "Führer" always wanted to decide everything himself, determine everything himself—what to do and when. And now to negotiate the cession of the Sudentenland to the Reich? "A. H. [Adolf Hitler] can scarcely contain himself when the word negotiation is mentioned," on 27 September 1938 the British naval attaché in Berlin, Captain R. N. T. Troubridge, recorded in his diary, the impression of his diplomatic colleague Ivone Kirkpatrick, who as interpreter had taken part in Hitler's conversations with Chamberlain at Bad

*According to the terms of the Treaty of Versailles, the Saar was separated from Germany and placed under the administration of the League of Nations for fifteen years, at the end of which period its inhabitants were to choose between continuation of the League government, incorporation into France, or return to Germany. The plebiscite of 13 January 1935 produced an overwhelming vote in favor of the latter.

†There was a well-nigh universal feeling in Germany that the terms of the peace imposed by the victorious Allies in the Treaty of Versailles had been unduly harsh.

Godesberg and Munich. And on 23 October Troubridge noted his own impression of the events surrounding the Munich Conference: "It is indeed more and more apparent that the man wanted his war and is furious at having been done out of it. There is a story going around the chancelleries that he said to the King of Bulgaria that he wanted a war while he was young enough to enjoy it. Not at all unlikely." Britain's disillusionment was growing and it was becoming ever clearer that to pursue a policy of pure appeasement would be disastrous for Europe.

In this atmosphere, the horror and revulsion provoked by the attack launched—"at a stroke" in the Nazi manner—against Jewish life and property by Dr. Joseph Goebbels on 9 November 1938 disturbed me even more.* It was the evening before my departure from Berlin for London and I was eating in the famous Cantina Romana, when my waiter, suddenly gone white as a sheet, shocked me with the words, "Have you heard? The synagogue next door is burning!" Together with the other guests, I rushed out of the restaurant. In the Kurfürstendamm I saw that groups of hooligans armed with tire irons and crowbars, assigned to sectors like assault troops, were destroying and looting Jewish stores and had put the synagogue on the Fasanenstrasse to the torch. Confronted at such close range with the brutal face of naked force, I stared into the convulsive signs of the time, symptoms of the barbarity that had loomed over us for five years and was now a harbinger of still worse things to come. A subdued crowd, the living exemplars of a people kept politically disadvantaged for centuries, moved through this spectacle, silently or speaking in whispers admonished by the commands of an unseen speaker—"Keep moving! Don't stand around! No picture taking!" It was an oppressive scene.

But what distressed me above all else that evening, what tore me to pieces inside, was not the horror in the Kurfürstendamm, the atrocious individual acts, as much as the recognition, clearly gained here

---

*On 7 November 1938 a junior German diplomat at the Paris embassy was assassinated by a Jewish youth in protest of the anti-Semitic policies of the Third Reich. Minister of Propaganda Joseph Goebbels seized upon this act as a pretext to order the party's Storm Troopers (SA) to launch a "spontaneous" assault on Jewish property throughout the Reich on the anniversary of Hitler's Munich Putsch. The ensuing violence became infamous as *Kristallnacht*—Crystal Night (a term the author firmly rejects, in favor of "murderous pogrom," since Jews were also murdered)—on account of the number of shop windows shattered. Approximately 7,500 Jewish stores were plundered and 250 synagogues burned.

in Berlin, of the true nature of the so-called "Third Reich," the Reich which I had to serve. Germany, since 1933 had been transformed into nothing more than the stage for a dictator, a political actor, who through successive assaults, beginning with the Emergency Decree for the Protection of the People and State of 28 February 1933,* had long ago changed the technical legality of his accession to power into an illegality, striking the instruments of a state of law out of the hands of the Germans, one after the other, like superfluous toys. Germany had become a theater directed by a dictator. It was outwardly dazzling—but on account of the parallel internal systems of coercion and repression, the grotesque racial nonsense, the fundamental immorality of the Brown rulers, which no oratorical demagoguery could conceal—internally rotten, self-destructive, and thus, in the last resort, worthless, heightening the political fall for the Germans when the Hitler-bewitchment ended. Germany was now the arena for an intoxicating Hitler-rhetoric that paid lip service to national interests while the actual policy, serving only the maintenance of the "Führer's" power, irresponsibly placed these very interests at risk and rejected the values of Western civilization, Bolshevik fashion. Here and now I had for the first time seen the regime unmasked; henceforth I could never again misunderstand it.

Individually to oppose the bans of ruffians in the streets, especially in view of the passivity of the police—obviously on orders—what a hopeless thought. That would lead only to one's own obliteration without doing any good for anyone and thus would be senseless. Besides, I did not have enough blind heroism for that. To be sure, I felt my toleration of these visible wrongs to be a humiliating civic failure, a growth of complicity to have unresistingly accepted another act by Hitler injurious to the interests of our nation and the German reputation in the world—but in this advanced phase of the consolidation of state terror an individual could not accomplish anything. Since 1933 the German people, with a very few exceptions, had with rejoicing capitulated to Hitler by surrendering the stations of a civilized state, never even recognizing the capitulation as such. The ad-

---

*On the evening of 27 February 1933 the Reichstag building was gutted by a fire apparently set single-handedly by a mentally disturbed young Dutchman. Portraying this event as the harbinger of Communist insurrection, the next day the National Socialist government issued an emergency decree (allowed by Article 48 of the Weimar Constitution) suspending habeas corpus, the rights of freedom of assembly and expression, and other civil liberties. The decree was never rescinded.

herents of a liberal state of law could accomplish nothing more here and would have to wait until the system of terror collapsed of itself.

But this would lie in the unforeseeable future, and it would be a long way, and for those with eyes to see, a lonely one, until that time came. How very lonely—and that, too, brings one particular memory to mind. It goes back to a day in December 1938, on which the naval attaché and I journeyed from London to The Hague so that I could present my credentials to the Dutch government, to which we were also accredited. After the official part of the day was over, I spent about an hour strolling through the city by myself, past inviting shops, pausing outside the bookshops to leaf through some of the volumes set out for inspection.

In so doing, I stumbled on authors from whom nothing had been heard for a long time in Germany and whom I could barely remember—exiled authors, in whom the publisher Fritz Helmut Landshoff of the Querido Press in Amsterdam had taken an interest. One of Ernst Toller's works came to hand, *Eine Jugend in Deutschland** with a chapter titled "Blick 1933,"† whose text included the words, "Whoever wishes to understand the collapse of 1933. . . ." Ernst Toller—the Communist, whose "Maschinenstürmer"‡ I recalled from my school days—did it have to be he to confirm that, through the years of doubt in which I had tormented myself about my countrymen's political sense, I had been entirely correct in my estimate of the Nazi system? We could scarcely think the same way, he and I—an active-duty naval officer and dyed-in-the-wood anticommunist; but I was not thinking in terms of party politics. The "collapse" that I had in mind was Hitler's so openly attempted disassociation of the German people from the last two thousand years of human culture, and insofar as I interpreted Toller in this manner I was in complete agreement with him.

How extraordinary, this glance at Toller's text; at this time, in this place, to which nature had contributed a dense fog, as if keeping "Big Brother" from peering over my shoulder and threatening me: "Listen, you, you're committing intellectual high treason, come along!" I wandered the streets still further, deep in thought, considering how ironic it was that of all people, I—descended from an unpolitical

---

*"A Youth in Germany."
†"Spotlight 1933."
‡"Machine Stormer."

11

family of officers and civil servants with a conservative outlook going back for generations, brought up in a strict boarding school after the death of my father, shielded by the military profession from the daily cares of civil life, politically naive and inexperienced—had been endowed with instinct enough to recognize early that Hitler's path was the wrong path, a dead-end. And thereby like a fallen leaf blown astray, I became estranged from my countrymen, who in their overwhelming majority were Hitler's followers.

But, my thoughts returning to the Kurfürstendamm, I felt then that if there was a ray of hope it was that the next day I would leave the arena of such barbarities and journey to England. I would be spared the sight of the swastika flag for a time that I wished would never end.

Under the impression of the pogrom of 9 November, of Hitler's last three speeches, and of his talks with foreign correspondents during these weeks, Troubridge noted in his dairy on 15 November 1938 that according to the opinion of American circles in Berlin, the Jewish pogrom of 9 November would have a negative effect twice that of the sinking of the *Lusitania* in 1915. He continued:

This has really been rather a significant day in the relations between England and Germany, for on this day I finally and irretrievably decided that whilst National Socialism in its present form remains in power there is not the slightest chance of an accord. For over two years I have thought it possible, but now I regret to say I must side with the majority. I am very sorry for Chamberlain, who has done more than anyone in his position could be expected to do but he has received no response whatever from here. The Führer has not made one conciliatory gesture since Munich. He has made three speeches in a row attacking Churchill and Co. and "democrats with umbrellas" (very good taste!) but has uttered not one word of hope. So far as I am concerned, the die is cast.

It is this foresight that leads the reader of Troubridge's diary back to the ominous words of one of the first entries in it, when in July 1936 he wrote of the launching of the Berlin Olympics:

Prophets who aver that Germany is rushing into an abyss of bankruptcy, self-immolation and dragging the rest of Europe with her in one glorious (?) downward plunge appear on the surface (?) to have some justification for their gloomy predictions. Where comes the money for this lavish entertainment, the new buildings one sees everywhere, new

Vice Admiral Sir Thomas Troubridge, who as a captain served as British naval attaché in Berlin from 1936 until 1939, was a sharp-sighted observer of the German political scene. (Photograph courtesy of Tom Troubridge, London.)

uniforms, new soldiers—ships—aeroplanes, all on a Babylonian scale of splendor and beneficence? First impressions [Troubridge had just entered his post as naval attaché] are lasting. Clean children. . . . Do they want a war, if so, with whom and what about? How is it all done economically? . . . this re-accession of strength that the Olympics symbolize?

Early on the morning of 11 November, I reached London in a spotlessly clean British railway car. The lead article in *The Times*, "A Black Day for Germany," unreservedly condemned the violence. It voiced my opinion exactly; I could have signed every sentence. It was terribly depressing to be starting out on my first mission abroad under these circumstances, and I was grateful to my British friends for being so tactful as not to mention to me the events in the Reich that must have shamed all decent German patriots.

Germany took another politically significant step in December 1938, this time concerning the German naval construction program, which then conformed to the terms of the Anglo-German Naval Treaty of June 1935. In this agreement, Germany pledged not to increase the strength of its fleet to more than 35 percent of the strength of the British fleet. This percentage applied not only to the total strength of the fleet, but to individual ship categories, as well. Although the treaty granted Germany the right to parity in submarine strength, the Reich professed its willingness not to go beyond 45 percent of British submarine strength. Should it ever appear necessary to exceed these limitations, the matter was to be discussed. At the time it was signed, the treaty was accepted with satisfaction in Germany, because it overturned the limitations set by the Treaty of Versailles and made possible the building of a bigger and a balanced fleet.

Now, in December 1938, the Reich called the attention of the British government to the clause in the treaty that allowed Germany to exceed the 45 percent limit on its submarine strength if "a situation arose" which, in the opinion of Germany, made it necessary to do so. Such a situation, Berlin informed London, now existed. The government of the Reich, therefore, intended to build up its submarine tonnage to parity with the British. Simultaneously, it announced its intention to arm two cruisers under construction more heavily than had been originally provided.

Technically, the German claims were perfectly in order. But were they being made at a politically propitious moment? The British, aware of the capacity of Germany's shipyards, were bound to know that the Reich would not have its increased submarine tonnage available for several years. And political opinion in Great Britain, already disturbed by the Munich Agreement, was such that the presentation of Germany's claims at this moment could only work to the political disadvantage of the Reich: this view was frequently expressed in conversations in London at the time and widely voiced by the British press. Therefore, why not patiently await the tactically correct moment? It was actions such as this that made it possible to read aggressive intent into everything Germany did, even when it was not there.

The next crisis came in the spring of 1939, and it was a serious one.

In mid-March, Hitler forced the Czech government to conclude a treaty making the provinces of Bohemia and Moravia a German protectorate. In violation of the Munich Agreement, he then occupied that area and incorporated it into the Reich. Czechoslovakia, as such, disappeared from the map. This action shook Europe like an earthquake. "It is evident," Troubridge wrote in his diary on 17 March, "that Chamberlain's policy of appeasement is now gone by the board and all Sir Nevile's work [Sir Nevile Henderson, British ambassador to Germany] gone west, too. I saw him at the embassy this afternoon pacing up and down his study like a caged lion using 'quarterdeck' language. I am not surprised. His rather too optimistic telegrams of a month ago (we all thought them a bit too much) have now been shown to be complete nonsense."

The British government and public were the hardest hit; the policy of appeasement towards Germany appeared to be shattered once and for all. Thereafter, many circles of British society avoided all contact with official representatives of the Reich. For the first time, Hitler's act of force was not taken quietly in London. Germans were no longer allowed to set foot in the Czechoslovakian embassy building. It now served the newly organized Czechoslovakian government in exile, which immediately recognized the former British diplomatic representative in Prague. The German embassy tried desperately to find a way of interpreting the event to its host country. I realized that a political turning point had been reached.

At the end of March, I attended a social gathering in the HMS *Calliope*. This venerable sailing ship was used for training the Tyne Division of the Royal Naval Volunteer Reserve. Her home port was Newcastle. The affair was to commemorate the fiftieth anniversary of the Samoan hurricane of 1889, which the *Calliope* had been fortunate enough to survive. Because some German and American fighting ships were also caught in the storm, the naval attachés of both countries were invited to the ceremony.* The American attaché was represented by his assistant, Lieutenant Robert Lord Campbell, with whom I traveled to Newcastle. On the way, I wondered what effect events in Czechoslovakia would have on the gathering in the *Calli-*

---

*The typhoon that broke over Samoa in March 1889 has entered Pacific history as the "Samoan Hurricane." Of the ships of various nationalities then anchored in the harbor, only the British corvette *Calliope* was not lost, thanks to her powerful engines. Of the German ships, the cruiser *Adler* and gunboat *Eber* were smashed on coral reefs and the corvette *Olga* was stranded in the mud but could be salvaged. Ninety-three German seamen were lost.

ope. I need not have worried. I had a pleasant evening of good comradeship, only slightly dampened by Germany's treatment of its new protectorate. In his welcoming address, the British host spoke of "troublous times" but did not go into particulars, and the evening's planners saw to it that no one else spoke. "It's a shame," Campbell said to me afterwards, "I had thought of a few things to say and would have been more than happy to do so." I could not exactly share his regret.

I also remembered Campbell because of the increasingly intense verbal attacks that his loathing of National Socialism occasionally led him to launch against the Reich. During a casual conversation one day he suddenly changed the subject and very aggressively upbraided me for the harsh conditions that our imperial government had imposed on Russia in the so-called Peace of Brest-Litovsk in March 1918. After he had finished his remarks, which were delivered like an oration, I tried—although I did not have the historical details in my head—to ground our conduct at that time on the need to safeguard ourselves in the east so long as the war was still underway in the west. I hardly convinced him of that, and, indeed, I myself had known for a long time that our territorial annexations and demands for indemnities had turned out to be highly unwise. But as a national-minded German with a sense of political obligation to Germany toward the outside world, I had chosen to give a substantive answer in preference to the immature alternative—recently become fashionable in such cases—of referring to the fact that I was seven years old at the time and demonstrably devoid of civic responsibility.

Only a month after the events in Prague, more alarming diplomatic signals came from Berlin. In his speech to the Reichstag on 28 April Hitler gave notice that he was canceling two treaties: the German-Polish Nonaggression Pact of 1934 and the Anglo-German Naval Treaty of 1935. Hitler had convened the Reichstag on this date basically to answer a note from President Franklin Delano Roosevelt, in which on 15 April the latter had proposed certain common steps for the preservation of world peace. First, however, Hitler devoted himself to European affairs, including relations with England, which he attacked sharply. He referred to a remark Prime Minister Chamberlain made following the German march into Prague, that trust could no longer be placed in Germany's promises, and accused England of a policy of encircling Germany, which violated the provisions of the naval agreement. He had decided to notify the British government of this today.

Troubridge had seen the cancellation of the naval agreement coming for some time. In his diary entry for 19 March, he wrote:

> The German papers have now concentrated their counterattack on England in the usual familiar fashion and hint at tearing up the Naval Agreement. This I think quite likely and it may well be followed by our breaking off diplomatic relations. A treaty more or less means nothing to this country and I have consistently reported that the A.G.N.A. [Anglo-German Naval Agreement] would go west when the moment was ripe. . . . [And on 30 April] Adolf Hitler tore up the A.G.N.A., which was little surprise to me and also his treaty of non-aggression with Poland. So the decks are cleared. I do not think there is any doubt that he intends to settle the [Polish] corridor question in the very near future. . . . The British people are undoubtedly fed up with A.H. and would, I believe, be ready even to the extent of going to war to put an end to a situation which is altogether intolerable. The Germans have their two motorized divisions close to the Polish frontier.

In Great Britain, the cancellation of the naval treaty was seen as the prelude to an unrestrained expansion of the German fleet; while that of the pact with Poland appeared to augur another dangerous political adventure. Hitler had switched the course of European affairs onto another track. Whether the tremendous international risks that he was taking, his principle of making territorial demands by ultimatum, permitted the preservation of peace or meant war, and, if war, whether Britain would take part in it, were questions about which observers in London became increasingly contradictory. Were there indices of the British attitude? Yes, I discovered one in the office of our naval attaché, who on 28 September 1938 telephoned a report to the Oberkommando der Kriegsmarine in Berlin:

> British fleet mobilized at midnight. Order for general mobilization is signed, the date left open. Security measures of all sorts and partial mobilization of the armed forces and civil population in full swing. Mobilization orders of all sorts also given for civil defense services. Women's auxiliary service understood to be in process of formation. From Chamberlain's speech appears that the British Empire will take arms, not for Czechoslovakia, but against any use of force for a goal which in British opinion is attainable without use of force. That is the new watchword for the struggle. Deadline of demand and rejection of Chamberlain's last offer will be seen as intolerable pressure on England under which it is resolved not to negotiate. From this arises the firm decision to fight in event of German use of force.

In reply to a question from the Oberkommando if the mobilization of the British fleet was to be understood as a complete mobilization, the attaché declared that he could not say. That same day Troubridge noted in his diary: "Also news of the mobilization of our fleet which ought to impress them here but will not simply because the people will not hear of it."

That the political leaders of the Reich had not reckoned on a firm attitude on the part of the British government is more than sufficiently well known today. Such a view was again communicated to me, although quite peripherally, on 1 September 1939, when the staff officer assigned to the staff of the Mürwik Naval School, Fregattenkapitän Heinrich Ruhfus, shouted, apparently from the deepest conviction, to the midshipmen assembled on the parade ground on the occasion of the outbreak of war that he did not believe Great Britain and France would declare war on Germany.

During the days when I was trying to find the answer to this question, I often thought of an unforgettable meeting I had in London not long before. In the British Admiralty, the Director of Naval Intelligence, Rear Admiral J. A. G. Troup, a rather taciturn Scot, was responsible for liaison with the accredited naval attachés. His assistant in this duty was the cosmopolitan, suave Commander Casper S. B. Swinley, who handled the day-to-day business of liaison. At a routine official gathering soon after my arrival in London, Troup said to me, "Baron, one day soon you and I will dress in our cutaways, put on our top hats, climb into a taxi, and visit Lady Jellicoe." I replied, "Admiral, it would be a great honor." At that time no German naval officer had to be told who Lady Jellicoe was. But that was long ago, so I should explain that she was the widow of Admiral of the Fleet Lord Jellicoe, who died in 1935. Lord Jellicoe commanded the British Grand Fleet at the Battle of Jutland in May 1916 and was later First Sea Lord. He enjoyed great esteem in German naval circles as well as in his own country.

Troup's first invitation to visit Lady Jellicoe was, however, not followed up, and I almost forgot about it. Then, at another meeting, Troup again said, "Baron, soon you and I will dress in our cutaways, put on our top hats, and go in a taxi to visit Lady Jellicoe." I said, "Admiral, I would be delighted." But once again it seemed that nothing was going to happen. Then one day Troup called me up: "Be at my house in the designated dress tomorrow afternoon. We'll drive to Lady Jellicoe from here." And so we did.

Lady Jellicoe received us in her tastefully furnished London flat.

The drawing room was decorated with many souvenirs of her husband's long and distinguished naval career, notably a silver model of his flagship the *Iron Duke*.

"I am delighted that Admiral Troup was so kind as to bring you to me," Lady Jellicoe told me, "and I bid you a cordial welcome." Then we discussed the two navies, the events of the world war at sea, the promising start towards an Anglo-German understanding around the turn of the century, its breakdown, and the subsequent, unhappy course of events. We parted with the mutual hope that peace between our two countries would be preserved—and that was more than an empty wish. I thought about this visit for a long time afterwards. Why had Lady Jellicoe wanted to see me? Ever since the end of the world war, her husband had been convinced that a political settlement with Germany would be in Britain's best interest. He had worked for it with all his strength to the last, and this was the spirit in which Lady Jellicoe talked to me.

On a daily basis, most of my duties as assistant to the German naval attaché were performed in the office. My dealings with the Royal Navy were limited to liaison with the Admiralty; I did not visit any British ships. I evaluated the daily and monthly press, professional periodicals, and literature on naval topics, and I cultivated my contacts with the assistant naval attachés of other countries. I assisted my chief in his reporting activities, one of which was to observe the effects of Franco's declaration of a blockage of the Republican coastal areas during the Spanish Civil War. Implementation of the 1935 naval treaty was naturally a very important facet of Anglo-German relations. Although the main business connected with that was not conducted in the office of the German naval attaché in London, correspondence on the subject came to our attention. In it, the two governments informed one another of the most important data regarding the warships they had under construction and had completed. This is how we learned the names of new British ships; for example, the battleships *King George V* and *Prince of Wales* and the aircraft carriers *Ark Royal* and *Victorious*. A report from our consulate in Glasgow in the summer of 1939 stated that the twenty-two shipyards on the Clyde would be working to capacity on new naval construction into the winter, and some of them for more than two years. When the *Prince of Wales* was launched at Birkenhead on 3 May 1939, the London agency of the German News Bureau reported: "This morning in Birkenhead the battleship *Prince of Wales* left the stocks, christened by the sister of the king. She is one of the fastest and most powerful ships in the British fleet. She has a displacement of 35,000 tons and is armed with ten 14-inch guns in three turrets, sixteen 5.25-inch guns in eight twin mounts, and numerous smaller guns. Her speed is said to be greater than that of the battleship *Nelson*, which makes 23 knots. The *Prince of Wales* is the second ship of its class to leave the stocks. The first was the *King George V,* which left the stocks in the presence of the king in February. Three more ships of the same class will follow."

That is where my reminiscences ended. Now, these "ships on paper" were about to take on tangible form, and my ship, the *Bismarck*, would certainly meet one or another of them at sea. But the veil of the future still lay over the when and the where.

My time in London lay barely twelve months back. How could it so quickly have come to this? At the end of June 1939 I was ordered to a fire control officers' course for heavy caliber guns at Kiel. Later the scene of this course was shifted to the sea room around the Isle of Rügen. In our free hours during that hot summer we incubated on the beach at the seaside resort of Binz. What peace seemed to lie over the holiday makers assembled there, who had no idea of how their fate had already been decided—a last, deceptive idyll, during which in the state chancelleries of Europe the false peace was finally winding to a close.

Then signs of uncertainty over the continuation of the course came through official channels; not that we learned anything about the underlying, genuine reason therefor, the orders—subsequently revoked—to attack Poland on 26 August; no, we were kept quite in the dark insofar. At any rate, our class was discontinued, and on the evening of 23 August I was again underway in my auto, driving back to Kiel. Over the car radio I heard the unfathomable news of the German-Soviet Nonaggression Pact and reached Kiel in a state of inward excitement over the question of what this could mean. The members of the course were released to their parent units and, as for me a return to London was out of the question in the midst of the crisis, I was appointed a company commander of the midshipmen at the Mürwik Naval School.

In the following days, the radio and press reports kept me in a state of growing unrest and drove me to the newspaper displays in the city of Flensburg, where on 28 August, I read in the *Flensburger Nachrichten* an exchange of letters, just released by the German News Agency, between Hitler and the French premier, Daladier. Daladier had appealed to Hitler to exert his peaceful intentions in a last attempt for a settlement between Germany and Poland, without doing any harm to German honor. "If," Daladier had written in declaring France's solidarity with Poland, "German and French blood flows anew as it did 25 years ago, in an even longer and more deadly war, each of the two peoples will fight in the confidence of its own victory. Destruction and barbarism will most certainly triumph."

In his reply, Hitler once more stressed the need for a revision of the Versailles treaty and wrote "that it is impossible for a nation of honor to renounce nearly two million human beings and see them mistreated on its own border. I have therefore made a clear demand: Danzig and the Corridor must return to Germany. The Macedonian condition on our eastern border must be resolved . . . settling . . . the question one way or the other . . . but I see . . . no possibility before us of being able to work with Poland in a reasonable sense to correct a situation which is intolerable to the German people and the German Reich."

"To resolve the question one way or the other . . . intolerable," enough of the familiar Hitler vocabulary, this time threatening and framing an ultimatum. Yes, of course, Versailles must be revised. What national-minded German has not demanded that; but to say Versailles and mean something quite different as you do, am I not right, Herr Hitler?—and thus I began my silent dialogue with him— Versailles as a convenient cover for one's megalomania: and announcing, "but I see . . . no possibility . . . of being able to work with Poland in a reasonable sense," because you really don't want to see it. This speech of yours already *is* war. You want *it*, in every line, between every line. When Daladier appealed to your peaceful intentions, it was to a phantom.

And while I read and reread the *Flensburger Nachrichten*, it came back to me, Hitler's saying: "Yes, gentlemen, I still must conduct a European war," spoken to a group of high-ranking military officers in Berlin in 1935 and related to me by a friend, the son of the later Generalleutnant Paul-Willy Körner, one of the officers who was informed of it at the time. Yes, whoever wanted to know it, could have known that Hitler was bent on war.

From the same source I learned of the memorandum of July 1938, in which the chief of the General Staff, General der Artillerie Ludwig Beck, warned the high command and the government of Hitler's aggressive policy, which was endangering world peace. Beck had resigned in August of that year after Hitler's announcement that in the coming weeks he would solve the Sudeten question with force. Of the admonition Beck then gave the commander-in-chief of the army, Generaloberst* Walter von Brauchitsch, I did not learn until after the war, but its sentiment is so exemplary and its language so noble that I cannot see it in print often enough:

> The decisions made now will affect the fate of the nation. History will charge its leaders with a capital crime if they do not act according to their professional and political knowledge and conscience. Their soldierly obedience reaches its limit at the point where their knowledge, their conscience and their responsibility prohibit carrying out a command. If in such situations their council and their warnings do not receive a hearing, they have the right and the duty, before the people and before history, to resign from their offices. If they all act with one firm will, the execution of warlike actions is impossible. They have thereby saved their Fatherland from the worst, from ruin. It is lack of stature and recognition of the task when a soldier in a high position in such times sees his duties solely in the restricted framework of his military tasks, without becoming aware that his highest responsibility is to the whole people. Extraordinary times call for extraordinary actions.

But there was no other suitably high-ranking officer of Beck's stature in the Wehrmacht.

I had admired Beck since 1938 as the model of a soldier and a man who had truly understood it all, even if he, too, had misjudged the regime in the beginning. But some others—to be sure, only a few—from politically sensitive circles had understood Hitler very early. Hubertus Prinz zu Löwenstein and the Karl Bonhoeffer family are examples. As early as 30 January 1933 they said, "Hitler means war, he will be a misfortune for Germany."

Despite my own mistrust, sharpened by the serial murders on and after 30 June 1934,† I had still welcomed the reintroduction of the universal military obligation in March 1935 and the remilitarization

---

*Colonel General; an intermediate rank between general and field marshal for which there is no American or English equivalent.

†Between 30 June and 2 July 1934 the leadership of the Nazi Party's Storm Troopers and other of Hitler's past and present opponents were murdered in the so-called Blood Purge. In the speech in which Hitler defended this action as necessary to avert a counterrevolution, he gave the number of dead as seventy-seven, but, in reality, at least twice that many people had been killed.

of the Rhineland a year later, although it grieved me to have to accept such gifts from Hitler, of all people. Finally, in 1937–38, after two more years in an atmosphere of increasing domestic violence, with the inevitability of the utter ruin of a Germany whose course was set by Hitler before my eyes, and in despairing certainty of being unable to change anything, anything at all, the only thing left for me was psychological flight into an inner emigration from my nation and a passive waiting until one day the regime's inevitable fall would enable Germany to back out of its dead-end. Until then, I would hold out! Yet I was not one of those sharp-sighted intellectuals with high powers of discrimination; I had simply decided to use the common sense that nature had bestowed on me as far as it would go. And it had easily sufficed to see through the tricks that Hitler was playing.

On 1 September 1939 Hitler spoke to the Reichstag of his "love of peace" and "endless forbearance" and then said: "Last night for the first time Poland fired on our own territory with regular troops. Since 0545 hours we have been firing back! And from now on, bombs will be answered with bombs!"

So he finally had it, *finally*, his war—that was how I felt when I heard it over the radio. My God, how happy the man must be, released from the torment of the long wait for *his* war. And two pictures, published shortly thereafter in the German press, have haunted me ever since and will continue to haunt me throughout my life. The first: German troops forcibly opening a Polish border barricade, unsuspectingly throwing open the door to the destruction of the Reich. The other: Hitler observing through a stereotelescope the burning of Warsaw, the result of the destruction which he now served to the east, and whose later return from there to Germany, with interest and compound interest, was to push him into shabby suicide—his stealing away from responsibility—a desperado's exit, worthy of his desperado deeds. What a world of difference between him and the statesman after whom he had dared to name a great warship so as to create a quasi-personal connection with him.

And now war was on the march, the war of an impatient Hitler, who had managed to have his people—a people certainly not without living space, but without patience—swear unconditional allegiance to him. Soon the name "Great German Freedom Fight" was given to this war. Freedom Fight! Freedom! My God, what business did the idea of freedom have anywhere near Hitler? As the goal of a regime, which since 1933 had publicly made itself manifest through murder, terror, and repression? What else could Hitler want than to continue these horrors inside Germany and expand them outwards as far as the military conquests of the Wehrmacht would enable him to do so? No, Herr Hitler had no message of freedom, no real message at all, no progressive goal for mankind—he, who embodied a historical low in public morality. Everywhere I saw his cherished motto, "The strong devour the weak," his lurking wish to wreck the religious life of our people and our civic state of law, his ever clearer manifestation as the destroyer of Western culture that he, of all people, pretended to have to safeguard against bolshevism.

What remained as a personal consequence? To fulfill the tasks assigned to me, but beyond that, insofar as I could influence them, to keep my rank and my duty assignments low and my sphere of responsibility small, and not to strive to get ahead. For the higher the position, the more important its support of Hitler, and the more significant the support of Hitler, the greater the harm to the German people. To speak to the men as little as possible about Hitler, so as not to have to lie too often. To such consequences six years of Hitler could drive one: from the retrospect of 1938, already one could only mourn for Germany—what an insane joke, what a bleak perspective and depressing hopelessness.

My leave flew past, and at the beginning of June I arrived in Hamburg in typical "Hamburg weather"—rain. I registered at a hotel and awaited the morrow, when I was to report for duty to the commanding officer of the *Bismarck*, Kapitän zur See* Ernst Lindemann. Lindemann's reputation as a naval officer was distinguished; he was known as an outstanding gunnery expert, but also as a strict superior, and so it was with some nervousness that I anticipated my first encounter with him.

Ernst Lindemann was born in Alenkirchen/Westerwald in 1894 and entered the Imperial German Navy on 1 April 1913. Because he was not very strong physically, he was accepted only "on probation." With the tenacity and energy that already characterized him, however, he weathered the hardships of a year of cadet training under a particularly strict officer in the heavy cruiser *Hertha* as well as did any of his comrades. Later, one of his classmates who served side by side with him as a naval cadet, wrote me: "His zeal and his concept of duty were exemplary; I cannot recall that he ever fell into disfavor or aroused the anger of our cadet officer." When one thinks what trifling

*Captain

Kapitän zur See Ernst Lindemann, commander of the battleship *Bismarck*. During the training and trial periods he demanded a great deal of his crewmen, but won their admiration and respect. (Photograph courtesy of Hans H. Hildebrand, Hamburg.)

misdemeanors could expose the cadets of that period to censure, it becomes obvious that Lindemann had unusual concentration and strength of will. "Yet he was definitely not a careerist in the negative sense; he was an unselfish, helpful, and popular human being," wrote the same classmate, who also praised his strict and uncompromising concept of the personal and professional obligations of a naval officer. Nevertheless, he was not lacking in ambition. When in later years, Lindemann, who had in the meanwhile become an acknowledged gunnery expert, was told by his classmate that he, Lindemann, would certainly become Inspector of Naval Gunnery some day, he replied: "I still hope at least to become commander of the first battleship squadron in the Kriegsmarine." But there was not such a squadron again in his lifetime.

Lindemann went to the Mürwik Naval School in April 1914. Owing to the outbreak of the world war, this assignment had to be broken off and the examination usually given at the end of training was not held. Like his classmates, he was given sea duty and in 1915 was promoted to Leutnant zur See. In the rank list for 1918 he stood fifth among his approximately 210 classmates, and later in the Reichsmarine and Kriegsmarine he ranked second in his class.

Most of Lindemann's service was in large combatants, on staffs, and at the Naval Gunnery School in Kiel. Early in his career, he made gunnery his specialty and he studied every aspect of it. In 1920, as an Oberleutnant zur See, he was posted to the fleet section of the Naval Staff in Berlin, and thereafter to the predreadnought *Hannover*. By 1925, he had been promoted to Kapitänleutnant and was on the admiral's staff at the Baltic Sea Naval Station in Kiel. When that tour ended, he went as second gunnery officer in the predreadnoughts *Elsass* and, later, *Schleswig-Holstein*. "Lindemann always performed his duties with the same industry and the same conscientiousness," said the classmate quoted above. "For example, as second gunnery officer of the *Elsass* he took paperwork home with him, even though that billet in a predreadnought was generally considered a relatively soft job." After a tour as an instructor at the Naval Gunnery School in Kiel and after being promoted to Korvettenkapitän* in 1932, Lindemann became first gunnery officer in the pocket battleship *Admiral Scheer*. It was at about this time, when more than twenty years of very successful service lay behind him, that he once told some friends that, actually, he was still "on probation," because he had never been advised of his final acceptance into the navy! In 1936, he was assigned as a Fregattenkapitän† to the operations section of the Naval Staff, and, in 1938, as Kapitän zur See, he became Chief of the Naval Training Section in the Naval High Command. This post was followed by one that was a high point in his long and successful career as a gunner, command of the Naval Gunnery School. Without doubt, given

*Commander
†An intermediate rank between commander and captain for which there is no American or English equivalent.

Kapitän zur See Ernst Lindemann, shown here as director of the Ships' Gunnery School at Kiel, prior to his appointment on the *Bismarck*. The photo was taken at the 1939–40 New Year's Eve party at the Gunnery School. (Photograph courtesy of Evelyn Martin, sister of Paul Döring, who fell in the *Bismarck*.)

his specialization in ordnance and his other professional and personal qualities, he was destined to have command of the newest, biggest, and most heavily armed German battleship: the *Bismarck*. The appointment reached him in the spring of 1940.

The morning after my arrival in Hamburg Lindemann awaited me in the captain's cabin aboard ship. I appeared, as was usual in such cases, in "small service dress," that is, a blue jacket with rank stripes around the cuff, and blue trousers. Lindemann, of medium height and build, with sharply chiseled features, stood, similarly dressed, before his desk and looked at me intently with his blue eyes as I announced, "Kapitänleutnant von Müllenheim reporting aboard for duty, as ordered."

"I thank you for your report and bid you welcome aboard," he replied with a friendly smile and gave me his hand. "My objective," he continued, "is to make this beautiful, powerful ship ready for action as rapidly as possible, and I expect your full cooperation. Be-

The author, adjutant to the *Bismarck*'s commanding officer and fourth gunnery officer, shown here as an Oberleutnant zur See. (Photograph from the author's collection.)

cause of your training in the fire control of heavy guns, your action station will be the after fire-control station, as you already know. But that won't be enough to keep you busy before the ship is commissioned and for a while after that, so I've decided to make you my personal adjutant; you've been an adjutant before and also had an interesting tour in London." I was surprised—and very pleased—to hear that I was to be adjutant. He went on to explain what he expected of me. "This duty won't occupy more than your mornings, and in the afternoons you'll be at the disposal of the first gunnery officer, who'll tell you just what he wants you to do. This will be your schedule until the maintenance of the combat readiness of the ship requires you to work all day in gunnery. As adjutant, your main job will be to prepare records and reports, supervise correspondence, and carry out whatever orders I might issue." After a short pause, Lindemann added: "One more thing. In the future, I would prefer to hear people on board use the masculine form when speaking of the *Bismarck*. So powerful a ship as this could only be a *he*, not a *she*." I resolved to accede to his wish and, although I have had a few slips of the tongue, have done so ever since.*

Then Lindemann gave me his hand again, wished me well in my new assignment, and the interview was at an end. As I closed the door of the cabin behind me, I was certain I had just met a very impressive personality, a man who would carry out his new assignment intelligently and conscientiously. Lindemann's manner was in all respects professional.

Being an adjutant was good duty under any circumstances, but in this particular case it would also lead me into a close working relationship with an obviously ideal commanding officer.

*Out of respect for the one and only commanding officer of the *Bismarck*, this rule has also been followed in the German edition of this book.

2

The *Bismarck* Joins the Kriegsmarine

24 August 1940: commissioning day for the *Bismarck*!
Beneath a cloudy sky, a strong, chilly wind from the east bank of the Elbe was raising whitecaps in the river and sweeping over the stern of the ship, whose port side was still made fast to a wharf of the Blohm & Voss building yard. The sun was not shining but, at least, I thought to myself, with the wind coming from that quarter, the ceremony would not be spoiled by rain, and that was something to be thankful for. The crew, in pea jackets and service caps, was lined up three or four deep on either side of the upper deck, from the quarterdeck to the forecastle, the officers and senior petty officers wearing their ceremonial daggers, and the officers their silver-brocade belts, as well. The division officers drew up their men along the joints in the deck's planks and reported to the First Officer, Fregattenkapitän Hans Oels, that their divisions had been formed. The ship's staff officers stood in a body slightly aft of the starboard gangway, opposite which was the honor guard, with a drummer and a bugler. The fleet band was ready on the quarterdeck. Farther forward, under the barrels of the aftermost 38-centimeter turret, representatives of Blohm & Voss added a civilian touch to this otherwise thoroughly military scene.

"Attention! Face to starboard," barked Oels as a sleek white motorboat bearing the battle ensign and the commission pennant came into view, and the bugler sounded the appropriate signal. All eyes were fixed on the boat, which slowed down and came alongside the gangway. The honor guard presented arms and the commanding officer was piped aboard by the bosun. "Crew formed for commissioning

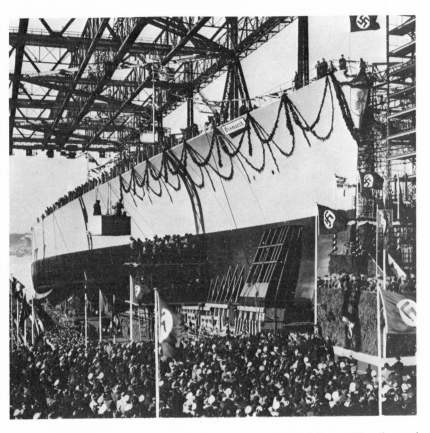

After being christened by Frau Dorothea von Loewenfeld, granddaughter of Prince Otto von Bismarck, the *Bismarck* begins her slide down the ways. Just as the champagne bottle smashed against her bow, a huge sign was lowered to reveal her name and the family crest on her bow was uncovered. Before the ship was completed, the crest was removed and the straight stem was replaced by a flared "Atlantic" bow. (Photograph courtesy of Württembergische Landesbibliothek, Stuttgart.)

ceremony," reported Oels. Followed by Oels and myself as adjutant, Lindemann reviewed the crew, then mounted a podium on the quarterdeck to deliver an address. The men, now standing in ranks eleven or twelve deep, faced their commanding officer and the flagstaff at the stern. Two signal petty officers held the halyards taut, ready to raise the battle ensign.

The ensign is hoisted for the first time on the *Bismarck*, formally placing her in commission in the Kriegsmarine. The horizontal and vertical stripes and the Iron Cross in the upper lefthand corner are reminiscent of the white ensign flown by ships of the Imperial German Navy. In the background is the ocean liner *Vaterland*, which was launched earlier the same day. (Photograph from Bundesarchiv, Koblenz.)

"Seamen of the *Bismarck*!"* Lindemann began. "Commissioning day for our splendid ship has come at last." He called on the crew, on each individual, to do his best to make her a truly effective instrument of war in the shortest possible time, and thanked Blohm & Voss for having worked so hard that she had been completed ahead of schedule. He spoke of the significance of the hour at hand, which demanded a military solution to the fateful questions facing the na-

---

*Lindemann actually said, "Soldiers of the *Bismarck*." The Germans refer to their naval seamen as "soldiers," but use "seamen" when referring to men in their merchant marine.

Kapitän zur See Lindemann, followed by the First Officer, Fregattenkapitän Hans Oels, and the author, reviews one of the ship's divisions during commissioning ceremonies. (Photograph from Bundesarchiv, Koblenz.)

tion, and quoted from one of Prince Otto von Bismarck's speeches to the Reichstag, "Policy is not made with speeches, shooting festivals, or songs, it is made only by blood and iron." After expressing certainty that the ship would fulfill any mission assigned to her, he gave the command, "Hoist flag and pennant!" The honor guard again presented arms and, to the strains of the national anthem, the ensign was hoisted on the flagstaff at the stern and the pennant on the mainmast. Both waved smartly in the wind. The battleship *Bismarck* had joined the Kreigsmarine.

Laid down on 1 July 1936 and launched on 14 February 1939, the *Bismarck* had a net displacement of 45,928 metric tons and a full-load displacement of 49,924.2 metric tons.* Her overall length was 251 meters, her beam 36 meters, and her designed draft was 9.33 meters or, at maximum displacement, 10.17 meters.

Of special interest is the fact that, in comparison with most large warships of the period, her beam was relatively wide in proportion to her length. This characteristic ran counter to the prevalent desire for ever more speed, which called for the least beam possible in relation to length. However, the *Bismarck*'s wide beam seemed to work to her overall advantage, because it lessened any tendency to roll in a seaway and, thus, increased her value as a gun platform. It also reduced her draft, which could be important in the shallow waters of the North Sea. Furthermore, it allowed a more efficient use of space, better placement of armor, a greater distance between the armored outer shell and the longitudinal torpedo bulkheads, which protected the ship against underwater explosions, and simplified the arrangement of the twin turrets of the secondary battery and of the heavy antiaircraft guns.

More than 90 percent of the *Bismarck*'s steel hull was welded. As added protection against an underwater hit, her double bottom extended over approximately 80 percent of her length. Her upper deck ran from bow to stern, and beneath it were the battery deck, the armored deck, and the upper and middle platform decks. A lower platform deck ran parallel with the stowage spaces, which formed the overhead of the double bottom, almost throughout. Longitudinally, the ship divided into twenty-two compartments, numbered in sequence from the stern forward.

---

*According to calculations from her designers (Mr. Otto Reidel), whose records include the construction specifications of both the *Bismarck* and the *Tirpitz*, when the *Bismarck* was completed, her full-load displacement was 50,933.2 metric tons, while the *Tirpitz* was 50,955.7 metric tons.

Armor comprised the highest percentage of the ship's total weight, some 40 percent, and qualitatively as well as quantitatively it was mounted in proportion to the importance of the position to be protected. The upper deck was reinforced by armor that ran almost its entire length. This armor was only 50 millimeters thick but it provided protection against splinters and would slow down an incoming projectile so that it would explode before striking the armored deck below, which protected the ship's vital spaces. The armor on this deck was from 80 to 110 millimeters thick and ran longitudinally between two armored transverse bulkheads, 170 meters apart. At the stern, the armor thickened into an inclined plane to protect the steering gear. Between the transverse bulkheads, the ship's outer shell was covered by an armored belt, whose thickness varied up to 320 millimeters and which protected such important installations as the turbines, boilers, and magazines. Higher up, the armor was between 120 and 145 millimeters thick and it formed a sort of citadel to protect the decks above the armored deck. The two-story forward conning tower, the elevated after section of which served as the forward fire-control station, was also armored with 350 mm on sides and 220 mm on roof.

Since as a weapon system the *Bismarck* was almost exclusively a gun platform, protection of her guns was of the utmost importance. Her main turrets were protected by armor that ranged in thickness from 150 to 360 millimeters. Her secondary armament was less heavily protected; indeed, the relatively light armor in those areas left something to be desired as protection against heavy projectiles.

The arrangement of the superstructure was very similar to that of the *Prinz Eugen* and other German heavy cruisers. There were four decks forward and three aft. The tower mast was on the forward bridge, and atop it were the main fire-control stations for both the antiaircraft gun and the surface batteries.

The propulsion plant, which comprised 9 percent of the total weight of the ship, consisted of three sets of turbines for which twelve high-pressure boilers supplied steam. The plant was designed to provide a top speed of 29 knots at a total horsepower for the three shafts of 138,000, but at the normal maximum of 150,000 horsepower the speed was 30.12 knots. By the time she had been completed, the *Bismarck* was one of the fastest battleships built up to that time.

Her maximum fuel-oil capacity was 8,700 tons, which gave her an operating range of 8,900 nautical miles at a speed of 17 knots, and 9,280 nautical miles at 16 knots. This was a remarkable range for a turbine ship of that day, and it shows that, from the outset, the

In the course of her construction, the *Bismarck* went into a giant floating dry dock at Blohm & Voss so that work could be done on her external hull fittings. (Photograph from Bundesarchiv, Koblenz.)

Bismarck was intended for high-seas operations. However, it was some 1,000 nautical miles less than the range of the preceding *Scharnhorst*-class of turbine battleships, and it might be that this relative lack of endurance contributed to the *Bismarck*'s unhappy end.

Electric-drive steering gear controlled two rudders mounted in parallel, each with an area of 24 square meters.

A big-gun ship such as the *Bismarck* needed an enormous amount of electrical energy. To supply it, there were four generating plants comprised of two 500-kilowatt diesel generators and six steam-driven turbo-generators. In total, these generators delivered approximately 7,900 kilowatts at 220 volts.

While the *Bismarck* was in dry dock, her three propellers, which were almost five meters in diameter, were installed. The workman sitting on the hub of the starboard propeller gives an idea of its size. In the foreground are the ship's twin rudders, her Achilles' heel. (Photograph from Bundesarchiv, Koblenz.)

The battleship's main armament consisted of four double 38-centimeter turrets, two of which, Anton and Bruno, were mounted forward, and two, Caesar and Dora, aft. Their maximum range was 36,200 meters. For these guns, her normal load was 840 rounds, her maximum load 960, each of which consisted of the shell (weighing 798 kilograms), a primer, and a principal charge. The shells were so heavy that they had to be conveyed from the magazines on the middle platform deck to the turrets by means of a mechanical hoist. Secondary armament consisted of twelve 15-centimeter guns (weighing 43.3 kilograms per shell) in six twin turrets equally divided on either side of the ship. They had a maximum range of 23,000 meters. The normal ammunition supply for these was 1,800 rounds. Antiaircraft defense consisted of heavy, medium, and light guns. As heavy flak, the *Bismarck* carried sixteen 10.5-centimeter quick-firing guns in twin mounts, with a maximum range of 18,000 meters. Sixteen 3.7-

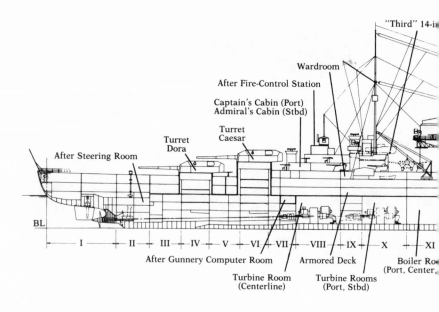

"Third" 14-in

Wardroom

After Fire-Control Station

Captain's Cabin (Port)
Admiral's Cabin (Stbd)

Turret
Caesar

Turret
Dora

After Steering Room

BL

I — II — III — IV — V — VI — VII — VIII — IX — X — XI

After Gunnery Computer Room

Armored Deck

Boiler Ro•
(Port, Center,

Turbine Room
(Centerline)

Turbine Rooms
(Port, Stbd)

centimeter semiautomatic guns in twin mounts provided medium flak, and eighteen 2-centimeter in ten single and two quadruple mounts provided light flak.

Since a battleship is essentially a floating gun platform, a description of the *Bismarck*'s gunnery equipment and procedures may be helpful, especially because these differed from navy to navy. Her surface fire-control system was installed in armored stations forward, aft, and in the foretop. Inside each station were two or three directors. A rotating cupola above each station housed an optical range finder and served as a mount for one of three radar antennas.

The director, which was basically a high-powered telescope, was used to measure bearings for surface targets. In contrast to most other navies, the Kriegsmarine did not mount its directors in the rotating range-finder cupola, but below it, inside the fire-control station. The director was designed like a periscope so that only the upper lens protruded slightly above the armored roof of the fire-control station.

Not only the optical range finders but also the radar sets were used to measure range to the target. German radar had a shorter range and poorer bearing accuracy than the optical equipment. It gave exact range information in pitch darkness or heavy weather, but it was extremely sensitive to shock caused by the recoil of heavy guns. Range and bearing information from directors, range finders, and ra-

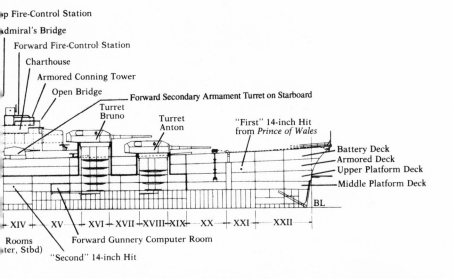

dar were received in two fire-control centers, or gunnery-computer rooms, which provided continuous solutions to ballistic problems.

Control of the guns was primarily the task of a gunnery officer. His personality, as expressed by his choice of words and tone of voice, could influence the morale of his men. Either the main battery or the secondary battery could be controlled from any one of the three stations, whose directors were brought to bear on a target by two petty officers under the direction of a gunnery officer who observed the fall of shot. In each station, there was a "lock-ready-shoot" indicator whose three-colored lights showed the readiness of the battery, the salvo, and any possible malfunctions in the guns. When the battery was ready, the petty officer on the right side of the director would fire by pressing a button or blowing into a mouthpiece. It was also possible to actuate the firing system from any of the computer rooms.

The gunnery officer could order a "test shoot," to find the range, or he could order a series of full or partial salvos. Rather than waiting to spot each splash between salvos of a "test shoot," he could use a "bracket" to find the target. A "bracketing group" consisted of three salvos separated by a uniform range, usually 400 meters, and fired so rapidly that they were all in the air at the same time. On the *Bismarck* it was customary to fire "bracketing groups" and, with the aid of our high-resolution optical range finders, we usually succeeded in

A view of the tower mast and bridges from the forward upper deck, taken while the ship was still outfitting at Blohm & Voss. The platform jutting out from the open bridge was for navigating in such confined waters as canals. It could be folded aft when not in use. Just forward of the two 15-centimeter gun turrets is a group of men in training. In the immediate foreground is turret Bruno. (Photograph from Bundesarchiv, Koblenz.)

boxing or straddling the target on the first fall of shot. The gunnery officer was aided in spotting the fall of shot by one of the gunnery-computer rooms, which signaled him by buzzer when the calculated time of projectile flight had expired.

Once the range and bearing had been found, the gunnery officer in control would order, "Good rapid." He could choose to fire full salvos of all eight guns or partial, four-gun salvos fore and aft. In either case, the "firing for effect" was as rapid as possible.

Firing could also be controlled by the individual turret commanders. This allowed great flexibility in case of battle damage. However, in action it was most important for the senior gunnery officer to retain control of the batteries for as long as possible, because central fire control with the help of computer rooms was far superior to independent firing under the control of the turret commanders.

The forward superstructure of the *Bismarck*. The first level at left is the open bridge. Just aft and to the right is the armored conning tower containing the protected wheelhouse and forward fire-control station. On the next level is a twin 3.7-centimeter antiaircraft gun mount. Just above it is the admiral's bridge. On top of the tower mast is the foretop fire-control station. Two of the three directors in each of these fire-control stations can be seen protruding through the roofs. The rotating range-finder cupolas have not yet been fitted. (Photograph from Bundesarchiv, Koblenz.)

As defense against magnetic mines and torpedoes, the *Bismarck* was equipped with a Mineneigenschutz.* This device consisted of a series of cables that encircled the ship inside the outer hull below the waterline. It was supposed to dissipate the magnetic field generated by the ship so that the enemy's magnetic mines and torpedoes would not detonate.

For reconnaissance, the spotting of shot, and liaison with friendly forces, the *Bismarck* carried four single-engine, low-wing Arado-196 aircraft with twin floats, which also served as light fighters. Two of these machines were stored in a hangar beneath the mainmast, the other two in ready hangars that held one aircraft each on either side of

*Degaussing gear

A view of the forward main-battery turrets from the forecastle. Just aft of and above turret Bruno is the open navigation bridge and the armored conning tower. The enclosure with large windows is the admiral's bridge. Aft of the wave-breaker, to starboard, a detachment of men is assembled. On the wharf, to port, is one of the Blohm & Voss workshops. (Photograph from Bundesarchiv, Koblenz.)

the stack. The planes were launched by means of a catapult located between the stack and the mainmast. This installation ran laterally across the deck as a double catapult, so that launching could be to either starboard or port.

The crew consisted of 103 officers, including the ship's surgeons and midshipmen, and 1,962 petty officers and men. It was divided into twelve divisions, whose numerical strength varied from 180 to 220 men. The battle stations of Division 1 through Division 4 were the main and secondary batteries. Division 5 and Division 6 manned the antiaircraft guns. Division 7 consisted of what we called "functionaries," that is, such specialists as master carpenters, yeomen, cooks, and cobblers. Division 8 consisted of the ordnancemen, and Division 9 combined signalmen, radiomen, and quartermasters. Division 10 through Division 12 were the engineers. During our opera-

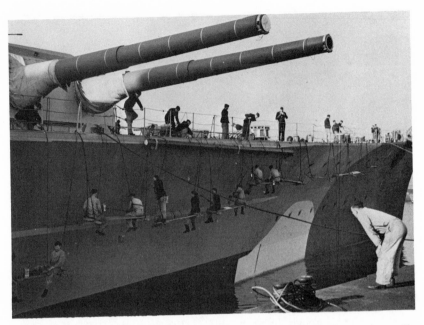

The dark color on the *Bismarck*'s gun barrels is red lead. It was normally applied when the barrels' gray paint blistered and peeled from the heat of extensive firing and had to be scraped. The rings around the guns hold a cable connecting a coil (visible at the muzzle) to an instrument in the turret which measures each shell's time of flight. (Photograph from Ferdinand Urbahns.)

tional cruise, Division 1 through Division 6, reinforced by approximately half of Divisions 7 and 8, occupied every other action station, checkerboard-style. When "Clear for action!" was sounded, the free watch occupied the vacant action stations.

The pilots and aviation mechanics we had on board belonged to the Luftwaffe and wore Luftwaffe uniforms. The air observation people were naval officers who were experienced in the recognition and evaluation of events at sea and had been detailed to the Luftwaffe; they served also as radiomen. When we departed on our Atlantic operation, the fleet staff, prize crews, and war correspondents raised the total number embarked to more than 2,200. On 27 May 1941, when the *Bismarck* sank, only 115 of them were saved.

At the time I joined the ship, her entire crew had not yet been ordered aboard. Some sixty-five technical officers, petty officers, and

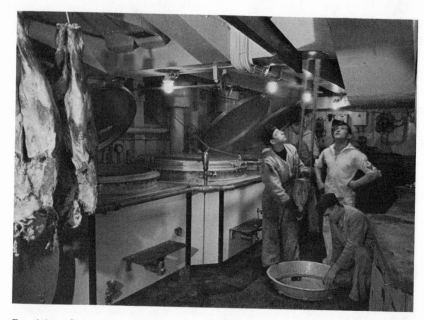

Provisions being brought up to the ship's galley from the meat locker below. The *Bismarck*'s cold-storage spaces could hold 300 sides of beef and 500 dressed pigs. (Photograph from Ferdinand Urbahns.)

men had been on board since around the middle of April, and sixty or so members of the gunnery department arrived in June. These men were subjected to what was called a building course, the purpose of which was to familiarize them with the ship's equipment from the keel up. Many of them, when they first saw the *Bismarck*, with her mighty guns and heavy armor-plating, said to themselves, "Well, nothing can happen to me here, this is really floating life insurance!" The petty officers buried themselves in the intricacies of the engine rooms, the weapons, the trunking and valves, then made drawings and prepared lectures for the instruction of the men. Because of the building work that was still going on, the crew was not, at this time, living on board. Most of them were housed in two barracks ships, the *Oceana* and the *General Artigas*.

Training began, and the petty officers and their men were assigned their stations. In order to get to know their ship, the men moved through her in small groups, crawling through the hold and ventilation shafts, climbing the bridge and the tower mast, and making

A tailor at work in the *Bismarck* during routine hours. When general quarters was sounded, the tailors, like everyone else, would go to assigned battle stations. (Photograph from Ferdinand Urbahns.)

themselves familiar with the double bottom, the stowage spaces, the bunkers, and the workshops. Instruction was given on general shipboard duties, on individual areas of competence, and on procedures for clearing for action. So-called emergency exercises began early. We were already at war, so first of all, we had aircraft- and fire-alarm exercises, then damage-control and clear-for-action exercises. These were gone over again and again, always at an increased tempo.

Signalmen and radio operators, corpsmen, cooks, and stewards began arriving. It was a very young crew; the average age of its members was around twenty-one years, and very few of them had ever been in combat. For many, the *Bismarck* was their first ship. The daily routine was reville at 0600, breakfast at 0630, sweep the decks and clean

The *Bismarck* had a complete cobbler's shop. (Photograph from Ferdinand Urbahns.)

up at 0715, muster at 0800, then either instruction or practical work at such things as maintenance of the ship and stowing the masses of provisions that were being taken aboard at this time—flags, signal books, binoculars, charts, foul-weather gear, enciphered documents, typewriters, medications, food, drink, everything needed for a ship's company of more than 2,000 men. The noon break was from 1130 to 1330, after which duties similar to those of the morning continued until 1700, when the evening meal was served. At 1830 the deck was cleaned again, then the duty day came to a close. The call to swing hammocks was sounded at around 2200.

During this period, Lindemann lived only to accomplish what he had identified as his primary objective when I reported aboard; to have his ship combat-ready, in terms of both men and material, in the shortest possible time. He had his officers report to him regularly on the progress being made in training the crew and outfitting the various departments, but he did not rely solely on these reports. He was frequently to be seen around the ship, satisfying himself on the spot, attending training, supervising whatever construction remained to be

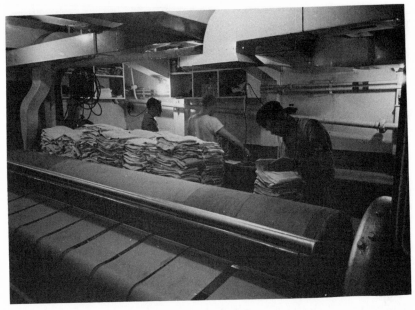

The steam press in the *Bismarck*'s laundry. (Photograph from Ferdinand Urbahns.)

done, asking cogent questions, giving orders, and meting out praise and censure. In addition to these activities, he spent a great deal of time on his paper work, especially reports on questions concerning the ship's guns, with which he was so familiar. I can still see the clear, steep handwriting in which, in polished terms, he explained his requests and wishes, amended the drafts of other people's correspondence, or put proposals that would lead to the earlier combat-readiness of the ship into a style that made them irresistible.

As a rule, Lindemann gave me his orders when I reported to his cabin in the morning. Shortly after I took up my duties, he told me to prepare a schedule of official visits, on which I would have to accompany him, to Hamburg's civil and military authorities. In due course, we visited the senate of the Free and Hanseatic City in Hamburg's venerable Rathaus, or town hall, called on the admiral of the Hamburg Naval Headquarters, and on various military commanders and headquarters important to the ship. In August and September 1940 Hamburg was already a target of quite frequent but not very heavy British night bombing raids. Whenever possible, the *Bismarck*'s guns

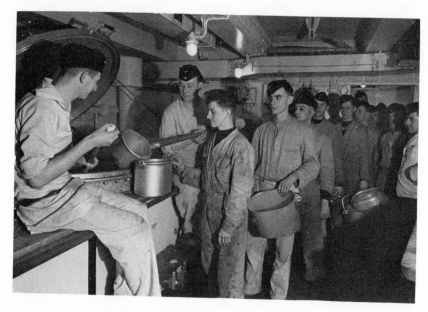

A mess cook ladles food from a giant cauldron into pots that were then carried to the mess decks of the *Bismarck*. (Photograph from Ferdinand Urbahns.)

joined in the city's antiaircraft defenses, and so one of our calls was on the commander of Hamburg's air defenses, Brigadier General Theodor Spiess, in his roomy offices on the Aussenalster. During visits such as this, wartime security put something of a constraint on the subjects of our conversation, but nevertheless we gained an insight into the morale of official Hamburg. Optimism and confidence in victory were universal. What else, indeed, would one expect, right after the fall of France?

Most of the visits involved a boat ride across the Elbe from the Blohm & Voss yard. The first time we made this crossing, Lindemann suddenly asked, "Do you know how big the *Bismarck* really is?" He asked this because the *Bismarck* was officially rated at 35,000 tons, and very few people knew her true tonnage. "Well," I answered, "35,000 tons plus fuel and water, I think." Not without pride, Lindemann said, "53,000 tons, fully equipped." When he saw how much that impressed me, he added, "But that is strictly secret information!" Of course, I promised not to divulge it and didn't until the end of the war.

Members of the *Bismarck*'s crew at mess. The large pot was used to bring hot food from the central galley. (Photograph from Ferdinand Urbahns.)

How far this secrecy extended in practice on board was another matter. There was a machinist chief petty officer who regularly began his briefing on the ship thus: "The *Bismarck* is a movable sea-tank of 53,000 tons. For public consumption and to third parties, the first two numbers change places, so they read 35,000 tons, and that's what you tell outsiders."

However, the British government, to whom the *Bismarck*'s construction data were transmitted in accordance with the Anglo-German Naval Agreement in July 1936, had accepted the tonnage figure of 35,000 as entirely true. Even naval attaché Troubridge personally had not doubted it and after the war justified himself by the facade of honest sincerity behind which Raeder had repeatedly assured him of Germany's firm determination to observe strictly the stipulations of the agreement. Nevertheless, with the political perspicacity characteristic of him, as early as the end of 1936 Troubridge had taken the view and repeatedly reported to London that "when the moment comes, the Anglo-German Naval Agreement will go the way other treaties have before—but not at the moment."

The *Bismarck* made fast to the main outfitting wharf of Blohm & Voss, Hamburg, which she left for the first time on 15 September 1940. After initial trials, she returned to the yard on 9 December 1940 to get her "finishing touches." She had to remain there until 6 March 1941 because the Kiel Canal was blocked by a sunken ship. (Photograph courtesy of Blohm & Voss.)

I found Lindemann a thoroughly competent naval officer and gunnery man, one who not only quoted but lived by Prince Otto von Bismarck's motto, *Patriae inserviendo consumor* (I am consumed in the service of the fatherland). He seemed to be always on duty. When his name came up in the wardroom, it invariably evoked high respect and there was a feeling that it would be impossible to equal his almost ascetic-seeming devotion to duty. Nevertheless, the man had a big heart, a characteristic he was more inclined to exhibit to his men than to his officers, and a radiant smile that greatly contributed to the affection he enjoyed among the crew. Maschinengefreiter* Hermann Budich said later: "I completed a year's building course in the *Bismarck* and was then steward to the Rollenoffizier,† Korvet-

---

*Seaman Apprentice (Machinist)

†The Detailing Officer, who assisted the First Officer in distributing the seamen of the ship's company among the battle stations, as called for by the battle or clear-for-action drills. The composition of the divisions was determined and drill stations were assigned on this basis. Every member of the crew had to be berthed in a space as near as possible to his action station so that he could reach it without interrupting the ship's traffic patterns.

tenkapitän Max Rollmann, who occupied a cabin in the *General Arti-gas*. Here I encountered many officers, and began to know and esteem Kapitän zur See Lindemann. When one bumped into an officer in the confines of the barracks ship, 90 percent of the time a bawling-out resulted. When the 'Old Man' came aboard, he radiated an aristo-cratic but not overbearing calm. If there was any excitement, he immediately took charge. In short, the ordinary sailor came to trust this man, despite his 'piston rings.'"*

*Captain's stripes

 51

Sea Trials
and Battle Practice

The day came for the *Bismarck* to leave the Hanseatic City for the first time and undergo her trials, which were to be conducted in the eastern Baltic. She had been lying with her stern to the Elbe, but on 14 September 1940 tugs turned her 180 degrees. A day later she slid into the channel and steamed through a mass of ships and launches, past the familiar landscape of the village of Blankenese, to the lower Elbe. How often I had passed this way on ships in peacetime, when the banks were full of people waving friendly greetings. But now it was wartime; the *Bismarck*'s sailing had not been announced, and the banks were empty. Early in the evening we dropped anchor in Brunsbüttel Roads, in order to enter the Kiel Canal the next morning. Naturally, the first time we anchored, I wanted to watch the operation. The anchor chain ran out with what to those who were forward of the navigation bridge sounded like a great roar but, because of the length of the ship, was scarcely audible to those aft. Furthermore, since the hull of the ship remained completely motionless, which is far from the case when a cruiser drops anchor, anchoring must have seemed to the men aft like something that was going on in "another part of town." After darkness fell, the air raid alarm sounded; the "Brits" were back. Aided by the light of a searchlight ashore, the *Bismarck* joined in the antiaircraft fire. But there was no visible result.

On 16 September, we entered the canal with the ship in a state of "heightened watertight integrity." In the highest state of readiness, that is, "cleared for action," all passageway doors and ventilation fittings, both intake and outlet, were closed, so that the *Bismarck*

On 15 September 1940, the *Bismarck* cast off from the wharf at Blohm & Voss and got under way for the first time. She is seen here going down the Elbe with the aid of a tug. (Photograph courtesy of Württembergische Landesbibliothek, Stuttgart.)

was divided into eighteen watertight compartments and a number of hermetically sealed spaces. In "heightened watertight integrity," which was usually ordered when navigation was hazardous, passage-way doors and ventilation fittings remained open. There was also an intermediate state, "wartime steaming condition," which was used when there was a high risk of encountering the enemy.

The transit of the canal took two days and on the evening of 17 September we made fast in Scheerhafen, near Kiel. For the young engineers who had their hands on levers controlling 150,000 horse-power, bringing this giant of a ship through the narrow canal on her maiden voyage was a great achievement. The slightest error on their part could have had disastrous consequences for both the ship and the canal. And so, when we got to Kiel, Lindemann came on the ship's loudspeakers and congratulated the men in the boiler rooms and engine rooms.

The following week was devoted to aligning the ship's batteries. After spending a few more days at a harbor buoy, on 28 September we steamed under the escort of *Sperrbrecher 13** for Arkona, on the

---

*A Sperrbrecher was a converted merchant ship, whose function was to sweep mines that the Kriegsmarine's regular minesweepers might possibly have missed. One such vessel was generally assigned to protect large German warships in waters where there was a high risk of mines. The ship being protected followed in the Sperrbrecher's wake.

The *Bismarck* going down the Elbe on her first voyage. At one point, she collided with the lead tug *Atlantik* but sustained no damage. (Photograph from the author's collection.)

island of Rügen, then went on to Gotenhafen (now Gdynia) without escort.

We spent fully two months at the Gotenhafen naval base, trying out the ship and her systems in the Gulf of Danzig. After testing her degaussing gear, we made measured-mile, endurance, and high-speed runs and tested her general maneuverability. Not until 23 October were the engines cleared for full speed.

Our ship did very well in all these tests. She was extremely steady, and rolled and pitched very little, even in a seaway. Her rudder response was almost immediate, and she did not heel excessively when she made a turn; when backing, even at speeds close to bare steerageway, she turned so easily that she could get out of tight spots without the help of tugs. We also tested to see how maneuverable she would be if only her engines were used in case her steering gear and rudders should be put totally out of action during an engagement. It was found that with both rudders locked in an amidships position, the *Bismarck* could be held on course only with great difficulty. The

reason for this was that the convergent design of her propeller shafts provided only a weak turning movement, even with the outboard shafts rotating in opposition at full power. No one aboard at the time could have had any idea of the fateful effect this flaw would one day have.

Lastly, with the thought that only the powered steering gear might be disabled while the rudders could still function, turning the rudders by manpower alone was practiced. For such manual steering, the crews of both after 15-centimeter turrets, a total of thirty-two men, would have to proceed as expeditiously as possible to Compartment II of the upper platform deck, where the manual steering gear was located. Of course, full speed could not be maintained with manual steering because of the pressure of the water against the rudders. The upper speed limit under these conditions was about 20 knots.

To us in the ship, high-speed runs were the most exciting of the tests. Then, the giant warship would surge forward with the full power of her engines at play, yet she lay steady in the water, making but a small bow wave. On the upper deck, there seemed to be hardly any vibration, but sometimes the men on the living decks had to hold their plates and utensils on the tables to keep them from bouncing to the floor. This shaking did not occur at the highest speeds, however, but at a slightly lower, so-called critical speed, at which the vibrations of the different parts of the ship were mutually reinforced and created maximum vibration throughout the ship. Earlier, when I was serving in the *Königsberg*, she sometimes vibrated so violently that the optical fire-control instruments could not be used. Ultimately, the problem was remedied by keeping away from the critical speed so as to minimize the reinforcement effect. But I never experienced anything like that in the *Bismarck*.

The speed trials continued into November, a speed of 30.8 knots being recorded on one occasion. That exceeded the designed speed! Not only were there joy and pride on board, but an appreciation of the tactical advantage that such a speed might provide during the coming operation in the Atlantic. The crew's already boundless confidence in their ship was once again justified.

One day, after a series of measured-mile runs, we had an unusual experience. In a fairly rough sea, we were entering the harbor of Gotenhafen when we suddenly suffered a minor malfunction of our steering mechanism, and came to a full stop to repair it. Nearby was a fishing boat, lying low in the water and laboring along. So low, in fact, was she lying that her abundant catch was obviously about to be spilled back into the water. By megaphone, she called to the *Bismarck*: "Could you give us lee? Our catch was so good that we can't stow it safely." Briskly, Lindemann ordered the officer of the watch to do as requested, and we escorted the boat into the calm waters of Gotenhafen Roads. Next day the *Bismarck* had fish on the menu!

Along with the mile runs, we carried out intensive training in the safe operation of the ship at sea. The green crew found their sea legs and became thoroughly familiar with their new surroundings. Emergency drills were followed by more emergency drills, or Rollen schwoof,* as the men called them. The word would be passed to "Make fast the passageways!" which meant "Set the cleared-for-action state of watertight integrity." Or, "Fire!" When that word was passed, the source of the flames would be sealed off and hoses made ready to extinguish them. Or, "Man overboard!" In this exercise, a life buoy would be thrown over the side to mark the spot where the man fell. A lifeboat would be launched with all possible speed, pick up the buoy, and then be hoisted in. Every man had to know his station and, at drill, proceed to it at once and perform his duties as instinctively as a sleepwalker. Emergency drills often began on the

*Emergency rushes

quarterdeck, where the off-duty section of the crew, some 1,600 men, would be mustered. Alarm bells would sound an emergency signal—for example, *tuy-tuy-tuy-tuy-tuy* (make fast the passageways!)—and these 1,600 men would storm down assigned companionways to their posts. Step lively! Step lively! but not on the head or fingers of the man below you. Two steps down, get a good grip, swing down, spring off to the right, always faster, lively, lively. So well practiced did the crew become that five minutes after the word was passed, the bridge had a report from every station.

Hermann Budich and two of his comrades, wanting to be first at their station in Compartment IX of the lower platform deck and therefore to avoid the choked companionways, sought a different route. They discovered a little-used companionway aft. Hanging onto the inner edge of the hatch, they took their usual two steps down, let go, and flew, rather than ran, for their station—all this with heavy tools stuck in the belts of their work clothes. Out of breath, they reached their goal, the first to do so, and reported it "clear." But hadn't Budich brushed against something soft at the bottom of the companionway? What could it have been? The men's division officer, Kapitänleutnant (Ingenieurwesen)* Werner Schock, did not attend the critique that followed the drill, but when it was over they were ordered to report to his cabin at once. There, a corpsman was applying cold compresses to a beautiful black eye. "Gentlemen," he began what promised to be an unpleasant interview, "if it weren't that everyone looks so much alike in work clothes, I would have caught you earlier. I know you move fast, but you don't have to ram your tools down my throat! Be more careful! Now, get out!" They did shout "Wahrschau!"† before they jumped, but that was to alert anyone who might have been there to move out of the way, not to tell him to stay put.

During emergency drills First Officer Oels had heavy responsibilities. His station at such times was in a secondary command center that had been set up in Compartment XIV of the upper platform deck. Since he was primarily responsible for the defense of the ship against fire, gas, and flooding, as well as for the maintenance of buoyancy and trim, the damage-control center was in the same compartment. There, also, was the ship's security station, in which were kept plans that showed all the ways in which the pumping, flooding, fire-

*Lieutenant Commander (Engineering)
†Used in the German Navy for "gangway!"

Immediately after coming aboard the *Bismarck*, her commanding officer re-
ceives a salute from the ship's honor guard. Behind Lindemann is the author,
wearing the aiguillette of adjutant to the commanding officer. (Photograph
from Bundesarchiv, Koblenz.)

extinguishing, and ventilation systems could be used to combat the
above-mentioned dangers. This area was the heart, so to speak, of the
ship, where vital information was delivered and equally vital decisions were made.

In mid-October Lindemann made an operational-readiness inspection. He ordered the most important emergency drills, then went
around to each station, watched how the men handled their equipment, and asked pertinent questions. What he saw satisfied him.
"Seamen of the battleship *Bismarck*," he said in closing his critique,
"this day has convinced me that you have made good progress.
Thanks to your instructors and to your own enthusiasm, the *Bismarck* is well on her way to becoming operational." The crew had
completed a kind of crash course. In peacetime, it took as a rule two
years to bring a warship from commissioning to combat-readiness
but, because of urgent missions to come, the *Bismarck* could count
on no more than nine months.

My tour of duty as Lindemann's adjutant ended about this time. The change, which I foresaw from the start, was brought about by my assignment to a three-week gunnery course at the Naval Gunnery School in Kiel, in November 1940. At the end of August 1939, the school's course on fire control for large-caliber guns, which I was then taking, was interrupted by the threat of war. Now it was to be revived as the completion of gunnery training. At an "all men aft" assembly held for some special reason at the beginning of November, Lindemann remarked that on account of my "valuable" professional training I would henceforth serve in gunnery only. My place as adjutant was taken by Leutnant zur See* Wolfgang Reiner. Although I left Lindemann most unwillingly, I realized it was a move that had to be made. As operational deployment approached, all that mattered was the combat-readiness of the ship, and that required that the utmost advantage be taken of everyone's specialty.

The second half of November was spent in more tests of the *Bismarck* and her engines. The only thing new was that gunnery drill was added to the routine. Not only were the brand-new guns tested for steadiness, the smooth working of their mechanisms, ballistic performance, and accuracy, but the resistance of the ship's components to recoil was also tested. Practice firings served to train the gunlayers in the best way of keeping on target. These drills could be carried out satisfactorily at close range with 8.8- or 5-centimeter subcaliber guns inserted into the barrels of the heavy and medium guns. Because the shells and powder charges used were relatively light, this kind of firing was economical. At the same time, it gave the gunnery officers practice in fire control.

Full-caliber firing! Unforgettable was the day the *Bismarck*'s heavy guns fired their first full salvo. How far, how violently would the recoil cause the ship to heel over, how quickly would she right herself? Below, in the engine rooms, where steam pressure was fifty-six times that of the atmosphere, the seconds passed slowly. A single crack in the main steam line caused by the shock of firing could result in the death of everyone in the engine room. Boom! The ship seemed to be abruptly jarred sideways, a few loose objects came adrift, a few light bulbs shattered, but that was all. Topside and in the control centers, it was quite different. Up there, the sideways movement was scarcely noticeable. Of course, the concussion had already been felt throughout the ship. Her steadiness in the water showed the *Bismarck* to be an ideal gun platform.

*Ensign

The *Bismarck* shows her rakish, modern lines in Kiel Bay in late 1940. A censor slightly altered her appearance by removing the radar antenna from her foretop range-finder cupola. (Photograph courtesy of Blohm & Voss.)

At the end of her trials, the ship was scheduled to return to Blohm & Voss in Hamburg so that the yard could give her the "finishing touches" it had not been able to complete by September. On 5 December, therefore, the *Bismarck* departed Rügen under escort of *Sperrbrecher 6* and steamed for Kiel. Passage of the canal again took two days, and on 9 December we were back in Hamburg.

On 17 December, Reich Minister Dr. Joseph Goebbels spoke in a shipyard workshop to the employees of Blohm & Voss, who had been assembled for a plant rally. His listeners also included some of Hamburg's leading personalities, among them the chief of the Hamburg naval station, Vizeadmiral Ernst Wolf.

Goebbels began by thanking the workers for their stalwart conduct and disciplined labor in the face of the British night air raids. He called the shipbuilders and the yardworkers soldiers of labor in a Germany that was conducting a total war, a people's war "in the best sense." The Führer had not wanted this war, had for long years called upon Europe to be sensible and made peace proposals. Nothing had

availed. But now, when England had forced the nation into war, Germany would stake everything on ending it victoriously. In this war, in which as in any conflict the victor creates legal title by force of arms, the German people had the opportunity to make good the mistakes of four hundred years of German history. While other peoples had divided the world among them, Germany had become Europe's battleground. But today the politically and racially united German Reich was proclaiming its rights. The dictate of Versailles had circumscribed German living space to an intolerable extent after the German leadership had failed at the decisive hour. That sort of failure was impossible today, because it was the Führer's unshakeable will to win the war for the whole Folk. Germany would finally have its just share of the world's riches, and above all be able to solve its social problems in a generous and exemplary manner. For the attainment of this goal the Führer had personally made himself the guarantee, and in Germany only his word had weight.

The employees of the Blohm & Voss yard enthusiastically joined in the "*Sieg heil!*" to Hitler with which the minister closed his address.

Well, now, Herr Goebbels, you've really let the cat largely—if not completely—out of the bag, I thought when I read excerpts of his speech in the *Völkischer Beobachter* (Hamburg edition) the next day. Of course Goebbels had repeatedly offered the elimination of Versailles as an alibi for the war; but then he had said something very different and exceptionally honest: "In this war, in which as in any conflict the victor creates legal title by force of arms, the German people has the opportunity. . . ."

Donnerwetter, that was clear: the formulated primacy of might over right, certainly over the "right to a homeland," which in the eyes of the Brown despots did not belong to the "subhumans" of the East, and for which, after the German military disaster, the displaced German nationals who had conveniently forgotten Hitler's and Goebbels's principles of conquest would strive as a God-given right.

"To make good the mistakes of 400 years of German history . . . its just share of the world's riches." Certainly, that was it.

Four hundred years ago there had been a vast Kingdom of Poland, a Grand Duchy of Lithuania stretching almost to Smolensk, and later an even further-reaching Kingdom of Poland.

Owing to my family history I had carried a map of the east inside by head since childhood. My forebear Gebhard had come to the east in the seventeenth century as a result of the masterful huntsmanship that made him known far beyond the borders of his Alsatian homeland—where in the German Imperial Free City of Strassburg his ancestor Burcard had received and quartered in his mansion Kaiser Rudolf von Habsburg and his retinue in 1284 and the latter's son King Albrecht in 1300.

While still a youth Gebhard was called by Kaiser Ferdinand II to be chief hunting master at the Vienna Hofburg and, upon the emperor's recommendation, to the court of Warsaw in order to introduce German-style hunting in Poland. With letters patent dating from 1625 he had served Prince Wladislas Sigismund (subsequently King Wladislas IV) and his successor Johann II Casimir as a master of the hunt and of falcons in the Grand Duchy of Lithuania and as a royal Polish chamberlain, attaining Polish indigenous rights in 1635. In his new homeland Gebhard was granted extensive landed properties. He became Starost* of Bersteningken, Striowken, and Masselingken. He acquired estates in Prussia as well, becoming hereditary lord of Puschkeiten, with Schleidanen, Meisterfelde, Stockheim, Dommelkeim in Samland, Frisching and Palpasch in what later became the District

---

*The recipient of a fief from the Polish crown, who was invested with police and juridical powers.

Prussian Eylau, Podollen in District Wehlau, and Moritzkehmen and Plauschwarren in District Tilsit. Gebhard also served Wladislas in his campaigns against Moscow and the Turks. The Cossack rebellion, the invasion of Poland by 200,000 Tartars who plundered and burned almost to Warsaw, and growing social and political unrest in Poland, cumulatively led him to lay down his Polish offices in 1668 and go back to Prussia, where he died in 1674 and was buried in the Sackheim Church in Königsberg.

To burst into the east already scarred by the bloody migration of peoples, to conquer, plunder, and practice "racial hygiene," to put forward the revision of Versailles as a curtain raiser for territorial conquests—a military hors d'oeuvre—one could have gradually grasped that to be Hitler's goal whether or not one had read *Mein Kampf*, and I had not.

Hitler's supreme goal was "total war"—the military expression that since the publication of Ludendorff's *Der totale Krieg* in 1935 had been embraced by the totalitarian regime as the mark of a "heroic" new era and had become a sponsored slogan. It was a war in which the entire personal, material and spiritual strength of a people would be used against the entire enemy people, not just its armed forces. After years of preparation this now to be considered "total" war was underway. It had exploded with growing force and would predictably become increasingly ruthless, ruled more and more by feelings of hate and revenge; thus, it must appear ever more inappropriate for bringing about any kind of acceptable settlement.

But moderation was not Hitler's concern. To the contrary, as legal title to the conquests he expected in enemy territories, Goebbels had only paraded the same cherished thesis, according to which in total war the role of policy was merely to serve military realities: that the place one's infantry reached in the enemy homeland would dictate the content of policy. That was it, the absolute immoderation of Hitler's policy, once more displayed by Goebbels—to those who saw, anyway.

Among those who had recognized Hitler's immoderation early was Eric Arthur Blair, later to become famous as George Orwell. In March 1940, he had written in *The New English Weekly*: "Suppose that Hitler's programme [in *Mein Kampf*] could be put into effect. What he envisages, a hundred years hence, is a continuous state of 250 million Germans with plenty of 'living room' (i.e., stretching to Afghanistan or thereabouts), a horrible, brainless empire in which, essentially, nothing ever happens except the training of young men for war and the endless breeding of fresh cannon-fodder." Exaggerated, certainly, but scarcely moreso than Hitler's sick visions.

I had to think of the man for whom my ship, the *Bismarck*, was named. One of my relatives had worked as chief nurse in the colonial hospitals at Tanga and Dar-es-salaam in German East Africa from 1911 to 1913 and subsequently animated me to study our colonial history. I had come to understand with what extreme, endless caution, what intense watchfulness, what understanding of the whole European scene, and with what a fine sense of international risks Bismarck had dared to take even the smallest step of colonial expansion. "The papers are full of the launch of the *Bismarck*, so named because of the Führer's love of him," Troubridge wrote in his diary for 15 February 1939: "Let us hope that they follow Bismarck's policy, which was one of friendship for England or at any rate avoidance of a clash." What a striking contrast between the insatiable conqueror Hitler and the statesman Bismarck, whose name the Brown despot had so shamefully misused through his christening of my ship.

It seemed to me a confirmation of my thoughts, my conception of Hitler as a conscienceless gambler, when, a day after Goebbels's speech, he spoke to officer aspirants at the Berlin Sports Palace of "the necessity of struggle in general," the need "to beat, or you will be beaten—kill, or you will be killed" and characterized the world as a "traveling cup" that was continually awarded anew to the bravest people. There was at present no world power that possessed so great a core of racially homogenous people as the German Folk, which he had made ready for this war, resolved to do nothing halfway and stake everything on the turn of the card. Should the 85 million Germans in national solidarity succeed in making good their claim to life, Europe's future would belong to them—if not, then this people would fade away, it would sink back, and it would not be worthwhile to live among this people.

Living in an environment in which there was no room for a critic of Hitler, I could again react only with impotence, choke back my cold rage at the tyrant, and withdraw still more deeply into myself. This is your war, Herr Hitler, I thought, not the German people's. You've got it all backwards—only when you and your system have one day disappeared, only then, when hopefully we will again be ruled by a statesman rather than a gambler, only then will it again be worthwhile to live.

Over Christmas, we were given leave. For most of us, this was our last chance to be with our families. Those who could not get away

v. Müllenheim - Rechberg.

v. Gross - Pfetsfeld.

J. Nacher

Schloss Puschkeiten near Königsberg, seat of the Prussian branch of the von Müllenheim-Rechberg family, 1647–1742. (Engraving from the author's collection.)

The *Bismarck* returns up the Elbe in December 1940 to complete her yardwork at Blohm & Voss. Her range-finder cupola and radar antenna have been installed above the foretop, but the cupola has not yet been mounted on top of her forward fire-control station. (Photograph courtesy of Blohm & Voss.)

were able to spend a few more hours in hospitable Hamburg. I enjoyed two weeks of marvelous skiing in the Bavarian mountains.

On 24 January 1941, the finishing touches to our ship were completed, but we could not immediately return to the Baltic to continue our trials and battle practice, as we had intended to do. A sunken ore ship was blocking the Kiel Canal, and the thick ice that had formed during this exceptionally severe winter was delaying salvage work. The idea of our making the long detour around Jutland was rejected by Berlin. I used the prolonged stay in Hamburg to take a special course in the English language in the fields of law and economics, in which I had a long-standing interest. I had the great luck to find a teacher who could look back on many years' residence in the British Commonwealth and possessed a truly sovereign knowledge of English. Moreover, we understood one another politically from the start. When I asked him how the newly fashionable Nazi "buzz-word" *gleichschalten* could best be translated, he scornfully offered, "to boil down to the same level," and the "down" in this formulation had at once indicated that we saw things the same way. In the Hamburg branch of the Reich Federation of Interpreting Organizations—through which, on his advice, I took a translator and interpreter's examination—he had long been on the blacklist on account of his political opinions, and one day one of the federation's functionaries warned me against being around him too much. "If you only knew," I thought, "against whom unfortunately Germany was not warned in time."

I also had great luck during these months through a social connection with an outstanding Hamburg hostess, who maintained an international circle even in wartime. When one was with her—let her be remembered with gratitude here—it was balm to be able once more to talk reasonably and easily about God and the world, secure against eavesdropping, and so wonderfully far from all the cramping of conversations in so-called national circles. It happened that I had received an invitation to one of her gatherings scheduled for the time Hitler was to give his speech of 30 January 1941, and I fully resolved to accept it and for once to escape Hitler's tirade, his "baying into the ether," as I always called it. But unfortunately a strict order came from the First Officer for us to assemble around the loudspeaker in the officers' mess for Hitler's speech, and it seemed to me better to avoid the complications in the offing for an unexcused absence. The speech was broadcast from the Berlin Sports Palace and on account of its length I took in only those points for which over the years I had developed a special sensitivity.

After the usual retrospective of the "desperate situation of the Reich" eight years earlier, Hitler launched his first attack on the nature of the English as unsocial, born capitalists and reactionaries, to whose account the outbreak of the First World War also should be debited. Yet for Germany the year 1918 had been exclusively the result of an exceptional accumulation of personal incompetents in the leadership of our people, which would "never" be repeated. He himself had drawn up his foreign policy program at an early date: "The destruction of Versailles!" He had not been able to make it clear to a certain Jewish-internationalist capitalist clique that 85 million

Germans were indeed a world power. National Socialism would determine the next millenium of German history; the last part of 1939 and 1940 had already practically decided the war. If our enemies were pinning their hopes on America, well, he had also taken that possibility into his calculations. And if they should have other hopes, let's say that Italy would desert the Axis, well, these gentlemen should not invent a revolution in Milan but should rather take care that none break out among themselves. The Duce and he were neither Jews nor businessmen and when they gave each other their hands it was the handshake of men of honor. And if the enemy was hoping that the German people would be weakened by hunger, the Four Year Plan had taken care of that, too. These German people would go through thick and thin with him. The Germans' spirit of fanatical readiness would enable them to pay back every blow they received with interest and compound interest. Thus we were going into the new year with the best-equipped Wehrmacht in German history. At sea the U-boat war would begin this spring and there, too, the enemy would see that we had not been sleeping—"the year 1941 will be, of this I am convinced, the historical year of a great New Order in Europe . . . and will contribute . . . to securing a reconciliation among peoples. . . . And I may not forget my earlier indication that if the world were to be plunged into a general war by Jewry, all Jewry will have played out its role in Europe! . . . The coming months and years will show that here, too, I have seen rightly."

The promise of a New Order in Europe was becoming increasingly common in speech and print; there were no longer any bounds on the phantasy and the megalomania. The threat of the obliteration of the entire Jewish population hung more darkly than ever over Europe.*

Because of the blocking of the North Sea Canal our sailing date was set for 5 February and until then we conducted training and battle drills in Hamburg Harbor. When that day came the canal had still not been cleared, but we could not have left, anyway, because some of our pressure gauges and electrical lines to the boiler-room ventilators had been damaged by the extreme cold, and we were not ready for sea. Although this situation was remedied by 16 February, the canal remained blocked and our departure had to be postponed again, this

---

*When Hitler spoke in January 1941, the extermination of the Jews had already begun, although the formal decision to liquidate the Jewish population of Europe was not made until the Grosse Wannsee conference on 20 January 1942 resolved the Jews in German-occupied Europe be exterminated (the "final solution of the Jewish problem").

Korvettenkapitän (V) Rudolf Hartkopf, chief administrative officer of the *Bismarck*, and his assistant, Oberleutnant (V) Günther Tischendorf, supervise the loading of provisions at Scheerhafen in March 1941. "V" (Verwaltungs) designated an administrative officer. (Photograph from Ferdinand Urbahns.)

time to 5 March. At the end of February, Lindemann complained in the War Diary: "The ship has been 'detained' in Hamburg since 24 January. Five weeks of training time at sea have been lost!"

On 6 March, we cast off from the wharf at the Blohm & Voss yard, steamed out into the Elbe, and once again headed downstream. As the familiar silhouette of Hamburg slowly sank astern, I had the feeling that this time our absence from the beautiful Hanseatic City would be longer. For part of the way, the admiral commanding the Hamburg Naval Headquarters did us the honor of escorting us in his flagship. Scattered passers-by waved from the banks of the river. At midday we dropped anchor in Brunsbüttel Roads. Three fighters flew air cover for us and an icebreaker and two Sperrbrechers anchored nearby to protect us against possible aerial torpedo attacks. We entered the canal the next day and, on the eighth, reached Kiel, where we spent a few days in Scheerhafen again aligning our batteries. Also, we had to take

The *Bismarck's* camouflage is touched up at Scheerhafen in March 1941. (Photograph by Ferdinand Urbahns.)

aboard ammunition, two of our four assigned aircraft, provisions, fuel, and water. Leaving Kiel, we continued our voyage east. Because of the thick ice in the western Baltic, the predreadnought *Schlesien*, a veteran of the Imperial Navy, went ahead of us to act as an icebreaker. Behind her came *Sperrbrecher 36*, then the *Bismarck*. On the afternoon of 17 March we once again dropped anchor at Gotenhafen, which was to be our principal base until we sailed on our first operational cruise.

The following days saw a great deal of activity. We conducted more high-speed trials and endurance runs and tried out our hydrophone gear. This apparatus emitted a sound impulse, by whose echo the range, bearing, nature, and conduct of its contact could be determined. A well-trained listener could even identify the type of vessel the echo came from. I still remember the report from the *Prinz Eugen*, our companion on our Atlantic sortie, on 24 May 1941 before the battle off Iceland. It was made by Leutnant zur See Karlotto Flindt, a technically proficient and talented listening officer, who was sitting at the hydrophones when around 0440 he picked up turbine noise and reported to the ship's bridge: "Noise of two fast-moving turbine ships at 280° relative bearing." The ships proved to be the *Hood* and the *Prince of Wales*.

The most important thing now was intensive testing of our batteries. Practice firing for the instruction of the fire-control officers and gun crews alternated with carrying out projects for the Gunnery Research Command for Ships, an organization that ran its own trials on new ships with a view to improving the ordnance of various ship types. For me, as a gunnery officer, these tests were exciting but for the crew they just meant drill and still more drill. Battle practice in the daytime, battle practice at night! The men did not complain, however; they were in the swing of things and were becoming more and more anxious for our first operation at sea to get under way.

On 19 March, Lindemann learned from the captain of our younger sister ship, the *Tirpitz*, that, according to a directive issued by the Seekriegsleitung,* the *Bismarck* was to be ready for her first mission from three to four weeks earlier than originally intended—now she was to be ready at the end of April. This meant that Lindemann had to cut short the program of the Gunnery Research Command for Ships. He arranged for it to end on 2 April, after which time we conducted our own surface and antiaircraft firing practices. We also spent more time than before in "clear for action" drills and in training our air crews. Since the *Prinz Eugen*, which was commissioned three weeks earlier than the *Bismarck*, was to be our escort on the upcoming operation in the Atlantic, we conducted tactical exercises with her. We also exercised with the 25th U-Boat Flotilla and, with the help of the tanker *Bromberg*, we practiced refueling at sea. It was at this time that we started doing searchlight drills. We carried seven searchlights: one was on the forward edge of the tower mast, two were atop the main hangar, and the other four were high up on either side of the stack. They were directed to their target through the use of large high-powered binoculars mounted in posts on the sides of the forward battle command station. The purpose of these drills was to provide practice at picking up an indicated object at first try and keeping the light on it.

Besides the frozen lines to the boiler-room ventilators mentioned earlier, we were having a few other problems with the propulsion plant: some hairline cracks in superheaters; a broken ball-bearing ring on the middle main coupling; a loose sleeve in one of the main

*Naval War Staff

The heavy cruiser *Prinz Eugen* steaming at high speed on her trials before joining the *Bismarck* for exercises in the Baltic. Only a practiced eye could tell the silhouettes of the two ships apart. (Photograph courtesy of Robert O. Dulin, Jr.)

steam lines; salt in one of the turbines. All these insignificant defects in the plant were repaired in short order, but in the War Diary Lindemann complained that they tended "to tarnish the good impression previously gained of its reliability." When Naval Group Command North, to which the ship was subordinate, read his comment in the middle of April, it added: "Considering that this is new construction, the engine malfunctions were very minor. In fact, the propulsion plant has been running more smoothly than expected." Lindemann must have felt increasingly impatient to be able to report to the Seekriegsleitung that his ship was ready for operational deployment.

Over Easter, which fell on 13 April that year, the *Bismarck* went in to Gotenhafen for four days. There, we were to take on more ammunition and have some work done on our engines.

When we were at sea, the routine was still battle practice, more battle practice, and battle problems. In a battle problem, a particular tactical situation was assumed: we were, for example, covering an attack by the *Prinz Eugen* on a British convoy that was escorted by a battleship. We went into action with the battleship, in the course of which we received two hits. The damage done to the *Bismarck* would be presented as realistically as possible: electrical breakdowns by removing fuses, fires by using some bombs, gaseous fumes by using tear gas, and so forth. In the case of damage that could not be portrayed, "damage notices" would be posted in the relevant parts of the ship; for example, "To the commander of the port II 15-centimeter turret: Turret destroyed by a direct hit. Your gun crew has been wiped out." That turret commander and his men would then cease to take part. In partially destroyed compartments, there was feverish activity: fire hoses were hooked up, openings were sealed tight, alternate piping routes established, and all damage was brought under control. Obermaschinist* Oskar Barho, of the main electrical control station, enjoyed the breakdowns and kept calm in the face of them. He gave precise instructions and repeatedly told his men: "If I become a casualty, you must keep everything going exactly the same way, regardless of your grade! If you think one of my orders is incorrect, report it!"

The officers told their men again and again: "If only two or three are still alive at your station, carry on. That's right, carry on! Execute the required emergency procedures at once!" This could be somewhat difficult for a young seaman or stoker who received a damage notice and had to decide how to deal with it himself. He would then have to give orders, which previously had been done by officers—how often they had practiced that! Superiors intervened only when lack of experience led the men into making serious mistakes. Not a bad way to accustom a young man of thinking and acting on his own.

Or another battle problem, which Maschinengast† Josef Statz would never be able to get out of his mind. He was ordered on board in April 1941 and assigned for duty to Stabsobermaschinist‡ Gerhard Sagner, whose specialty was indicated by his title of Pumpenmeister—Pump Master. Sagner had welcomed Statz, a draftsman trained in skyscraper and bridge construction, with the words, "You're just the man for me!" and carefully acquainted him with his duties. Statz was happy with his transfer to the *Bismarck*, and with the personal style of his immediate supervisors—his division officer, Oberleutnant (Ingenieurwesen) Karl-Ludwig Richter, the second damage control officer, and Pumpenmeister Sagner. He also hit it lucky with his mess; its members were all old hands. Of the five machinist seamen, four had already been sunk once, in the cruiser *Karlsruhe*.§ Among them he had become especially close to Erich Seifert, generally known as "Fietje." And Fietje enjoyed telling him

---

*Warrant Officer (Machinist)
†Machinist
‡Chief Warrant Officer (Machinist)
§The *Karlsruhe* was torpedoed by a British submarine in the Skaggerak on 10 April 1940.

repeatedly and forcefully of his experiences in the *Karlsruhe:* "If any-thing like that ever happens with the *Bismarck,* keep all your things on, especially your leather clothing, and your money in your pocket!" At the time, he had neglected to do either.

But now to the battle problem, the most important Statz would experience during his training period in the *Bismarck.* As the "dam-age control center runner" he had to carry a message to turret Bruno, to which command of the ship had been transferred upon the hypo-thetical destruction of the forward conning tower. Statz encountered the captain there and tried to make the report to him—but Linde-mann did not react at all. "Don't you see?" someone shouted at him. "The captain's dead!" Statz replied, "But the captain's standing right here!" And at the same time he looked at Lindemann, who, despite every outward sign of indifference, showed a sly smile. "Well, Slim, are you from Cologne?" he heard, in the same voice as before, from Oberleutnant zur See Friedrich Cardinal, a Rhinelander like Statz. Then Cardinal said, "Give me the message and come to the bridge!" And the two of them had stood on it, no one else, for all the others in the area had supposedly become casualties. Cardinal explained: "All the men who are pretending to be casualties put their caps on side-ways, so they can be recognized most quickly. You must take notice of that!" They could not know, Statz and Cardinal, that a month later this sort of battle problem, complete down to the details, would overtake them in reality.

After a battle problem, there would be a muster on the quarterdeck. Under the leadership of the captain, the damage done and the coun-termeasures taken were discussed in detail. Lindemann understood how to ask the right questions. Not only was he thoroughly conver-sant with the duties of naval officers and with his own specialty, naval ordnance, but he had a good understanding of technical mat-ters. When the engines were the subject of discussion, he was quick to expose excuses for mistakes and attempts to gloss them over. Be-ing a competent judge of these things, he would close the muster by distributing praise and censure. But his tone was always objective. The point of it all was that every man should learn and should have his confidence in himself and his ship built up. "When we made a mistake," said Maschinengefreiter Budich, "we did not hear angry words from our superiors."

From time to time, the ship went in to Gotenhafen Roads to catch her breath. When the sky was clear and a gentle wind blew over the ship, we experienced some truly enchanting nights there. Once,

Lindemann reviews machinist petty officers. The geared wheel on the sleeve of the man at the end of the front row indicates his career specialty. The device on his collar shows that he is a petty officer, first class. (Photograph from Bundesarchiv, Koblenz.)

when the full moon drew a broad silver track across the mirror-calm water, Matrose* Paul Hillen was on watch on the upper deck. Seeing the captain coming towards him, he prepared to make his report, but Lindemann waved it aside and said: "Isn't that a wonderful sight? Many people would give a great deal of money to see it, and we have it for free." Later, Hillen, who had only recently come aboard, said, "It was the first time I heard, not an order, but a personal remark from a high-ranking officer." Yes, Lindemann had a winning way, which inspired affection. Many of the ship's survivors have testified eloquently to that. One of them put it this way: "We admired, indeed we loved, our commanding officer, Kapitän zur See Lindemann. He was like a father to us. He always had an open ear for the cares and needs of his crew."

One day, after being at sea a long time, we dropped anchor and the

*Seaman Recruit

signal was piped: "Work details to the forecastle!" That could mean only that the mailboat was coming out from Gotenhafen. And there it was, already quite close. Suddenly it was too close, and we heard a crash. Commented the chief bosun, "Shit, no mail!" Sadly he watched over the stern post as the boat, already taking on water dangerously, and its longed-for cargo returned, stern first, to Gotenhafen.

Lindemann's entry in the War Diary for the month of April was: "In sum, all our time was taken up in training. Heavy emphasis was placed on how the crew would perform in the upcoming operation. The men seem to have come to recognize for the first time the magnitude of our mission, which they still don't know, but easily guess." He was right. Rumors were rife that we were about to depart on a mission. Watchwords surfaced, were whispered from man to man, then disappeared to make room for new ones.

The *Tirpitz* appeared in the Gulf of Danzig for her own working-up exercises and that provoked speculation that we were about to form a task force with her.

Plans for
Commerce-Raiding

At the beginning of the war, for which the navy was not prepared, the inferiority of the German fleet in relation to the British was incredible. The ratio was around one to ten. All we had ready for immediate deployment in the Atlantic were two pocket battleships, the *Deutschland* (soon renamed *Lützow*) and the *Admiral Graf Spee*, and twenty-six U-boats, and that small number of ships could not be expected to have a decisive effect on the war. The commander in chief of the Kriegsmarine, Grossadmiral Erich Raeder, who was taken completely by surprise by the outbreak of war with Great Britain, commented, "Our surface forces are still so inferior to the British in numbers and strength that, should they become fully committed, the only thing they could show is that they know how to die gallantly." At least initially, the only naval bases Germany had at her disposal were in the southeast corner of the North Sea, as had been the case in the First World War; whereas, thanks to their geographical position and worldwide bases, the British could control every important sea lane and impede the passage of German warships to and from the Atlantic. However, when Germany occupied Norway and France in 1940, the Seekriegsleitung had advance bases to the north and west, which made it easier to deploy our surface forces and U-boats on the oceans.

"The Kriegsmarine is to carry out commerce warfare, and it will be aimed primarily against England." Overnight, this statement, contained in Directive No. 1 for the Conduct of the War of 31 August 1939, became the basis of the Seekriegsleitung's strategic objectives.

The weakness of her fleet obliged Germany to confine herself to conducting economic warfare and to design an appropriate strategy. The Seekriegsleitung was convinced that, by cutting Britain off from her Atlantic supply lines, Germany could win the war, providing *all* resources were concentrated on this objective. To Raeder, "all resources" meant all naval resources which, in turn, meant that our long-range, heavy surface units—battleships and pocket battleships—were to conduct commerce warfare on the high seas. This strategy was intended not only to disrupt Britain's trade but to tie down her forces and keep them from concentrating: when German commerce-raiders appeared in a certain ocean, Britain would have to move naval forces there, thus denuding some other area. In this way, it was hoped, other German operations such as a ship's breakout into the Atlantic or its return to port would be facilitated.

This offensive reached its high point in the first quarter of 1941. Between January and March, the battleships *Scharnhorst* and *Gneisenau*, under Fleet Commander Admiral Günther Lütjens, spent eight weeks operating against British commerce in the Atlantic. The total of shipping sunk was relatively low, 122,000 gross register tons, but the mere presence of German battleships in the Atlantic had forced the British Admiralty to take inconvenient countermeasures. It had to deploy significant forces in the ocean areas menaced by the *Scharnhorst* and *Gneisenau* and in the northern passages into the Atlantic, and the whole convoy system was thrown into disarray because, now, every convoy had to be escorted by at least one battleship. The Seekriegsleitung responded with a plan to form a four battleship task force—the *Bismarck*, *Tirpitz*, *Scharnhorst*, and *Gneisenau*—and send it into the Atlantic to prey on convoys. Although the intention was to send this force out as soon as possible, it turned out that the *Tirpitz*, commissioned on 25 February, could not be operational until the late fall, and in the meantime the Seekriegsleitung would have to be content with the *Bismarck*, *Scharnhorst*, and *Gneisenau*. No wonder it was anxious for the powerful *Bismarck* to be operationally ready.

The expectation with which the *Bismarck* was awaited was matched by a corresponding anxiety on the British side. To the Admiralty, it was clear that, when the German commerce-raiders in the Atlantic were joined by the *Bismarck*, the situation could only get worse. Therefore, it watched the *Bismarck's* progress towards operational readiness very closely and apprehensively. It was reported at one point that the *Bismarck* in company with light forces had passed

Skagen on a northwesterly course on 18 April 1941. That day the *Bismarck* was still training in the Gulf of Danzig.

British interest in the *Bismarck* went back further than that, however. Since the beginning of the war, Winston Churchill, first as First Lord of the Admiralty and, after May 1940, as Prime Minister, had repeatedly pointed out the danger inherent in the German fleet being reinforced by the addition of the *Bismarck* and had taken part in discussions as to how this danger could best be countered. In February 1941, the *Bismarck* still not being operational, he tried to foresee what the Seekriegsleitung would do. He reasoned that it would not make a move until the *Bismarck* and the *Tirpitz* had been completed—and up to that point, he guessed Berlin's intentions correctly. It seemed to him that Germany could not make better use of these great ships than to keep them in the Baltic and, every now and again, start a rumor that they were about to depart for the Atlantic. This would compel Great Britain to keep a powerful force at Scapa Flow, the Home Fleet's main base, to the detriment of other missions. It would also give Germany the advantage of being able to select her own timing for any operation; she would not have to keep her ships in constant readiness. And since the British ships would naturally have to go into the yard from time to time, it would be very difficult for the Admiralty to maintain superiority over the German commerce-raiders at all times.

Two months later, Churchill coupled a reference to the serious damage that the *Scharnhorst* and *Gneisenau* had done to British trade at the beginning of the year with the remark that the situation would shortly be made worse by the appearance of the *Bismarck*. Several times since the war began, he had pointed out the necessity of mounting air attacks to delay the construction of the *Bismarck* by at least three or four months, and said that success in such a mission would be helpful to British fleet dispositions worldwide. In August 1940, he wrote to the British Air Minister, "Even a few months' delay in *Bismarck* will affect the whole balance of sea-power to a serious degree."* And in October, he wrote to the Combined Chiefs of Staff, "The greatest prize open to Bomber Command is the disabling of *Bismarck* and *Tirpitz*."†

However, these hopes about the fate of the *Bismarck* were not to be fulfilled before she put to sea on her first operational cruise.

---

*Winston Churchill, *The Second World War*, Vol. 11 p. 578.
†Churchill, p. 445.

 **5**

Operation Orders
for Exercise Rhine

The success of the *Gneisenau* and *Scharnhorst* as commerce-raiders naturally led the Seekriegsleitung to intensify its conduct of this form of warfare with heavy ships. On 2 April 1941, as the *Bismarck* approached combat-readiness, it issued an operational directive that read in part:

During the past winter the conduct of the war was fundamentally in accord with the directives of the Seekriegsleitung . . . and closed with the first extended battleship operation in the open Atlantic. Besides achieving important tactical results, this battleship operation showed what important strategic effects a similar sortie could have. They would reach beyond the immediate area of operations to other theaters of war (the Mediterranean and the South Atlantic). The goal of the war at sea command must be to maintain and increase these effects by repeating such operations as often as possible.

We must not lose sight of the fact that the decisive objective in our struggle with England is to destroy her trade. This can be most effectively accomplished in the North Atlantic, where all her supply lines come together and where, even in case of interruption in more distant seas, supplies can still get through on the direct route from North America.

Gaining command of the sea in the North Atlantic is the best solution to this problem, but this is not possible with the forces that at this moment we can commit to this purpose, and given the constraint that we must preserve our numerically inferior forces. Nevertheless, we must strive for local and temporary command of the sea in this area and gradually, methodically, and systematically extend it.

During the first battleship operation in the Atlantic the enemy was able always to deploy one battleship against our two on both of the main supply lines. However, it became clear that providing this defense of his convoys brought him to the limit of the possibilities open to him, and the only way he can significantly strengthen his escort forces is by weakening positions important to him (Mediterranean, home waters) or by reducing convoy traffic.

As soon as the two battleships of the *Bismarck* class are ready for deployment, we will be able to seek engagement with the forces escorting enemy convoys and, when they have been eliminated, destroy the convoy itself. As of now, we cannot follow that course, but it will soon be possible, as an intermediate step, for us to use the battleship *Bismarck* to distract the hostile escorting forces, in order to enable the other units engaged to operate against the convoy itself. In the beginning, we will have the advantage of surprise because some of the ships involved* will be making their first appearance and, based on his experience in the previous battleship operations, the enemy will assume that *one* battleship will be enough to defend a convoy.

At the earliest possible date, which it is hoped will be during the new-moon period of April, the *Bismarck* and the *Prinz Eugen*, led by the Fleet Commander, are to be deployed as commerce-raiders in the Atlantic. †At a time that will depend on the completion of the repairs she is currently undergoing, *Gneisenau* will also be sent into the Atlantic.

The lessons learned in the last battleship operation indicate that the *Gneisenau* should join up with the *Bismarck* group, but a diversionary sweep by the *Gneisenau* in the area between Cape Verde and the Azores may be planned before that happens.

The heavy cruiser *Prinz Eugen* is to spend most of her time operating tactically with the *Bismarck* or with the *Bismarck* and *Gneisenau*.

In contrast to previous directives to the *Gneisenau-Scharnhorst* task force, it is the mission of this task force to also attack escorted convoys. However, the objective of the battleship *Bismarck* should not be to defeat in an all-out engagement enemies of equal strength, but to tie them down in a delaying action, while preserving her own combat capability as much as possible, so as to allow the other ships to get at the merchant vessels in the convoy. The primary mission of this operation also is the destruction of the enemy's merchant shipping; enemy warships will be engaged only when that objective makes it necessary and it can be done without excessive risk.

The operational area will be defined as the entire North Atlantic

---

*The *Bismarck* and the *Prinz Eugen*
†The *Scharnhorst* was undergoing a lengthy overhaul of her engines.

north of the equator, with the exception of the territorial waters (three-nautical-mile limit) of neutral states.

The Group Commands have operational control in their zones. The Fleet Commander has control at sea.*

The Group Commands mentioned in the above directive were Naval Group Command North in Wilhelmshaven and Naval Group Command West in Paris. Both commands, each of which was then headed by a Generaladmiral,† were responsible for the conduct of operations in their geographically defined areas of authority. They were immediately subordinate to the Seekriegsleitung in Berlin, and the senior officers afloat were subordinate to them. This form of organization was adopted for several reasons: a headquarters ashore would have the best intelligence available; it would have much better communications than the senior officer afloat; and its communications systems was less vulnerable. The Fleet Commander has control over all tactical matters and, obviously, in action.

The directive had no sooner reached the Fleet Commander, Admiral Lütjens, than it was out of date. On 6 April, the *Gneisenau*, then undergoing repairs in Brest, was hit by a British aerial torpedo and a few days later by four bombs. She would not be available for a long time. The task force was now reduced to the *Bismarck* and the *Prinz Eugen*. Nevertheless, Lütjens proceeded to issue orders for the overall operation, and Group North and Group West did the same for their respective areas of authority. Group North was responsible until the task force entered the Atlantic, at which point Group West took over.

In his order of 22 April, Lütjens gave the forthcoming operation the code name Rheinübung (Exercise Rhine),‡ and set forth his strategy: taking every precaution not to be detected, the task force was to steam through the Great Belt, the North Sea, and the Denmark Strait to the North Atlantic, where it would attack convoys on the Halifax-England route. Subsequent missions would depend on what the situation was, but munitions and stores would be replenished at a port in western France.

---

*"Weisung für weitere Unternehmungen von Überwasserstreitkräften." Skl. 1 Op 410/41 Gkdos Chefsache, 2. IV. 1941. For the full text, *see* Appendix A.

†An intermediate rank between admiral and fleet admiral for which there is no American or English equivalent.

‡"Operationsbefehl des Flottenchefs für die Atlantikoperation mit 'Bismarck' und 'Prinz Eugen' (Deckbezeichnung 'Rheinübung')," Flottenkommando B. Nr. Gkdos 100/41 Al Chefsache o 22. IV. 1941, Annex I: "Allgemeiner Befehl für die Atlantikunternehmung," is reproduced in Appendix B.

Under Lütjens's command were to be the *Bismarck* and *Prinz Eugen*; the U-boats operating along the north-south Atlantic routes; after the end of May, the four U-boats on the Halifax-England convoy route; the scouts *Gonzenheim* and *Kota Penang*; two fleet supply ships; and five tankers. For protection, *Sperrbrecher 13* and *Sperrbrecher 31* would precede the force on its way from Arkona to the Great Belt, and the 5th Minesweeping Flotilla would escort it through the Skagerrak minefield. Thereafter, it would have a destroyer escort consisting of the *Z-23*, *Z-24*, *Hans Lody*, and *Friedrich Eckoldt*. Independently operating forces such as reconnaissance planes and fighters were to provide cover as prescribed by Group North and Group West.

Group North timed the task force's passage through the Great Belt so that it would transit the channel in the outer Kristiansand-South minefield around 2030 on the third day of the operation and enter Korsfjord (now Krossfjord), near Bergen, the following morning. After spending that day in the fjord, which would allow the *Prinz Eugen* and the destroyers to refuel from a tanker, at nightfall the formation would depart through the northern exit of Hjeltefjord and steam at high speed for a point thirty nautical miles west of Sognefjord. Thereafter, it would continue at its own discretion.

Group North recommended that, weather permitting, the force should straightway enter the Atlantic through the narrow Iceland-Faeroes passage, keeping far away from the coast of Iceland. Should that not be possible, it should wait in the Norwegian Sea for more favorable weather and make use of the opportunity to fuel from the tanker *Weissenburg*, which would be in the area.

Group West allowed the Fleet Commander a free hand in carrying out the mission in the area of operations, but stipulated that, although the *Prinz Eugen* was to spend most of her time operating in tactical combination with the *Bismarck*, she would be subject to being sent on special missions at the direction of Group West or at the discretion of the Fleet Commander. It stated that if the breakout into the Atlantic should be detected, the mission would remain the same, being shortened or broken off, as necessary. Group West emphasized that the important thing was to preserve the combat-readiness of the ships; combat with enemy forces of equal strength should therefore be avoided. Contact with a single battleship covering a convoy was permissible only if it could be done without fully engaging her and if it gave the cruiser a chance to engage successfully the remaining escort or the convoy. If combat was unavoidable, it was to be conducted as forcefully as possible.

Two points in the above directives require comment. One point is that the Seekriegsleitung's admonition that our forces strive "gradually, methodically, and systematically" to establish command of the sea in the North Atlantic, even "local and temporary" command, was, in view of our limited surface strength, unrealistic. Apparently, it was born of a certain euphoria in Berlin.

The other point is that the brevity with which the directives treated the matter of a sortie being undetected might give the reader the impression that this aspect of an operation, though desirable, was almost incidental. Such was far from the truth, but the few lines devoted to it sufficed because it was axiomatic with German naval officers at that time that if they could get out into the Atlantic without being detected the chances of their operations being successful were enormously improved. Indeed, concealment was their highest priority, at least until the first attack had been made on a convoy. For our side, the weaker side, surprise was half, if not more, of the battle. And it must be said that surprise in later phases of an operation was equally important. Once the position of a German commerce-raider had been disclosed by a contact with the enemy, the raider might just as well make for remote areas of the high seas, from which it could later emerge with renewed surprise. An undetected sortie was the first link in this hoped-for chain of surprise, and was recognized as a prerequisite to the success of our surface ships in the Atlantic.

On the other hand, and this also should be noted, the Seekriegsleitung did not go so far as to make concealment a sine qua non of a sortie. If it had done this, every time a force was detected its commander would have had to immediately break off or at least delay his operation. And this in turn would have meant aborting any serious threat to Great Britain from the very form of warfare upon which the Seekriegsleitung had just decided. There was no getting away from the fact that Germany had to live with the risk of her intentions being prematurely disclosed because Great Britain was strategically situated on the routes to the Atlantic. It was left to the force commanders to decide whether to proceed immediately or to turn back and try again later.

On the morning of 25 April the *Bismarck* received orders to depart Gotenhafen in company with the *Prinz Eugen* on the evening of the twenty-eighth. The 6th Destroyer Flotilla was to escort the task force. This order had hardly arrived on board when we were informed that our departure on Exercise Rhine would be postponed by from seven to twelve days because, as the *Prinz Eugen* was making her way to Kiel, a mine exploded near her and did her considerable damage.

Lütjens spent 26 April in Berlin, conferring with Raeder on Exercise Rhine. The mishap on the *Prinz Eugen* gave the two admirals an opportunity to go over once more the composition of our surface task forces in the Atlantic. Lütjens declared that if there was to be no change in the plan to send the *Bismarck* and *Prinz Eugen* out as a pair, either it should be done as soon as the latter was repaired, or they should wait for the next new moon after the one just waning. But there were also valid reasons for awaiting the availability of the *Scharnhorst*, which was still in the midst of an engine overhaul, if not for the *Tirpitz*, which was nearing completion, as well. The appearance of all four would make the operation much more effective than it would be with a "teaspoon" deployment now. Lastly, if one of our new and powerful battleships were to appear now as a commerce-raider, the enemy would have time to take countermeasures that would reduce the prospect for success when joint operations became possible. Nevertheless, it was deemed wiser to resume the Battle of the Atlantic as soon as possible: in plain language, the *Bismarck* and *Prinz Eugen* should not await reinforcement, they should go into action right away.

And with this return to the original operation order, Lütjens came to agree fully and completely with the basic thinking of Raeder. In Raeder's opinion, any interruption in the battle against Great Britain's Atlantic commerce could only strengthen the enemy. Furthermore, in the northern latitudes the passing season was bringing ever shorter nights and every delay increased the difficulty of reaching the Atlantic under cover of darkness. But, he told Lütjens: "Deliberate, careful operations are indicated. It would be a mistake to risk a heavy engagement for limited and perhaps uncertain results. Our objective with the *Bismarck* and, later, the *Tirpitz* must be continuous, sustained operations."

Act boldly against convoys—keep heavy British escorts tied down but don't get into action unless it serves the primary mission and can be done without excessive risk—if battle becomes unavoidable, conduct it with full force—operate deliberately and carefully—such were the conflicting demands laid upon the Fleet Commander. How often was Lütjens going to have the heavy responsibility of deciding when to forgo an irretrievable tactical opportunity and when to take it. His mission was far from simple.

After his meeting with Raeder, Lütjens stopped briefly in the office of the future Rear Admiral (Engineer) Hans Voss, who was then assigned to the Oberkommando der Marine. "Voss," he said, "I'd like to make my farewells; I'll never come back." When Voss looked at him questioningly, he added, "Given the superiority of the British, survival is improbable."

6

Another Postponement and Last Liberty

"Anxiety to get into our first battle," wrote a twenty-four-year-old petty officer, "reached fever pitch, and tension was kept high by numerous rumors that we were about to go into action."

By the end of April the *Bismarck* was provisioned for three months at sea. This meant that, among other things, she had embarked enough pork and beef to feed a city of 250,000 inhabitants for one day. On the twenty-eighth, Lindemann reported to the Oberkommando der Kriegsmarine, Naval Group North, Naval Group West, and the Fleet Commander that his ship was fully operational in terms of men and material. In the War Diary, he noted: "The crew, from whom it is impossible to keep our approaching departure secret—war correspondents, prize crews, and B-Dienst* teams come aboard daily—still does not know that our departure has been postponed. Everyone is working on the final preparations with enthusiastic energy. I fear a considerable setback in morale if the delay is long." Then again:

The first stage of the ship's life since her commissioning on 24 August 1940 has come to a successful conclusion. Our goal has been attained in eight months, only 14 days more than the original schedule (Easter) allowed, and that was only because we had to wait in Hamburg for six weeks because the Kiel Canal was blocked and ice was creating a problem.

*Funkbeobachtungsdienst (radio intelligence)

The crew can be proud of this feat. It was achieved because the desire to come to grips with the enemy as soon as possible was so strong that I had no hesitance in making extraordinary demands on the crew over long periods of time, and because the ship and her systems suffered no major malfunction or damage, despite heavy demands and very little time in port. The level of training is equivalent to that attained by big combatants preparing for the annual battle practice inspection in a good peacetime year. Even though my crew, with few exceptions, has had no combat experience, I have the comforting feeling that, with this ship, I will be able to accomplish any mission assigned to me. This feeling is strengthened by the fact that, in combination with the level of training achieved, we have—for the first time in years—a ship whose fighting qualities are at least a match for any enemy.

The delay in our departure, whose approximate date obviously could not be kept from the crew, is a bitter disappointment to everyone concerned.

I will use the waiting time the same way as before, to acquire a still higher degree of training, but I will allow the crew more rest, and give more time to divisional exercises and the external conditioning of the ship, activities that have understandably had to be severely restricted in recent weeks.

The following days were devoted to continuing battle drills, maintenance, and division drills. Statz had his hands full; he inspected the shafts for the engine battle circuits, lubricated the bevel wheel connections, and saw for the first time the little white box with the red letters "Procedure V"* in the pumping room for setting off the scuttling charges if that became necessary. The idea that it would ever have to be used was as remote as the stars. "Soon we were so keyed up," the then twenty-four-year-old petty officer wrote later, "that we burned to see our first action. The numerous rumors and watchwords of an imminent operation heightened this tension from day to day."

It was announced that the fleet staff would embark in the *Bismarck* on 12 May and conduct a practical test of its collaboration with the ship's command in a clear-for-action drill at sea the following day. The staff numbered approximately sixty-five men. It consisted of the Fleet Commander, Admiral Günther Lütjens, his chief of staff, Kapitän zur See Harald Netzbandt, with whom he had been close friends for years, three other senior officers, the fleet engineer, the fleet surgeon, the officer in charge of the B-Dienst, and a few junior officers, plus petty officers and men.

*The "V" stood for *Versenken*, the German term for 'scuttle.'

Kapitän zur See Harald Netzbandt, Admiral Lütjens's chief of staff. (Photograph courtesy of Hans H. Hildebrand.)

Then fifty-one years old, Lütjens was an undemonstrative man, tall and thin, with dark, serious eyes. He entered the Imperial Navy as a cadet in 1907 and first saw the world from the heavy cruiser *Freya* the same year. After completing the required courses at the Naval School and graduating twentieth out of a total of 160 midshipmen in his class, in 1909 he had his first sea duty in a position of responsibility in a big ship. That tour was followed by many years in the sort of training assignments with which he was to be repeatedly entrusted, officer training and development of the torpedo-boat flotillas. Thus,

Günther Lütjens, right, shown here as captain of the cruiser *Karlsruhe*. This photo, taken as his ship neared the equator on 24 November 1934, records Admiral Triton's visit on board in preparation for the appearance of King Neptune the next day. From left to right: Admiral Triton's aide-de-camp; Admiral Triton; a chief petty officer; the *Karlsruhe*'s First Officer, Korvettenkapitän Schiller; and Lütjens. (Photograph from the author's collection.)

from 1911 to 1912 he was the officer in charge of naval cadets in the heavy cruiser *Hansa*. During the First World War he served in torpedo boats, winding up as a commanding officer and half-flotilla leader of the Flanders Torpedo Boat Flotilla. In the years following the war, he commanded torpedo-boat flotillas, served on the Naval Staff in Berlin, and was captain of the *Karlsruhe*. In the year 1937, as a rear admiral, he became Chief, Torpedo Boats. Soon after the Second World War broke out, Lütjens, then a vice admiral, was in command of reconnaissance forces in the North Sea. As a deputy of the Fleet Commander, he led the covering forces, the *Scharnhorst* and *Gneisenau*, during the invasion of Norway. In July 1940 he assumed command of the fleet and was promoted admiral in September of the same year. In February and March 1941, he gained operational experience striking at British supply lines in the previously mentioned Atlantic

From left to right: Dr. Hans-Günther Busch, Dr. Hans-Joachim Krüger, and Dr. Rolf Hinrichsen, the ship's dental officer, on the bridge of the *Bismarck*. (Photograph courtesy of Frau Erika Busch.)

sortie of his flagship *Gneisenau* and the *Scharnhorst*. This experience proved useful to him in a new operation aboard the mighty *Bismarck*.

Throughout his career Lütjens was seen by both his superiors and his peers as a highly intelligent, able, and courageous man of action. Although his serious, dry disposition and reserve made it difficult for his more outgoing comrades to get close to him, this forbidding exterior concealed a noble and chivalrous character. When he spoke, which he did in a quick and lively manner, it was evident that his thought processes were equally lively.

On the morning of 13 May, the fleet staff conducted the tests on board, as had been announced, and inspected and tried out the ship's internal communications facilities. A morning was ample time for that. When at noon the staff disembarked to return to Gotenhafen in the tender *Hela*, the newcomers among our crew were an experience richer. They had seen how, just as in times past a commander led his troops into battle, so now, in the Nelson tradition, the Fleet Com-

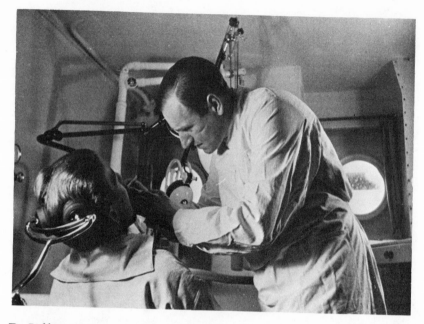

Dr. Rolf Hinrichsen treating a dental patient on board. (Photograph courtesy of Frau Erika Busch.)

mander would exercise command in action. He would be as close to death as anyone else on board. He would have no more of a rear echelon in which to take refuge than would a corpsman.

In many ways, it must have seemed to the greenhorns in the crew that their ship belonged less to the world of war than to the world of modern industry. Many of them worked in confined spaces, far from the light of day, their eyes on pressure gauges and indicators, their hands on valves and levers, as they struggled to keep a wandering pointer at the proper place on a dial. Bound to their stations, they would have to manipulate their precision instruments with cool deliberation, even in the heat of battle. Their world was not that of the infantryman, who can release tension during an attack by such satisfying means as firing his rifle; it was a stationary world of highly specialized technology. The hardest test of their physical and psychological endurance, of course, would come in actual combat.

By order of the Fleet Commander, that same afternoon the *Bismarck* again exercised at refueling over the bow with the *Prinz*

In the *Bismarck's* dispensary, bars kept the bottles of medicines and drugs from falling off the shelves in heavy seas or when the big guns fired. (Photograph courtesy of Frau Erika Busch.)

Eugen. Lütjens was particularly concerned that the ships be letter-perfect at this maneuver, because of the circumstances to be anticipated in the operational zone. In the event the enemy should appear when the *Bismarck* had fuel lines over her bow, she was to be released immediately from the tanker so that she could make her way unhindered.

On 14 May, we carried out reconnaissance and combat evolutions with the light cruiser *Leipzig*, which was then training in the Gulf of Danzig. The reconnaissance was conducted by our aircraft, whose crews took the opportunity to get in some more practice by "attacking" one another. In the midst of these exercises one of the cranes used for hoisting in aircraft suddenly broke down and all practice came to a premature end. Since repair of the crane was urgent and could not be done with the means available in the ship, we went in to Gotenhafen, where it was to be offloaded. This was by no means our first experience with a malfunctioning crane. Indeed, in the War Diary Lindemann described our cranes as "extremely susceptible to damage and unreliable." He reported this new incident to higher headquarters, adding that he could not yet predict when his ship would be back to a state of operational readiness. In the wardroom First Officer Oels and the electrical engineer, Korvettenkapitän (Ingenieurwesen) Wilhelm Freytag, resumed their grumbling about the sorry state of our cranes, but this time the trouble was remedied surprisingly fast. We had gone to all the trouble of offloading oil so that the ship could pass through the shallows at the entrance to Gotenhafen Harbor, but it proved unnecessary to remove the crane. A mechanic from the crane's manufacturer came aboard and repaired the damage in about an hour. Meantime, however, Group North had reacted to Lindemann's message by postponing our departure for Exercise Rhine for at least three days.

In those beautiful May days of 1941 we were only too glad to be able to spend our free hours ashore. We found Gotenhafen rather dreary, however. Originally named Gdynia by the Poles and later called Gdingen by the Prussians, it was a small fishing village until after the First World War, when it was incorporated into Poland and developed into a naval base and commercial port. It had 130,000 inhabitants when in 1939, following the conquest of Poland, the Germans named it Gotenhafen and began to convert it into a major naval base. Being beyond the range of enemy bombers at the outset of the war, it made an ideal base for ships in battle training.

We preferred to go to Danzig or to Zoppot, which was still closer but, because of wartime conditions, rather deserted. The beach and pier at Zoppot invited visits. Both these places were easy to reach by rail, and my good friend Kapitänleutnant (Ingenieurwesen) Emil Jahreis, nicknamed "Seppel," and I spent many happy hours together in one or the other. Bar-hopping in Danzig one evening, we were asked by an acquaintance, "When won't we see you again? Of course, we know you can't say. One day you just won't come, and then maybe we'll read about you in Wehrmacht reports."

Another time, after a tour of the bars in Zoppot, we returned to our hotel very late. When we woke up, the sun told us that the *Bismarck* must have long since sailed for her at-sea exercises. Springing out of bed, we made for Gotenhafen with lightning speed. Would we have the undeserved good luck to find a neighborly tug in the harbor? We did. As we neared the *Bismarck*, which had stopped for us, we saw, standing on the upper deck, where we would have to go alongside, a man we had no great desire to see at that moment: Hans Oels who, as First Officer, was primarily responsible for the discipline of the ship.

Kapitänleutnant Emil Jahreis, right, shown here as an ensign (engineering) performing an experiment in chemistry class at the Naval College at Kiel-Wik in 1931 or 1932. (Photograph from the author's collection.)

If at all possible, everyone, whether officer, petty officer or enlisted man, made a circuit around Hans Oels, the unapproachable, whom the crew called the loneliest man on board. This time, with his usual aloofness, he let matters rest by saying: "The captain awaits you on the bridge."

"Well," said Lindemann, with a kindly smile, when we rather sheepishly appeared on the bridge, "go on about your duties!"

Seppel Jahreis from Öttingen, Bavaria—he loved life and was always cheerful. In those last weeks in Gotenhafen, however, a change came over him. He became unusually quiet and seemed depressed. I had the feeling that a foreboding of what was to come weighed on him. Most of all, however, he suffered, even if he didn't say so, from his sudden and to him incomprehensible transfer from the post of turbine engineer to that of chief of damage control. Since the beginning of the building course he had become so familiar with "his" turbines and so humanly close to the turbine crew that the mandatory change tormented him. It was a fateful change. His successor in the engine room survived the sinking of the ship.

 **7**

Hitler Comes Aboard

On 1 May, the Fleet Command received a telephone call from Hitler's naval aide, Fregattenkapitän Karl Jesko von Puttkamer, advising that the "Führer" intended to inspect the *Bismarck* and *Tirpitz* at Gotenhafen on the fifth. That day, Hitler, Feldmarschall* Wilhelm Keitel, von Puttkamer, Oberst† Nicolaus von Below, Hitler's Luftwaffe aide, and the rest of the party arrived on Gotenhafen Roads aboard the *Hela*. Grossadmiral Raeder was conspicuously absent. The fleet commander conducted the tour of the ship and the "Führer's Standard" waved over the *Bismarck* during the four hours that Hitler was on board. The crew was mustered on the upper deck in greeting, Oberbootsmann‡ Kurt Kirchberg with beads of sweat on his forehead from the exertion of cleaning up the last traces of a bucket of paint that had been spilled on the starboard side of the upper deck aft a moment before Hitler came aboard.

Hitler, looking somewhat pale, and Keitel, followed by Lütjens and Lindemann, reviewed the crew. The party then inspected some of the ship's equipment, which gave the responsible officers a chance to brief the "Führer" in their own areas. Hitler remained for an especially long time in the after gunnery computer space, where an extremely capable gunfire-plotting officer, Oberleutnant zur See Friedrich Cardinal, explained how the various intricate-looking devices

*Field Marshal
†Colonel
‡Warrant Officer

controlled gunfire. Keitel as well as Hitler seemed to be much impressed by Cardinal's presentation, but neither asked any questions.

After touring the ship, Hitler, Lütjens, and a small group adjourned to the admiral's quarters. There, Lütjens told of his experiences in action against British commerce in the Atlantic with the *Scharnhorst* and *Gneisenau*, expressed optimism about an operation of this type with the *Bismarck*, and explained his immediate intentions. He considered it an advantage that in the *Bismarck*, which was more powerful than the *Scharnhorst* class, he would no longer be forced to avoid well protected convoys. This, however, did not solve his most difficult problem: getting his force out into the Atlantic without being spotted by the enemy. When Hitler suggested that, apart from anything else, the numerical superiority of the British fleet presented a great risk, Lütjens pointed to the *Bismarck*'s superiority over any single British capital ship. Her hitting and staying power were so great that he had no apprehension on that score. After a pause, he added that breaking out to the high seas would not by any means be the end of our worries. Quite clearly, torpedo planes from British aircraft carriers were a great danger that he would have to reckon with all the time he was in the Atlantic. Little did he know how directly his words bore on the impending fate of his flagship.

Apart from his remark about the superiority of the British fleet, Hitler remained silent throughout Lütjens's presentation. This was probably no surprise to Lütjens. He must have been aware that Hitler, who was strictly a landsman, knew nothing whatever about the unique features of war at sea. Whenever the big ships were at sea, Hitler worried that they might be lost, which would be bad enough, and that their loss would damage his prestige, which would be still worse. While he viewed commerce-raiding as a deviation from the proper mission of warships, he often assessed its risks more realistically than did the experts. Be that as it may, he remained remote from matters concerning the sea and naval warfare. This characteristic was demonstrated that day aboard the *Bismarck*, when Hitler, who was very much interested in military technology, could not find a single word to say about this masterpiece of naval construction and weapon technology. He was not moved to comment.

At this time the Seekriegsleitung was afraid that Hitler might suddenly forbid any ocean operation for the *Bismarck*, a fear it had had in similar cases. Could that have been the reason why Lütjens did not tell Hitler that she was scheduled to sail in two weeks' time? Had he and Raeder decided to keep quiet about it? Quite possibly so, because

Raeder did not report the departure of the *Bismarck* and *Prinz Eugen* until 22 May, by which time the ships had been at sea for four days and were nearing the Denmark Strait, having entered the North Sea long before. Even with the operation that far under way, to get approval for it to continue, he would still have to overcome Hitler's very considerable reservations. The latter who, as Puttkamer later reported, became extremely nervous following the report of the sailing, immediately responded, "Herr Grossadmiral, if at all possible, I would like to recall the ships." Raeder objected that the preparations for the operation had already gone too far; no one would understand a recall at this time. The ensuing conversation was ended by Hitler with the words, "Well, perhaps now you have to leave things the way they are, but I have a very bad feeling." No protocol would record these remarks; one would read only, "The Führer agreed . . ."

After the presentation in the admiral's cabin, luncheon was served in the wardroom. Hitler's preference for meatless fare being known, it was a vegetarian, one-course meal. For security reasons, Hitler was served by an SS-man, and said hardly anything while he ate. Afterwards, however, he started to talk. It was almost a monologue; only occasional comments came from others. I was seated a long way from the high-ranking people, but from what I could hear, Hitler spoke first about the German minority in Romania. He said that he intended "to haul these people back into the Reich in short order" if the government in Bucharest did not stop "harassing" them. On the subject of the United States, he expressed his belief that there was no question of her coming into the war, which, at any rate, would be decided in the Mediterranean. He declared that the Americans remembered the First World War and the unpaid debts of their former allies only too well: they were hardly likely to get themselves involved in another such undertaking and would gladly renounce sacrificing their soldiers in Europe again.

Lindemann disagreed with this point of view. He said he was not by any means prepared to write off the possibility that the United States would enter the war. Fregattenkapitän Oels was obviously extremely embarrassed by this contradiction, as it were, of the "Führer": misgiving showed all over his face. At the end of these proceedings, Lütjens stood up and made a brief address. He talked about how the war at sea was going and the tasks that lay before the *Bismarck*. The objective, he said, was and always would be to beat the British wherever they showed themselves. There was no response.

8

Departure from Gotenhafen

On 16 May 1941, Lütjens reported that the *Bismarck-Prinz Eugen* task force would be ready for Exercise Rhine on the eighteenth. Accordingly, Group North ordered him to enter the Great Belt at nightfall on the nineteenth. At about the same time, two freighters moved into the Atlantic to act as scouts, and a store ship and five tankers steamed for the Norwegian Sea and the Atlantic where they would resupply the task force.

Aboard the *Bismarck* on 18 May, Lütjens went over the operational details of the exercise with Lindemann and Kapitän zur See Helmuth Brinkmann of the *Prinz Eugen*. It was decided that, if the weather was favorable, they would bypass Korsfjord and make directly for the Norwegian Sea to rendezvous with the *Weissenburg*; then, if possible, go on through the Denmark Strait. There, they would be under cover of the Arctic fog yet, with the help of radar, able to maintain high speed. If enemy cruisers and auxiliary cruisers should appear in our path, they might have to be attacked. Paramount, however, was the preservation of the *Bismarck* and *Prinz Eugen* so that they could spend maximum time in the area of operations. They were to proceed independently to the island of Rügen, where the task force would be formed on the morning of 19 May.

His operation order of 22 April shows that Lütjens favored the route through the Denmark Strait; from the outset, he gave it priority over any other. Hadn't he done pretty well when he broke out through the Denmark Strait in the *Gneisenau* in early February? Why shouldn't the poor visibility that prevails there most of the year help him again?

Apparently, that was how Lütjens thought—although I do not know for certain.* In any case, he apparently just took no notice of Group North's recommendation that he use the Iceland-Faeroes passage. That command had warned against use of the Denmark Strait for what it viewed as very good reasons: its channel was relatively narrow, which made it easier for the enemy to watch; it would be simpler for the British to maintain contact in the north, because their forces there could draw their southern patrols into the search, which would not work in reverse; time and fuel would be saved if, immediately after leaving Norway, Lütjens took the nearer and shorter southern course; and on the southern course he would be able to gain a greater lead over the British ships that would sortie from Scapa Flow when word of the attempted German breakout was received.

The intensification of preparations for the approaching operation, the embarkation of the fleet staff with all its gear, the bunker-cleaning to which the entire crew was assigned on 17 May—all these developments made it clear that our departure from Gotenhafen was imminent.

Bunker-cleaning—a filthy job! A petty officer and a seaman, armed with a fresh-air pipe to enable them to breathe and a safety lamp, had to go into each bunker to clean out the sludge. They collected the muck in buckets, which were than passed from hand to hand, via the upper deck, to barges made fast alongside. Many a bucket reached the upper deck empty, its black contents having wound up on the men's working uniforms somewhere along the way. The dirtiest work was done by Polish forced laborers, with whom the language difference made communication difficult. But after twenty-four hours the job was done, and the bunkers were spanking clean and ready to take on a new supply of fuel. The Polish workers were rewarded with schnaps and cigarettes.

Liberty was canceled as of noon 17 May. Towards midday on the eighteenth the *Bismarck* left the wharf at Gotenhafen. The fleet band stationed on the upper deck struck up *"Muss i denn,"* the tune traditionally played on large warships leaving for a long cruise. I must admit that I was more than a little surprised by this musical advertisement that Exercise Rhine had begun. I think it highly doubtful that either our Fleet Commander or our captain knew we were to have this musical program. In all likelihood, it did not occur to any

*There being nothing in writing on this matter, I asked Vizeadmiral Helmuth Brinkmann if this was the case but he could not recall that Lütjens gave his reasoning.

responsible officer that such a thing would happen, and therefore nothing was done to stop it. The bandmaster, aware that our departure was imminent, probably just automatically chose that song without giving the matter another thought. We did not put to sea immediately, however, but dropped anchor in the roadstead, in view of Gotenhafen. Great masses of provisions and fuel oil still had to be taken aboard. Although thousands of tons of fuel flowed into our bunkers, we could not fill them completely, because a hose ruptured, causing the fueling operation to be called off so that the mess could be cleaned up. By that time, our schedule forced provisioning to be brought to an end. The ship was not far short of being fueled to capacity, and no one then suspected how important this shortfall would become. The *Bismarck* sailed at 0200 on 19 May.

The crew was in the state of tense anticipation that comes when a long period of preparation is finally over and the action for which it was designed is about to begin. Their faith in their captain and their ship was boundless, even though they knew nothing about the operation on which they were embarking. Now, they heard Lindemann announcing over the loudspeakers that we were going to conduct warfare against British trade in the North Atlantic for a period of several months. Our objective was to destroy as much enemy tonnage as possible. This message confirmed what the men had long suspected. Their apprehension about the unknown was replaced by certainty. Below, the gentle vibration of the engines reminded them of the tremendous power that made their ship a deadly weapon.

Our passage to the west, under a cloudy sky, with medium wind and seas, was uneventful. Escorted by the destroyers *Z-23* and *Friedrich Eckoldt* and preceded by Sperrbrecher, the task force sailed as a unit after leaving Rügen and reached designated positions on schedule. Around 2230, the *Hans Lody*, carrying the commander of the 6th Destroyer Flotilla, Fregattenkapitän Alfred Schulze-Hinrichs, joined the formation and we steamed north through the Great Belt. To maintain the secrecy of our mission, the commander of the Baltic security forces announced that the Great Belt and the Kattegat would be closed to commercial traffic on the night of 19–20 May and the following morning.

Next day, when we were in the Kattegat, the *Hans Lody* sounded our first aircraft alarm. We in the *Bismarck* assumed that we had been sighted by British reconnaissance planes. However, they turned out to be our own fighters, of whose arrival we had not been informed.

In contrast to the preceding day, 20 May was clear and sunny. It was

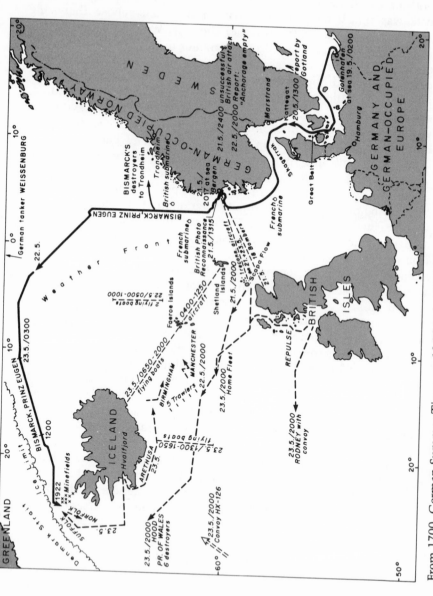

From 1700, German Summer Time, on 18 May to 2000, German Summer Time, on 23 May. The beginning of Exercise Rhine. (Diagram courtesy of Jürgen Rohwer.)

perfectly beautiful. The shimmering green sea, corded with the light blue of many small swells, stretched to the far horizon. As we passed the small, flat island of Anholt to port, the tall, slender lighthouse on its northeastern end was clearly visible. This radiant weather might have been seen as a good omen for our operation. If only we hadn't had to steam in such clear view of the Swedish coast and among innumerable Danish and Swedish fishing boats. They seemed to be everywhere, these little white craft with their chugging motors, some of them bobbing up and down beside us. Not only that but steamers from all sorts of countries were passing through the Kattegat. If this wasn't a giveaway of what we were doing here, what was? Surely the appearance of our task force in Scandinavian waters would attract attention that might well work to our disadvantage. Would Sweden's neutrality, which at that time was benevolent towards Germany, avert the military damage that the vigilant Norwegian underground was certainly eager to inflict on us? It was not exactly a secret that the Norwegian underground was in touch with London. But more than that. As our Seekriegsleitung was well aware, Stockholm and Helsinki were hotbeds of British intelligence, and British naval attachés there reported all known German ship movements and other German military operations to London. Indeed, we knew that on 15 March 1941, the British naval attaché in Stockholm informed the Admiralty that an organization had been set up to observe ships passing through the Great Belt and that its reports could reach him in twelve hours. Captain Troubridge, too, had thought about navigation in these waters when he made a duty visit to the area in July 1939. "I should think," he confided to his diary, "it would not be difficult to slip through unseen on a dark night provided the ship was darkened. It would be the obvious place for a S/M [submarine] patrol in time of war."

It ran through my head that enemy agents were being handed a unique opportunity to identify and report our task force just as it was putting to sea. On top of that, the weather was perfect for aerial reconnaissance. I could not see how Exercise Rhine could possibly be kept secret. I became still more concerned when around 1300 the Swedish aircraft-carrying cruiser *Gotland* came in view to starboard against the Swedish coast. The *Gotland*, in accordance with a long-standing training program, was just then on her way to gunnery practice off Vinga, that is, in Swedish territorial waters directly west of Göteborg, and even steamed on a parallel course to us for a while. Assuming that the *Gotland* would inform the Swedish Admiralty that we had been sighted, Lütjens radioed Group North, "At 1300 aircraft-carrying cruiser *Gotland* passed in clear view, therefore anticipate formation will be reported." The commander in chief of Group North, Generaladmiral Rolf Carls, replied: "Because of the strictly neutral conduct of Sweden, I do not think the danger of being compromised by the Swedish warship is any greater than from the already present, systematic enemy surveillance of the entrance to the Baltic."

But if Lütjens did fear that we had been dangerously compromised, it was he, not Carls, who was right. Captain Ågren, of the *Gotland*, immediately sent a secret radio signal reporting our passage through the senior naval officer at Göteborg to the commander of the west coast naval district at Nya Varvet, who in turn notified naval headquarters in Stockholm.*

---

*It was not this report, however, that gave naval headquarters in Stockholm the first news of the German operation. Knowledge of it had already been gained by an aerial reconnaissance, during which five picket vessels had been sighted about 1200 around twenty nautical miles west of Vinga, followed about ten nautical miles astern by a task force described as three *Leberecht Maass*-class destroyers plus a cruiser and a very large warship (*Bismarck?*)—ten or twelve aircraft had overflown this task force, which was holding a northerly course. For her part, the *Gotland* reported having sighted two German battleships and three *Maass*-class destroyers to Nya Varvet about 1300. Thereafter she had raised steam in all boilers and followed the German task force on a northerly course along the edge of Swedish territorial waters. Around 1545 the *Gotland* reported that the German ships had gone out of sight on a northwesterly course.

9

A British Naval Attaché in Stockholm

Early in 1941, a few high-ranking officers in the Swedish intelligence service privately came to the conclusion that a weakening of Germany would be greatly to the advantage of their country. They considered the German invasion of Denmark and Norway an outrageous attack on the sovereignty of all Scandinavia, and, after February 1941, worked closely with the Norwegian underground. Some of their contacts with this movement were through the Norwegian government-in-exile's military attaché in Stockholm, Colonel Roscher Lund, who had become a friend and trusted informant of the British naval attaché there, Captain Henry W. Denham.

On the evening of 20 May, Roscher Lund learned from Lieutenant Commander Egon Ternberg,* who belonged to the Swedish secret intelligence service, the so-called Bureau C of the armed forces' high command in Stockholm, that, during the day, two large German warships and several merchantmen had passed through the Kattegat on a northerly course under air cover. He hastened to the British embassy, where he was told that Denham was at a certain restaurant in the city. He pursued him there and gave him the important news. Both returned immediately to the embassy and, with reference to an earlier observation that day, cabled the Admiralty in London: "Kattegat

---

*Roscher Lund never divulged the name of this officer. He spoke of him as his "source." Lieutenant Egon Ternberg had retired not long before but was recalled because of the war and assigned to Bureau C. In 1941 he was promoted to commander. He is likely to have had excellent contacts with Roscher Lund.

today 20th May. (a) This afternoon eleven German merchant ships passed Lenker North; (b) at 1500 two large warships, escorted by three destroyers, five escort vessels, ten or twelve aircraft, passed Marstrand course north-west 2058/20." On 23 May, Denham wrote Roscher Lund a letter of thanks:

> Your very valuable report of enemy warships in the Kattegat two days ago, has enabled us to locate in the fjords near Bergen on 21st
> one Bismark [sic] battleship
> one Eugen cruiser.
> Naturally there is no harm in your making use of this to enlighten your source.
> Thank you so much for your very helpful efforts—let us hope your friend will continue to be such a valuable asset.

Ternberg had seen the *Gotland*'s sighting report in the Admiralty in Stockholm and immediately advised Roscher Lund of its contents, but for security reasons he did not reveal the source of his information. And it was routine for the *Gotland* to report the presence of foreign warships in or near Swedish territorial waters.

Of course, at the time, I did not know of these events, but even so, it did seem to me on 20 May that there had been far too many opportunities for our formation to be sighted and, when I thought about what this might do to our mission, I felt that a shadow had fallen over it.* I doubt that I was the only one in the ship who had such thoughts, yet none of my younger shipmates, at any rate, said anything about it. What good would it have done? Nothing could be changed. The only thing to do was hope for the best. No one in the *Bismarck* had any inkling of the rapidity with which the news would reach the British Admiralty or of the energetic and successively wider-reaching steps the sea lords would take.

---

*That indications of the *Bismarck*'s departure on an operation reached the British and Swedish by other means besides aerial reconnaissance and the sighting by the *Gotland* was worked out at an international conference of the Study Group for Military Research (Arbeitskreise für Wehrforschung) in Stuttgart in 1978. The relevant finding reads: "The Swedish intelligence service, which was also very active in code-breaking, had tapped the German telegraph lines to Norway, which had to run partly through Swedish territory, and obtained important information from them. Swedish intelligence officers who sympathized with the Allies gave this information to the military attaché of the Norwegian government in exile, who in turn relayed it to the British attachés in Stockholm, and the latter transmitted it—though never verbatim—to London. In this way, for example, the first information regarding the sailing of the battleship *Bismarck* came into British hands." (Communication from Hans-Hennig von Schultz to the author.)

10

Grimstadfjord and the Journey North

Around 1600* on 20 May, we were escorted through our own minefields by the 5th Minesweeping Flotilla, which was under the command of Korvettenkapitän Rudolf Lell. When we arrived at our rendezvous with the flotilla, we were dismayed to find a number of merchant ships waiting to take advantage of the cleared channel. Their presence was liable to endanger the security of Exercise Rhine and, therefore, was extremely unwelcome. However, it gave the Swedish observers and their British friends the impression that our task force and the merchantmen were operating together. As has been said, they so stated in their reports. Consequently, in London the Admiralty put a lot of effort into puzzling over what the Germans could be intending to do with such a combination of ships and how they might counter whatever it was.

When we left the minefield, the minesweepers were detached and the *Bismarck* and *Prinz Eugen*, still escorted by destroyers, steered a zigzag course at 17 knots to avoid submarines. The south coast of Norway came into view during a magnificent summer sunset. The outlines of the beautiful, austere landscape, with the black silhouettes of its mountains raised against the red glow of the sky, enabled me to forget for a moment all about the war.

*This was German Summer Time (one hour ahead of standard Central European Time), which I have used throughout. It was the same as double British Summer Time used in the British ships and in all British accounts of the operation. I chose to adopt it in order to synchronize with British literature on this subject, even though the clocks in the *Bismarck* were set on Central European Time at noon of 23 May and remained so to the end.

Following the line of the coast, we turned westward. We would resume our northerly course after we had rounded the southwestern tip of Norway. Between 2100 and 2200 we passed through the southernmost channel in the Kristiansand minefield, then proceeded at a speed of 27 knots. At all times half the guns were manned.

I was off duty that evening and went to see the film that was showing in the wardroom, *Play in the Summer Wind*. We carried enough films to keep us entertained for the several months we were to be at sea but, after that evening, Exercise Rhine kept us so busy that we were never able to put on another program.

Little did we know, as we watched the only movie shown on the *Bismarck* during the operation, that, on the coast near Kristiansand, Viggo Axelsen, a member of the Norwegian underground, was watching our formation and that another Norwegian actually photographed it! Through his binoculars Axelsen observed our passage, noted: "20.30, a battleship, probably German, westerly course," and gave this report to his friend Odd Starheim who from a nearby hideout immediately radioed a coded report to London.* There it reached the desk of Colonel J. S. Wilson, Chief of the British Intelligence Service for Scandinavia, to whom all reports from the Norwegian underground were routed. He relayed it to the British Admiralty, where it provided confirmation of Denham's message.

Around thirty minutes after being discovered by Axelsen our task force was sighted by another member of the Norwegian underground, Edvard K. Barth, who was researching bird's nesting habits on Heröya Island, ten nautical miles southeast of Kristiansand. He saw our task force pass through a corridor in the mine field, turn on a westerly course, and proceed on at a slow speed of around ten knots. Using a

---

*That Axelsen's observations and the consequent radio signal were incomplete, owing to the omission of the cruiser *Prinz Eugen*, is proven by the observations and photographs made by Edvard K. Barth. The German occupation forces took a fix on the signal and made every possible effort to uncover the sender but without success.

Axelson's friend Odd Starheim had left Dundee on the orders of his superior, Colonel J. S. Wilson, in a collapsible boat in January 1941 and landed on the south coast of Norway, near Egersund. He made this daring trip despite a high fever and concealed himself in the coastal hills until it passed. His previous experience as a radioman in merchant ships, coupled with a special training course in England, qualified him for service as a radio operator in the Norwegian resistance movement. When he returned to London by way of Stockholm on 21 June 1941 his station had transmitted a total of ninety-five signals, including that concerning our task force. A high-ranking naval officer at the Admiralty who heard of Starheim asked, "Who is this lad? I'd serve with him anywhere."

Some of the *Bismarck* complement relax. (Photograph from Bundesarchiv, Koblenz).

telephoto lens, shortly before sunset he snapped the surprising picture that presented itself to him: the *Bismarck*, and *Prinz Eugen*, and two destroyers (the third remained just outside the camera field)— and through such a coincidence made the last photograph of the task force taken from shore.

Early the next morning the *Bismarck* went to general quarters. From then on, we would have to be on guard against British submarines, especially during the hours of twilight. Shortly after 0700 four aircraft came into view—mere specks against the sun. Were they British or our own? So quickly did they vanish that we wondered if we had imagined them. It was impossible to say, and the supposed sighting was soon crowded out of our minds by other events.

Not long thereafter, we reached the rocky cliffs near Bergen and before noon ran past barren, mountainous countryside and picturesque, wooden houses to enter Korsfjord under a brilliant sun. The *Bismarck* went into Grimstadfjord, south of Bergen, and anchored at the entrance to Fjörangerfjord, about 500 meters from shore. The *Prinz Eugen* and the destroyers went farther north, to Kalvanes Bay, where they took on fuel from a tanker. With the thought that, in the hazy visibility of these northern waters, our black-and-white stripes might stand out and betray us, both we and the *Prinz Eugen* painted

The efforts of the German Seekriegsleitung to have the task force break out without being observed suffered a setback. The ships *Bismarck* and *Prinz Eugen* leading, with two of the three destroyers behind, are observed, reported—and photographed!—by members of the Norwegian underground. This unique photograph originates from the ornithologist (later professor) Edvard K. Barth, who was conducting research on sea gulls on the island of Heröya, southwest of Kristiansand. As a member of a secret resistance group and in possession of a camera, nothing seemed to him more natural than to photograph the German task force during its advance. (Photograph courtesy of Edvard K. Barth.)

over our camouflage with the standard "outboard gray" of German warships.

Apart from that activity, we simply waited for the day to pass. The sun shone continuously and many members of the German occupation forces in Norway, understandably eager to see the new *Bismarck*, came out to visit us. One episode gave everyone who witnessed it a hearty laugh. A soldier, who apparently had run out of tobacco and assumed that we would have a great store of it, got a boat and came out to the *Bismarck*. As his cockleshell bobbed up and down beside

the giant battleship, our men lowered down to him on strings so many cigarettes and so much tobacco that, unless he shared his booty with his comrades, he had enough to smoke for a year!

We were quite close inshore and could feast our eyes on terra firma, from which many Norwegians stared at us. Through our range finders, we could see them having breakfast in their little cottages on the mountainsides. I couldn't help wondering how many of them were looking with something more than idle curiosity. "Frightful, when you think in a week everyone sunning here on board today could be dead!"—Maschinengast Statz heard that said by someone whom he did not know and was already turning to go. A fateful week later he saw him again in British captivity, and learned that it was Maschinengefreiter Budich who had spoken these words.

Two Messerschmitt-109 fighters flew cover over the *Bismarck* all day, and I can still remember the feeling of security they gave us. A little after 1300 the antiaircraft watch sounded the alarm, but the *Bismarck* was not attacked and our guns did not go into action. The British plane that may have caused this alarm had an objective other than an attack. At 1315 Flying Officer Michael Suckling of RAF Coastal Command, near the end of his reconnaissance mission, was circling 8,000 meters above us in his Spitfire when he spotted and photographed "two large German warships." Later that same day, thanks to Flying Officer Suckling, the British were able to identify a *Bismarck*-class battleship and an *Admiral Hipper*-class cruiser* in the vicinity of Bergen—thanks were also due to Roscher Lund, as is shown in Captain Denham's congratulatory letter to him of 23 May. And we, in our ignorance, were just happy that nothing came of the alarm. I did not learn of Suckling's success until the summer of 1943, when I was a prisoner of war in Bowmanville, Ontario, Canada. One morning I picked up the paper to which I subscribed, *The Globe and Mail*, and there on the front page was an enlargement of Suckling's photograph of the *Bismarck* at anchor in Grimstadfjord. I have never forgotten my astonishment.

As we lay at anchor the entire day, I was perplexed—this is not hindsight, I remember it very clearly—as to why the *Bismarck* did not make use of what seemed like ample time to refuel, as did the *Prinz Eugen*. Of course, I did not know that the *Bismarck*'s operation orders did not call for her to refuel on 21 May, but I did know that we had not been able to take on our full load in Gotenhafen, and I thought it was imperative to replenish whenever possible, so as it put to sea on an operation of indeterminate duration with a full supply of fuel. The operations order even foresaw that the *Prinz Eugen*, which had a smaller operational radius, might take on fuel from the *Bismarck* while underway!†

---

*The *Prinz Eugen* belonged to the *Admiral Hipper* class.

†Histories of the *Bismarck* allude to a "contradiction" between our stopover in Norway and the intention Lütjens expressed in Gotenhafen on 18 May to continue across the Norwegian Sea without stopping to join up with the *Weissenburg* (see Jochen Brennecke, *Schlachtschiff Bismarck*, 4th edition, pp. 66, 278; Ludovic Kennedy, *Pursuit*, p. 40). I do not see that there was any contradiction. According to the *Bismarck*'s War Diary, at the commanders' conference Lütjens said that he intended to continue if the weather was "favorable." Perhaps he defined what he meant by "favorable." I was not present at the conference, but I take it that he meant he would continue without a halt only if the visibility were poor enough to give him a chance of making the critical passage between the Shetlands and Norway without being observed by enemy aerial reconnaissance. If I am correct, our entry into the fjords in the beautiful sunshine of 21 May was precisely in accordance with his original intention. Indeed, he could not have done anything else.

The fact that, in spite of the fighter cover we requested and were given during our day at anchor, a high-flying British reconnaissance plane photographed us and the *Prinz Eugen* has nothing to do with it. After all, Bergen and its surroundings were within reach of British short-range aerial reconnaissance.

This photograph of the *Bismarck* in Grimstadfjord, taken by Flying Officer Michael Suckling of RAF Coastal Command, confirmed the British Admiralty's suspicions that German heavy ships were preparing to break out into the Atlantic. (Photograph from the Imperial War Museum, London.)

At 1930 the *Bismarck* weighed another and headed north to join the *Prinz Eugen* and the destroyers outside Kalvanes Bay. The formation then continued on its way. As we slid past the rocky promontories at moderate speed, I was in a small group of the younger officers on the quarterdeck. We wanted to enjoy the Norwegian scenery at close range before we put out into the Atlantic. While we were standing there, the chief of the fleet staff's B-Dienst team, Korvettenkapitän Kurt-Werner Reichard, passed by, a piece of paper in his hand. Eager for news from his interesting duty station, we asked him what he had and he readily told us. It was a secret radio message from B-Dienst headquarters in German, according to which early that morning a British radio transmission had instructed the Royal Air Force to be on the lookout for two German battleships and three destroyers that had been reported proceeding on a northerly course. Reichard said that he was taking the message straight to Lütjens. I must admit that we found this news somewhat of a damper because we junior officers had no idea that the British were aware of Exercise Rhine. Now we felt that we had been "discovered," and that was something of a shock. Surely, I immediately began to theorize, Lütjens would now change his plans. For instance, he might go into the Greenland Sea and stay there long enough for the British to relax the intensity of their search. The whole business of making an "undetected" breakthrough pressed into my thoughts and once again I reviewed what seemed to me to be the breaches of security to which we had been subjected since leaving Gotenhafen: casting off from the wharf at Gotenhafen to the strains of "Muss i denn"; our passage through the—despite its name— narrow Great Belt; the swarms of Danish and Swedish fishing boats in the Kattegat; being in plain view from the coast of Sweden; the Swedish aircraft-carrying cruiser *Gotland*; passing so close to the Norwegian coast near Kristiansand; the sunny, clear day at anchor in Grimstadfjord, with the soldiers coming and going. How could Exercise Rhine really have been kept secret? Might it not have been better to enter the North Sea by way of Kiel Canal and rendezvous with the *Weissenburg* when the timing was best, without touching at Norway? There would have been a risk of detection on this route, too, but probably much less than in our day-long cruise through the narrows of the Kattegat and Skagerrak. But what good did it do to speculate now? In any event, we did not let Reichard's news get us down and decided to keep our knowledge to ourselves. Passing it on to our men would not have helped anyone.*

At this hour there was still a visitor on board, whom Lindemann graciously permitted to leave on the pilot boat after the ship put to sea. Around noon that day the telephone rang in the office of Ober-

---

*The secret British radio transmission reported by B-Dienst headquarters had been intercepted and deciphered by the *Prinz Eugen's* B-Dienst team around 0640 that morning. This signal furnished the first official confirmation that the German task force had been identified and reported by the enemy.

The execution of Exercise Rhine was seriously threatened thereby, for it was to be assumed that the British would use every available means in the attempt to prevent the task force from breaking out into the Atlantic. Thus the continuation of the operation from Norway had already become a great gamble.

feldarzt* Dr. Otto Schneider, who was then stationed in Bergen, and a familiar voice said, "Would you like to visit your brother Adalbert on the *Bismarck*? We don't know what she's doing, but she's lying in a nearby fjord at this very minute." He did not have to think twice about the answer and soon he and two companions were under way in a speedboat. "After a short, fast ride," he later wrote, "we turned into a bay and saw a bewitching sight. Before us, the *Bismarck* lay like a silver-gray dream from *The Thousand and One Nights*. In spite of her mighty superstructure, gun barrels, and armor, her silhouette was a thing of beauty, almost as though it were worked in filigree." Then he saw his brother waving for him to come on board. After a joyous, hearty greeting Otto mentioned, not without pride, that the speed of the boat that brought him out was 32 knots, only to hear in reply, "We can do that with the *Bismarck*, too, and a little more, besides! We're faster than anything stronger and stronger than anything faster, so really nothing can happen to us, and our assignment is just like life insurance." For Otto Schneider this was an interesting indication of the technological capability and superiority of the *Bismarck*. He found the morale of both officers and men to be outstanding in every respect. "Until now, up to the time we got to Norway," several officers told him, "our operation was nothing but a pleasure cruise." In the wardroom, over which in retrospect Otto Schneider sensed "an almost eerie, spooky atmosphere," they discussed the operational and tactical aspects of the ship's forthcoming mission, although they knew hardly anything about it. In any case, his brother Adalbert absolutely radiated optimism. In his brother's stateroom, Otto admired a photograph of Adalbert's three small daughters. Later, he was invited to have dinner with Adalbert. The brothers also wrote some joint postcards, which Otto offered to take back to Bergen. By the time those cards reached their addressees, the fate of the *Bismarck* had long since been sealed, and the messages were like greetings from the other side of the grave. That night, as they cruised past the rocky cliffs, Adalbert and Otto talked about this and that operation, such as the airborne assault on Crete, but not a word, of course, was said about Hitler's imminent attack on the Soviet Union, because they had no idea it was about to take place. Otto asked how Adalbert, confident as he was, evaluated the danger of the ship being attacked from the air. Adalbert answered with a smile that her defences and

*Major, Army Medical Corps

armor protection made her almost invulnerable to air attack. When they were training in the Baltic, he said, the Luftwaffe had not been able to score a single hit! For the approaching breakout, Adalbert only wanted there to be as much rain and fog as possible. He apparently knew nothing whatever about the state of British radar.

Then it was time for Otto to say good-bye to his brother and also to the captain who had made this visit possible. When he reported to the latter, Lindemann stood alone, leaning against the forward conning tower. They shook hands and Schneider looked into a pale, calm face with deep-set eyes. "Looking back," Otto Schneider said later, "I believe that at this moment Lindemann was well aware of the great dangers that the *Bismarck* faced and I think he considered my prospects of ever seeing my brother again very slight. It seemed that he and the Oberkommando der Kriegsmarine differed in their estimates of the situation."

Had the message relayed by Reichard from B-Dienst headquarters contributed to Lindemann's mood? Had it caused him to regard the evening of 21 May as the last possible chance to make what he regarded as the necessary changes in the task force's breakout tactics? And did he realize, with a heavy heart, that such a change, the power to make it lying, as it did, within the jurisdiction of the fleet commander, was scarcely to be expected in view of Lütjens's personality?

Meanwhile, the weather had worsened and the sky became completely overcast. A sharp wind from the southwest chased heavy rain clouds before it and raised whitecaps in the waters of the fjords. Foggy haze hung between the mountains. At about 2300 we turned away from the rocky shoreline, the destroyers in the lead, followed by the *Bismarck* and the *Prinz Eugen*, and resumed our war watches. When we began to head north, shortly before midnight, the wind was blowing out of the south-southwest at Force 4. Looking back, we saw alternating white, yellow, and red lights flickering in the clouds over the mainland. Group North informed us later in the day that five British planes had flown between the cliffs ten kilometers north of Bergen and dropped flares and bombs over Kalvanes Bay. Their attack was the result of Flying Officer Suckling's midday reconnaissance, of which we were still unaware. The beams of the searchlights ashore and the flashes of the antiaircraft batteries had heightened the light effects in the sky. I did not learn until very much later that, because of the weather, the British could make out hardly anything and dropped their bombs simply on suspicion.

According to plan, around 0500 on 22 May, Lütjens released the destroyers that had shielded our formation from British submarines. We were in the latitude of Trondheim, and I can still see the three ships disappearing towards the coast in the morning mist. For the first time I felt that we really had left home and Exercise Rhine had begun. From now on, the *Bismarck* and the *Prinz Eugen* were alone.

As I write this story, I have to remind myself repeatedly that the young officers on board that morning had no knowledge whatever of the defensive measures that the British were then taking against Exercise Rhine. However, having been told by Reichard the previous evening about the alerting of the British air force, I assumed that the enemy's naval forces would also be looking for us. And the mere thought of that inspired a prickly anxiety over what being in these narrow waters, the outposts of British sea power, under those conditions might entail. On the other hand, it was not long since the intercepted British radio order had gone out, so the probability of our being rediscovered soon was slight.

At 0930 or so, Lütjens was informed by Group North that, according to B-Dienst, neither the sailing of his task force nor the British orders to search for "the battleships" had produced any perceptible consequence, other than intensified British aerial reconnaissance in the northeastern sector. Group North believed that the enemy was concentrating its search of Norway and the Norwegian Sea too far to the south to find our task force. Thus, it appeared that this leg of our journey had not been detected by the enemy.

Steaming at 24 knots in hazy weather under an overcast sky, the task force reached a position approximately 200 nautical miles from the Norwegian coast, in the latitude Iceland-Norway, at about noon. Weather conditions, which seemed settled, were just what Lütjens hoped to encounter when he attempted to break out into the Atlantic through the northern passage. Accordingly, he advised the *Prinz Eugen* that he intended to proceed through the Denmark Strait, adding that, in the event the weather cleared up, which would reduce the task force's prospects for a breakthrough, he would first rendezvous with the *Weissenburg.*

At 1237, the *Bismarck* sounded her submarine and aircraft alarms—a periscope-sighting had been reported. The task force turned to port and steered a zigzag course for half an hour, but nothing transpired and at 1307 it resumed its former course. The weather was still favorable; in fact, it seemed inclined to become our best ally. By 1800 it was raining and a southwesterly wind was blowing at Force 3. Visibility fell to between 300 and 400 meters, and patches of fog appeared. A damp cold gripped us, and the *Bismarck* glistened all the way to her foretop under a silvery sheen of moisture. It was a wonderful sight. In order to maintain contact and station, both ships turned on their signal lights or small searchlights every now and again, and, when the fog was particularly thick, the *Bismarck* shone her big searchlights astern to help the *Prinz* keep station. We were now in the northern latitudes, where the nights are almost as light as the days, so we could stay in a tight formation and maintain 24 knots even in poor visibility. Our passage was truly ghostly, as we slid at high speed through an unknown, endless, eerie world and left not a trace. The setting might have been created for the "perfect" breakout.

Low, dark rain clouds driven by a steady wind from astern ran with us like sheltering curtains. They were moving faster than we were, and it was only because there were so many of them that, as one overtook us, it was quickly replaced by the next, giving us virtually unbroken protection from hostile eyes. Despite the dampness, when I was not on watch I went for a stroll on the quarterdeck. The fleet staff's meteorologist, Dr. Heinz Externbrink, happened to be doing the same thing, and I fell in with him. I could not resist asking him if he agreed that we should increase speed, so that we could keep up with the clouds and take advantage of their cover for as long as possible. He replied: "You've no idea how many times I've suggested that to Lütjens. I've warned him repeatedly that if we don't do so we'll have to count on unpleasantly good visibility in the Denmark Strait. But he won't budge. He simply rejects the idea without giving any reasons." Externbrink was worried sick, and the next day proved that his fears were not groundless.

After 2300 on this 22 May, Lütjens received three very important radio messages from Group North. The first, practically a repetition of the one he'd received that morning, read, "Assumption that breakout has not yet been detected by the enemy reconfirmed." The second based on aerial reconnaissance of Scapa Flow, stated: "Partly visual reconnaissance Scapa 22.5. Four battleships, one possibly an aircraft carrier, apparently six light cruisers, several destroyers. Thus no change from 21 May and passage through the Norwegian Narrows not noticed."* Didn't "no change" once more confirm that the *Bis-*

---

*A penciled note regarding this report in MGFA-DZ III M 307/5, "Preparatory Directives and Operational Orders of the Seekriegsleitung," page 281, reads: "This visual reconnaissance must be very strongly doubted on the basis of *later* knowledge. The manner in which it was relayed is not apparent to me. Should it have caused the fleet *marck* and the *Prinz Eugen* had left Norway without being detected? What renewed confidence Lütjens must have gained from that! Wasn't his intention to break through in the north without delay absolutely correct? And at 2322 he ordered a course change to the west: a course toward the Denmark Strait.

Shortly thereafter, the third signal arrived. In it, Group North reported that no operational commitment of enemy naval forces had yet been noted and that in the past days our U-boats had scored great successes south of Greenland. The landings in Crete, which we had begun on 20 May, were going according to plan and, in view of the sinking of several British cruisers off Crete, an *early* appearance of our fleet on the Atlantic sea lanes promised to inflict serious new damage on the British position at sea.† Naturally, this message

---

commander to attempt the breakthrough into the Atlantic, without pausing in the north, it can only be described as fateful. LNB MVO (signature illegible)." Later, in October 1942, the Naval High Command commented in its MDV 601 on the results of this Luftwaffe reconnaissance flight: "Subsequent determinations allow it to be taken for certain that the visual reconnaissance of 22 May, according to which four battleships lay in Scapa Flow, was in error."

In his book Brennecke adds to the commentary of the Naval High Command in MDV 601 (p. 79) note 131, according to which the Luftwaffe had probably let itself be deceived by British dummy battleships at Scapa Flow. Accordingly, in note 132 he supposes that the "four battleships" mentioned in the partly visual reconnaissance of Scapa Flow on 22 May must have been the *King George V, Victorious*, and two dummy battleships. Kennedy advances a similar argument on pp. 50–51 of his book, where he goes into the presence of the dummy ships at Scapa Flow and reproaches the Luftwaffe for sloppy reconnaissance.

Kennedy's remarks apparently go back to an article by the (since deceased) Professor Marder in Supplement 5 of the *English Historical Review* for 1972 on the question of dummy ships, which were built, upon Winston Churchill's insistence, as they had been in the First World War. Dummy ships were in fact anchored in Scapa Flow from March 1940, but for only a few months. As they failed completely in their purpose of misleading the Luftwaffe, in August 1940 they were removed to Rosyth upon the recommendation of Admiral Sir Charles Forbes, then commander in chief of the Home Fleet, to remain there in "care and maintenance" status.

Hence, it can be asserted that, contrary to Brennecke and Kennedy, there were no dummy ships in Scapa Flow in May 1941.

†Admiral Carls noted in the War Diary of Group North: "I gave this latter information to the fleet, not only because I expected its speedy appearance in the Atlantic to have the result indicated, but because the danger to ships in the north when they do not have the cover of darkness will increase with every delay. I also wanted to indicate that, if the Fleet Commander still had a choice between the Denmark Strait and a southern passage, the latter appeared preferable to me because it would be shorter and quicker." But Lütjens did not really have a choice, because when he received this message he was already in the latitude of the Denmark Stait.

strengthened Admiral Lütjens resolve—indeed, it made him feel indirectly ordered—to carry on with Exercise Rhine without the slightest delay.

The truth of the matter was that our departure from Norway had been noticed by the enemy, and the German report on the ships at Scapa Flow was wrong. We were soon to discover all that the hard way.

11

Alarm in Scapa Flow

As early as the beginning of May, the British noted an increase in German aerial reconnaissance in the far north and over Scapa Flow. The commander in chief of the British Home Fleet, Admiral Sir John Tovey, suspected that this activity portended another German surface operation in the Atlantic. His first precautionary measure was to instruct the cruiser *Suffolk*, which was patrolling the Denmark Strait, to keep a sharp watch for a possible German attempt to break out. At the same time, he ordered the cruiser *Norfolk*, flagship of the commander of the First Cruiser Squadron, Rear Admiral W. F. Wake-Walker, and then lying at a base in Iceland, to relieve the *Suffolk* as necessary.

In the early hours of 21 May, Denham's report of the sighting of eleven German merchant ships, two large warships, three destroyers, and five escorting vessels on a northwesterly course in the Kattegat reached Tovey aboard his flagship *King George V* at Scapa Flow. He immediately attached great significance to this report and began speculating as to what ships were involved, what they were up to, and what was the purpose of the reported merchantmen.* The admiral thought of the *Bismarck*, of whose recent trials in the Eastern Baltic the British intelligence service had kept him advised. Naturally, he could not be certain that she was one of the "large warships" sighted, but it seemed wise to base his plans on the assumption that she was.

---

*Since Denham's message made no mention of merchantmen, Tovey was probably told about them in a separate message.

If it turned out that his assumption was false—well, so much the better!

Tovey and his staff worked out four possibilities as to what might be the mission of the reported combination of ships:

The warships were escorting a supply convoy to Norway, and when the latter reached its destination, they would return to Germany.

The warships were escorting the merchant ships to the north, in order to use them for replenishment during their own operations.

The warships were escorting the merchant ships northwards in preparation for a landing in Iceland or the Faeroes, for which they would provide cover.

The warships were escorting the merchant ships only as a secondary mission, their prime one being to get out into the Atlantic.

All these mental gyrations were brought on by our purely accidental meeting with some merchant ships at the entrance to the channel through the Skagerrak minefield!

Since the last of the four hypotheses would be the most threatening to him and at the same time the one the Germans could most quickly implement, that is what Tovey prepared for. He reckoned that any measures he took to counter that threat would be bound to serve as some defense against a landing in Iceland or the Faeroes, if that was what the Germans intended. But which of the five possible routes to the Atlantic would they choose this time? There was the Denmark Strait between Iceland and Greenland, which, in May, was narrowed by pack ice from 200 nautical miles wide to probably 60 nautical miles; the passage between Iceland and the Faeroes, 240 miles wide; the passage between the Faeroes and the Shetlands, 140 miles wide; the Fair Island Channel between the Shetlands and the Orkneys; and the narrow Pentland Firth, between the Orkneys and the coast of Scotland, which for practical purposes could be counted out.

After carefully weighing the pros and cons, Tovey concentrated on the Denmark Strait, but did not ignore the three more southerly routes. At his immediate disposal were the battleships *King George V* and *Prince of Wales*, the battle cruiser *Hood*, the heavy cruisers *Suffolk* and *Norfolk*, eight light cruisers—including the *Galatea*, flagship of the commander of the Second Cruiser Squadron, Rear Admiral A. T. B. Curteis—and twelve destroyers. Upon receipt of Denham's report, the Admiralty also assigned him the aircraft carrier *Victorious* and the battle cruiser *Repulse*. The *Prince of Wales* and *Victorious* had been in commission for only two months and were not fully combat-ready.

Tovey at once deployed his ships to meet the situation. He ordered the *Norfolk* and the *Suffolk* to patrol the Denmark Strait together, rather than alternately, sent three cruisers to watch the passage between Iceland and the Faeroes, and divided the rest of his force into two task groups: the *Hood* and the *Prince of Wales* under the command of Vice Admiral Lancelot Holland; the *King George V*, the *Repulse*, and the *Victorious* under his own command.

In the midst of all this planning, the interpretation of Suckling's photography arrived; so it was the *Bismarck*! She and a *Hipper*-class cruiser in the fjords near Bergen. Tovey's hunch had not played him false. The same evening he sent Holland's task group and six destroyers to watch the passages into the Atlantic, especially those north of 62° latitude. In order to avoid wasting fuel on superfluous searches, he decided not to take his own group to sea until it had been determined that the *Bismarck* and her accompanying cruiser had left Norway. He then had almost twenty-four hours of anxious waiting because the bad weather of 22 May was as great a handicap to British aerial reconnaissance as it was an advantage to the German ships, which that day were steaming across the Norwegian Sea. Late in the afternoon of 22 May a plane left the Orkneys on a daring, low-level, reconnaissance flight across the water and over the hilly coast of Norway. That evening Tovey got the report he wanted: the German ships had left Norway. At 2200 he put to sea on a northwesterly course to cover the breakout routes south of the Faeroes.

Winston Churchill cabled President Franklin D. Roosevelt:

Yesterday, twenty-first, *Bismarck*, *Prinz Eugen*, and eight merchant ships located in Bergen. Low clouds prevented air attack. Tonight [we find] they have sailed. We have reason to believe a formidable Atlantic raid is intended. Should we fail to catch them going out, your Navy should be able to mark them down for us. *King George V*, *Prince of Wales*, *Hood*, *Repulse*, and aircraft-carrier *Victorious*, with ancillary vessels, will be on their track. Give us the news and we will finish the job.*

*Winston Churchill, *The Second World War*, Vol. III, p. 272.

12

Lütjens's Operational Decisions

At midnight on 22 May, as British and German forces converged on the northwestern passages into the Atlantic, it is interesting to compare the premises on which the two commanders were basing their actions.

Tovey had had the German task force identified, knew it had left Norway, and anticipated that it would try to enter the Atlantic through the Denmark Strait.

Lütjens knew that the opening stage of Exercise Rhine had become known to the enemy. The several signals he received from Group North on 22 May, however, led him to believe that his northward passage had not been detected and that most of the British Home Fleet was still concentrated at Scapa Flow.

It should here be pointed out that Lütjens, his staff officers, and the diaries of both the fleet and the ship having been lost in the *Bismarck* on 27 May, the considerations and estimates that determined tactical decisions after we left Grimstadfjord on the evening of 21 May cannot be known for certain. Neither the surviving turbine engineer, Kapitänleutnant (Ingenieurwesen) Gerhard Junack, nor I, in charge of the after fire-control station, knew what was going on in the minds of the fleet and ship commands. Like everyone else, we could follow closely only the events that took place in the immediate vicinity of our duty stations. All we knew about Exercise Rhine was what Lindemann had told the ship's company over the loudspeakers on 19 May. Even such basic matters as the route we were planning to take and where we might stop, being components of a secret operational plan, were not

Kapitänleutnant (Ingenieurwesen) Gerhard Junack, the turbine engineer during Exercise Rhine, whose action station was in the middle turbine room. On the evening of 26 May he took part in the attempt to repair the *Bismarck*'s rudder. He is among the handful of survivors. After the war he served in the Federal German Navy, attaining the rank of Kapitän zur See. This photograph was taken at Prisoner-of-War Camp 30 at Bowmanville, Ontario, Canada. (Photograph courtesy of Josef Statz.)

made known to the junior officers ahead of time. Fähnrich (B)* Hans-Georg Stiegler, who was doing a petty officer's duty in the engines' internal command and communications post and assigned to the after E-Group,† received his own sample of secrecy. On an off-duty stroll around the ship during the passage through the Kattegat, he reached the charthouse, where his classmate Friedrich-Wilhelm Dusch was in process of tracing the ship's course. "Just don't look at

---

*Midshipman (B) designated officers with a career specialty in naval construction (Baulaufbahn).

†Electrical team.

The Fleet Commander, Admiral Günther Lütjens, a man not given to confiding his reasoning or intentions. (Photograph from Bundesarchiv, Koblenz.)

the chart," Dusch shouted at him, "that's all secret!" But Stiegler had already noticed that the ship's course was plotted to the Norwegian fjords and thus obtained information that far exceeded his need to know, but resolved to keep it strictly to himself.

Lütjens's taciturnity probably ensured that deliberations at his level were restricted to a very small circle, anyway. Finally, the fact that we were at general quarters almost continually from the time we entered the Denmark Strait on 23 May until the end on 27 May made conversation among the officers next to impossible.

The tactical conduct of the operation must, therefore, be based primarily on the *Bismarck*'s War Diary as it was reconstructed from whatever material was available at installations ashore.* Obviously a document so produced cannot be entirely satisfactory because, for example, it cannot show whether the embarked B-Dienst team or shipboard radio and listening equipment provided Lütjens information that Group North and Group West did not have and, if so, what that information was. Nor can the reconstructed diary show why and how new decisions brought about by significant developments in the course of the operation were reached.

*On the orders of the commander in chief of the Kriegsmarine, Grossadmiral Raeder, at the beginning of July 1941 the *Prinz Eugen*'s chief wireless officer, Kapitänleutnant Hans-Henning von Schultz, was detailed to Naval Group Command West (Paris) for three weeks to reconstruct the *Bismarck*'s War Diary in respect to technical signals matters. He had the help of the originals of all radio messages received by the *Prinz Eugen* during the Exercise Rhine, the visual signals traffic between the *Bismarck* and the *Prinz Eugen*, and the B-Dienst reports received.

13

First Contact
with the Enemy

Early on the morning of 23 May, in foggy, rainy weather, the *Bismarck* and *Prinz Eugen* entered the Denmark Strait. Around 0800 the wind, which had been blowing from the south-southwest, veered to the north-northeast, and thus again came from astern on our new, westerly course. Around noon a new weather forecast from home promised that weather favorable for our undetected passage of the strait would continue on the twenty-fourth: "Weather 24. Area north of Iceland, southeasterly to easterly wind, Force 6–8, mostly overcast, rain, moderate to poor visibility." In spite of this welcome message, in the afternoon visibility increased to fifty kilometers, but before long intermittent heavy snow caused it to vary considerably between one point on the horizon and another: to port, in the direction of Iceland, heavy haze hung over the ice-free water; on our bow, in the direction of Greenland, there were shimmering, bluish-white fields of pack ice and the atmosphere was clear. The high glaciers of Greenland stood out clearly in the background, and I had to resist the temptation to let myself be bewitched by this icy landscape longer than was compatible with the watchfulness required of us all as we steamed at high speed through the narrowest part of the strait, with our radar ceaselessly searching the horizon. We would not have welcomed this clear visibility even if we had not been expecting intensified British reconnaissance. I could not help thinking of the warnings Externbrink had given Lütjens.

Suddenly, at 1811, alarm bells sounded throughout the *Bismarck*: vessels to starboard! The task force turned to port but the "vessels"

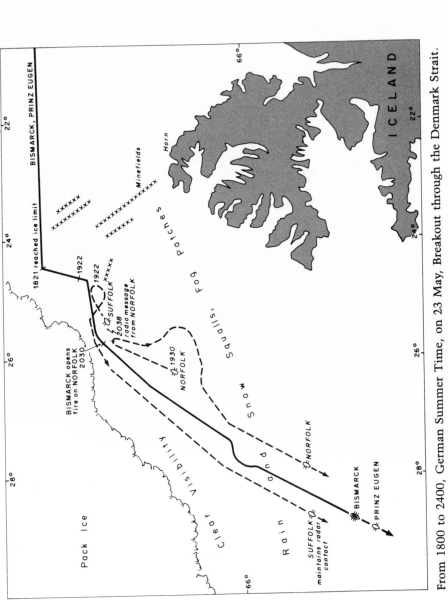

From 1800 to 2400, German Summer Time, on 23 May, Breakout through the Denmark Strait. (Diagram courtesy of Jürgen Rohwer.)

Battleship *Bismarck*

revealed themselves to be icebergs. Ice spurs and ice floes piled one on top of another frequently led young men, unaccustomed to recognizing objects at sea, to report nonexistent ships and submarines. Excusable, but dangerous, because when a man had made several incorrect observations he might be afraid to report any sighting. But that wasn't all. Sometimes the air over the glaciers of Greenland caused mirages that fooled even the old sea dogs. When that happened, the officers on the bridge were liable to see ships and shapes that were not there.

Shortly before 1900 we entered the pack ice. From then on, we had to steer a zigzag course through heavy ice floes that pressed hard against the ship's side and could have damaged our hull. In an area three nautical miles wide, visibility ahead and to the edge of the ice to starboard was now completely clear. To port, there was haze in the distance and, in front of the haze, there were patches of fog.

It was 1922 when the *Bismarck's* alarm bells sounded again. This time our hydrophones and radar had picked up a contact on our port bow. I stared through my director but could not see anything. Perhaps the contact was hidden from me by the ship's superstructure. Our guns were ready to fire, awaiting only the gunfire-control information. It never came. Whether the "contact" was a shadow on the edge of a fog bank or a ship bow-on or stern-on, perhaps very well camouflaged, we saw it too fleetingly to fire on it. Our radar registered a ship heading south-southwest at very high speed and plunging into the fog. As the contact moved out of sight, the shadowy outline of a massive superstructure and three stacks was discernible for a few seconds. That was the silhouette of a heavy cruiser—as we learned later, the *Suffolk*. Thereafter the hydrophone and radar bearing of the vanished enemy soon shifted astern and the range increased. With exemplary speed, the B-Dienst team in the *Prinz Eugen* deciphered the radio signal by which the *Suffolk* had reported us in the course of her turn: "One battleship, one cruiser in sight at 20°. Range seven nautical miles, course 240°." Lütjens reported to Group North the sighting of a heavy cruiser. When shortly afterwards we saw the *Suffolk* clearly and for some time, she was at the limit of visibility. Her small silhouette revealed that she was trailing us astern.*

---

*The chief wireless officer of the *Prinz Eugen*, Hans-Henning von Schultz, informed me in 1984: "The report intercepted and deciphered by the *Prinz Eugen*'s B-Dienst team at 1922 on 22 May of the sighting of the task force by the British cruiser *Suffolk* initiated a series of very exact contact reports that continued the whole night through.

130

The County-class heavy cruiser *Suffolk*, the ship that shadowed the *Bismarck* by maintaining radar contact from the evening of 23 May until the early morning of 25 May. She is down here wearing camouflage and patrolling the North Atlantic in the spring of 1941. (Photograph from the Imperial War Museum, London.)

There was another alarm in the *Bismarck* at 2030 and "full speed ahead" was ordered. Our forward radar had made a new contact. Over the loudspeakers, Lindemann informed the crew, "Enemy in sight to port, our ship accepts battle." Looking through my director in the indicated direction, at first I could see nothing at all. Then the outline of a three-stack heavy cruiser emerged briefly from the fog. It was the *Norfolk*—summoned by the *Suffolk*, to which we had come alarmingly close. The *Norfolk* had suddenly discovered her alarming proximity to our big guns. Flashes came from our guns, which were now trained on her, and in a moment we could see the splashes of our shells rise around the cruiser, which laid down smoke and turned away at full speed to disappear into the fog. According to the *Norfolk's* after-action report, three of our five salvos, all that we could

---

With surprise we had to conclude that this was possible only with the aid of shipboard radar, which on our part was not known to be aboard British warships. To the contrary, on the German side it was believed that the British were behind in this area. On the other hand, it was known that land radar installations had been built on the British coast."

With her guns trained abeam, the *Bismarck* released a salvo in the battle off Iceland. (Photograph courtesy of Paul Schmalenbach.)

fire in so short a time, straddled their target. A few shell fragments landed on board but no hits were scored. The *Norfolk* stayed hidden in the fog for a while, then reappeared astern to join the *Suffolk* in shadowing us. The word was passed to our crew. "Enemy cruisers are sticking to our course in order to maintain contact."

It now developed that the jolts caused by the firing of our big guns had put our forward radar out of action and, since the *Bismarck* was in the lead, our task force was blind to any threat from ahead. In order to overcome this disability and also to have the ship with the heavier guns near the shadowers astern, Lütjens ordered a "number change," which meant that the *Prinz Eugen*, her forward radar intact, would take the lead. In the Kriegsmarine number changes were routine evolutions: the ship in the rear pulled out of the line and increased speed, while the leading ship slowed down until the overtaking one had taken her place at the head of the line. That was supposed to happen this time, but instead of a routine maneuver we had a little excitement. Lindemann happened to be inspecting my battle station and asking questions about this and that, when he received a report from a talker on the bridge. Hurrying forward, he was confronted with an alarming sight: the *Bismarck* and the *Prinz Eugen* were on a collision course! Without waiting to get back to the bridge, he had his orders to the helm relayed—and the danger passed.

Thus the thing we most wanted to avoid, an encounter with British naval forces, had happened at the very beginning of Exercise Rhine. As I have probably emphasized enough already, such an encounter was highly undesirable because an undetected breakout was so important to the success of our commerce warfare in the Atlantic. We younger officers still did not know that Tovey was expecting us to be in this area and had strengthened his surveillance of the Denmark Strait two days earlier. Nor did we know that there had been no German aerial reconnaissance of the strait since a Focke-Wulf had flown over it four days before, on 19 May, and had not observed anything unusual. Not only being unaware of these things but counting on the fact that our departure from Norway was still a secret, this sudden encounter with British cruisers came as a shock to me, especially as it was reasonable to assume that there would be other enemy ships in these rather narrow waters. But at the same time, I regarded it as only the opening act, and naturally we were confident that we would be able to ward off the threat. Lütjens's next moves were aimed at either shaking off our pursuers or sinking them.

Now, the *Suffolk* and the *Norfolk* were both maintaining contact with us from astern and at the limit of visibility—the *Suffolk* to starboard, where visibility was good; the *Norfolk* to port, where there were long stretches of fog. Most of the time, I had a good view of the *Suffolk* and occasionally could see them both. Since at least the tip of a mast was always visible on the horizon, it gradually dawned on us that these annoying hangers-on must have better means of maintaining contact than optical instruments.

Through dark gray seas and white wave crests, the pursuit continued. At almost 30 knots we sped through the half-light of the Arctic night, through fog banks, rain squalls, and snow squalls, every now and again adding to the cover the elements gave us by laying down smoke. In an attempt to shake off our pursuers, we changed course and sought the shelter of every patch of haze; but it did no good. The British cruisers were continuously informed of our position, course, and speed, which they radioed to Tovey. Their reports were intercepted by our B-Dienst team and in five minutes were laid before Lütjens. They read like a minute-by-minute account of the movements of his task force—this phase of his operation was an open book to Tovey. What a depressing beginning for Exercise Rhine!

Lütjens decided to take the offensive. Around 2200, under cover of a rain squall, he had the *Bismarck* make a 180-degree turn. He intended to surprise the *Suffolk* by suddenly running out of the squall and attacking her when she came into view, but when we emerged, there was no enemy to be seen. It looked as though the cruiser had seen through our maneuver in time; in any case, she had turned and moved away from us at high speed. For a while we pursued her, in the hope of getting her in sight. Then Lütjens gave up, not wanting to be drawn too far back to the east, no matter what the enticement. He ordered the *Bismarck* to turn back and resume her former position in the task force. The *Suffolk* eventually caught up with us, but Lütjens did not take the offensive again. He assumed that it would not turn out any differently, and he was undoubtedly correct.

We had another excitement when the word was passed, "Aircraft off port beam!" In the far distance, a Catalina flying boat, evidently from Iceland, was banking as it searched the area; then, apparently unsuccessful, it turned away and disappeared. We could see it clearly outlined against the sky, but for its crew the gray hulls of the *Bismarck* and *Prinz Eugen* probably blended into the leaden hue of the Arctic sea.

Shortly before midnight our task force was enveloped in a heavy snow storm, into which our followers soon ran. Visibility shrank to a nautical mile, and the cruisers' signals ceased. On our bridge the atmosphere was tense: perhaps there would be no more. Were we to be lucky for once? But the respite lasted only three hours. Lütjens concluded that the British had an efficient long-range radar system, a conclusion that threw his whole concept of surface warfare in the Atlantic into a disturbing new dimension.

In fact, only shortly before, the *Suffolk* had had a modern, traversable radar installed, by means of which she could reconnoiter up to 22,000 yards. It was blind only in a small sector astern of the ship, where its impulses were blocked by the ship's superstructure. The *Norfolk* had to get along with an older and less efficient, non-traversable radar.

Although we continued to hope that somehow we would succeed in shaking off our shadowers, we were haunted by concern as to what other ships they might have called on to join them.

14

The *Hood* Blows Up

The early morning of 24 May brought radiantly clear weather and moderate seas. Steaming in the same order as the previous evening, the *Prinz Eugen* in the lead, the *Bismarck* in her wake, we were following a southwesterly course at a speed of 28 knots. Below, in the three turbine rooms, a warrant officer (machinist), two petty officers, and six stokers were on duty at all times. The warrant officer, the senior petty officer, and one stoker stood on the control platform, the second petty officer and the other five stokers tended the auxiliary engines and the fresh-water generator. Every lever and every control had to be examined again and again to make sure that the 150,000-horsepower propulsion plant was performing precisely as it should. Because of the high steam pressures at speeds such as we were then making, the slightest error in handling could have catastrophic consequences. And everyone on board sensed that the hours to come would bring great decisions.

The watch on the bridge and all the lookouts paid particular attention to the southeastern horizon, from which direction other enemy units were most likely to come. And we were certainly not disappointed.

Not long after 0500, the hydrophones in the *Prinz Eugen* picked up ship noises to port, and at 0509 Group North radioed that shortly before 0500 the *Suffolk* had again reported our position, course, and speed to Scapa Flow. It must have been around 0545, the rising sun having already lit up the horizon, when the smoke plumes of two ships and then the tips of their masts came into view on our port

The mighty *Hood*, whose elegant lines can be seen in this photograph taken in late April 1938, was the pride of the Royal Navy for two decades. In May of 1941 she looked much the same, except that her 5.5-inch guns had been removed, numerous antiaircraft weapons had been added topside, and she was painted a darker gray. (Photograph from Marius Bar, Toulon.)

beam. General quarters was sounded on the *Bismarck*. Through my director, I watched as the masts in the distance grew higher and higher, reached their full length, and the silhouettes of the ships below them became visible. I could hear our first gunnery officer, Korvettenkapitän Adalbert Schneider, speaking on the fire-control telephone. His hour had come, and all our thoughts and good wishes were with that competent, sensible man. How was it that a young seaman in the *Bismarck* had summed up his own and his comrades' feelings? "Next to the captain, the first gunnery officer, Korvettenkapitän Schneider, has all my respect and confidence!" Now I heard Schneider saying he thought the approaching ships were heavy cruisers and giving targeting information on the lead one; I heard our second gunnery officer, Korvettenkapitän Helmut Albrecht, who was in the forward control station, expressing first mildly, then definitely, doubt that the ships were heavy cruisers and saying that he thought they were battle cruisers or battleships. Then the turrets were

trained, the 38-centimeter guns loaded, and all we needed was the Fleet Commander's permission to fire.

Meanwhile, the enemy ships were rapidly closing their original range of more than 30,000 meters. I estimated that they were steaming at about the same speed we were, 28 knots. To approach nearly bow-on, as they were doing, appeared to me absolutely foolhardy; it reminded me of an enraged bull charging without knowing what he's up against. But, since the British admiral obviously knew that, his impetuous approach must, I thought, have something to do with gunnery. Presumably, he wanted to close the range rapidly, so as to get out of the way of plunging fire.* But there was not time to ponder such considerations at this moment. Whatever the British tactic was,

---

*Captain S. W. Roskill writes in *The War at Sea*, Vol. I, p. 398: "Admiral Holland must also have considered whether it would be to his advantage to fight the enemy at long or short ranges. He had no information regarding the ranges at which the *Bismarck* would be most vulnerable to the gunfire of his own ships, but he did know that the *Prince of Wales* should be safe from vital hits by heavy shells from maximum gun range down to about 13,000 yards, and that the *Hood* should become progressively more immune from such hits as the range approached 12,000 yards and the enemy shell trajectories flattened. At long ranges the *Hood*, which lacked heavy horizontal armour, would be very vulnerable to plunging fire by heavy shells. There were, therefore, strong arguments in favour of pressing in to fight the *Bismarck* at comparatively short ranges."

Korvettenkapitän Adalbert Schneider, first gunnery officer of the *Bismarck*, who, from the foretop fire-control station, directed the gunfire that sank the *Hood* and damaged the *Prince of Wales*. (Photograph courtesy of Frau Ilse Schneider.)

the exciting reality was that the ships were getting nearer and nearer to us.

The clock showed 0553. The range, I figured, was less than 20,000 meters. There were flashes like lightning out there! Still approaching nearly bow-on, the enemy had opened fire. *Donnerwetter!* Those flashes couldn't be coming from a cruiser's medium-caliber guns. Certain that we would immediately return the fire, I braced myself for "Permission to fire" and the thunder of our guns that would follow. Nothing happened. We in the after station looked at one an-

The *Bismarck*, running at high speed, has just fired a salvo at Admiral Holland's force. The large bow wave and the thin stream of smoke forced high out of her stack attest to her speed. Note that she is on the starboard quarter of the *Prinz Eugen*. (Photograph courtesy of Paul Schmalenbach.)

other in bewilderment. Why weren't we doing something? The question hung in the air. Schneider's voice came over the telephone. "Request permission to fire." Silence. Schneider again: "Enemy has opened fire," "Enemy's salvos well grouped," and, anew, "Request permission to fire." Still no response. Lütjens was hesitating. The tension-laden seconds stretched into minutes. The British ships were turning slightly to port, the lead ship showing an extremely long forecastle and two heavy twin turrets. On the telephone I heard Albrecht shout, "The *Hood*—it's the *Hood!*" It was an unforgettable moment. There she was, the famous warship, once the largest in the world, that had been the "terror" of so many of our war games. Two minutes had gone by since the British opened fire. Lindemann could restrain himself no longer and he was heard to mutter to himself, "I will not let my ship be shot out from under my ass." Then, at last, he came on the intercom and gave the word, "Permission to fire!"

Both the German ships concentrated their fire on the *Hood*, while she, deceived, as our enemies often were by the similarity of design of all our ship types, was firing at the *Prinz Eugen*, in the belief that she was the *Bismarck*. The captain of the other British ship, which turned out to be the battleship *Prince of Wales*, realizing what had happened, began firing at the *Bismarck*, despite Admiral Holland's

Turrets Caesar and Dora fire on the *Prince of Wales*. The *Bismarck* has pulled to port of the *Prinz Eugen* and her guns now point at a bearing of about 310 degrees. Note the position of the foretop range-finder cupola. (Photograph courtesy of Paul Schmalenbach.)

order to concentrate fire on the leading German ship. About four minutes after the firing began and after six salvos had been aimed at the *Hood*, Lütjens ordered the *Prinz Eugen* to take the *Prince of Wales*, which he referred to as the *King George V*, under fire. Having been ordered to keep our old fellow travelers, the *Norfolk* and *Suffolk*, under continuous observation in case they launched torpedoes at us, I could no longer watch what was going on off our port beam. I had to depend on what I could hear over the fire-control telephone.

Lindemann's permission for us to open fire was immediately followed by our first heavy salvo. The *Bismarck* was in action, and the rumble of her gunfire could be heard as far away as Reykjavik, the capital of Iceland.* I heard Schneider order the first salvo and heard

---

*In 1953, as the chargé d'affaires ad interim of the Federal Republic of Germany, I was invited to a state dinner at which the foreign minister of Iceland, Bjarni Benediktsson, told me that he was in Reykjavik and clearly heard the sound of the battle.

his observation on the fall of the shot, "short." He corrected the range and deflection, then ordered a 400-meter bracket.* The long salvo he described as "over," the base salvo as "straddling," and immediately ordered, "Full salvos good rapid." He had thus laid his battery squarely on target at the very outset of the engagement.

I had to concentrate on watching the *Suffolk* and *Norfolk*, but I must say I found it very difficult to deny myself glimpses of the morning's main event. The cruisers, still twelve to fifteen nautical miles astern, followed on our course, a little to one-side of our wake. There was no evidence that they were preparing to launch a torpedo attack. The *Suffolk* fired a few salvos, but they fell hopelessly short. Wake-Walker in the *Norfolk* appeared to have left the battlefield completely in the hands of the senior officer, Holland, in the *Hood*. I continued to hear Schneider's calm voice making gunnery corrections and observations. "The enemy is burning," he said once, and then, "Full salvos good rapid." The forward gunnery computer room was telling him at regular intervals, "Attention, fall."

Ever since the action began, I had been wondering whether I would be able to distinguish the sound of the enemy's shells hitting us from

*The lateral fall of shot was corrected by adjusting the bearing.

the sound of our own firing—with all the noise that was going on, that might not always be easy. Then I heard Schneider again: "Wow, was that a misfire? That really ate into him." Over the telephone I heard an ever louder and more excited babble of voices—it seemed as though something sensational was about to happen, if it hadn't already. Convinced that the *Suffolk* and *Norfolk* would leave us in peace for at least a few minutes, I entrusted the temporary surveillance of the horizon astern through the starboard director to one of my petty officers and went to the port director. While I was still turning it toward the *Hood*, I heard a shout, "She's blowing up!" "She"—that could only be the *Hood!* The sight I then saw is something I shall never forget. At first the *Hood* was nowhere to be seen; in her place was a colossal pillar of black smoke reaching into the sky. Gradually, at the foot of the pillar, I made out the bow of the battle cruiser projecting upwards at an angle, a sure sign that she had broken in two. Then I saw something I could hardly believe: a flash of orange coming from her forward guns! Although her fighting days had ended, the *Hood* was firing a last salvo. I felt great respect for those men over there.

At 0557 one of our observers had spotted a quick-spreading fire forward of the *Hood*'s after mast: the second salvo from the *Prinz Eugen* had set fire to rocket propellant for the U. P. Projectors.* Four minutes later, a heavy salvo from the *Bismarck* hit the *Hood* and sent a mountain of flame and a yellowish-white fireball bursting up between her masts and soaring into the sky. White stars, probably molten pieces of metal, shot out from the black smoke that followed the flame, and huge fragments, one of which looked like a main turret, whirled through the air like toys. Wreckage of every description littered the water around the *Hood*, one especially conspicuous piece remaining afire for a long time and giving off clouds of dense, black smoke.

Another observer, on duty in the charthouse as an assistant to Korvettenkapitän Wolf Neuendorff, the navigator, described what he saw:

---

*A U.P. Projector was a mortar-type weapon that fired a 76-millimeter rocket into the air. Once the rocket reached a certain height, it released a parachute with a mine attached. The device was intended for defense against attacking aircraft. When the planes flew into a barrage of these devices, the parachutes would drag the mines against the wings or fuselage and the mines would explode. The rocket propellant was cordite, which had a low flash point. After this incident all U.P. Projectors were removed from British warships.

The *Hood* blows up. A giant column of black smoke marks the spot where the battle cruiser had been. The smoke at left is from the guns of the *Prince of Wales*. (Photograph courtesy of Paul Schmalenbach.)

"Straddling," boomed out of the loudspeaker. I was standing with Kapitän Neuendorff in front of the chart on which we were continuously recording our course. We put our instruments down and hurried to the eye-slits in the forward conning tower, looked through, and asked ourselves, what does he mean, straddling? At first we could see nothing but what we saw moments later could not have been conjured up by even the wildest imagination. Suddenly, the *Hood* split in two, and thousands of tons of steel were hurled into the air. More than a thousand men died. Although the range was still about 18,000 meters, the fireball that developed where the *Hood* still was seemed near enough to touch. It was so close that I shut my eyes but curiosity made me open them again a second or two later. It was like being in a hurricane. Every nerve in my body felt the pressure of the explosions. If I have one wish, it is that my children may be spared such an experience.

In my director I now saw the after part of the *Hood* drift away and quickly sink. Her forward section sank slowly, and soon there was nothing to be seen where the pride of the Royal Navy, the 48,000-ton* "mighty *Hood*," had so suddenly suffered the fate Admiral Holland had in mind for the two German ships. From the time the firing began, only six minutes passed before a shell from the *Bismarck* penetrated the *Hood*'s armor protection at a point never definitely established and detonated more than 100 tons of cordite in the am-

*Full-load displacement in 1941

munition room of one of her after main turrets. How reminiscent of what happened to the battle cruisers *Queen Mary, Indefatigable,* and *Invincible* at the Battle of Jutland in 1916! The *Hood* met her end in the midst of battle. She left only three survivors in the ice-cold waters, and they were picked up by a British destroyer and landed at Reykjavik.

At their battle stations, our men were kept informed of the course of the action by the ship's watch. They heard, "Enemy in sight"— "Opponent has opened fire"—they waited to hear the response of our own guns. A few minutes later it came, and each salvo made the ship shudder. Salvo after salvo was leaving the *Bismarck*'s guns and her engines were running smoothly, when the men below heard, "*Hood* is burning," and, a little later, "*Hood* is exploding." They just stared at one another in disbelief. Then the shock passed and the jubilation knew no bounds. Overwhelmed with joy and pride in the victory, they slapped one another on the back and shook hands.

In the damage-control center adjacent to the command center, the First Officer's action station, Josef Statz saw a more exuberant Oels than he would have believed possible. Oels thrust the top half of his body through the pass-through between the two centers and, thrilled to the core, shouted, "A triple *Sieg Heil* to our *Bismarck!*" The superiors had a hard time getting the men back to work and convincing them that the battle wasn't over and that every man must continue to do his duty.

When the *Hood* had gone, our heavy guns were ordered to "Shift to left target." That meant combining our fire with that of the *Prinz Eugen* which, along with our own medium guns, had been firing at this target for some minutes. The *Prince of Wales*, which, in obedience to Admiral Holland's last command, was turning 20 degrees to port when the *Hood* blew up, had to change direction to avoid the wreckage of her vanished leader. She was then at approximately the same range and on the same course as the *Hood* had been. Consequently, Schneider could continue the action without adjusting the firing data. Because our courses were converging, the range soon closed to 14,000 meters and the *Prince of Wales* was being fired upon by both German ships. By this time I was back watching for a torpedo attack from the *Norfolk* and *Suffolk*, listening over the telephone to Schneider's firing directions. The action did not last much longer. Clearly, it was telling on the *Prince of Wales* and she turned away to the southeast, laying down a smoke-screen to cover her withdrawal. When the range increased to 22,000 meters, Lütjens gave the com-

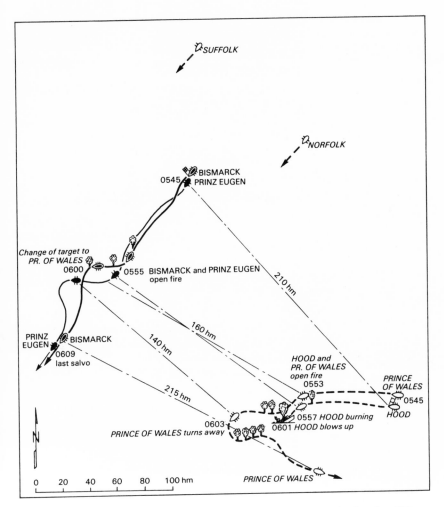

From 0545 to 0609, German Summer Time, on 24 May. The battle off Iceland. (Diagram courtesy of Paul Schmalenbach.)

mand to cease firing on the *Prince of Wales*. She, too, must have been hard hit, how hard we had no way of knowing at the time. Nevertheless, I will tell here what we learned later.

The *Prince of Wales* took four 38-centimeter hits from the *Bismarck* and three 20.3-centimeter hits from the *Prinz Eugen*. One 38-centimeter shell struck her bridge and killed everyone there except

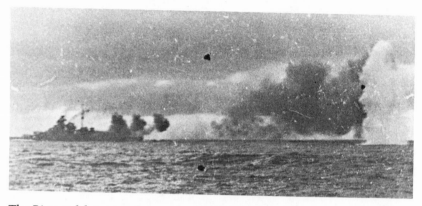

The *Bismarck* has turned to starboard of her cruiser consort. Her guns trained astern, she has just fired a salvo. The smoke from a previous salvo and a column of water from one of the *Prince of Wales*'s 14-inch shells to the right. The splash of a major-caliber projectile could easily reach seventy meters in height. (Photograph courtesy of Paul Schmalenbach.)

the captain and the chief signal petty officer. Another put her forward fire-control station for the secondary battery out of action, and a third hit her aircraft crane. Number four penetrated below the waterline, did not explode, and came to rest near one of her generator rooms. Two 20.3-centimeter shells went through her hull below the water-line aft, letting in some 600 tons of water which flooded several aft starboard compartments, including a shaft alley; the third entered the shell handling room of a 13.3-centimeter gun and came to rest there, without exploding. One of the crew of this mount instantly carried the shell to the railing and threw it overboard. Besides the damage done by these hits, the *Prince of Wales* was suffering from increasingly frequent trouble with her main turrets, which had been in operation for only two months, so that she was able to get off scarcely a salvo with its full load of shells.

It was in the stars that the shell that struck the bridge of the *Prince of Wales* would not explode until it had passed through, a fact that later brought me the friendship of one of its victims. Lieutenant Esmond Knight, Royal Naval Volunteer Reserve, an actor by profession and a painter and ornithologist by avocation, was keeping lookout through a pair of German Zeiss binoculars. His station was in the unarmored antiaircraft fire-control position above the bridge, and he was protected only by his steel helmet. He heard something like "a

To the left, the wreckage of the *Hood* still burns as the *Prince of Wales* comes under fire by the *Bismarck*. Between the *Prince of Wales* and the burning remains of the *Hood* are splashes from the *Prince of Wales*'s shells, which fell hundreds of meters short. (Photograph courtesy of Paul Schmalenbach.)

violently onrushing cyclone," then someone said, "Stretcher here, make way." He had the feeling that he was surrounded by corpses and he smelled blood. People were approaching him and asking, "What happened to you?" He looked in the direction of the voices and saw nothing—a shell splinter had blinded him. In 1948, after a visitor to Germany brought me greetings from him, he wrote me, "I was blind for a year, but now I am back in my old profession at the theatre, which makes me very happy." In 1957 I was a surprise guest in the episode of the BBC's television program "This is Your Life" that was devoted to Esmond Knight. That is when we met for the first time, and we have been friends ever since.

But back to the *Bismarck*.

Today, I greatly regret that, especially from this time forward, I was not a party to Lütjens's deliberations, his conferences within the fleet staff, and his conversations with Lindemann, and did not even have any means of hearing about them secondhand. Nothing of them reached me in the after fire-control station. I can only record the statements of survivors to the effect that Lütjens and Lindemann had a difference of opinion regarding breaking off the action with the *Prince of Wales*. Apparently, Lindemann wanted to pursue and destroy the obviously hard-hit enemy, and Lütjens rejected the idea. Lütjens may have feared that if he continued the action he would be drawn in a direction from which other heavy British units might be

To Bākkō ~
In fond memory of
our second meeting, 16
years later!
Esmond Knight
April · 195

Former Royal Naval Volunteer Reserve Lieutenant Esmond Knight was blinded by a German hit on the *Prince of Wales* during the battle off Iceland. An actor by profession and an ardent amateur painter and ornithologist, he was able to return to his old profession after he regained his sight. This picture shows author's meeting with Knight in London in 1957 on the occasion of the BBC Television program "This Is Your Life" devoted to him. (Photograph courtesy of the *Daily Express*, London.)

advancing. German aerial reconnaissance had not, at that time, provided him with accurate information on the disposition of the British Home Fleet. Therefore, he would be running the risk of getting into more action, using up more ammunition, and, of course, having his own ships damaged—none of which prospects he could have welcomed in view of his principal mission, "war against British trade." He would have viewed it as necessary to forgo the destruction of another British battleship, which must have been tempting to him also. But the chances are that his reserve prevented him from explaining his decision to Lindemann. "Differences of opinion" generally result in arguments and, according to one survivor, there was an argument between Lütjens and Lindemann about breaking off the action. It is not clear what the survivor meant by an argument, but it is highly unlikely that there were loud words in the presence of third parties. In view of the personalities of the men involved, it seems certain that whatever took place would have been conducted with military formality. The only thing definite about this is that someone overheard an officer of the fleet staff telling Fregattenkapitän Oels over the telephone that apparently Lindemann had tried to persuade Lütjens to pursue the *Prince of Wales*. According to other reports, there was "heavy weather" on the bridge for a while. It seems likely that the "argument" was more evident in the atmosphere than in an exchange of words.*

In any event, the men below found it absolutely incomprehensible that, after the destruction of the *Hood*, we did not go after the *Prince of Wales*. They were upset and disappointed. Upon the report of the battle off Iceland Hitler expressed himself to the same effect. "If now," he said to his retinue, "these British cruisers are maintaining contact and Lütjens has sunk the *Hood* and nearly crippled the other, which was brand new and having trouble with her guns during the action, why didn't he sink her, too? Why hasn't he tried to get out of there or why hasn't he turned around? That's really what he was thinking of. But then he would have run into the arms of the Home Fleet."

The battle off Iceland was over and we had used astonishing little ammunition: the *Bismarck*'s 38-centimeter guns had fired 93 shells and the *Prinz Eugen*'s 20.3-centimeter guns had fired 179. Many shells fell close to the *Prinz*, but she was not hit; the *Bismarck* received three 35.6-centimeter (14-inch) hits. My action station was high up and in the tumult of the battle, I was not aware of any incoming hits, but the men in the spaces below found them easily distinguishable from the firing of our own guns. "Suddenly," a petty officer (machinist) wrote of our first hit from the *Prince of Wales*, "we

---

*In *The Bismarck Episode*, p. 85, Russell Grenfell reports another disagreement on the bridge: "It became known afterwards that there had been a hot and prolonged argument between the German Admiral Lütjens in the *Bismarck* and the Captain of the ship, Lindemann, the latter arguing strongly for a return to Germany, the Admiral insisting on a continuance westward." I regard this account as greatly exaggerated. Nothing has ever suggested to me that Lindemann did any more than urge that the action with the *Prince of Wales* be continued.

sensed a different jolt, a different tremor through the body of our ship: a hit, the first hit!"

That first hit, forward of the armored transverse bulkhead in the forecastle, passed completely through the ship from port to starboard above the waterline but below the bow wave. It damaged the bulkheads between Compartments XX and XXI and Compartments XXI and XXII and left a one-and-a-half-meter hole in the exit side. It also ripped up several wing and double bottom tanks. Before long we had nearly 2,000 tons of seawater in our forecastle.

The second hit struck beneath the armored belt alongside Compartment XIV and exploded against the torpedo bulkhead. It caused flooding of the forward port generator room and power station No. 4, and shattered the bulkheads between that room and the two adjacent ones, the port No. 2 boiler room and the auxiliary boiler room. Later, it was discovered that this hit had also ripped up several of the fuel tanks in the storage and double bottom.

The third shell severed the forepost of one of our service boats, then splashed into the water to starboard without exploding or doing any other apparent damage. The crew of an unarmored antiaircraft gun nearby was very lucky; although the hit sent splinters of the boat flying in every direction, none of them was injured. Happily, no one was hurt by any of the hits we took at this time.

Our damage-control parties* and machinery-repair teams made a detailed inspection of the damage that had been done by the two serious hits and set about making what repairs they could.

Forward, the anchor windlass room was unusable and the lower decks between Compartments XX and XXI were flooded. Consequently, the bulkhead behind Compartment XX was being subjected not only to the pressure of static water, but, on account of the big hole in our hull, to that created by our forward motion. To keep it from giving way, a master carpenter's team shored it up while the

---

*We had six twenty-six-man damage-control parties—one each for Compartments I–IV, V–VII, VIII–X, XI–XIII, XIV–XVII, and XVIII–XXII. Each party was led by a warrant officer (machinist), who was assisted by a petty officer. The petty officer of each team assigned most of his men to important points in the area under his supervision but always kept from four to six men with him to take care of emergencies. In the event of a hit or any severe shock, each man checked the various tanks and spaces assigned to him and reported by telephone to the petty officer. The latter gave all the reports of his team to the warrant officer, who relayed a consolidated report to the command center in Compartment XIV on the upper platform deck, where the First Officer received it. Thus, the ship's command was informed of damage in the shortest time possible.

action was still going on. After the action, a work party led by the second damage-control officer, Oberleutnant (Ingenieurwesen) Karl-Ludwig Richter, attempted to enter the forward pumping station through the forecastle in order to repair the pumps so that the contents of the forward fuel storage tanks could be transferred to the service tanks near the boiler rooms. But the pumps in Compartment XX were under water, those in Compartment XVII did not help much, and the valves in the oil lines in the forecastle were no longer serviceable. When an effort to divert the oil via the upper deck also failed, we realized that the 1,000 tons of fuel in the forward tanks were not going to be any use to us. Lütjens turned down Lindemann's suggestion of heeling the ship first to one side and then the other and reducing speed in order to allow the holes in our hull to be patched. Later, however, we did slow to 22 knots for a while, which at least allowed matting to be placed over the holes, and the flow of water into the ship was reduced.

Eventually, we had to shut down power station No. 4, in Compartment XIV. We still had sufficient energy for all our action stations, but our 100 percent reserve capacity was cut in half. The damage-repair parties stuffed the shattered bulkheads in the port No. 2 boiler room and the auxiliary boiler room with hammocks to keep the water in check. Oberleutnant Karl-Ludwig Richter was again on the scene, the never-out-of-sorts officer who always had a good word for everyone, together with his Oberzimmermeister,* the best pair of damage-control men in the ship! Yet in spite of all they could do to seal the bulkhead, the water level rose throughout the day until Richter was standing in it up to his chest and the boiler had to be shut down.

As a result of the flooding, the *Bismarck* was down 3 degrees by the bow and had a 9-degree list to port. The tips of the blades of her starboard propeller were already turning above water. The leader of Damage-Control Team No. 1, Stabsobermaschinist Wilhelm Schmidt, was ordered to flood the flooding and trimming tanks in Compartments I and III, and this improved the situation somewhat.

The lasting effect of the hits in Compartments XIV an XXI was that, mainly because of water pressure on the forward bulkheads, our top speed was restricted to 28 knots. We were now leaving a broad streak of oil in our wake, which was undoubtedly going to help the enemy's reconnaissance and pursuit. The oil was leaking from the

---

*Warrant Officer (Carpenter)

service tanks in Compartment XIV and possibly also from the storage tanks in Compartments XX and XXI.

After the "all clear" was sounded around 0830 the off-duty officers assembled in the wardroom to congratulate our first gunnery officer on the sinking of the *Hood*. Schneider was his friendly and unassuming self as we gathered around to empty a glass of champagne in his honor. His brilliant success made us forget for a few minutes any worries we had about the *Suffolk* and *Norfolk* hanging onto us and the hits we had suffered. None of us grasped the gravity of the damage we had sustained and certainly no one suspected that this would be our last big gathering in the wardroom during Exercise Rhine. Quite obviously, the *Bismarck* was holding her breakout course into the Atlantic and those of us assembled had no reason to think that our operation would not continue according to plan. If anyone doubted the correctness of the Fleet Commander's decision to go on, he did not say so.

At 0632, the battle being over, Lütjens reported to Group North: "Battle cruiser, probably *Hood*, sunk. Another battleship, *King George V* or *Renown*, turned away damaged. Two heavy cruisers maintain contact." Atmospheric conditions in the waters off Greenland were so poor that this message was not received in Wilhelmshaven until 1326. When the minutes passed and it was not acknowledged, Lütjens had it repeated continually. At 0705 he enlarged upon it in a brief report, which also failed to reach Group North, "Have sunk a battleship at approximately 63°10' North, 32°00' West." At 0801, Lütjens advised the Seekriegsleitung of the damage he had received, adding: "Denmark Strait 50 nautical miles wide, floating mines, enemy two radars" and "Intention: to proceed to St. Nazaire, *Prinz Eugen* [to conduct] cruiser warfare."

15

Lütjens's Alternatives

The dispatch of his third radio signal, at 0801 on 24 May, shows that within an hour or so after the action off Iceland, Lütjens had decided to make for St. Nazaire. That was too soon for him to have had a complete picture of the damage the *Bismarck* had suffered or, most important, of what shipboard repairs we would be able to make. The time of his signal shows further that even as we in the wardroom were rejoicing in the assumption that the operation would continue as planned, he had already informed the Seekriegsleitung that such was not his intention. Not until noon, when we changed course from southwest to south, did the news go around, to the officers' considerable surprise.

Before that, I had been wondering, as I'm sure the other officers had too, what Lütjens's decision would be when he knew the full extent of our damage and could tell how, if at all, the enemy's situation had changed. I, of course, had no idea what redeployment of his forces Tovey might consider necessary, but Lütjens had probably already received information on this subject from the B-Dienst in the *Bismarck* and *Prinz Eugen* and in Germany. Therefore, I was sure he would have weighed all the factors he would have to take into consideration in deciding whether to continue the operation immediately, to disappear into the Atlantic and make emergency repairs, to make for a tanker and resupply, to make for a port in western France, to return to Norway, or even to return home.

The only thing clear to me at the moment was that our operation had not gone at all according to our hopes: our breakthrough was anything but undetected, in fact we had been in a battle. It was true that we had scored a tactical victory over two warships, but we had lost the element of surprise, which was so important to the success of our commerce raiding on the high seas. On top of that, even though the battle was over, we still had our unwelcome companions astern. Would we be able to shake them off—now that our speed had been reduced?

I then took to wondering whether we had any chance of commerce raiding after our breakthrough under the eyes of the enemy. What ships would the enemy bring against us and how long would it take to get them there? What was the fleet staff thinking? What did Lindemann think, and what suggestions had he made to Lütjens? Question after question came to mind, but there was no one from whom to expect answers. They would have to be deduced from the execution of Lütjens's new decisions.

The answer came around midday, in the form of our change of course to the south. So, Lütjens had decided to make for western France. But what had so suddenly moved him to try to reach port when he had just decided against the highly promising pursuit of the wounded *Prince of Wales* in order to conduct commerce warfare—the commerce warfare he now had obviously decided not to pursue?

Although, when he ordered our course change, Lütjens could hardly have been absolutely certain what repairs could be made on board, he must have known how alarming the damage was: two holes in our hull, 2,000 tons of water in our forecastle, our speed reduced by 2 knots, the threat that two of our boilers would have to be shut down, 1,000 tons of fuel oil inaccessible in our forward storage tanks, the steady leakage of fuel, and the loss of some of our electric power. It would not have taken him long to realize that little could be done about these things aboard ship and, therefore, decide to look for a port. But that was not all. It was no secret in the ship that Lütjens was much impressed by the excellent performance of the radar carried by the two British cruisers. That the *Suffolk* and *Norfolk* had been able to stay in contact at long range through the rain, fog, and snow of the Denmark Strait made him think that the British definitely had a technological superiority in this area. This is why he mentioned "enemy two radars" in his radio signal to the Seekriegsleitung at 0801. Furthermore, he was probably disheartened by the fact that the few salvos fired at the *Norfolk* the night before had put the *Bismarck*'s forward radar out of action. Shipboard repair of the radar was obviously impossible.

Around 1000, in the course of a semaphore exchange with the *Prinz Eugen*, it came to light that several radio signals sent by Group North in the previous two days had not been received by the *Bismarck*. The *Prinz Eugen* then passed the messages on to us by visual means.* They contained information about the enemy in the Atlantic, mostly the position and course of escort groups, but also what U-boat attacks were doing to them. Lütjens had not suffered any operational disadvantage by not having this information, but the fact that the *Prinz Eugen* had received the signals and his flagship had not must have given him still another cause for concern. His own radio signal of 0632 about the sinking of the *Hood*, in spite of being repeated several times, had apparently not been received by Group North. The two incidents may have shaken his faith in the *Bismarck*'s radio operators and equipment, upon whose flawless functioning during a month-long operation in the Atlantic he had to rely heavily.

Why did Lütjens choose to make for St. Nazaire, 2,000 nautical miles away? He could have gone back to Norway, via the south coast of Iceland. Bergen was only 1,100 nautical miles away and Trondheim was 1,300. Or, he could have returned to Norway by way of the Denmark Strait, on which course Trondheim was 1,400 nautical miles distant.

Viewed in terms of the weather, the Denmark Strait, with its generally poor visibility, should have been the most inviting. But hadn't Lütjens just discovered that in spite of poor visibility the British

---

*In 1984 the chief wireless officer of the *Prinz Eugen*, Hans-Henning von Schultz, gave me the following information concerning this exchange of signals between the *Bismarck* and the *Prinz Eugen*: "After the action the commander of the *Bismarck* informed the commander of the *Prinz Eugen* of his situation with the following semaphore signal: 'I have received two serious hits, one in Compartment XIII–XIV, causing the loss of power station No. 4, the port boiler room taking on water, which can be controlled; second hit in Compartment XX–XXI in the foreship, entry from port, exit to starboard, above the armored deck. British hit through a boat without importance. Otherwise I'm fine. Five slightly wounded.'

"Following a question from the commander of the *Prinz Eugen* as to how the commander of the *Bismarck* estimated the enemy situation in the Atlantic it became evident that the *Bismarck* had not received *three* radio signals from Group North. They were transmitted to the *Bismarck* by visual means. Why these messages were not received by the *Bismarck* will never be explained. One can only guess between technical defects in the receiving set and human error. (In the *Prinz Eugen* the frequency of Ship-Group North/West and vice-versa was permanently manned in two radio rooms [B and A]—that is, double manned—for the duration of Exercise Rhine in order to ensure that *all* entering messages were picked up. These radio messages were numbered and recorded in the action radio room or the action signals center.)"

maintained contact? Might not going back through the strait be a repetition of the pursuit, this time in the opposite direction? The *Suffolk* and *Norfolk* were still very near us. What forces would they call up this time? The British Home Fleet had been alerted. Where were Tovey's other big ships, anyway? All Lütjens knew was that they were somewhere between us and Scapa Flow. And mustn't he have remembered how he had been misled by Group North only two days ago—"Assumption that breakout has not yet been detected by the enemy reconfirmed," they had told him, and then sent him an erroneous report on the ships still at Scapa Flow. The appearance of the *Hood* and *Prince of Wales* had told him a different story. On the evening of 23 May, Group North had informed him that the weather had made aerial reconnaissance of Scapa Flow impossible that day. The picture, as he saw it, could not have been exactly rosy: any information he had about the enemy was suspect; our top speed had been reduced; it was light both day and night in northern waters at this season; the British would probably be making aerial reconnaissances over the Norwegian Sea; we were leaving a telltale trail of oil in our wake; the effectiveness of British radar and radio direction finders had been demonstrated; a second attempt to get out into the Atlantic, after completing repairs, would be even riskier than the first. It would be much better not to return to Norway.

A reconstruction of the overall situation made later by the Oberkommando der Kriegsmarine showed that the best thing the Fleet Commander could have done was go back through the Denmark Strait. Yet that was hindsight and was based on knowledge of where the British naval forces were deployed, which Lütjens, naturally, did not have.

Although St. Nazaire was 600 nautical miles farther away than Trondheim, we would be on a southerly course, where there would be more hours of darkness, and we would not be in narrow waters. On the high seas we would have a better chance of shaking off our pursuers, and we might be able to get some support from our U-boats or to fuel from one of our tankers positioned in the Atlantic. Other things in favor of St. Nazaire were that it had a dry dock large enough for the *Bismarck* and it would be a good point of departure for operations against enemy commerce in the Atlantic.

That Lütjens regarded his visit to St. Nazaire as an interruption of Exercise Rhine and not its end, I can only surmise, but his actions up to this point make it almost certain that he did: he had not hesitated to go on with the operation after the day in Grimstadfjord, even though the enemy was known to be alerted; he had maintained course after the first encounter with the British cruisers in the Denmark Strait, instead of reversing it, as he did in a similar operation with the *Gneisenau* and *Scharnhorst* three months earlier; he had broken off the pursuit of the *Prince of Wales* in favor of carrying out his principal mission of commerce warfare. The rumor that the operation would be "continued" after the repairs there went around the ship in the course of the day.

These speculations about St. Nazaire lead back to Lütjens's rejection of Lindemann's suggestion that we reduce speed and heel the ship so that the holes in our hull could be patched. I have not been able to find out why Lütjens did this, nor do I know precisely when he and the captain had this exchange. It must, however, have been after Lütjens decided to make for St. Nazaire, because, once he had done so, there would have been no point in doing anything that would delay our getting into port. It might, of course, have been possible for us to do an at-sea repair job on the two shell holes and thus restore our ability to steam at top speed. But would that have made sense when the loss of the two boilers in our forward boiler room, which seemed imminent and actually occurred barely twenty-four hours later, could easily have canceled out the advantage? Would it have been worth the risk of reducing speed, perhaps for a considerable length of time, while we were still within range of our shadowers, who were in a position to get help from powerful ships? The wisdom of doing so would have been questionable for many reasons and, if Lütjens viewed the pros and cons as I have presented them, I can sympathize with him.

16

Parting with the *Prinz Eugen*

Shortly before 1000, Lütjens ordered the *Prinz Eugen*, which had been steaming ahead of the *Bismarck*, to drop back and examine the battleship's trail of oil. As the ships passed one another during this change of station, Lindemann asked Brinkmann, his classmate at the Naval School, to signal the results of his observations. The slick was still visible, Brinkmann reported, and was spreading over the surface of the water so rapidly that it was impossible to estimate, even approximately, its extent. The giveaway streak seemed to want to stay with us, and give us away it did, because before long a Sunderland flying boat began cruising back and forth over our wake, beyond the range of our antiaircraft guns. It notified the *Suffolk* that we were trailing oil and kept her informed of the situation. When the *Prinz Eugen* had completed her inspection of the oil slick, she took the lead again and resumed her radar search of the area ahead.

Throughout the morning of the twenty-fourth the *Suffolk* and *Norfolk* hung on and around noon the *Prince of Wales*, directed by a Catalina flying boat, came into view again at extreme range. The cruisers detected every change of course and speed we made and immediately passed on the information by radio. We had come to accept the three ships as our standing escort. Morale on board did not suffer, however. On the contrary, the crew was optimistic, or seemed to be, that somehow we would shake them off.

Group North, still knowing nothing of any action off Iceland,*

---

*Lütjens's radio signal of 0632, reporting the action, had not yet reached Group North; the repeat sent at 0705 never did get there.

After the battle off Iceland, the *Bismarck* pulls into line astern of the *Prinz Eugen*. Her guns, now silent, are again trained fore and aft. (Photograph courtesy of Paul Schmalenbach.)

signaled Lütjens at about 0830 that it assumed he intended to drive off his shadowers so that the *Prinz Eugen* could refuel, and above all that he would try to lure the enemy to our U-boats. It also noted that, at 1200, operational control of Exercise Rhine would pass to Group West—a transfer that took place on schedule. Other signals received in the course of the morning relayed to the Fleet Commander information B-Dienst had collected about the success the British were having in keeping up with us. This merely reconfirmed to him that his task force was under constant surveillance by the *Suffolk*, *Norfolk*, and *Prince of Wales*.

Somewhere about 1100 the weather suddenly worsened and the sea rose. Rain squalls began to alternate with haze, and broad banks of fog loomed ahead, but now and again the sun broke through. Visibility varied between eighteen and two nautical miles. Difficult as it was for the British shadowers, operating at a distance of around 30,000 meters, they never lost contact.

Shortly before 1400 Lütjens reported to the Seekriegsleitung and to GroupWest: "*King George V* and a cruiser keep contact. Intention: if no action, to attempt to lose them after dark." Obviously, he was still

The *Bismarck* passing the *Prinz Eugen* during a change of station. She is down by the bow and pitching heavily as a result of a hit forward. When the *Prinz Eugen* had taken station astern, she tried to determine how much oil was leaking into the *Bismarck's* wake. This photograph, shot on the morning of 24 May, is the last one of the *Bismarck* taken from the German side. (Photograph courtesy of Paul Schmalenbach.)

mistaking the *Prince of Wales* for her sister ship, the fleet flagship *King George V.* And the reason why he mentioned only one cruiser was that the *Norfolk's* course took her through fog banks and she was lost to sight for considerable periods of time, which was the case when the message was sent.

In a semaphore message sent to the *Prinz Eugen* some twenty minutes later, Lütjens amplified what he had told Group North at 0801: "Intend to break contact as follows: *Bismarck* will take a westerly course during a rain squall. *Prinz Eugen* will hold course and speed until forced to change or for three hours after separating from the *Bismarck.* Then released to fuel from the *Belchen* or *Lothringen,* thereafter to conduct cruiser warfare. Execute on code word *Hood.*"

Lütjens explained his other intentions in a radio signal to the Commander in Chief, U-Boats, who already knew from our shadowers' radio messages where the task force was. The latter was instructed to position whatever boats he had in the west in a line south of the southern tip of Greenland. Lütjens planned to lead his British shadowers over the waiting U-boats on the morning of 25 May. The positioning of the U-boats, relatively far to the west of us, indicates that, in order to escape enemy aerial reconnaissance as long as possible, Lütjens intended to steam well out into the Atlantic before turning in a great southwesterly curve towards St. Nazaire. He still thought he had enough fuel for such a detour. At 1508 he gave the Seekriegsleitung and Group West more details about the action off Iceland: "*Hood* destroyed at 0600 this morning in a gunnery action of less than five minutes. *King George V* withdrew after being hit. *Bismarck's* speed reduced. Down by the bows a result of a hit in the forecastle."

About this time an aircraft came into view astern. At first, it was taken for a Dornier flying boat and, later, some of the men said that it even gave the German recognition signal in answer to our calls. I have not been able to learn the source of this rather questionable assertion. When the plane closed to around 4,000 meters, however, our antiaircraft officer, Kapitänleutnant Karl Gellert—my good friend from officer candidate and gunnery schools, with whom I had spent happy times—clearly recognized it as American. It was a PBY Catalina flying boat. He immediately sounded the aircraft alarm and almost simultaneously our antiaircraft batteries opened up. The Catalina withdrew. Several times thereafter it tried to maintain contact at close range, but was driven off by our fire. Around 1630 it disappeared for good—as we know today, because of engine trouble.

We entered another heavy rain squall. Visibility declined and Lütjens, deciding that the moment had come for us to leave the *Prinz Eugen*, gave the signal, "Execute *Hood*." It was about 1540. The *Bismarck* increased speed to 28 knots and turned to starboard, in a westerly direction. But our breakaway did not succeed. We were out of sight for a few minutes, than ran out of the squall, right back into the sight of one of our pursuers. We simply completed a circle and, coming up from astern at high speed, rejoined the *Prinz Eugen* some twenty minutes after we'd left her. By visual signal, we told her, "*Bismarck* resumes station here, as there is a cruiser to starboard." Almost three hours later, when we were in a fog bank, Lütjens repeated the code word *Hood*. We executed the same maneuver as before and separated ourselves from the *Prinz Eugen*, this time for good. Turning first to the west and then to the north, we ran into a rain squall, pretty confident that the enemy had not observed the dissolution of our task force. The second gunnery officer of the *Prinz Eugen*, Kapitänleutnant Paul Schmalenbach, later described the parting:

> The signal to execute the order for the two ships to separate is given for the second time at 1814. As the *Bismarck* turns away sharply, for the second time, the sea calms. Rain squalls hang like heavy curtains from the low-lying clouds. Watching our "big brother" disappear gives us a melancholy feeling. Then we see him again for a few minutes, as the

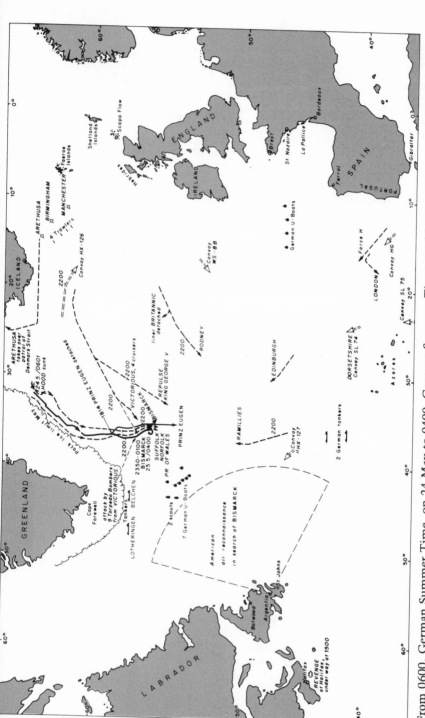

From 0600, German Summer Time, on 24 May to 0400, German Summer Time, on 25 May. Movements of the opposing forces between the battle off Iceland and the loss of contact with the *Bismarck* early on 25 May. (Diagram courtesy of Jürgen Rohwer.)

flashes of his guns suddenly paint the sea, clouds, and rain squalls dark red. The brown powder smoke that follows makes the scene even more melancholy. It looks as though the ship is still turning somewhat northward.

In the fire of his after turrets, we see clearly again the outline of the mighty ship, the long hull, the tower mast and stack, which now look like one solid, sturdy building, the after mast, at the top of which the Fleet Commander's flag must be waving. Yet, because the distance between the two ships is rapidly increasing, it can no longer be made out. On the gaff below, waves the battle ensign, still recognizable as a dot.

Then the curtain of rain squalls closes for the last time. The "big brother" disappears from the sight of the many eyes following him from the *Prinz*, with great anxiety and the very best of wishes. According to orders, which could still be transmitted by signal light, the *Prinz Eugen* reduces speed. We are to act as a decoy, proceeding on the same course as before at a somewhat lower speed, in order to help the *Bismarck*, whose speed has been impaired, to escape from the British shadowers.

We in the *Bismarck* also had heavy hearts as we parted with the faithful *Prinz*. Only reluctantly did we leave her to her own destiny. In retrospect, it must be considered fortunate that we did, for against the concentration of heavy British ships that we later encountered we could not have been of much help to one another. Had we not separated, we probably would have lost the *Prinz Eugen* as well as the *Bismarck* on 27 May. As it was, she was able to reach the port of Brest undamaged on 1 June.

17

Direct Course for St. Nazaire

The *Bismarck's* gunfire, to which Schmalenbach refers, was being directed at our persistent shadower, the *Suffolk*. We met her in the course of our turn, and opened fire at a range of 18,000 meters. She immediately turned away and laid down smoke, but the *Prince of Wales*, which was farther away from us, opened up with her 356-millimeter guns. We turned to our originally planned southerly course and continued the gunnery duel with the *Prince of Wales*. But the extreme range at which we fought, 28,000 meters, coupled with the glare of the sun on the surface of the water and the clouds of stack smoke, made observation from the main fire-control center in the foretop so difficult that Schneider was able to fire only single salvos at long intervals. Since the enemy was astern of us, he eventually ordered me to take over the fire control. Apparently he thought that I, in my station aft, could see better. Such was not the case. The range was too great for me to make reliable observations, either. I told Schneider this, and after a few salvos had been fired at my direction we got the order to cease fire. Neither side scored a hit in this sporadic exchange of salvos. At 1914 Lütjens, still under a misapprehension about the identity of the British battleship, reported to the Seekriegsleitung, "Short action with *King George V* without result. *Prinz Eugen* released to fuel. Enemy maintains contact."

Since leaving the *Prinz Eugen*, the fact that we were alone gradually sank into our consciousness and there was mounting tension as we wondered what surprises the coming hours and days might bring us. Something, we did not even have to wonder about. If for no other reason than to make up for the shame of losing the *Hood*, the British would do everything they possibly could to bring an overwhelming concentration of powerful ships to bear on us. How many and which would they be? Where were they at the moment and in what combination? These uncertainties created tension and were the most important objects of our speculation. A great deal, if not everything, would depend on our shaking off our shadowers and getting as far as possible along the projected great curve towards western France without being observed. Our fuel supply being tight because of the 1,000 tons cut off in the forecastle, we reduced speed to an economical 21 knots. With a little luck, we would reach St. Nazaire without having to fight.

Shortly before 1900 Lütjens received Group West's answer to the radio signal he had sent early that morning saying that he intended to take the *Bismarck* to St. Nazaire and to release the *Prinz Eugen* to conduct cruiser warfare. Group West concurred and had already made arrangements for the *Bismarck* to be received at St. Nazaire and also at Brest. The auxiliary arrangements at Brest had been made in case it became impossible for any reason for the *Bismarck* to go in to St. Nazaire.

Group West made the suggestion that, in the event enemy contact had been shaken off, the *Bismarck* make a long detour en route to port, obviously hoping that this would wear out the British pursuers. It was not a bad idea, and it is more than likely that Lütjens had considered doing just that. What Group West did not know was that the *Bismarck's* fuel situation had been changed by the damage she had suffered—a fact that had not been reported. Therefore it must have been surprised to receive Lütjens's radio signal of 2056: "Shaking off contact impossible due to enemy radar. Due to fuel steering direct for St. Nazaire."

Why Lütjens considered our fuel situation so much more serious on the evening of 24 May than he had at midday, I do not know. Perhaps he had finally accepted the fact that there was no way we could draw on the fuel oil stored in the forecastle.

The Fleet Commander's decision to make "direct for St. Nazaire" had immediate and important results. The Commander in Chief, U-Boats, supposing his instructions to form a line of U-boats south of Greenland to be thereby canceled, adjusted his dispositions to the *Bismarck's* new course towards France. Appropriate instructions were sent to the *U-93*, *U-43*, *U-46*, *U-557*, *U-66*, and *U-94*. The *U-556* was ordered to act as a scout.

18

Attack by Swordfish Torpedo Planes from the *Victorious*

Since the fruitless action with the *Prince of Wales*, which took place a little after 1900 on 24 May, the *Bismarck* had held steady on her southerly course. Before long a report came over the ship's loudspeakers that there was probably an aircraft carrier in the area. All our antiaircraft gun crews immediately went on full alert.

Then, around 2330—it was still light as day*—several pairs of aircraft were seen approaching on the port bow. They were beneath a layer of clouds and we could see them clearly, getting into formation to attack us. Naturally, we did not know it then, but they were from the *Victorious*, the carrier that accompanied Tovey's force out of Scapa Flow on the evening of 22 May. Tovey's objective was to intercept the German task force southwest of Iceland, in the unlikely event that, after Admiral Holland's attack with the *Hood* and *Prince of Wales*, interception would still be necessary. It was.

Aircraft alarm! In seconds every antiaircraft gun on the *Bismarck* was ready for action. One after the other, the planes came towards us, nine Swordfish, torpedoes under their fuselages. Daringly they flew

---

*It was light as day at midnight because, as pointed out earlier, we were on German Summer Time (one hour ahead of standard Central European Time). At 35° west longitude, about where we were during the air attack, German Summer Time was more than four hours ahead of the true local time. This means that when German Summer Time showed midnight, it was not a true 2000. At our position, approximately 57° north latitude, the sun does not go down until after 2000.

through our fire, nearer to the fire-spitting mountain of the *Bismarck*, always nearer and still nearer. Watching through my director, which, having been designed for surface targets, had a high degree of magnification but only a narrow field, I could not see all the action. I could see only parts of it, and that only so far as the swirling smoke of our guns allowed. But what I could see was exciting enough.

Our antiaircraft batteries fired anything that would fit into their barrels. Now and again one of our 38-centimeter turrets and frequently our 15-centimeter turrets fired into the water ahead of the aircraft, raising massive waterspouts. To fly into one of those spouts would mean the end. And the aircraft: they were moving so slowly that they seemed to be standing still in the air, and they looked so antiquated. Incredible how the pilots pressed their attack with suicidal courage, as if they did not expect ever again to see a carrier.

In the meanwhile, we had increased speed to 27 knots and begun to zigzag sharply to avoid the torpedoes that were splashing into the water. This was an almost impossible task because of the close range and the low altitude from which the torpedoes were launched. Nevertheless, the captain and the quartermaster, Matrosenhauptgefreiter* Hans Hansen, who was steering from the open bridge, did a brilliant job. Some of the planes were only 2 meters above the water and did not release their torpedoes until they had closed to 400 or 500 meters. It looked to me as though many of them intended to fly on over us after making their attack. The height of impudence, I thought.

The enemy's tactics were such that torpedoes were coming at us from several directions at the same time and, in trying to avoid one, we were liable to run into another. Back and forth we zigzagged. All at once the sharp, ringing report of an explosion punctuated the roar of our guns and the *Bismarck* gave a slight shudder. At the moment, I was only aware that whatever had caused it must have taken place forward of my duty station. Although I silently cursed what I supposed was a torpedo hit, my immediate reaction was that it had not done much harm. Undoubtedly launched at close range, it could not possibly have reached its set depth—it would have been dangerous to us if it had—but had probably struck in the area where our armor belt was strongest: at the waterline amidships. That armor, I was sure, would not be bothered by a little aerial torpedo. Nonetheless, I took a careful look at the speed and rudder-position indicators. They showed that the engines and rudder were intact—thank God!

*Seaman

What had happened? A torpedo, perhaps the last one launched, and a surface runner at that, had struck the armor belt amidships on the starboard side and exploded, creating a tall waterspout. It was delivered by a pilot who left his wingman and came in, unnoticed by us, in the glare of the setting sun. The concussion of the hit hurled Oberbootsmann Kurt Kirchberg, who was handling ammunition in the immediate vicinity of the explosion, against something hard. He was killed instantly: the first man to die on board the *Bismarck*. We sewed up his corpse in sailcloth and laid it in a boat. His death made a deep impression on all his shipmates in that he was the only fatality, but it was especially distressing to those who had come to know him as a strict but capable and understanding superior.

Below, the explosion made it seem as though the ship had been thrust sideways with much greater force than had been the case when the shells hit that morning or than was created by the recoil of our own guns. In the command and damage-control center the lights went out for a minute or two; everyone thought, "It's all over now." Then the ship returned to her normal trim, the damage-control parties inspected their areas and their telephoned reports buzzed into the damage-control center. The men there were still a little pale but otherwise calm. "Look here," Pumpenmeister Sagner called to them encouragingly, "only the dear God can sink our ship!" Only the young talker in the command center had lost a little of his nerve. He put on his lifejacket and wanted to inflate it, fidgeting around—all this under the eye of the First Officer. The latter gave him a terrific dressing down, but the seaman had the wind up so badly that he could not take in any of it. Comrades brought him to a nearby compartment used as a holding station where he could calm down. In the record time of three minutes the ship's command knew the situation in every sector. Hardly any material damage had been done, although Artillerieobermechaniker* Heinrich Juhl and five other men had broken bones. In action station "E" in Compartment IX on the lower platform deck, the shock threw Maschinengefreiter Budich crossways across the compartment to the main instrument panel. Stupified silence reigned. Obermaschinist Barho broke it by asking, "But Budich, where are you going in such a hurry?" The release of laughter and entering reports quickly dissolved the momentary tension.

Shortly before the attack began, Matrosengefreiter† Georg Herzog,

---

*Warrant Officer (Ordnance Engineer)
†Seaman Apprentice

of the port third 3.7-centimeter mount, spotted three planes to port and sang out, "Three aircraft approaching at 240 degrees." "I had the feeling," he said later, "that the British were putting their all into this attack and were coming in with exceptional daring to deliver their torpedoes. It seemed to me that they came within 15 meters of the ship before they turned away."

Matrosengefreiter Herbert Manthey, of the starboard fifth 2-centimeter mount, noticed that, at first, the incoming planes tried to make a concentrated attack on our port side, then they separated to attack from different directions. When he asked Oberleutnant zur See Sigfrid Dölker, his section commander, about this he was told that three squadrons of torpedo planes had participated in the attack. Our constant zigzagging to avoid torpedoes had greatly complicated his efforts to bring his guns to bear. And towards the end of the attack he heard the explosion to starboard.

Morale in the ship after the attack, whose end was easily told by the cessation of antiaircraft fire, was outstanding. The crew felt even better when they heard that five enemy aircraft had been shot down. In fact, none had been.

Although we weathered it quite well, it cannot be said that we came out of the Swordfish attack unscathed. When we increased speed to 27 knots, water pressure increased correspondingly and that, together with our violent zigzags, caused the matting in the forecastle to rip, and water began rushing in again. The result was that we were still more deeply down by the bow. Furthermore, vibration from our gunfire and the shock response of the starboard torpedo hit enlarged the gash in the bulkhead between port boiler room No. 2 and the adjacent electric power station, which had flooded after the shell hit that morning, to such an extent that the boiler room also flooded and had to be given up. We reduced speed and steamed at 16 knots long enough for the matting in the forecastle to be made watertight again. Meanwhile, we resumed course towards St. Nazaire.

Sometime after midnight Lütjens reported home, "Attack by torpedo planes. Torpedo hit on starboard," and around 0200, "Torpedo hit not important."

Soon after the air attack, we became engaged in a brief sea fight, again with the *Prince of Wales*, which had reappeared on the horizon. She fired two salvos from around 15,000 meters. Schneider answered two or three times with our big guns, but fading light made observation difficult for both sides. The British battleship steamed out of sight and the intermezzo was over.

19

The Admiralty Steps Up the Pursuit

The air attack on the *Bismarck* was the last of the measures that Tovey had planned before leaving Scapa Flow on the evening of 22 May. Despite the impressive performance of the *Suffolk* and *Norfolk* in maintaining contact, the German task force had not been destroyed nor had its speed been so drastically reduced that it would be possible, without doing anything else, to bring other big ships up against it. Nor were there any such ships near enough to be brought up right away. For Tovey and the Admiralty, the failure as such was bad enough, but the loss of the *Hood* made it doubly hard to bear. The *Hood* was not just any battle cruiser. To the Royal Navy, and indeed to the nation, she was the incarnation of British sea power. Wake-Walker had succeeded Holland as senior naval officer on the scene, and his laconic report, "*Hood* has blown up," hit London like a bolt of lightning. If it had been necessary to sink the *Bismarck* before, the loss of the *Hood* made it even more so.

On the evening of 23 May, Tovey with the Home Fleet, consisting of the *King George V,* the *Victorious,* the *Repulse,* several cruisers, and some destroyers, was about 550 nautical miles southeast of the German task force. He had chosen a course to the northwest so that he would be in a position to intercept the German ships whether, after the expected action with Holland's force, they went back through the Denmark Strait or, although heavily damaged, continued to make for the Atlantic. Now, everything was different, and Tovey had very little hope of being able to engage the German task force as long as it continued to the southwest at high speed.

What would the German Fleet Commander do in the changed circumstances? As Tovey saw it, Lütjens was likely to do one of three things: rendevous with a tanker off the west coast of Greenland or near the Azores; if the *Bismarck* had been damaged in the action with Holland's ships—there were no reports that she had—seek out a port in western France for repairs; return home. Not only was Germany the best place for repairs to be made but, more important, the return of the heroes would give the German propaganda machine material that it could use to excellent effect—the alternative that Winston Churchill later declared would have been the best for the Germans. The three courses of action being equally probable, Tovey decided to compromise and take a course towards the southern tip of Greenland. In doing this, he hoped to guard against what was in his eyes the most dangerous eventuality: the German ships getting out into the Atlantic, where they would be able to interdict supply routes vital to Great Britain. And where the *Bismarck* could inflict damage that he of all people would rather not think about.

In London, the Admiralty reacted to the morning's catastrophic report by making a number of important and far-reaching decisions. There were at this time ten convoys in the North Atlantic, escorted by battleships, cruisers, and destroyers. To rob them of their protection when a German task force was at large would expose them to deadly danger, but it was a risk that had to be taken. All that mattered was to deploy against the *Bismarck* every warship then in the Atlantic or anywhere nearby—and deployed they were, every one of them!*

Vice Admiral Sir James Somerville's Force H, consisting of the battle cruiser *Renown*, the aircraft carrier *Ark Royal*, the cruiser *Sheffield*, and six destroyers, was at Gibraltar, waiting to escort a troop convoy. It was released from this mission and instructed to proceed north for operations against the German task force. The cruiser *London*, which was escorting a convoy from Gibraltar to Great Britain, received orders to change course to intercept the *Bismarck* and *Prinz Eugen*. The cruiser *Edinburgh*, which only shortly before had captured a German blockade-runner near the Azores, was also and without regard to her fuel supply deployed against the German formation. Hundreds of nautical miles to the northwest, the battleship *Ramillies* was instructed to leave the convoy she was escorting and take a course to intercept the German task force. Thousands of miles to the

*See Appendix C.

west, in Halifax, the battleship *Revenge* was directed to take over the escort of the convoy the *Ramillies* had left. West of Ireland, the battleship *Rodney*, which was en route to the United States for repairs, was escorting the troop transport *Britannic* across the Atlantic. She, too, received orders to begin operations against the *Bismarck* and *Prinz Eugen*. Three destroyers were assigned to screen her on this new mission. Among them was the *Tartar*, on whose bridge the previous evening Sub-Lieutenant Ludovic Kennedy, the officer of the watch, had received from the hands of a signalman the *Norfolk's* first report of having sighted the German task force in the Denmark Strait. Ludovic Kennedy, whose book *Pursuit* tells the story of the search for the *Bismarck*, is the son of Captain E. C. Kennedy, who had met a seaman's death as commander of the *Rawalpindi* in action against the *Gneisenau* and *Scharnhorst* in November 1939, when I was fourth gunnery officer of the *Scharnhorst*, the same billet I now held in the *Bismarck*.

Within six hours of the loss of the *Hood*, the British had deployed against us four battleships, two battle cruisers, two aircraft carriers, three heavy cruisers, ten light cruisers, and twenty-one destroyers. And so there began a chase which, in terms of the area involved (more than a million square nautical miles) and the number and strength of the ships engaged, is perhaps unique in naval history.

~20

Contact Shaken Off

In the afternoon of 24 May, Lütjens learned from Group West, which had been informed by a Spanish source,* that the *Renown*, *Ark Royal*, and a *Sheffield*-class cruiser—in other words, Force H—had sailed from Gibraltar the previous evening, course not known. What Group West did not know, and therefore could not tell Lütjens, was that these ships had left Gibraltar on a convoy-escort mission but had subsequently been redirected against our task force. Lütjens would have assumed the latter objective, anyhow. Whether or not our B-Dienst team gave him any more information about the enemy that same afternoon, I do not know.

It was not until around noon the next day that the Fleet Commander told us anything at all about the drastic measures the British were taking, and then he told us only in general terms. Up to that time every man had made up for the lack of information by using his own imagination. I recall that my imaginings were very vague. It was just as well that some things were not known. That way, we could still have our moments of hope and, should a critical situation arise, we would deal with it, as before, to the best of our ability. Our young crew was inherently optimistic and, surely, the preservation of optimism for as long as possible could only be to the good. An exact

---

*The information came in a radio message from the Spanish intelligence service to the appropriate German headquarters. This message was intercepted and decoded by British intelligence.

awareness of the enemy armada being assembled would have had anything but a healthy effect on the ship's morale.

Midnight gave way to Sunday, 25 May, Admiral Lütjens's birthday, and over our loudspeaker system the ship's company offered him congratulations. Darkness had fallen and our shadowers, the *Suffolk*, *Norfolk*, and *Prince of Wales*, were once again forced to rely on the *Suffolk's* invaluable radar. Since late the day before, all three of them had been off our port quarter, the *Suffolk* at times being as little as ten nautical miles away from us.*

Lütjens, undoubtedly having been informed that our listening devices and radar showed no hostile ships to starboard, evidently decided it was high time to try to break contact. Shortly after 0300, we increased speed and turned to starboard. First, we steered to the west, then to the northwest, to the north, and, when we had described almost a full circle, we took a generally southeasterly course in the direction of St. Nazaire. I was not aware of these maneuvers, either because I was in my completely enclosed control station and in the darkness did not notice the gradual turn, or because I was off duty at the time. The maneuver carried out the intention that Lütjens had radioed to the Seekriegsleitung the previous afternoon and that had grown increasingly urgent, "Intention: if no action, to attempt to break contact after dark."

Fate seemed to have a birthday present for the Fleet Commander. The *Suffolk*, steering a zigzag course as a defense against possible U-boat attacks, had become accustomed to losing contact with us when she was on the outward leg of her course and the range opened, but regaining it as soon as she turned back towards us. At 0330 she expected to regain the contact she had lost at 0306. She did not.

Lütjens's great chance had come! But he didn't recognize it. He must have believed that, despite his maneuvers, the *Bismarck's* position was still known to his shadowers. He cannot have been aware that by transmitting messages he might be enabling the enemy's

---

*It seems curious that Admiral Wake-Walker kept all three of his pursuing ships off the *Bismarck's* port quarter, the *Suffolk*, with her superior radar, nearer to the *Bismarck* than the *Prince of Wales* and *Norfolk*. At first, he intended to have the *Prince of Wales* engage the *Bismarck* with gunfire from time to time, in the hope that the defensive maneuvers the latter would be forced to take would draw her to the east, the direction from which Tovey's task force was approaching. But this plan did not work out and was soon abandoned. Keeping his three ships to port enabled Wake-Walker to command them as a unit, but how seriously he considered the risk that the German battleship might be able to slip away to starboard, I am unable to say.

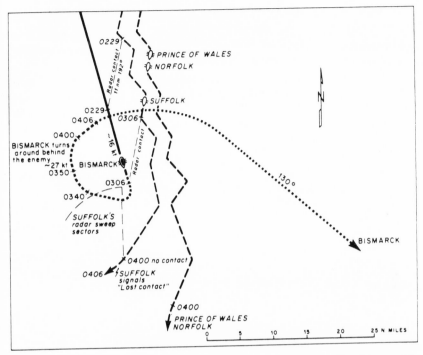

From 0229 to 0406, German Summer Time, on 25 May. The *Bismarck*'s changes of course that led to the loss of contact. (Diagram courtesy of Jürgen Rohwer and Vice Admiral B. B. Schofield.)

direction finders to renew contact with her. After all, his position had been known to the *Suffolk* and *Norfolk* ever since he first encountered them more than twenty-four hours earlier, and radio signals, even long ones, would not really tell the enemy anything new about the position of his flagship. Therefore, he saw no reason for maintaining radio silence, or even any need to use the Kurzsignalverfahren,* which at that date was still immune to direction-finding.

It cannot be definitely determined, but this must be how he thought because at around 0700 he radioed Group West, "A battleship, two heavy cruisers continue to maintain contact."†

When the *Suffolk* was unable to renew contact with the *Bismarck*, she and the *Norfolk*, going on Wake-Walker's assumption that the

*Short-signal procedure
†This message reached its destination at 0908.

175

battleship had broken away to the west, changed course in an attempt to pick her up again. Therefore, by 0700, they had been steaming for several hours in first a southwesterly then a westerly direction. If the *Suffolk*'s radar, with its range of 24,000 meters, could not regain contact with the *Bismarck* at 0330, what chance did it have of doing so at 0700, by which time the *Bismarck* had been steaming for hours in a southeasterly direction? As for the battleship whose presence Lütjens reported, around 0600 the *Prince of Wales* turned to a southerly course in compliance with orders that she join the *King George V.* Therefore, she also had moved too far away from the *Bismarck* to know the latter's position at 0700.

Shortly after 0900 Lütjens radioed to Group West:

> Presence of radar on enemy vessels, with range of at least 35,000 meters,* has a strong adverse effect on operations in Atlantic. Ships were located in Denmark Strait in thick fog and could never again break contact. Attempts to break contact unsuccessful despite most favorable weather conditions. Refueling in general no longer possible, unless high speed enables me to disengage. Running fight between 20,800 and 18,000 meters. . . . *Hood* destroyed by explosion after five minutes, then changed target to *King George V*, which after clearly observed hit turned away making smoke and was out of sight for several hours. Own ammunition expenditure: 93 shells. Thereafter *King George* accepted action only at extreme range. *Bismarck* hit twice by *King George V.* One of them below side armor Compartments XIII–XIV. Hit in Compartments XX–XXI reduced speed and caused ship to settle a degree and effective loss of oil compartments. Detachment of *Prinz Eugen* made possible by battleship engaging cruiser and battleship in fog. Own radar subject to disturbance, especially from firing.†

In the first four sentences of this signal Lütjens reported the perplexing new dimensions that during his passage of the Denmark Strait he had seen looming for the operation of our heavy ships in the Atlantic.

In the course of the past hours Group West got a completely different and correct impression of the scene around the *Bismarck*. Reports sent out by the British shadowers and received by Group West after the dissolution of our task force had, at first, shown some confusion on the part of the enemy. They were still reporting contact with both

---

*Lütjens overestimated the range of the *Suffolk*'s radar by 11,000 meters.
†This signal reached its destination at 0942.

the *Bismarck* and *Prinz Eugen* at 2230, 24 May, in spite of the fact that the ships had separated shortly after 1800. From 2230 until 0213 the next day, they reported contact with the *Bismarck* alone, then their reports ceased. When several hours passed and no more reports of contact were picked up, it seemed clear that contact had been broken, and at 0846 the Group signaled Lütjens: "Last report of enemy contact 0213 *Suffolk*. Thereafter continuation of three-digit tactical radio signals but no more open position reports. Have impression that contact has been broken."

How incomprehensible it must have been for Group West, after 0900, to receive two radio signals from Lütjens reporting that the enemy was still in contact.

The *Bismarck's* signals appeared equally incomprehensible to those aboard the *Prinz Eugen*, which was now far distant but still able to pick up her transmissions. Their shipboard B-Dienst team had long realized from decoding British radio traffic that the British had lost contact with the *Bismarck*. The painful certainty grew on them that this loss of contact had escaped the *Bismarck* and that she had placed herself in danger, great danger, of being located by radio direction-finding. But why?

Why did he still believe his position was known, when even Group West had the impression that contact had been broken? There are four conceivable explanations, in one of which, or in a combination of which, the answer must lie.

First, perhaps the *Bismarck* was still detecting enemy radar pulses, and that made Lütjens think that contact had been maintained. Besides her three radar sets, the *Bismarck* had a radar detector, a simple receiver designed to pick up incoming pulses of enemy radar. Upon receiving such pulses, the detector allowed the wavelength, the frequency and strength of the pulse, and the approximate direction of the sender to be determined. Precise direction-finding, however, was not possible. If such incoming pulses were actually still being picked up at 0700 that day, they could not have been useful to the originating ships, since the pulse reflections had to return to the shadower's radar transmitter to be registered. For if, as previously mentioned, the range had already become too great for the reflections from the *Bismarck* to return to the *Suffolk's* radar at 0330, because of the ships' diverging courses, by 0700 the range must have been much too great. Possibly the *Bismarck's* operators were picking up weak radar pulses beyond effective range of the radar transmitter—in the case of the *Suffolk*, 22,000 meters. Merely to receive a pulse, however, does not necessarily mean that the sender has fixed the target's position. Radar operators must be especially careful to observe and evaluate the strength of an incoming pulse. The ability to do that requires expert training and practice, and whether the *Bismarck*'s radar operators had those qualifications, I cannot say. I am not an expert in this area. In any case, it should be borne in mind that all radar was still in its infancy and there was not much experience to go on. I leave the question open. I think that by 0700 on 25 May our distance from the *Suffolk, Norfolk,* and *Prince of Wales* must have been too great for us to pick up even weak pulses from them. Moreover, the three erstwhile shadowers assumed that the *Bismarck* had turned to the west and therefore adjusted their search patterns in that direction. Would they not have used their radar to search the area ahead of them, to the west, rather than behind them, to the east, where the *Bismarck* really was? It is difficult for me to believe that radar pulses were still being picked up by the *Bismarck* at 0700.*

Second, the interception of enemy radio traffic might have given Lütjens the impression that his position was still known. It may be that the signals of his shadowers were still so strong that it did not occur to him that there had been any change in their proximity. The possibility is purely theoretical. Nothing concrete concerning it has come to my attention.

Third, it is possible that during these hours our B-Dienst team gave Lütjens information that he took or had to take as an indication that the enemy was still in contact. Had the B-Dienst misinterpreted British tactical signals or operational transmissions? Did it play any other role in this connection? That possibility cannot be excluded.

Fourth, Lütjens might have been so deeply under the spell of what he took to be the superiority of British radar that he was no longer able to imagine anything else. Can the two radio messages he sent on the morning of 25 May therefore have a purely psychological explanation, his feeling of resignation? As stated, it is conceivable. In view of the first four sentences of his second signal, it is even probable.

---

*Hans-Henning von Schultz told the author in 1984: "The *Prinz Eugen* also was equipped with radar detectors. These were passive radar sets, with which the beams of a radio-location set (radar impulses) could be detected in a then still-inexact direction only. And since radar detectors would register radar impulses at great distances while the range of shipboard radar was still short, the great distance that existed between the *Bismarck* and her shadowers after contact had been lost excludes any chance that she was still being located by enemy radar. That was not technically possible at the time."

To draw a convincing conclusion from four such diverse alternatives is difficult. I would, however, like to exclude the first. The second and third I can neither assert nor exclude. Not having any direct knowledge of how Lütjens reacted during the most critical phase of the operation so far, from the beginning of the pursuit by the *Suffolk* and *Norfolk* in the Denmark Strait to the morning of 25 May, I am not in a position to transfer the fourth alternative from the realm of the conceivable into that of the believable. In my view, a veil must remain over the reason why Lütjens supposed that the *Bismarck*'s position was known and therefore did not regard the enemy's ability to take a fix on a radio signal as a new and serious danger to his ship.

After 1000 the *Bismarck* did observe radio silence, and Group West then realized that the signal it sent to Lütjens at 0846 had shown him his error concerning enemy contact. But his attempt to correct his mistake by maintaining radio silence was not enough to repair the damage done by the dispatch of his two radio signals.

21

The British Compute the *Bismarck*'s Position

Around 1030, barely an hour and a half after Lütjens sent his second message, Tovey received an urgent signal from the Admiralty informing him that the radio bearing of a ship, supposedly the *Bismarck*, had been picked up at 0852. It gave him the relevant bearings but did not include a determination of our position. This information was omitted because, before he left Scapa Flow, Tovey said he wanted such computations to be done in his flagship.

The bearings transmitted to him from stations in Great Britain, Iceland, and Gibraltar could only be computed by his navigation officer, Captain Frank Lloyd, on an ordinary mercator projection, however, as the flagship had not been outfitted with the gnomonic charts needed for such purposes. The result was that the computations made on the *King George V* were far from unequivocal. Faced with a choice of positions in which the *Bismarck* might be found, Tovey decided that the most northerly was the most probable. That position was, in fact, so far north that Tovey concluded the *Bismarck* was going home through the Norwegian Sea. When he transmitted it to his ships, most of them, with the *King George V* in the lead, turned to the north or northeast on courses that led away from the *Bismarck*'s true position.

Were we to have two chances of escape in one day, 25 May?

The Admiralty soon began to have doubts about the *Bismarck* steering a northerly course and that afternoon recalculated the coordinates with the help of a fix on another signal sent by Lütjens. As a result, it sent Tovey a more southerly position for the *Bismarck*, one that definitely showed her to be heading for the Bay of Biscay. Tovey meantime had had his computations reexamined and realized that a grave error had been made that morning. After another exchange of thoughts with the Admiralty, more hesitation, and briefly taking a compromise course to the east, he let himself be persuaded that the *Bismarck* was steering for the west coast of France. Accordingly, shortly after 1800 he turned to the southeast. For seven hours the *Bismarck* had been enjoying his gift of space and time, and now he was 150 nautical miles behind her on course for St. Nazaire. At 0400 that day, he was 100 nautical miles ahead of her in that direction.

22

A Fateful Sunday

Around the noon hour on 25 May, Lütjens spoke to the ship's company. The summons to assemble near the loudspeakers came on short notice and reached me while I was watch officer in the forward control station. I dismissed the men on watch with me so that they could listen to the talk but, not wanting to leave the guns completely uncovered, I remained at my station.

According to the *Bismarck*'s reconstructed War Diary,* Lütjens said:

Seamen of the battleship *Bismarck!* You have covered yourselves with glory! The sinking of the battle cruiser *Hood* has not only military, but also psychological value, for she was the pride of England. Henceforth, the enemy will try to concentrate his forces and bring them into action against us. I therefore released the *Prinz Eugen* at noon yesterday so that she could conduct commerce warfare on her own. She has managed to evade the enemy. We, on the other hand, because of the hits we have received, have been ordered to proceed to a French port.† On our way there, the enemy will gather and give us battle. The German people are with you, and we will fight until our gun barrels glow red-

*This reconstruction is based on statements made by survivors landed in France by the *U-74* and the weather ship *Sachsenwald* during their debriefing by Group West in Paris at the beginning of June 1941.

†Here the survivors' memories must have played them false. Lütjens can hardly have said anything about being ordered to proceed to a French port. It was his own decision to head for St. Nazaire.

hot and the last shell has left the barrels. For us seamen, the question now is victory or death!

I can still see the leading petty officer who operated one of my directors returning dejectedly from the loudspeaker and still hear him remarking that it was really all over. He and the others who heard the address regarded our chances of getting through to France as practically nil. The enemy, they told me the admiral had said, is concentrating his entire high-seas fleet, not only the ships in home waters, but those in any part of the Atlantic. In the face of such a mass, the fate of the *Bismarck* could only be victory or defeat.

The undertone of the men's remarks was clear. They had used both words, "victory" and "defeat." Yet, before them they saw only defeat. It was not easy to reassure and calm them. I said something to the effect that perhaps things really wouldn't be that bad and reminded them of our lightning victory over the *Hood*. Why shouldn't we do something else like that? But a shadow hung over the men: after all, it was the Fleet Commander who had said those things.

Kapitänleutnant (Ingenieurwesen) Gerhard Junack later reported that after Lütjens's address dejection spread throughout the ship, and it was obviously generated at the top. Staff officers began to wear unfastened life jackets. Senior ship's officers declared in the presence of their juniors that they now saw no way out. Senior petty officers appeared at their duty stations with open life jackets, although to do so was against regulations. The division officers tried harder than anyone to counter the contagious depression and had some success in cheering up their men. But the high morale that permeated the ship in the preceding days was irretrievably lost.

Junack continued: "Whether the Fleet Commander simply made a bad choice of words or whether the crew sensed his innermost fears must remain an open question. Needless to say, all the later rumors about people refusing to obey orders and so forth were invented out of thin air. Morale was low, however, and who can judge what tactical effects that had?"

Stabsobermaschinist Wilhelm Schmidt said: "It is understandable that immediately after this address some of the crew were depressed. The men were so young, some of them had come directly from the training centers and had been on board only six weeks. We warrant and petty officers, trusting in what fighting power we had left and in timely intervention by our long-range bombers, did everything we could to revive and sustain the men's morale."

And a few other voices. A junior gunnery officer: "The Fleet Commander should not have described the situation so baldly." A seaman gunner: "My comrades seemed downhearted and said that the Fleet Commander spoke well, but they interpreted his words to mean that we were already lost." A machinist: "The address had a depressing effect on the crew. Since morale was very high before the speech, the general opinion was that it would have been better if we had not been told anything about the situation we were in." A machinist petty officer: "The Fleet Commander's words had a devastating effect on us. They were taken to mean that we were sentenced to death, whereas we had already reckoned when we would arrive in France. No one looked at anyone else, for fear of betraying any weakness in himself. Deep depression enveloped the whole crew."

Quite obviously, Lindemann immediately perceived what the Fleet Commander's words and tone were bound to do to the spirit of his crew. There were already whispers that the two had their differences. About an hour after Lütjens spoke, the captain made a brief address over the loudspeakers, in which he said exactly the opposite: we would put one over on the enemy and soon reach a French port. Also, in conversations with groups of men, he did his best to counteract the effect of Lütjens's words. He succeeded in dispelling the gloom. The men went back to their duties cheerfully. "I remember," a survivor wrote me, "how their faces brightened after the captain's address, they showed that the men had got their courage back."

Junack's impression that, after Lütjens's address, the dejection seeped down from the top, confirms that our crew, being very young on the average, was overwhelmingly optimistic by nature. At first, some of the younger men were not particularly depressed by the Fleet Commander's warnings. Later they made such comments as, "We were all young and believed in victory," or "The Fleet Commander's address didn't give us the slightest idea that anything could happen to this powerful ship." Another youngster had to overhear a conversation between two older members of the ship's company before he understood "that worse awaited us and that the near future was not nearly as rosy as it appeared to us young sailors."

The *Bismarck's* reconstructed War Diary concludes: "After this address by the Fleet Commander, which made the crew aware of the situation of the ship and the intentions of its command, the morale of the crew, outstanding until then, suffered a certain setback."

Information regarding the latest dispositions of the British fleet, on which his address was based, was evidently given to Lütjens by the B-

Dienst at home and perhaps also by our own B-Dienst team. He continued to get this kind of information and periodically had the crew told about it. "Intercepted and decoded radio signals must have kept our leadership very well informed as to British positions and intentions," remarked a survivor. Thus the crew learned, among other things, that Force H had left Gibraltar; that the British battleship damaged by us in the action of 24 May was not the *King George V*, but the *Prince of Wales*; and that the *Bismarck* was now being sought and pursued by the *King George V*, *Rodney*, *Ramillies*, and *Repulse*, plus cruisers and destroyers, eager to avenge the loss of the *Hood*.

In the course of the day Lütjens received two personal messages from home. One was from Raeder: "Hearty congratulations on your birthday. After the last great feat of arms, may more such successes be granted to you in your new year. Commander in Chief of the Navy." The other, dry and aloof, came from the "Führer." "Best wishes on your birthday. Adolf Hitler."

During my off-duty time that afternoon I went up to the bridge to have a chat about what was going on with whomever I could. I also hoped to find out some details of the situation, which Lütjens had only outlined in general terms. The officer of the watch was Kapitänleutnant Karl Mihatsch, the Division 7 officer. Even today I can see us standing side by side on the starboard side of the bridge, our mighty ship running through a following sea with the wind from astern.

Mihatsch knew no more than I did, so we could talk only in general terms. We both thought that in spite of the enemy's intensified efforts to intercept us, we had a good chance of reaching St. Nazaire. We reckoned that the lead we had over the main British force plus the fact that we could still do 28 knots gave us a better than fifty-fifty chance. We were fully aware that, besides the pursuers coming up astern and Force H to be expected ahead, other ships, if not formations, would be approaching from other directions. It all depended on which ships they were and how fast, where they were at the moment, and what radius of operations they had left. Only one thing could not be allowed to happen under any circumstances: the *Bismarck* must not lose speed or maneuverability. If that were to happen, the slow but heavily armed British ships presently astern would be able to close and concentrate more fire power on us than we would be able to withstand. Of course, the most serious threat was an air attack, such as we had experienced from the *Victorious* the evening before. But was there an aircraft carrier close enough to launch an attack? That was the really big question. We decided, rather lightheartedly, that we had little to fear from other quarters: we regarded submarines, which in any case we were not likely to meet until we got near the French coast, as a secondary danger that did not seriously enter our calculations. And so ended our little "council of war." It did not produce anything sensational, but it was good to talk to someone, and we parted with contented optimism.

Late in the morning the word went round the ship like a streak of lightning: Contact has been broken! Broken after thirty-one long, uninterrupted hours! It was the best possible news, a real boost to confidence and morale. Exactly how this blessing had come about and where the British ships were at the moment, we did not know. Other things we did not know were that around 0400 Tovey's task force had intersected our course 100 nautical miles ahead of us and two hours later the *Victorious* and four cruisers had done the same behind us; and, since 0800 we had been standing to the east, away not only from both those formations, but also from the cruisers *Suffolk* and *Norfolk*, which were looking for us to the west. We probably would not even have wanted to know that much detail. Content with the momentary respite, we kept expressing to one another the hope that we would not catch sight of the enemy again before we got to St. Nazaire.

As the time since Lütjens's address increased and the long day passed into night, the thoughts of those who were not up to date on the enemy situation came to be dominated by the idea that contact had been broken and there was only an extremely small chance that it would be reestablished. The very pleasant contrast between the sound of the guns on Saturday and the calm of Sunday contributed to this feeling. So, too, did human nature, which allows pessimism to fade fast and offers us the welcome support of hope.

What significance did 25 May have for the continuation of Exercise Rhine? No exciting actions took place and by nightfall we had not seen a single enemy either on the sea or in the air, nor did we throughout the night of 25–26 May. But, it could hardly have been a more fateful day.

In the morning the enemy lost contact with us—Lütjens didn't realize it and sent two radio messages—Group West informed him of its impression that contact had been broken—Lütjens accepted this finding and instituted radio silence—the enemy took a bearing on the two messages he did send, but, their coordinates having been incorrectly evaluated in the *King George V*, our pursuers turned in the wrong direction—Tovey's loss of time and space was our gain—in the afternoon Tovey returned to the correct course—the British net drew together again—preparations were made for an air search for the *Bismarck* at her supposed position—our prospects of reaching St. Nazaire rose in the morning and sank in the afternoon, but were still real at the end of the day.

23

The *Bismarck's* Dummy Stack

On the afternoon of 25 May, we devised a small strata- gem whose purpose was to make our adversaries, when next we met them, mistake us for a British battleship. *King George V*-class ships had two stacks, so orders were given to build a second stack for us.

Even with such a change, our silhouette would, of course, give us away to an expert observer on the surface. But we expected that the next enemy to spot us would be in the air. From there it is not easy to recognize ship types, and a second stack could cause real confusion. If it did nothing else, our camouflage would cost the enemy recognition time, especially if visibility worsened, and time became increasingly valuable as our fuel supply became increasingly precarious. So small a thing as delaying our being recognized would be a gain because, once we were recognized, we might be forced, in self-defense, to steam at high speed or to steer an evasive course, either of which measures would strain our fuel supply. Everything, literally every- thing, counted—and not the least was the fact that the longer it took Tovey's ships to find the right course, the better was the chance that one or another of them would run low on fuel and have to give up.

Our dummy stack seemed to me to be a feeble trick because, for one thing, unless our ship's command knew what visual recognition signals the British exchanged when they met, it would not be effec- tive. Perhaps they did know them. I cannot say. Not only that, but British battleships operating on the high seas were usually escorted by destroyers, and the *Bismarck* had no screen, which would certainly make any enemy scout think twice. However, a feeble trick was better than none at all.

Lütjens must have bitterly regretted not having taken the opportunity to fuel in Grimstadfjord or from the *Weissenburg* after we got under way. Ever since it had been determined that part of our fuel supply was inaccessible, more than twenty hours earlier, the *Bismarck* had had to proceed at an economical 20 knots. Had we been making the 28 knots of which her engines were capable, we would have been 160 nautical miles nearer to St. Nazaire and under cover of the Luftwaffe. We would not have had to worry about camouflaging ourselves, either.

With sheet metal and canvas, we built a dummy stack and painted it gray to match the real stack. It was to be set up on the flight deck forward of the hangar. Men from the workshops went at this unaccustomed task with enthusiasm until darkness fell; for them, it was a welcome change from the routine of long war watches.

Our chief engineering officer, Korvettenkapitän (Ingenieurwesen) Walter Lehmann, who took a personal interest in the dummy stack, naturally wanted to see for himself how his men were going about their task. From the first, he had established a close and confidential relationship with them. It was reinforced by the bull sessions he held, preferably near turret Dora, whenever anyone did something wrong. He would take the culprit aside and, to put him at his ease, growl, "No formalities!" As a survivor put it, "You had to walk round the turret with him and could say whatever was on your mind." In Gotenhafen, while liberty was canceled in preparation for our departure, a young stoker learned that his mother was dying. He was heartbroken. A sympathetic comrade took him to Lehmann. The boy blurted out, "Please, Papa," then, overcome by emotion, fell silent. "Now tell Papa," Lehmann said, "it doesn't matter, what's got you down?" Before long, all his men were calling him "Papa Lehmann."

So Papa Lehmann came and took a look at what was going on with the stack. "We really must," he said, "fix it so that it will smoke as it should." The ship's command took up his jesting idea, and word was passed over the loudspeakers, "Off-duty watch report to the First Officer's cabin to draw cigars to smoke in our second stack!" The hilarity that this order caused did a lot to raise morale.

When the dummy stack had been completed it was left lying on the deck. It was not to be rigged until the order was given. In the meanwhile, I helped to compose several English-language Morse signals for use in the event of an enemy contact.

Korvettenkapitän Walter Lehmann, chief engineer of the *Bismarck*. (Photograph courtesy of Frau Ursula Trüdinger.)

Lehmann's big worry that day was not so much the fuel shortage created by the oil in the forecastle being cut off, as it was the danger of saltwater getting into the boilers. As a result of the flooding in port No. 2 boiler room, the feedwater system of turbo-generator No. 4 had salted up and the same danger was threatening power plant No. 3. If seawater got into the boiler through the feedwater system, unevaporated water might be carried into the propulsion turbines along with the steam and, in no time at all, destroy the turbine blades and lead to "blade salad." Therefore the feedwater in all the turbo-generators must be changed immediately. But our high-pressure boilers took so

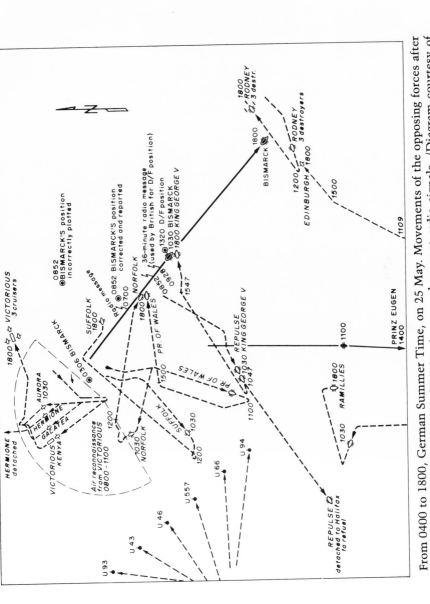

From 0400 to 1800, German Summer Time, on 25 May. Movements of the opposing forces after the loss of contact and Admiral Lütjens's two subsequent radio signals. (Diagram courtesy of Jürgen Rohwer.)

much feedwater that we had trouble producing enough to keep pace with the demand. An all-out effort to make our four fresh-water condensers and auxiliary boiler produce enough was successful and by the evening of 25 May the danger had passed.

In the afternoon we reduced speed to 12 knots to facilitate the repair work still being done in the forecastle. With much difficulty, men in diving gear climbed into the completely flooded forward compartments and opened the oil-tank valves, which gave us a few more hundred tons of fuel.

Marinebaurat* Heinrich Schlüter suggested that we jettison the forward anchors and anchor chains. His idea was to lighten the forward section so as to adjust the forward trim that we had had since the flooding that began during the battle off Iceland. The ship's command rejected the suggestion, presumably because it foresaw that the anchors would be essential for mooring in St. Nazaire.

Group West informed the Fleet Commander at about 1930 that the Luftwaffe was ready to cover the approach of the *Bismarck* in force: bombers as far out as 14 degrees west, reconnaissance planes to 15 degrees west, and long-range reconnaissance planes to 25 degrees west; and three destroyers were ready to meet her. The message advised him that the approaches to Brest and St. Nazaire were under strict surveillance and, in an emergency, he would be able to go in to La Pallice. When he passed 10 degrees west longitude, he was to report it promptly.

At about 0430 on 26 May an announcement came from the bridge: "We have now passed three-quarters of Ireland on our way to St. Nazaire. Around noon we will be in the U-boats' operational area and within the range of German aircraft. We can count on the appearance of Condor planes after 1200." Joy reigned throughout the ship and morale climbed.

---

*Naval Constructor from the Construction Office, OKM (Oberkommando der Kriegsmarine)

24

Catalinas from Northern Ireland

Like everyone else on board, I knew nothing of the reconnaissance activities in which the Royal Air Force's Coastal Command was engaged during the night of 25–26 May.

At the beginning of May 1941, seventeen U.S. Navy pilots were sent to Great Britain under the strictest secrecy—the United States was not at war with Germany at this time—and distributed among the flying-boat squadrons of Coastal Command. Their mission was to familiarize the Royal Air Force with the American-built Catalina flying boat some of which had been put at the disposal of the British government under the provisions of the Lend-Lease Act. The arrangement was also to give the American pilots operational experience for the benefit of the U.S. Navy.

With a wingspan of 35 meters, the Catalina had what was at that time the unusually long range of 6,400 kilometers. At 0300 on 26 May, two of them left their base at Lough Erne in Northern Ireland on a far-reaching search into the Atlantic for the *Bismarck*. One of them was Catalina "Z" of Squadron 209. Its pilot was a Briton, Flying Officer Dennis Briggs, its copilot an American, Ensign Leonard B. Smith. Around 1015, in poor visibility and low-lying clouds, Smith saw a ship that he took to be the *Bismarck*, but could not be absolutely certain. Briggs maneuvered the plane into a position for better observation. From an altitude of 700 meters and at a distance of 450 meters abeam, Smith saw the ship again through a hole in the clouds. Was it the *Bismarck*? Minutes later, the Catalina began to transmit,

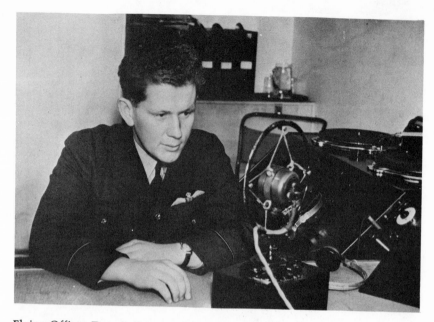

Flying Officer Dennis Briggs, pilot and aircraft commander of the Catalina flying boat that sighted the *Bismarck* on 26 May 1941 . This sighting reestablished the contact that had been lost for thirty-one hours. (Photograph from the Imperial War Museum, London.)

"One battleship bearing 240° five miles, course 150°, my position 49°33' north, 21°47' west. Time of origin, 1030/26."

That message showed Tovey how narrowly the *Bismarck* had been missed the previous day: the *Rodney* and her destroyer screen had missed her by some 50 nautical miles, the cruiser *Edinburgh* by around 45 nautical miles. A flotilla of British destroyers had crossed the *Bismarck*'s wake at a range of only 30 nautical miles. Now the *King George V* was 135 nautical miles to the north, the *Rodney* 125 nautical miles to the northeast, and the *Renown* 112 nautical miles to the east-southeast of the German battleship, which was still 700 nautical miles from St. Nazaire.

25

The *Bismarck* Is Rediscovered

The *Bismarck* maintained course and speed towards the west coast of France. As the night past had been, the early morning hours of 26 May were quiet. At 1025 Group West radioed Lütjens that our own aerial reconnaissance had started as planned, but that weather conditions in the Bay of Biscay prevented air support from going out. Thus for the time being we could not expect air cover until we were close to shore.

Suddenly, around 1030, a call came from the bridge, "Aircraft to port!" "Aircraft alarm!" All eyes turned in the direction indicated and a flying boat was indeed clearly visible for a few seconds before it disappeared into the thick, low-lying clouds. As soon as it reappeared we opened well-directed antiaircraft fire. It turned away, vanished into the clouds, and was not seen again. We assumed that it was staying in the cover of the clouds so that it could continue to observe us and report our position, preferably unseen. For a while, the bridge considered sending our Arado planes up against the Catalina. But because of the risks that would be incurred in recovering the float planes in such heavy seas, Lindemann would not allow them to be launched.*

---

*The Arado-196 had a 760-horsepower Bayerische Motoren Werke engine, a cruising speed of 240 kilometers per hour, a maximum speed of 275 kilometers per hour, a rate of climb of 300 meters per minute, a ceiling of 5,300 meters, and an endurance of three to five hours. It was armed with one 2-centimeter cannon in each wing and two machine guns. Under each wing it had a rack for one 50-kilogram bomb.

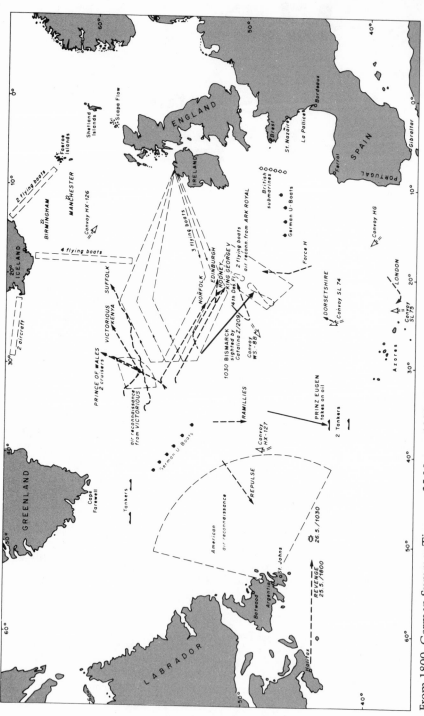

From 1800, German Summer Time, on 25 May to 1030, German Summer Time, on 26 May. After a day without sighting the enemy, the *Bismarck* was rediscovered at 1030, German Summer Time, 26 May. (Diagram courtesy of Jürgen Rohwer.)

Our B-Dienst team speedily decoded the Catalina's reconnaissance report and at 1156 Group West radioed it to Lütjens as well: "English aircraft reports to the 15th Reconnaissance Group: 1030, a battleship, course 150°, speed 20 knots. My position is 49°20′ north, 21°50′ west."

We had been rediscovered.

Obviously, the big flying boat had come from a land base a long way away, which led me to assume that it might be a long time before there were any perceptible reactions to its report. But I soon found out that I was wrong. As early as 1200, only an hour and a half after our encounter with the Catalina, Lütjens radioed Group West about the appearance of another aircraft: "Enemy aircraft maintains contact; wheeled aircraft; my position approximately 48° north, 20° west."*

A wheeled aircraft! So there must be an aircraft carrier quite nearby. And other, probably heavy, ships would be near her. Would cruisers or destroyers pick up contact before we ran into them? And were we now to experience a new version of our happily ended pursuit by the *Suffolk* and *Norfolk*?

We in the *Bismarck* had the realization forced upon us that another page had been turned. After thirty-one hours of almost unbroken contact, thirty-one hours of broken contact had now, perhaps for good, come to an end—an exactly equal number of hours, how remarkable! Did the carrier plane really signify a decisive turn of events? Morale sagged a little among those who could read the new signs.

Of course, we did not know then that the appearance of the carrier aircraft was not simply the visible result of the Catalina's reconnaissance. We had no idea that the radio signals transmitted by Lütjens the morning before had led the enemy to us. The two signals, the second of which was especially useful to enemy direction-finding stations ashore because of its length, became of interest when the operation was evaluated in Germany. At the time of their transmission, however, they were of no operational consequence. They only helped seal the fate of the ship and her crew.

---

*The position reported by Lütjens differs considerably from that reported by the Catalina shortly before. According to a subsequent reconstruction, both reports were in error as to our latitude, that of the Catalina by approximately twenty-five nautical miles, and that of the *Bismarck* by approximately eighty nautical miles. Such deviations can easily occur after long flights and cruises. (*See also* Ludovic Kennedy, *Pursuit*, pp. 154–55.)

The dummy stack still lay where it was built on the flight deck. It had not been rigged, and I have not heard a logical reason why not. If it was to serve its purpose, we would have had to set it up when we were out of sight of the enemy, so that the next time they saw us they would immediately think they were seeing a two-stack ship. Instead of playing our trick, we confirmed our identity by firing at the enemy aircraft. As we know today, we even spared him the trouble of making completely sure who we were! So we had decided in advance not to try our ruse or our prepared radio messages, and I could imagine only that this decision had something to do with the attitude of the fleet staff. They probably decided that the overall situation, which they sensed to be increasingly precarious, made it useless to try to camouflage ourselves. There was neither time nor opportunity to ask questions, so I kept my speculations to myself.*

---

*Jochen Brennecke, *Schlachtschiff Bismarck*, page 156, quotes the following excerpt from the first batch of raw material (1951) for my subsequent book, which reached him only through an indiscretion and was never authorized for publication: "I do not know why at this time (1030, when we were rediscovered by the Catalina) the second stack built to mislead the enemy had not yet been set up or, in the same connection, why afterwards (between the disappearance of the Catalina and the appearance of a wheeled aircraft from the *Ark Royal*) it was not set up. On the contrary, our fire confirmed that we were the enemy. There is no way of knowing whether the aircraft would have been taken in by this stratagem. . . ."

To this extract, Brennecke appends footnote 267, in which Konteradmiral Hans Meyer (Retired) says: "The whole business of the dummy stack is in my opinion a fantasy. The order to build a second stack was certainly given, but the situation that developed very soon made it clear that it could not be erected. *The very harsh criticism along the lines of, 'Only he who gives up is truly lost,' at least in connection with the dummy stack, I hold to be absolutely unjustified"* (my italics).

Surprised by this appraisal of a "criticism" I had not made, I consulted the first edition of Brennecke's book, published in 1960, and found, on page 307: "The mistaken attack [by aircraft from the *Ark Royal* on the evening of 26 May] on the *Sheffield* made one thing clear: the crucial value the second stack built on board the *Bismarck* could have had, if it had been set up. In the uncertainty that prevailed after this attack on the *Sheffield*, which did not look anything like the *Bismarck*, no British pilot would have dared attack a two-stack ship because the two-stack British ships *Renown*, *King George V*, and *Sheffield* were in the area. Perhaps the decisive hit [the hit on the *Bismarck*'s rudder later that evening] would not have been made. *Here, too, one might say, Only he who gives up is truly lost"* (my italics). Brennecke has deleted that passage, his own words, from his fourth edition. He simply attaches Meyer's negative evaluation to my words, which gave no occasion for it.

Furthermore, in the cited footnote Meyer says: "Bad weather also came up. The dummy would have hardly been able to withstand the wind pressure. It was a matter of surface area. The situation might have been different if the ship had reached the open Atlantic, where only single aircraft were to be anticipated, not a battle at any moment,

During the afternoon a Catalina flying boat joined the wheeled aircraft that was holding contact with us. It was the partner of our discoverer, which had earlier been obliged to break off the operation because of its fuel supply. The Catalina circled back and forth over our wake for a long time, out of range of our antiaircraft batteries. Occasionally the planes tried to come closer to us, but each time they were driven off by our flak. The bridge announced that an aircraft carrier was in the vicinity and all lookouts were to pay particular attention to the direction in which the wheeled aircraft disappeared, so that the position of the carrier could be ascertained. The flying boat vanished around 1800 but the carrier plane stayed with us and was soon joined by the cruiser *Sheffield*, which had newly arrived on the scene. At 1824, Lütjens reported the *Sheffield*'s position to Group West, giving her course as 115 degrees and her speed as 24 knots.

At 1903 he radioed Group West: "Fuel situation urgent. When can I count on replenishment?" The question must certainly have puzzled its recipients. Knowing as little as they did about the situation of the *Bismarck*, how could they tell him when and where a supply tanker could be deployed in the midst of the area of operations? It did not become clear until later that Lütjens was only trying to tell them that his fuel supply was critical. In order to keep his transmission brief, he used the so-called short-signal book for encoding, which permitted a report of the fuel situation to be given only in combination with a question about replenishment.

It is also of interest in this connection to recall the signal, also encoded in short-signal format, sent by the *Prinz Eugen*, which Lütjens had detached to conduct independent operations, to report a similar fuel problem on 25 May: "Fuel situation urgent, my position is. . . . " As a result of this signal, immediately received by Group West, the *Prinz Eugen* and the tanker *Spichern* were directed to a meeting point, so that the cruiser could take on fuel the very next

---

and where there would also have been time to tidy up the dummy. Presumably, the dummy was meant for this situation." My reply to that is: When the dummy was being built on 25 May and the following day the wind was blowing from astern. It was strong but, on our course, the wind pressure was light and would not have had the effect that Meyer assumes. Secondly, the dummy was certainly not intended for use in the Atlantic. We had to get to St. Nazaire by the quickest, i.e., the most direct, route. The order to build the stack proceeded, at least originally, from a feeling that we needed it immediately. After 24 May, most of the actions of the fleet staff and the ship's command were determined only by immediate needs.

morning. If the *Bismarck* had used the same short-signal group—that is, including her position—the battleship's approximate location would have become known to Group West, although, of course, the operational situation would have made it impossible for her to refuel. But the knowledge of the ship's approximate position would have been of value to Group West in planning the measures it initiated to assist the *Bismarck*.

26

Tovey's Hopes Are Pinned on the *Ark Royal*

In the meantime, several of the British ships were forced by their dwindling fuel supplies to abandon the pursuit towards the west coast of France. *The Prince of Wales*, the *Victorious*, their escorting destroyers, and the *Suffolk* dropped out of the race. The *Norfolk*, having been convinced from the start that the *Bismarck* was making for Brest, did not take the search course to the north, and was consequently in a quite favorable position. The *Rodney* was even more advantageously placed. She had proceeded on the same assumption as the *Norfolk*, but was too far to the south at the start ever to have joined in a pursuit to the north. The positions of the *Rodney* and *Norfolk* were only relatively favorable, however, because like the *King George V,* they were much too far behind the *Bismarck* on course for France to be any threat to her unless her speed were significantly reduced. When the hunt began, the *Ramillies* was not unfavorably placed, but she was withdrawn on account of her age and lack of speed.

At the moment, then, to attack the German battleship as soon as possible, Tovey had only Somerville's Force H, which was to the south. This task force and Tovey's had been steaming virtually towards one another since 24 May. In the beginning Tovey thought Force H was too far to the south to be able to take part in the pursuit. Now, it was the only force that was in a position to stop the *Bismarck*. And, that was certainly not because it included the *Renown* and the *Sheffield*. The loss of the *Hood* had shown the folly of pitting such ships against the *Bismarck* unless they had the support of heavier forces. It was upon the aircraft of the *Ark Royal* that he would have to rely. Their job was to cripple the *Bismarck* with their torpedoes so that Tovey's own big ships could come up for a decisive engagement—a situation that had to be created at once, because he was getting ever nearer to the effective range of the Luftwaffe. Tovey was aware that this was his one and only chance to avoid the barren alternative of calling off the days-long pursuit through the Atlantic. He had to remind himself that the attack by the planes of the *Victorious* on 24 May had not been successful, but their crews were young and inexperienced, whereas the *Ark Royal* had the best-trained and most experienced aircrews in the Royal Navy—with them, the prospects would be much better.

Since the morning of 25 May, Somerville had been going on the assumption that the *Bismarck* was heading for Brest. On the basis of running reports on the position of the German battleship, he launched ten of the *Ark Royal's* Swordfish for reconnaissance on the morning of 26 May. Six other Swordfish, equipped with auxiliary fuel tanks to increase their range, joined them. They were to shadow the *Bismarck* once she had been found. Following their launching around 0830 nothing was heard from them for two hours. Then, around 1030, the radiomen in the *Renown* and *Ark Royal* recorded an incoming message: "One battleship bearing 240° five miles, course 150°, my position 49°33′ north, 21°47′ west." It did not come, as the people in the carrier hoped, from one of the Swordfish, but from the Catalina. This did not diminish the warmth of its welcome, and when the Catalina lost contact after being fired on by the *Bismarck*, it was a Swordfish that found the battleship again and maintained contact.

Thereafter Somerville's objective was an aerial torpedo attack on the *Bismarck*. The first opportunity to launch from the *Ark Royal* came in the early afternoon and, regardless of the stormy weather, fifteen Swordfish took off at 1450. Around the same time, he sent the *Sheffield* to maintain contact with the *Bismarck*, because, with the weather deteriorating, it seemed to him risky to depend on observation from the air. Unaware that the *Sheffield* had been given this mission, the skipper of the *Ark Royal*, Captain Loben E. Maund, told his pilots that there would not be any ship in view between the *Ark Royal* and the *Bismarck*. Consequently, when they detected a ship on their radar, they dived through the clouds and launched their attack. Only three of the pilots at the last moment recognized their faithful old target ship *Sheffield* and withheld their fire. Defects in their magnetic detonators caused most of the torpedoes that were launched to explode harmlessly upon entering the water. Fortunately, by putting on full speed, the *Sheffield* avoided the handful of torpedoes that ran well. Nevertheless the aircrews returned to the *Ark Royal* in a gloomy mood, and were consoled only by the promise that they would be launched again that evening. In spite of the gloom, the incident had its bright side in that it revealed the failure of the magnetic detonators. For the next attack, the Swordfish fell back on their old, reliable contact detonators.

For Tovey, who had not been told that the planes had mistaken the *Sheffield* for the *Bismarck*, the *Ark Royal's* report of an unsuccessful attack was bitter news. He had little reason to think that another attack that same evening would be successful. Once more, he reviewed the whole situation. Unless the *Bismarck* could somehow be crippled on the night of 26 May, on the morning of 27 May she would have as good as escaped. In other words, an attack that evening would be the very last chance. Considering the continuing deterioration of the weather, he did not expect much from a night attack by the destroyers. Both the *King George V* and the *Rodney* were reaching the limits of their fuel endurance. Unless the next few hours brought a decisive change, the *King George V* would have to drop out of the race.

At 1820 Tovey signaled Somerville that if the *Bismarck's* speed was not reduced by midnight, the *King George V* would have to turn away to refuel. The *Rodney*, he said, could continue the pursuit, without destroyers, if need be.

It was hard for Tovey to send that signal. For four days and nights, over 2,000 nautical miles, he had pursued the *Bismarck*, from the Denmark Strait almost into the Bay of Biscay, with a great body of ships. Should this tremendous effort really have been for nothing?

At 1700 the *Sheffield* made out the German battleship at the limit of visibility. For the first time since the *Suffolk*, *Norfolk*, and *Prince of Wales* had lost contact, one-and-a-half days ago, a ship had visual contact with the *Bismarck*. The *Sheffield* did everything she could to avoid being seen by us. Her mission was only to help the second wave of carrier planes find the target and to maintain contact.

In the *Ark Royal*, hasty preparations for a second attack were being made. For one thing, the torpedoes' magnetic detonators were replaced by contact detonators. There was so much to be done that the originally intended launching time of 1830 slipped. It was 1915 when, under low cloud cover and in varying visibility, fifteen Swordfish were launched, one after the other, into the wind. Around 2000 they appeared over the *Sheffield*. She directed them, but wrongly at first, because in thirty minutes they were back, without having sighted their target. Directed anew, they flew off again, and the sound of the German antiaircraft fire that soon followed told the *Sheffield* that this time they had gone in the right direction.

27

The Mortal Hit

Daytime on the twenty-sixth passed into early evening. Twilight fell and, as far as we in the *Bismarck* were concerned, the dark of night could not come too soon. In spite of our experience as the object of the enemy's unerring means of reconnaissance, we were still inclined to feel nighttime brought some protection. Of course, ever since a Catalina rediscovered us that morning, a wheeled aircraft had maintained almost uninterrupted contact. Its presence indicated that a carrier was nearby, but eight hours had now passed and, to our surprise, we had not been attacked. Not having any means of knowing that her Swordfish had lost time by mistakenly attacking the *Sheffield* instead of us, we began to speculate. Could the wheeled aircraft be a reconnaissance plane with extraordinarily long range? Was the carrier too far away to launch an attack? Might we be spared one today, 26 May?

Below, the men's good spirits had returned and morale was high throughout the ship. Word had spread that an enemy force was about 100 nautical miles astern of us, but unless it was much faster than we were, how could it possibly overtake us? Some men pored over charts and calculated that the next morning we would be 200 nautical miles off the coast, within range of the Luftwaffe's protection. A report circulated that a tanker was on her way to meet us, so our worries about fuel would be over. Hope sprouted anew. I could not help remembering my conversation with Mihatsch: didn't we still have a good chance of making St. Nazaire? What was to stop us from outrunning the enemy?

We got the answer to that question around 2030—"Aircraft alarm!"

No sooner had the report that sixteen planes were approaching run through the ship than they were flying over us at high altitude. Then they were out of sight, and the order was given, "Off-duty watch dismissed, antiaircraft watch at ease at the guns." At ease, but not for long. In a few minutes another aircraft alarm was sounded, and this time it was a different picture. The planes dived out of the clouds, individually and in pairs, and flew towards us. They approached even more recklessly than the planes from the *Victorious* had done two days earlier. Every pilot seemed to know what this attack meant to Tovey. It was the last chance to cripple the *Bismarck* so that the battleships could have at her. And they took it.

Once more, the *Bismarck* became a fire-spitting mountain. The racket of her antiaircraft guns was joined by the roar from her main and secondary turrets as they fired into the bubbling paths of oncoming torpedoes, creating splashes ahead of the attackers. Once more, the restricted field of my director and the dense smoke allowed me to see only a small slice of the action. The antique-looking Swordfish, fifteen of them, seemed to hang in the air, near enough to touch. The high cloud layer, which was especially thick directly over us, probably did not permit a synchronized attack from all directions, but the Swordfish came so quickly after one another that our defense did not have it any easier than it would have had against such an attack. They flew low, the spray of the heaving seas masking their landing gear. Nearer and still nearer they came, into the midst of our fire. It was as though their orders were, "Get hits or don't come back!"

The heeling of the ship first one way and then the other told me that we were trying to evade torpedoes. The rudder indicator never came to rest and the speed indicator revealed a significant loss of speed. The men on the control platforms in the engine rooms had to keep their wits about them. "All ahead full!"—"All stop!"—"All back full!"—"Ahead!"—"All stop!" were the ever-changing orders by which Lindemann sought to escape the malevolent "eels."

As though hypnotized, I listened for the sound of an exploding torpedo mixing with the roar of our guns. It could be much worse than it was two days earlier. A hit forward of my station could be tolerated, but what about a hit aft? There was not much distance between me and our sensitive propellers and rudders, and it seemed as though these were our attackers' favorite targets. We had been under attack for perhaps fifteen minutes when I heard that sickening sound. Two torpedoes exploded in quick succession, but somewhere

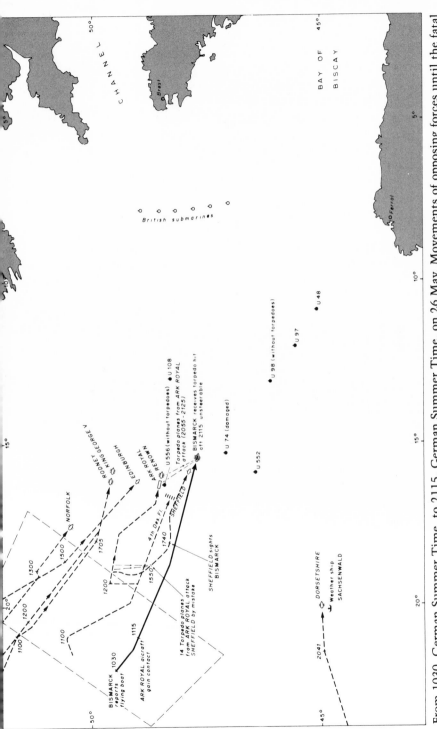

From 1030, German Summer Time, to 2115, German Summer Time, on 26 May. Movements of opposing forces until the fatal rudder hit on the *Bismarck*. (Diagram courtesy of Jürgen Rohwer.)

A Swordfish torpedo-spotter-reconnaissance aircraft returning to the *Ark Royal* after making an attack on the *Bismarck*. The Swordfish carried one 1,600-pound, 18-inch torpedo armed with a charge of 450 pounds of TNT. To deliver an attack, it had to fly at a speed of about 75 knots and an altitude of 50 feet or less. (Photograph from the Imperial War Museum, London.)

forward of where I was. Good fortune in misfortune, I thought. They could not have done much damage. My confidence in our armored belt was unbounded. Let's hope that's the end of it!

Soon after the alarm, Matrosengefreiter Herzog, at his port third 3.70-centimeter antiaircraft gun, saw three planes approaching from astern at an oblique angle, while the talker at his station was reporting other planes coming from various directions. Then, through the powder smoke, Herzog saw two planes approach on the port beam and turn to the right. In no time they were only twenty meters off our stern, coming in too low for Herzog's or any other guns to bear on them. Two torpedoes splashed into the water and ran towards our stern just as we were making an evasive turn to port.

The attack must have been almost over when it came, an explosion aft.* My heart sank. I glanced at the rudder indicator. It showed "left 12 degrees." Did that just happen to be the correct reading at that moment? No. It did not change. It stayed at "left 12 degrees." Our increasing list to starboard soon told us that we were in a continuous turn. The aircraft attack ended as abruptly as it had begun.

---

*My account of the number and sequence of torpedo hits differs from that given by the Fleet Commander in his subsequent radio reports. It is, however, my firm recollection that there were two explosions forward of my station before the one aft. The sequence and content of Lütjens's reports are, of course, important as evidence of what happened, but they are not incontrovertible proof.

I heard Schneider on the gunnery-control telephone give targeting information on a cruiser. She was the *Sheffield*, which had come back into view after a long interval. Schneider fired a few salvos, the second of which was straddling. The *Sheffield* promptly turned away at full speed and laid down smoke. The guns of the *Bismarck* fell silent.

Our speed indicator still showed a significant loss of speed because of the turn we were in. Our rudder indicator, which drew my gaze like a magnet, still stood at "left 12 degrees." At one stroke, the world seemed to be irrevocably altered. Or was it? Perhaps the damage could be repaired. I broke the anxious silence that enveloped my station, by remarking: "We'll just have to wait. The men below will do everything they can."

Hadn't we at least shot down some planes? I had not seen us do so, but we must have. Word that we had shot down several began to make the rounds. How could anyone be so specific, I wondered. Not until years later did I learn that all the Swordfish returned to their carrier.*

---

*The fact that the *Bismarck* did not on either 24 or 26 May shoot down a single one of the relatively large number of close, low-flying enemy planes has puzzled both experts and laymen. Ostensibly, such a complete failure simply "should not have happened," and I cannot offer any plausible explanation of this apparently poor performance. In this context, however, it may be helpful to refer to a passage from Alistair MacLean's *H.M.S. Ulysses*, quoted here by permission. It describes the crucial phase of German air attack on the British cruiser *Ulysses* in the Norwegian Sea:

Two bombers left now, pressing home their attack with suicidal courage, weaving violently from side to side to avoid destruction. Two seconds passed, three, four—and still they came on, through the falling snow and intensely heavy fire, miraculous in their immunity. Theoretically, there is no target so easy to hit as a plane approaching directly head on: in practice, it never worked out that way. In the Arctic, the Mediterranean, the Pacific, the relative immunity of the torpedo bombers, the high percentage of successful attacks carried out in the face of almost saturation fire, never failed to confound the experts. Tension, overanxiety, fear—these were part of the trouble, at least: there are no half measures about a torpedo bomber—you get him or he gets you. And there is nothing more nerve-racking—always, of course, with the outstanding exception of the screaming, near vertical power dive of the gull-winged Stuka dive bomber—than to see a torpedo bomber looming hugely, terrifyingly over the open sights of your gun and know that you have just five inexorable seconds to live. And with the *Ulysses*, of course, the continous rolling of the cruiser in the heavy cross sea made accuracy impossible.

The difficulty in aiming the guns on the *Ulysses*, caused by the ship's heavy rolling, corresponded to that experienced on the *Bismarck* due to the constantly changing target bearings and tilts produced by the maneuvering of the ship.

The torpedo hit shook the ship so violently that the safety valve in the starboard engine room closed and the engines shut down. Slowly the vibration of the ship ceased, accentuating individual vibrations. Above, the control station reopened the safety valve and we had steam again. The floor plates of the center engine room buckled upwards about half a meter, and water rushed in through the port shaft well. It did not take long, however, to seal off the room and pump it out.

Casualties in the area of Damage-Control Team No. 1 were kept to a minimum by the foresight of Stabsobermaschinist Wilhelm Schmidt who, when the attack began, ordered his men to cushion themselves against shocks by sitting on hammocks. After the blow that lifted her stern, the ship rocked up and down several times before coming to rest and Schmidt reported to the damage-control center, "Presumed torpedo hit aft." Inspection by his damage-control parties revealed that the hole blown in the ship's hull was so big that all the steering rooms were flooded and their occupants had been forced to abandon their stations. The water in those rooms was sloshing up and down in rhythm with the motion of the ship. In order to keep it contained, the armored hatch above the steering mechanism, which had been opened to survey the damage, was closed. But then the after depth-finder tube broke and water rushed through to the maindeck. Apparently because cable stuffing tubes through the bulkheads were no longer watertight and the after transverse bulkheads had sprung leaks, the upper and lower passageways on the port side of Compartment III and the centerline shaft alley were making water. An attempt to pump out the after steering room was delayed by an electrical failure that necessitated switching to a substitute circuit. As soon as that repair had been made, however, it was discovered that the water in the passageway to the steering mechanism had got into the pumps' self-starters and the pumps were unusable.

Under the supervision of two engineering officers, Kapitänleutnant Gerhard Junack and Oberleutnant Hermann Giese, the damage-control parties, assisted by a master carpenter's team, went to work. They shored up the transverse bulkhead on the approaches to the steering gear and sealed the broken depth-finder tube. They forced their way through an emergency exit on the battery deck that led to the armored hatch over the steering gear below. A master carpenter and a master's mate hoped that, with the help of diving gear, they would be able to reach the upper platform deck and there disengage the rudder-motor coupling. Very carefully, they opened the hatch.

Seawater shot up past them, as high as the emergency exit, then was sucked down and disappeared the next time the stern rose in a seaway. Like a falling stone, the stern plunged into the next trough. Once again the water shot up, threatened to overflow the emergency exit, was sucked down on the next wave crest, and disappeared. Giese, the officer supervising the work, was repeatedly called away by questions from the First Officer in the command center. The latter wanted to be informed almost continuously of how things were progressing and to know when the ship could finally resume way. It also appeared ominous that not enough technical personnel were familiar with the layouts of the hand rudder, steering gear, and rudder-motor compartments, that insufficient diving gear was available, and that the volunteers called for did not know how to use it very well. For some, the ship's abbreviated training period had been too short. Further effort was pointless. There was nothing to do but close the hatch. No one could force his way into the steering plant, much less work there. The attempt had failed.

Hours later, we managed to get a hand rudder coupled to the rudder yoke, and the crew of the starboard third 15-centimeter turret were ordered to man it. But they weren't able to get to it. Inside the room, they were confronted with swirling and tossing seawater and oil. They returned to their stations and reported to the bridge. The crews of the starboard second and third 15-centimeter turrets were then directed to go to the quarterdeck and place a collision mat over the hole in the ship's hull. But high seas frustrated their efforts and they, too, had to return to their stations without accomplishing anything.

Above, in the after fire-control station, all we could do was sympathize with the hard work of the men struggling to repair our damage. From time to time we asked what they were trying to do and what success they were having. Most of the answers we got were brief and not very informative. For example, we were told that some water had been pumped out of the ship. There was never any intimation as to whether they were having success or were on the verge of it. I had to suppress an urge to go and see for myself. Anyone who was not involved in making repairs obviously had to remain at his station because, although that air attack was over, there might be another, and enemy ships might appear. We were still at general quarters. We could not let down our guard even for a minute.

The circle we involuntarily made after our rudder was damaged had turned us around from our southeasterly course towards St. Nazaire, and we were moving to the northwest, into the wind and towards the enemy. The *Bismarck*'s hull shook noticeably as Lindemann tried various speeds and combinations of propellers in an attempt to bring us back on course. His orders from the bridge came in rapid succession: "Port engines half ahead, center and starboard engines stop"—"Port and center engines half ahead, starboard engines back slow"—"Port engines full ahead, starboard engines stop."

Below, the men did their best to regulate the turbines precisely and, instead of two of them standing on the control platforms, as was normally the case, there were three: one at the forward throttle, one at the backing throttle, and one ready to jump in and do whatever was needed. The minimum time prescribed for waiting between "Stop" and "Full power" was ignored. Boiler pressure was now the only thing the men turning the hand cranks had to go by and, inevitably, the safe maximum was sometimes overshot. Because we were in the cleared-for-action state of readiness, no doors or ventilators were open and the temperature in the engine room climbed to 50 degrees centigrade—this, with the men in leather clothing.

Lindemann desperately tried other combinations of speeds and propellers. Nothing did any good. When he did succeed in deflecting the ship from her course to the northwest, her jammed rudders brought her back into the wind. Increasing winds and rising seas made our useless rudders an even more critical factor. Nevertheless, we had to regard it as fortunate that, despite their proximity to the explosion, our propellers had not been damaged and we could still do a little maneuvering.

About an hour after the torpedo hit, we in the after station got word of the suggestion that we either send down divers to cut off our rudders or set charges to sever them. Getting rid of our rudders would have the same effect as having them jammed in the midships position, which would greatly facilitate steering with our propellers. The chief engineer and his staff assembled on the quarterdeck to investigate this possibility. It has been said that Lindemann took some part in these deliberations, but I cannot be certain that he did. In any case, both ideas were rejected.

Although there certainly would have been no lack of volunteers, approaching the rudders from outside the ship was not even considered. The seas were too high and the suction under the stern was too strong for free-swimming divers or for men to work their way down safety lines rigged under the stern. Before men were asked to risk their lives there had to be a reasonable chance of success. There was not. Blowing the rudders off from inside was rejected because it would be next to impossible to measure the explosive charge so exactly that it would have neither less nor more than the intended effect. In the latter case, it might damage the nearby propellers as well as other parts of the ship.

One working party volunteered to take off the hangar door and weld it to the starboard side of the stern at a 15-degree angle, which would correspond to a rudder position of 12 degrees. The thought was that this would counteract the effect of the rudders jammed in the port position and make it easier to steer with the propellers. But this plan, too, was rejected because of the bad weather.

High above the scene of the damage, in the after station, we could do no more than witness from afar the attempts at repair, one after the other of which appeared to fail. We could only worry and try to give one another hope and confidence. Serious as the jammed rudder was, I knew it was not the worst thing. But what was the use of adding to the worries of the men around me by telling them what really doomed us? It was that the *Bismarck*, reverting inexorably to a generally northwesterly course, was traveling back over a stretch of our passage towards St. Nazaire, on which our progress had seemed so promising. And more than that. The course we were on was leading us towards the overwhelming British forces that had been pursuing us. We were relieving Tovey of the job of pursuit. Naturally, there was no point in using the full power of which our engines were still capable. High speed would have only led the more quickly to the unwelcome encounter with the enemy. Therefore we maintained only enough speed to keep us from being blown about, between 5 and 7 knots.

The wind! Throughout the operation, its direction had been of varying degrees of importance. From the time we left the cliffs of Norway to the bitter end, no matter what course we were on, it blew from astern. On 22 May it did us the favor of providing us with a shield from hostile observation by driving rain clouds with us. But this evening, 26 May, the northwester, which developed into a real storm overnight, sealed our fate.

Our spirits were given a new lift when we heard that someone had succeeded in uncoupling the starboard rudder—Maschinengefreiter Gerhard Böhnel in the stern reported it through Maschinengefreiter Hermann Budich, the talker in action station "E," to Obermaschinist Oskar Barho. Reports that this was not so dampened all our hopes. It was true that several times men managed to force their way into the port rudder room also, but they could not reach the coupling. Seawater gulped in and out through the hole in the hull. When, after indescribable exertions, a diver did succeed in reaching the coupling, he found it so badly jammed he couldn't budge it. Several divers collapsed when they were pulled out of the rooms.

A machinist petty officer first class who had made a dive in the port rudder room appeared in the command center to deliver his report. After the man's report, Oels realized that there was a serious weakness in the ship's supply of diving equipment. The hoses of the so-called small diving suit had repeatedly become entangled with one another and created additional difficulties for the only partly trained divers, already shaken by the water's violent heaving up and down. Their air hoses were repeatedly pinched off and their faces turned blue from the effects of nitrogen poisoning. The so-called naval respirators could be used only in waist-high water and by no means in completely flooded compartments. Only underwater escape apparatus,* Oels concluded, would have given the men the necessary freedom of movement and a better view to all sides—but there was none on board.

A moonless, gloomy night had long since fallen over us. Incapable of maneuvering, we crept towards the superior forces coming to destroy us—a virtual journey to Golgotha. As the hours passed, our dying hope that somehow we would still find a way to escape was supplanted by the growing certainty that there was no escape. Sometime after midnight, the word spread that work on the rudder had ceased, and certainty became absolute.

---

*This was a small diving apparatus for escaping from sunken U-boats, for example. The air supply was carried to the diver from a flask of oxygen through a breathing mask by means of a mouthpiece. The operational endurance of the apparatus was approximately thirty minutes. The breathing mask, which was shaped like a ring and worn around the neck, also served as a life buoy. (For technical details, see: "Gebrauchsanweisung T2.1-2 Dräger-Tauchretter," November 1943, 10th edition, Drägerwerk Lübeck.)

28

Destroyers Ordered to Tovey's Support

When on the afternoon of 25 May Tovey realized that the *Bismarck* was making for a port in western France, he became concerned about his shortage of destroyers. As his battleships neared the coast, they would face an increasingly grave threat from German U-boats, and it disturbed him that his destroyer escort had had to turn back for lack of fuel and the *King George V* had been unprotected since morning. He knew that the *Rodney*, which had been placed under his command but had yet to join him, had three destroyers with her but he had no idea about the status of their fuel.

That evening, therefore, Tovey asked the Admiralty to provide the *King George V* and *Rodney* with a new destroyer escort. By the time it received this request, the Admiralty had already recognized the problem and decided how to handle it. The solution, which had not been easy to find because destroyers were in short supply in general, was to recall the 4th Destroyer Flotilla—the *Cossack, Maori, Zulu, Sikh,* and *Piorun**—from convoy duty. On the evening of 25 May, this flotilla, under the command of Captain Philip Vian, was some 300 nautical miles ahead of the *King George V,* which meant it would be able to join Tovey's battleships early the next afternoon. At 0200 on 26 May Vian in the *Cossack* received orders to close with the *King George V,* taking with him the *Sikh* and *Zulu.* He was to send the

*The destroyer *Piorun* left the building ways in Great Britain in May 1940 and was later transferred to the Polish government-in-exile in London. She served in the British fleet, but under the Polish flag and with a Polish crew.

Maori and *Piorun* to join the *Rodney.* Under way, Vian read the Catalina's report of the rediscovery of the *Bismarck*, which fixed her position to the southeast of his, and saw that the question before him was should he obey the letter of the Admiral's 's order or simply make for the enemy? Thinking his destroyers might help to intercept the *Bismarck* on her way to France, he decided to do the latter. He turned onto a pursuing course at maximum speed but a storm astern and heavy seas prevented him from maintaining it. Around 2200 on the twenty-sixth he sighted the *Sheffield*, which had been taken under fire by the *Bismarck* only shortly before and was now steaming north, and from her he learned the *Bismarck's* exact bearing. By 2230 both the *Piorun* and the *Zulu* had found the *Bismarck*. His destroyers could begin operating against the German battleship.

29

The Last Night on Board the *Bismarck*

For about an hour and a half after the air attack, the battle zone close around the *Bismarck* was deserted. Then, somewhere before 2300 we saw destroyers. Alarm bells sounded and, as usual, our 38-centimeter and 15-centimeter turrets were ready for action in seconds. "Permission to fire." Salvos of both calibers went off towards the nearest of the destroyers—the *Piorun*, as I learned later. Our guns must have been very well laid at the start, for the enemy turned away and got out of range.

We did not know how many destroyers there were around us. The pitch-blackness of the night and frequent rain squalls made it impossible for us to make out silhouettes, so we couldn't tell whether we were seeing a few destroyers over and over again or whether there was a great number of them. The only thing clear to us was that we could expect endless torpedo attacks. Everything was going to depend on extreme vigilance and the flawless functioning of our range finders. Fortunately for us, however, the attacks were not synchronized, that is, they did not come from different directions at the same time, which would have made our defense much more difficult. The wind and seas, which gave even the *Bismarck* trouble, probably handicapped the destroyers even more. With seas breaking over them and spray as high as the bridge—conditions that I experienced many times in German destroyers—they would often be compelled to reduce speed just when for tactical reasons they wanted to run at high speed.

Our range finders worked to perfection. From 8,000 meters down to 3,000 we tracked the destroyers. Tension in my station rose as the incoming ranges went down, 7,000 meters . . . 6,500 . . . 4,000. . . . In spite of the darkness, I could see through my director our shadowy attackers coming nearer and nearer, twisting to attack—each time, I thought, "Now the torpedoes are hissing out of the tubes"—then drawing off. They dared not stay near us for long because of the speed with which our gunnery found its targets. This, in spite of the fact that our fire control had to contend with occasional heavy rolling of the ship caused by seas coming in off our beam and with the even greater disadvantage of our inability to maneuver. Her jammed rudders made the *Bismarck* swing some eighty points between northwest and northeast. Changes in target bearing, always rapid at short range, were accelerated, not only by the swinging of the ship but also by the use of our propellers for steering, so that an oncoming destroyer might change from one side of the ship to the other during the same attack. This meant that Albrecht in the forward station had to keep switching between the port and starboard 15-centimeter turrets. The darkness, made worse by drifting rain squalls and clouds of undissipated powder smoke, made observation difficult for him as well as for Schneider in the foretop. As I waited at the ready in case I was needed on any battery, I saw shells bursting over enemy ships but I could never be sure that the flames indicated a hit. At times like this there is always the danger of "seeing" what one wants to see.

If the men in the engine rooms thought their turbines had reached peak performance during the two air attacks, they now learned better. They found out how those turbines could really perform. They went without pause from "Full speed ahead" to "Full speed astern." Scarcely was the forward throttle closed when two men wrenched open the reverse throttle. Looking back, it doesn't seem possible that our engines survived the strain.

The men, sweat oozing from every pore, had hardly a dry stitch on their bodies. A sweatband around the head, a slice of lemon in the right corner of the mouth, a cigar or pipe in the left—they looked comical and their mood matched their appearance.

At around 0100, a destroyer attack having just ended, the starboard turbine was ordered to "Stop," while the center and port turbines were ordered "Ahead." Therefore, the throttle of the starboard turbine was closed, shutting off the propelling steam. Even so, the turbine should have been turning at an idling speed, but it was not. The order came to start it just to see if it would turn. The second mate opened the throttle to supply steam for "Forward": first two, then three, four, and five times atmospheric pressure. Nothing happened! The turbine remained frozen in position. Even at ten, twenty, and thirty atmospheres of pressure it refused to budge. The engine-control station was advised of the situation. "Try everything!" was the reply, which meant "Get steam to it, by hook or crook." Steam pressure was increased to forty, fifty, fifty-eight atmospheres. One nozzle opened and injected steam against the rotors, stressing the turbine unevenly and dangerously—with steam pressure at fifty-eight times atmospheric pressure at 400 degrees centigrade. More steam! Then, the nozzle on the other side also began to register pressure: five, ten, twenty atmospheres. When it reached thirty, the turbine suddenly began to rotate: it did not break and it did not turn into "blade salad." From that time until the moment the ship went down the next morning, it kept on turning.

The seas were so heavy that we were not surprised by the long lulls between attacks. We supposed the destroyers were either trying to get in position to attack or were satisfied just to keep contact with us. In any case, we welcomed the lulls as moments in which, for however short a time, we could rest. Then, we would have totally illogical flashes of hope that despite everything we were going to escape. To St. Nazaire? On our enforced course to the northwest? But the destroyers always came back, and the noise of our guns brought us back to the immutable present. And so the cycle went, hour after hour: we sighted the enemy; he attacked; our guns went into action; awareness of our inability to maneuver made us afraid that we'd be hit; once again, we had been lucky; the enemy was lost to sight; hope returned.

Around 0100 something new was added. A star shell fired by a destroyer suddenly burst in the sky—the thought flashed through my mind that it was the handwriting on the wall. It exploded high in the air and a flare suspended from a parachute slowly floated down, illuminating a wide expanse of water. We thought it was too far off to do the enemy much good in calculating our exact position. But gradually, as more star shells were fired at long intervals, the range closed, until one of them came very near and seemed to be saying, "There's no escape!" Although others followed and lit up the scene for attacks, in the darkness between them, contact was lost—or did I imagine that? After one particularly long lull, we saw a flare coming down almost directly onto us. "Fire on the bow!" and men hurried to put it out.* For a moment, as it burned furiously, we were certain that it was revealing our position.

*Russell Grenfell, *The Bismarck Episode*, may have been describing this incident when, on page 168, he wrote: "As the *Maori* retreated those on board her were sure they saw a torpedo hit [on the *Bismarck*]. A bright glow seemed to illuminate the enemy's waterline and shortly afterwards another vivid glare appeared to betoken a second explosion."

After the sinking of the *Bismarck*, I learned from Captain Benjamin C. S. Martin, commanding officer of the heavy cruiser *Dorsetshire*, that the periodic firing of star shells after 0230 was ordered by Tovey, who was worried that the positions worked out in his battleships might differ greatly from those plotted in the destroyers. Tovey's hope was that this means of reconnaissance would provide continuous information on the *Bismarck*'s position.

Nevertheless, the firing of the shells died out around 0300. The destroyers that were firing them had to come within fairly close range of the *Bismarck* for the shells to be of any help, and when they did so they were promptly taken under fire. Captain Vian later wrote Tovey that, as he saw it, his duty was, "Firstly to deliver to you at all costs the enemy, at the time you wished. Secondly to try to sink or stop the enemy with torpedoes in the night if I thought the attack should not involve the destroyers in heavy losses."* In view of the *Bismarck*'s obviously hopeless situation, he certainly must have considered that to continue firing star shells would unnecessarily endanger his destroyers.

We were happy that darkness again prevailed and contact was broken. Or so it seemed, because when I looked through my director I did not see any destroyers. The coming of dawn seemed like a succession of curtains being opened, each of which instantaneously disclosed a more distant view. A little before 0600 it was light enough for me to see that the destroyers were back in position around us. Seeming quite suddenly to discover that they were dangerously near the *Bismarck*, they withdrew at high speed to a more salubrious distance. The last we saw of them, they were disappearing into the still numerous rain squalls.

It was announced over the loudspeakers that we had sunk one destroyer and set two on fire, but this turned out to be understandable wishful thinking, a phenomenon common to all sides in time of war. No one on either side knew it at the time, but the truth of the matter is that, as of about 0700, there had not been any torpedo hits on the *Bismarck* nor, despite many straddling salvos and near misses, any direct hits on the destroyers. In the crow's nest of the *Zulu*, Midshipman B. J. Hennessy, who had made out the *Bismarck* at the same time as the *Piorun*, saw our first salvo go into the water between the *Maori* and the *Cossack*. Later the *Zulu* was straddled by shell bursts from the *Bismarck* and numerous splinters struck her, wounding the

*Ludovic Kennedy, *Pursuit*, p. 184.

gunnery officer, Lieutenant Galbraith, and damaging his director. Now and again Hennessy heard our "overs" whistling overhead and marvelled at our "unbelievably" good shooting. The destroyer skippers boldly pressed their attacks through heavy German fire, while the torpedo officers tried to compensate for the violent rolling and pitching of their ships as well as the blinding effects of the *Bismarck*'s fire. The repeated flashes of the guns, probably, led both sides to assume that they were achieving results that never occurred. The British could have hardly been successful in any event, because the destroyers' torpedo officers overestimated the *Bismarck*'s speed and aimed accordingly. Yet at the time no one knew that they had not hurt the enemy.*

I was no longer concerned with the destroyers. They had managed to keep us under surveillance throughout the night, fired a lot of torpedoes at us, and surely reported our position to Tovey that morning. Our thoughts and our attention were now concentrated on the British battleships. Their hour had come, and I expected them to appear at any moment.

At 1954 on the twenty-sixth Group West radioed Lütjens that the *U-48* was near him and had been ordered to proceed at full speed to operate against the *Sheffield*. Lütjens sent the following sequence of radio signals to Group West:

2054: "Attack by carrier aircraft."
2105: "Have torpedo hit aft."
2115: "Torpedo hit amidships."
2115: "Ship no longer steerable."
2140: To the Oberkommando der Kriegsmarine and Group West: "Ship unable to maneuver. We will fight to the last round. Long live the Führer."

That last signal was sent only about half an hour after the hit that jammed our rudder and long before we had tried every means of repairing the damage. Of course, the content of the message proved correct, but I cannot help wondering what made Lütjens send such a premature and certainly, for the fleet staff and the radiomen, depressing message.

*In his book, *The Loss of the Bismarck*, Vice Admiral B. B. Schofield remarks on page 59 that the *Maori* observed one certain torpedo hit on the *Bismarck* during the night. On page 60, he writes, "The question of how many torpedo hits were obtained during these attacks will never be known with absolute certainty." I can certify that the *Bismarck* was not hit by a single torpedo from a destroyer that night.

At 2205 Group West informed Lütjens that the eight U-boats in the area had been ordered to close the *Bismarck*. Half an hour later he signaled, "Am surrounded by *Renown* and light forces."

In fact, the *Renown* did not participate in the destroyer action, and I do not remember seeing a ship of her size that night. Either Lütjens was laboring under an optical illusion or his B-Dienst team misidentified the *Renown*.

During the night the ship's command tried to keep the crew informed on the most important things that were going on. Information was relayed by loudspeaker and telephone as often as possible. The preceding signals were read out shortly after midnight, and later the following exchange of messages was announced:

2303 Group West to Fleet: "Complete aerial reconnaissance on 27 May between 46° and 48°30' north and sector from Brest northwest. Earliest possible start 0430, bombers 0630."

2358 Fleet Commander to Führer of the German Reich, Adolf Hitler: "We will fight to the last in belief in you, my Führer, and in unshakable confidence in Germany's victory."

2359 Fleet to Group West: "Ship is able to defend herself and propulsion plant intact. Does not respond to steering with engines, however."

0004 Commander in Chief, Group West, to Fleet Commander: "Our thoughts and good wishes are with our victorious comrades."

0014 Commander in Chief, Kriegsmarine, to Fleet Commander: "All our thoughts are with you and your ship. We wish you success in your hard fight."

0113 Group West to Fleet: "Tugs have been dispatched. Three Focke-Wulf 200 near the *Bismarck* at dawn. Three bomber groups start between 0500 and 0600."

Soon after the signal of 0113 had been read out, a report circulated that at daybreak eighty-one Junkers-88 bombers would take off from France to attack the British fleet. Where this precise figure originated, I have never been able to discover, but it may be that the Luftwaffe officer on his staff, Hauptmann* Fritz Grohé, told Lütjens that a bomber group consisted of twenty-seven aircraft. If he did, Grohé did not say and probably did not know how many of them were operational. In any case, the news gave the crew a big lift.

Radio signals continued:

*Captain (Army and Luftwaffe)

0147 Group West to Fleet: "*Ermland** leaves La Pallice 0500 to assist."

0153 Adolf Hitler to Fleet Commander: "I thank you in the name of the entire German people."

0153 Adolf Hitler to crew of *Bismarck*: "All Germany is with you. What can be done, will be done. Your performance of duty will strengthen our people in the struggle for its destiny."

0217 Fleet Commander to Commander in Chief, Kriegsmarine: "Recommend bestowal of the Knight's Cross on Korvettenkapitän Schneider for sinking *Hood*."

0221 Group West to Fleet: "Send directional signals on 852 meters wavelength for five minutes at 0 and 30 minutes every hour for U-boats."

0235 Commander in Chief, Group North to Fleet Commander and *Bismarck*: "We think of you all with loyalty and pride."

0351 Commander in Chief, Kriegsmarine, to Korvettenkapitän Schneider, Fleet Commander to be informed: "The Führer has bestowed Knight's Cross on you for sinking battle cruiser *Hood*. Hearty congratulations."

0419 Group West to Fleet: "For Luftwaffe, weather reports every two hours with cloud ceiling. First report needed immediately."

0443 Group West to Fleet: "For bombers send directional signals on 443 kHz. for five minutes at 15 and 45 minutes every hour. Begin at 0615."

0500 Fleet to Group West: "Partly overcast, ceiling 600 meters, [wind] northwest 7."

0542 Group West to Fleet: "Two Focke-Wulf 200 took off 0330. Reconnaissance 0445 to 0515. Three bomber groups 0530."

0652 Fleet to Group West: "Situation unchanged. Wind strength 8 to 9."

0745 Group West to Fleet: "Fifty-one bombers took off 0520 to 0645, appearance from 0900."

0835 Group West to Fleet: "Today, around 1100, Spanish cruiser *Canarias* and two destroyers leave El Ferrol [for the position of the *Bismarck*] as a precaution to render assistance. Speed 20 to 22 knots."

I do not recall the signal of 0835 being announced to the ship. When it arrived the *Bismarck* must have been in her battle with the *King*

*A supply ship

George V and the *Rodney*, which began at 0847. The cooperation of the neutral Spanish was the result of a request that the chief of staff of the Seekriegsleitung, Admiral Otto Schniewind, had transmitted to the Spanish Navy through the German naval attaché in Madrid, Kapitän zur See Kurt Meyer-Döhner.

    0900 Group West to Fleet: "Important for Luftwaffe. What is in sight where?"

This signal was not answered.

The destroyers' attacks, their maneuvers, and their firing of star shells naturally meant tension-filled, exciting minutes for us. They claimed our attention and all our actions were concentrated on defense. The news the Fleet Commander and the ship's command gave us over the loudspeakers took our minds off the hopeless situation, raised morale, and revived sinking hopes. However, defending ourselves and listening to reports of the radio traffic were only brief episodes and were interspersed with long, indeed endless-seeming, periods of inactivity, which gave us time to talk or think.

Most of the time during the lulls between destroyer attacks we proceeded at very low speed, but occasionally we stopped. At such times the *Bismarck* lay athwart the seas and rolled quite heavily. Of course, except for helping us to defend ourselves, it did not matter whether we made headway or not, because when daylight came on 27 May, Tovey's battleships would find us one way or another.

Besides the assigned midshipman, the fire-control petty officers, and an ordnanceman, there were at my station two prize-crew officers and one of the reporters assigned to cover Exercise Rhine. Fate had decreed that the prize officers would never take a captured enemy merchantman with a valuable cargo into a German port. And the journalist, who in his eight days at sea had collected a wealth of dramatic material for publication at home, would never be able to write his story. Naturally, we chatted about the prospects of our situation changing for the better. The men were full of hope and seemed convinced that somehow we would reach France. They lived in the expectation that the promises from home would be fulfilled and were sure that "our bombers will mop up in the morning." For the sake of the crew in my station, I had to show optimism, so I agreed. Actually, I assessed our situation quite differently, but could not share my deep uneasiness with anyone.

Finding it rather close in the station, when a lull in the battle allowed I walked out to the open searchlight-control station. In the darkness I could discern the outlines of our superstructure, but the sea was empty. It happened to be a moment when we were lying athwart the seas and rolling heavily. Some distance below me on the upper deck a heavy door was making a metallic clang as it swung open and shut in rhythm with the movement of the ship. It was enough to get on one's nerves. A symptom of slackening discipline? Of course not. A death knell for us? That was more like it. Thank goodness, someone finally closed it tight.

Thoughts rushed in on me. There we were, in the Atlantic 400 nautical miles west of Brest, in the most modern and most powerful German battleship of the time. A highly refined work of technology, she was virtually without equal, yet one small part of her, the rudder, was the cause of the situation we were in. It was amazing that our principle of carrying replacements for all important components apparently did not apply to the rudder. That omission proved to be a real Achilles' heel. There was nothing wrong with our propulsion plant and our hull was in good enough condition to get us to port. If only we had some sort of replacement rudder, a bow rudder or a rudder that could be lowered from the keel in deep water. Yes, if only we had! Then perhaps on this moonless night we could slip away from the enemy. But what use were these hypothetical reflections? They were only wishful thinking, illusions born of the abundance of time and the impossibility of doing anything.

The northwest wind increased steadily throughout the night and chased low rain clouds even faster across the water. I thought the likelihood that tankers and tugs would be able to bring us relief in the morning was nil. What about the eighty-one Junkers-88s? In weather like this and at the limit of their range? They would never find us. These doubts, too, I kept to myself. Suddenly it began to blow more violently. In a matter of seconds the wind strength seemed to increase by two or three numbers. It must now be Force 9. That would have to happen, I thought, to create still another complication. The wind howled through the signal halyards. Before I went back to my station, I glanced up at Leutnant zur See Hans-Joachim Ritter's flak-control station "C," where a lookout was on duty. How drafty it must be up there! A strange thought flashed through my mind—you up there, unknown shipmate, it will be all over for both of us on 27 May. In the gray of morning the British battleships will arrive long before help can get anywhere near us.

The minutes crept past. It didn't seem to want to pass, this sinister night of waiting, and waiting for nothing but the end. Enforced inactivity and the certainty of approaching defeat made it doubly depressing. The end must and indeed would come, but it was coming in agonizingly slow motion. Action was the only thing that could relieve the almost unbearable tension.

What did the men think about the situation they were in? For days they, too, had been at their action stations, cut off in their compartments and turrets from all but a few of their comrades, often without an officer near. They did have in common the experience of listening to what Lütjens had to say two days earlier about the predicament their ship was in, but his somber way of presenting things had created an atmosphere of depression. Lindemann's ensuing words gave some comfort and the intervening time had quieted many of their fears—but with the news of the jammed rudder, their dejection returned. They were told about all the efforts that were being made to repair the damage, but not in detail and only at long intervals. They could not have heard much that was encouraging, and so they had once again to prepare themselves to face the fate they had drawn. When, after midnight, it was announced that work on the rudders had ceased, hope evaporated. The older men took the news as a sentence of death for ship and crew. Everyone had to find his own way of dealing with the inevitable. Some fell into a mood of total indifference, in which nothing more could have any effect on them.

In the damage control center Kapitänleutnant (Ingenieurwesen) Jahreis had filled a sudden silence with the words, "We have some time now, let's think once more of the homeland!" and Pumpenmeister Sagner added, "Ja, and of wives and children most of all." Then Sagner lay his head on the table and shut everything out; absolute silence reigned in the compartment. Statz had already concluded that he would never leave the center, but after a minute or two everything was back to normal.

After the news of the cessation of the rudder repair every eye turned to the First Officer, as always in critical moments. But also as always, no word came from him, no word of reassurance or any kind of encouragement—only instructions in the line of duty, nothing about him had changed. A picture of devotion to duty, no doubt, a soldier out of a picture book. One look from him sufficed and everyone went back to work. Inwardly, the men in his area felt abandoned by him.

Later in the night permission was given for everyone to help himself to anything he wanted. This was a clear sign that the ship's command knew the end had come. And the men, above all the young ones, clung more than ever to the radio signals from home, to the promised help, the planes, the U-boats, the tanker, and the ocean tugs. Repeatedly, the word came over the loudspeaker, "Watch for our planes"—"Watch for our U-boats." Over and over again new hope was built.

Hope, so useful and so fragile, how often it had come and gone in these days and nights.

Down in the engine rooms, where endurance had been strained to the utmost during the destroyer attacks, things were calmer that morning. The tension and stress of the last hours gave way to irresistible fatigue. Four days without sleep were too much, and they had been followed by this frenzied night. Men, hardly able to stay on their feet, lay down where they were and slept the sleep of exhaustion. Some of them were aroused only by the firing of our guns and the explosion of enemy shells.

30

Attempts to Save
the Fleet War Diary

So sure was Lütjens that the *Bismarck* would not survive the approaching battle that early on the morning
of 27 May he decided to have the Fleet War Diary taken to safety in
France. He realized that it would be of inestimable value not only for
the Seekriegsleitung but for any analyst of Exercise Rhine to know:

Why he, an experienced and successful leader of Atlantic operations, did not take the B-Dienst's radio signal of 21 May, which told
him that the British had been alerted, as a warning that they would
intensify their surveillance of the Denmark Strait as well as to the
south of it, and adjust his plans accordingly. Did Group North's signals of 22 May, telling him that his departure from Norway had apparently not been noticed and that the British were searching too far to
the south, remove any concern he may have had about being detected
as he went north? Did he unquestioningly accept what these messages said?

Why he did not postpone Exercise Rhine and turn away when he
first encountered the *Suffolk* and *Norfolk*, as he did during the corresponding phase of his operation with the *Scharnhorst* and *Gneisenau*
three months earlier.

Why, when he held his course, he did not make an all-out attempt
to sink his shadowers.

Why he abandoned the pursuit of the obviously hard-hit *Prince of
Wales*, thereby renouncing the possibility of achieving another apparently easy and important victory.

Why he interrupted Exercise Rhine so soon after the battle off Iceland and tried to reach port.

Why, on the evening of 24 May, he suddenly viewed the *Bismarck*'s fuel situation as so critical that he had to steer for St. Nazaire by the shortest route instead of making a detour into the Atlantic, which might have been our salvation.

Why, on the morning of 25 May, he thought the enemy still knew our position.

The diary would also show exactly when on the night of 24–25 May and at what intervals the *Bismarck* made the gradual change of course to starboard that led to the breaking of contact.

Between 0500 and 0600 one of our planes was put on the catapult and made ready to carry the War Diary to safety. With full power, we maneuvered to turn the starboard end of the catapult into the wind so that the plane could fly off. Nothing happened. The compressed-air line to the catapult was bent. Another effort to launch was made, but again nothing happened. The track was unusable. We had no means of making the necessary repair and, after some discussion, the launching was canceled. Obviously, the Arado could not be left on the catapult, where in battle it would be a fire hazard. So, with its wings folded and holes made in its floats, it was pushed to the end of the track and tipped overboard. I watched it drift by and disappear.*

I don't know what damaged the catapult, but I suspect it was the hit that shattered one of our service boats during the battle off Iceland.

In another effort to get the War Diary to safety in the short time remaining before the final action, at 0710 Lütjens radioed Group West, "Send a U-boat to save War Diary." That was his last radio signal home.

---

*The *Bismarck*'s reconstructed War Diary states that, while we were trying to launch the Arado, waves were washing over the upper deck of the ship and some of the men of the 10.5-centimeter flak crews were washed overboard. Also, we were listing so far to port that our 15-centimeter turrets on that side were under water. I cannot reconcile this entry with reality. There being no action in progress or, as it appeared, in immediate prospect between 0500 and 0600, I went to watch the aircraft being launched. It is true that the ship was listing to port, but our 15-centimeter turrets were certainly not under water at the time. Furthermore, our beamy ship was doing so little rolling that it would not have been possible for any members of the flak crews to be washed overboard from the still-elevated superstructure deck. I did not observe conditions such as those described in the diary until about twenty minutes before the ship sank.

Send a U-boat! That was the last hope, the vague possibility of saving the War Diary. With the failure to launch the Arado, the *Bismarck* had exhausted her own means of carrying out that mission. And, with the dispatch of the message to Group West, there was nothing Lütjens could do towards the fulfillment of his wish but wait for the outside world to respond. Wait and wait.

At first, of course, Lütjens had reason to suppose that a U-boat would be sent. In fact, at 0801, Group West informed him, "*U-556* will pick up War Diary." But as the morning wore on, no U-boat appeared. Presumably, so I thought then, there was none near enough or none that had enough fuel to detour to us.

In order to understand why we never saw the *U-556* it is necessary to go back a day.

On 26 May, when dispositions were being made to support the *Bismarck* in her increasingly critical situation, new instructions were sent to the U-boats in the Bay of Biscay. One of those boats was the *U-556*, whose commanding officer, Kapitänleutnant Herbert Wohlfarth, was ordered to reconnoiter and operate in the area of the *Bismarck*'s most recently reported position. When Wohlfarth received those orders, he was on his way home from a patrol that began on 1 May. Therefore, he was low on fuel and, on his way to the *Bismarck*, he would have to be extremely economical with what he had left. Furthermore, he had expended all his torpedoes against British convoys.

Wohlfarth reached the immediate area around the *Bismarck* on the evening of 26 May. Around 1950 he saw the *Renown* and the *Ark Royal* coming out of the mist at high speed—the big ships of Force H. Nothing for it but to submerge. "Enemy bows on, 10 degrees to starboard, without destroyers, without zigzagging," as Wohlfarth later described it. He would not even have had to run to launch torpedoes. All he would have had to do was position himself between the *Renown* and the *Ark Royal* and fire, at both almost simultaneously. If only he had some torpedoes! He had seen activity on the carrier's flight deck. Perhaps he could have helped us. Yes, perhaps—that is what he thought at the time. But what he saw was the activity after the launching of the second and decisive attack on the *Bismarck*. So, even if he had torpedoes, he would not have been able to save us from the rudder hit. The Swordfish had long since banked over the *Sheffield* and were just about to attack us.

Fifty minutes later, at 2039, Wohlfarth surfaced and made a radio report: "Enemy in view, a battleship, an aircraft carrier, course 115°, enemy is proceeding at high speed. Position 48° 20′ north, 16° 20′ west." Wohlfarth intended his report to be picked up by any of his comrades who might be in the vicinity and able to maneuver to attack. Then he proceeded on the surface at full speed behind the *Renown* and the *Ark Royal*. Their course to the *Bismarck* coincided almost exactly with his own. Every now and again, he submerged and took sound bearings to both ships, but after 2200 he could no longer hear them. The race between his little boat and the two big ships was an unequal contest.

At 2330 Wohlfarth, then 420 nautical miles west of Brest, gave the alarm again. A destroyer came out of the mist at high speed. Once more, he quickly dove. He had reached a depth of thirty meters when the enemy passed him, her propellers making a devilish row. Relieved, he noted in his War Diary: "Fingers crossed again, no depth charges!"

It was probably one of Vian's destroyers, but at that moment she was not interested in a U-boat. She was too busy trying to shadow and torpedo the *Bismarck*.

Another entry in Wohlfarth's War Diary reads: "27.5.0000, [wind] northwest 5, seaway 5, rain squalls, moderate visibility, very dark night. Surfaced. What can I do for the *Bismarck*? I can see star shells being fired and flashes from the *Bismarck*'s guns. It is a terrible feeling to be near and not to be able to do anything. All I can do is reconnoiter and lead in boats that have torpedoes. I am keeping contact at the limit of visibility, reporting the position, and sending directional signals to call up the other boats."

At 0352: "I am moving around on the east side to the south, in order to be in the direction of the activity. I soon reach the limit of what I can do in view of my fuel supply. Otherwise I won't get home."

0400: "The seas are rising ever higher. *Bismarck* still fighting. Reported weather for the Luftwaffe."

Around 0630 Wohlfarth sighted the *U-74*, one of the other boats that had been in the Bay of Biscay. Optically and by megaphone, he transferred the mission of maintaining contact with the *Bismarck* to her commanding officer, Kapitänleutnant Eitel-Friedrich Kentrat. He gave Kentrat the *Bismarck*'s position, which he based on his observations of the star shells fired during the night, adding: "I have not seen her directly. You assume contact. I have no more fuel." And after blinking a greeting to Kentrat, he turned away.

In his War Diary Wohlfarth wrote: "Around 0630 gave last contact report, sighted *U-74*, by visual means gave *U-74* the mission of maintaining contact. I can stay on the scene only by using my electric motors at slow speeds. Above water I need fuel and would have to retire."

After transferring his mission, Wohlfarth promptly submerged and did not surface again until 1200, a time at which radio signals were routinely repeated. That was when he heard for the first time the order radioed to him between 0700 and 0800 to pick up the *Bismarck*'s War Diary. Having no more idea than had the headquarters ashore that in the meantime the *Bismarck* had sunk, he immediately asked Commander in Chief, U-Boats, to transfer this mission to Kentrat.* In the course of the morning Wohlfarth did hear a series of explosions, but had no way of interpreting their significance.

By the time Kentrat received the radio order issued in response to Wohlfarth's signal, "U-boat Kentrat pick up *Bismarck* War Diary," he could only search in vain.

I still see it as something more than a coincidence that the *U-556* was the boat ordered to pick up the *Bismarck*'s War Diary because, to us on board, the *U-556* was no ordinary U-boat. There was a very special bond between the little boat and the giant battleship. Both were built at Blohm & Voss and in the summer of 1940 they were often neighbors on the ways. When the *U-556* was commissioned, the mighty bow of the *Bismarck* towered over her. Wohlfarth, who was known in naval circles as "Sir Parsifal," decided that the commissioning ceremony would not be complete without a band and, since a U-boat certainly did not carry one, he would ask the big neighbor, which as Fleet Flagship had a band—called the Fleet Band—

---

*Wondering why on 27 May the *U-556*, which had been at sea for almost four weeks and was therefore presumably in a precarious fuel situation, was assigned to pick up the War Diary, in 1978 I wrote to ask Wohlfarth. He replied: "The U-boat operational command had only a general idea of my fuel situation from a report I sent when I was off Greenland that I was returning because of a shortage of fuel and did not know that, after I had been en route home for a day, I spent half a day operating at high speed against a convoy in a northwesterly direction, which used up my last reserves.

"Admiral Dönitz selected me for the pick-up because I had given running contact reports throughout the night. The *U-74*, to which I gave the mission of maintaining contact around 0600 that morning, would have automatically assumed reponsibility for carrying out the order. But I don't think the order was radioed until around 1000, so that Kentrat could not have performed the mission with the *U-74*, either.

"I was submerged from 0600 to 1200 and did not receive the radio signal until 1200, at which time radio signals were regularly repeated."

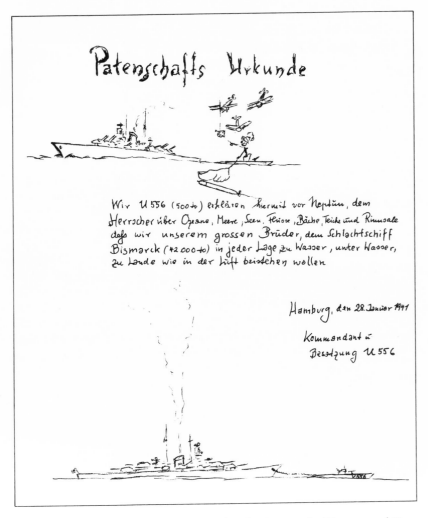

Patenschafts Urkunde

Wir U556 (500t) erklären hiermit vor Neptun, dem Herrscher über Ozeane, Meere, Seen, Flüsse, Bäche, Teiche und Rinnsale daß wir unserem grossen Bruder, dem Schlachtschiff Bismarck (+2000to) in jeder Lage zu Wasser, unter Wasser, zu Lande wie in der Luft beistehen wollen

Hamburg, den 28. Januar 1941

Kommandant u. Besatzung U556

The Patenschaftsurkunde of the U-556 for the *Bismarck*. (Courtesy of Herbert Wohlfarth.)

to provide the music. Accordingly, he went to see Lindemann, but he did not go empty-handed. In exchange, he offered the *Bismarck* the Patenschaft* of his boat. Lindemann readily accepted. Wohlfarth got

*Sponsorship, an informal, merely personal relationship between the two ships, based on the friendship between Lindemann and Wohlfarth

his band and thereafter his artistically designed Patenschaft-surkunde* hung in the *Bismarck*.

Lindemann and Wohlfarth became friends. At the beginning of 1941 the *Bismarck* and the *U-556* were together during gunnery exercises in the Baltic, and once even used the same target. The *U-556*, which Lindemann had allowed to precede him, damaged the target so badly with ten hits that the *Bismarck* could not use it that day. Lindemann, however, did not take it amiss and soon dispelled Wohlfarth's fear that he would be greeted with an ill-humored reaction, "I do not begrudge you that in the least. I wish that you may have as much and rapid success in the Atlantic and win the Knight's Cross for it." Relieved, Wohlfarth replied, "I hope we both receive the Knight's Cross in the common struggle in the Atlantic."†

Wohlfarth heard over the radio about the sinking of the *Hood* during the operation he had just ended against convoys. At first he could not believe it. Now, only two days later, the situation of the *Bismarck* was drastically different, almost hopeless. What did his Patenschaftsurkunde say? "We, the *U-556* (500 tons), hereby declare before Neptune, the ruler of the oceans, lakes, seas, rivers, brooks, ponds, and rills, that we will stand beside our big brother, the battleship *Bismarck* (42,000 tons), whatever may befall her on water, land, or in the air. Hamburg, 28 January 1941. The captain and crew of the *U-556*." One of the two sketches on the certificate shows "Sir Parsifal" warding off aircraft attacking the *Bismarck* with a sword in his right hand and stopping torpedoes coming towards her with his left thumb. The other sketch shows the *Bismarck* being towed by the *U-556*. It almost seemed as though Wohlfarth had the gift of prophecy when he prepared that certificate.

Help against aircraft and torpedoes, and then a tow. That was exactly what the *Bismarck* needed, and he, of all people, Godfather Wohlfarth, was near her. But he was powerless to help her.

---

*Certificate of Sponsorship

†Wohlfarth was, in fact, awarded the Knight's Cross, a decoration similar to the U.S. Medal of Honor, on 15 May 1941.

31

A Last Visit to the Bridge

The clock was crawling towards 0800. It had been bright daylight for a long time. I could not understand why there was still nothing to be seen of the enemy battleships. Hadn't they had time to catch up with us during the night? Where were they?

At the moment there was no specific order from the ship's command that I had to carry out and nothing important demanded my presence in the after fire-control station, so I decided to circulate a little and started with the wardroom. As I went in, for the first time I became strongly aware that we were listing to port. It was strange how much more pronounced the effect was in this closed room than elsewhere. A handful of officers, the senior of whom was Korvettenkapitän (Ing) Wilhelm Freytag, were sitting round a table. The names of the others escape me. On the opposite side of the room was a large tureen, its dippers hanging in a sweet gruel that sloshed back and forth with the rolling of the ship. The silence at the table was broken from time to time by a laconic, hopeless remark. How could it have been otherwise? After all, we were by ourselves—why continue to play games? We all knew what was to come. Finally, someone said, "Today my wife will become a widow, but she doesn't know it." It was depressing. Too depressing to stay there.

Next I went to the bridge, which struck me as pretty deserted. That was an illusion, because there were men stretched out in the corners. Lindemann was standing in the forward conning tower. He was wearing an open life jacket. I had to look twice to believe it.* His steward, Arthur Meier, was just handing him his breakfast and, while he ate it, he seemed strangely detached from his surroundings. He saw me coming, but he did not return my salute, which I held as I looked at him intently in the hope that he would say something. He did not say a word. He did not even glance at me. I was greatly disturbed and puzzled. After all, I had been his personal adjutant and the situation we were in seemed to me unusual enough to merit some remark. I would have given a great deal for a word from him, one that would have told me how he felt about what had happened. But there was only silence, and I had to try to interpret it for myself.

That was not the Lindemann we all knew. I thought back. In private conversations in the past year he told me how much he had always wanted to have command of a great battleship, and how happy he was to be appointed commanding officer of the *Bismarck*. He did say, however, that command of a flagship was not exactly what he had hoped for. Having an admiral embarked could, at critical moments, lead to differences that did not arise in a "brown" ship.† Naturally, the personalities involved would have a lot to do with that. Early in 1941 a classmate asked him, "How goes it with Lütjens?" His terse reply was, "Not easy." His only consolation, Lindemann also told me, was that if his ship, the flagship of the Fleet Commander, were ever to be put in unnecessary danger, the blame would be on the admiral and not on him. These words came back to me, loud and clear, as I watched him standing there: Was that the way he felt about what had happened? Was his demeanor intended to show that he accepted none of the responsibility for the situation into which his ship had been led? When command decisions were called for in the course of Exercise Rhine, wouldn't at least some of those he made have been different from those made by Lütjens, and wouldn't he have chosen differently from among the alternatives available? After the B-Dienst center's report about the alerting of the enemy on 21 May, for example, or when the *Suffolk* and the *Norfolk* were first

---

*Jochen Brennecke, *Schlachtschiff Bismarck*, note 329, quotes statements I allegedly made to the Zurich *Weltwoche* in 1959 on the subject of this meeting with Lindemann. I have never made any statement, either oral or written, to that newspaper. I disavow both the content and the form of the remarks ascribed to me there. My impression of Lindemann on this last morning and the thoughts I had about my meeting with him are described in this book.

†In the Kriegsmarine a "brown" ship was one in which no force commander (usually from the rank of Konteradmiral upwards) was embarked, and consequently the captain was the highest-ranking officer on board.

sighted? And what decision would he have made on the question of continuing the action against the *Prince of Wales* on the morning of 24 May? Mustn't my yearning to know his thoughts have been apparent to him, wouldn't it unlock his lips, wouldn't he say, "Müllenheim, if you live through this, tell them in Berlin how I would have conducted this operation"? Then his words would have come, terse and precise, would have engraved themselves in my brain until the day I reported in Berlin. So many "would's." . . . If just one question had been decided differently early in the game, the subsequent course of the operation could have been different in so many ways. There would have been no guarantee against defeats and losses, but the *Bismarck* might not have suffered such a lingering death.

The personalities of the two officers certainly played a role in what took place. Lütjens was deeply impressed with what he took to be the superiority of British radar and his mood varied between optimism and despondency. Lindemann judged matters more realistically and resisted the depression of the Fleet Commander until finally, in military submission, he capitulated.

Junack's impression of Lindemann was much like mine. Towards morning, he later said, "full power" orders to the engines gradually stopped coming and the atmosphere in the ship became somewhat calmer. Lehmann called him to the engine-control station to take over the watch for a little while. Just then the order came from the bridge, "All engines stop." When some time passed and no other order came, Junack began to fear that, after the strains of the past hours, the turbines might be warped by heat expansion. He therefore picked up the telephone and asked for the captain. Having reported his concern to Lindemann, he requested an order for "Ahead slow," and was greeted with the reply, "Ach, do as you like." That was not the Lindemann Junack knew.

Only four hours earlier Lindemann was a completely different person. Around 0400 he was standing silently beside Schneider in a corner of the bridge. Then he moved away, but a moment later returned, beaming with delight, and went over to Schneider. A radio signal announcing that Schneider had been awarded the Knight's Cross had just arrived, and Lindemann offered congratulations to his first gunnery officer. Cool and collected as ever—nothing about him betrayed his awesome worries. But, when I saw him at about eight o'clock, he had been on the bridge of his helpless ship for eleven hours straight. The rudder hit, the destroyer attacks—it was all too much.

Was this really, as it was to all appearances, the way Lindemann felt? In these tragic moments was he inwardly preoccupied, too preoccupied to break his silence, with reviewing his life and the fate by which his boyhood dream of commanding a ship had been fulfilled for only nine action-packed days, nine short days which had been overshadowed by depressing differences with his superior? The answer to that question was lost when he died two hours later.

Before I left to continue my tour of the ship, I threw a last glance at Lindemann and at Meier, who was still standing in front of him. The good Arthur Meier, who managed a pub in Hanover. When I was serving as Lindemann's adjutant, I saw him every day as he looked after the needs of his captain and brought him his Three Castles cigarettes. Arthur Meier was always ready for a little chat. He could imagine much nicer things than war and being in the navy, but, as he said resignedly, one had to serve somewhere, and being in the *Bismarck* was quite all right with him. Such a big ship and such heavy armor! It would be hard for anything to happen to him there. How often he said that. And now his last dawn had broken.

From the bridge I went down the small ladder to the charthouse. The atmosphere in there was ghostly. A lamp lit up the lonely chart on which no more courses would be plotted. The rest of the room was dark; apparently no one was there. Our position when we received the rudder hit the previous evening was marked on the chart. I could see where our course towards St. Nazaire ended. From there on, a serpentine line showed our swerving course to the northwest, into the wind. Where the line stopped must be where we were at the moment. Navigationally, everything was up to date. Was there really no one in there? Then, in a corner I saw two men stretched out on the deck. Well, they had nothing better to do. I quickly left the room.

As I passed the heavy flak guns on my way back to my station, I suddenly saw Lütjens. I had not seen him since Exercise Rhine began on 19 May. And now, in this situation! What would he say to me? For he would surely say something! Perhaps, in view of our long acquaintance, "Well, Müllenheim, now we're going down together, too," or something of the sort. Accompanied by his Second Staff Officer, Fregattenkapitän Paul Ascher, he came straight towards me, obviously on his way to the admiral's bridge. There was not much room to pass, so I stood aside and saluted. Lütjens looked at me, briefly, attentively, and returned my salute. But not a word came from him, either. He gave no sign of acknowledgment that we were in an extraordinary predicament—although we almost brushed together as he passed.

Disappointment, indeed, astonishment, at so much speechlessness and the certainty that I would never see Lütjens and Ascher again made me turn around and look after them as long as I could.

Günther Lütjens, Fleet Commander and my commanding officer in the *Karlsruhe* during her cruise to North and South America from 1934 to 1935. What memories he brought back!

As a Leutnant zur See in the *Karlsruhe* I was the range-finding officer and a divisional section officer. Lütjens attended divisional instruction more often than any other commanding officer I ever served with and paid closer attention. Having been chief of the Office of Naval Personnel in the Defense Ministry from 1931 to 1934, he took special interest in how his junior officers performed in the training of their men and wanted to see for himself.

Other images came before me. The tall, slim figure and the dignified bearing of the *Karlsruhe*'s commanding officer when he was representing his country on ceremonial occasions in foreign ports. He was not the kind of superior whom we junior officers would seek out for ourselves. He was too reserved for that; he seemed almost melancholy. Yet we were conscious of the integrity and reliability that he exuded.

And now as Fleet Commander? I had no firsthand knowledge. I had never served directly under him. But we in the officer corps were aware that Raeder had a very high degree of confidence in him.

And Ascher—one of those affected by Hitler's imbecilic Aryan Paragraph,* who in accordance with the exceptions it made was, as a veteran of the First World War, allowed to remain in the navy. In December 1939 he had been first gunnery officer in the pocket battleship *Graf Spee* and later told his friend Puttkamer of her battle with

---

*Paragraph 3 (the "Aryan Paragraph") of the "Law for the Reconstitution of the Civil Service" of 7 April 1933 read as follows:

Paragraph 3

(1) Civil servants who are not of Aryan origins are to be placed in retirement; insofar as honorary civil servants are concerned, they are to be dismissed from official connections.

(2) Section 1 shall not apply to civil servants who have been civil servants since 1 August 1914 or who fought at the front for the German Reich or its allies during the world war or whose fathers or sons fell in the world war. The Reich Minister of the Interior can permit further exceptions in agreement with the minister of the responsible department or the highest state authorities for civil servants abroad.

This law was also employed, in part arbitrarily, against members of the three branches of the armed forces.

the British cruisers *Ajax*, *Achilles*, and *Exeter* off the River Plate. "I never got to do any proper shooting," was how he put it, "because every time I had just range and attained bearings on one cruiser, another showed up, and that meant, 'Change target to the other!' The rate of fire of my 28-centimeter guns really wasn't that great, so it always took a while to get the new range and bearings. I wasted all my ammunition without real chances."

Lütjens and Ascher had long since disappeared out of sight. I looked at the clock. It was past 0830. Where were the Britons? They should have been here at daybreak at the latest. I still could not understand their delay. Hardly had I formulated that thought than the alarm bells began to ring shrilly. It seemed as though they would never stop.

The *Bismarck*'s last battle was about to begin.

32

Tovey Sets the Time of the Final Action

At about 2130, after the second air attack on the *Bismark*, its leader, Lieutenant Commander Tim Coode, reported to Admiral Tovey in the *King George V,* "Estimate no hits." It was bitter news, for it buried Tovey's last hope of being able to stop the German battleship. However, he found it strange that shortly before this the *Sheffield* had reported the *Bismarck* on course 340 degrees. A northwesterly course? Towards his own formation? Highly improbable, not to say unbelievable. For, after Coode's negative report, reason argued against the *Bismarck* making such a drastic course change, and Tovey sarcastically remarked to his staff, "I fear Larcom has joined the Recriprocal Club."* Scarcely had he said this than a message came in from one of the aircraft shadowing the battleship, "*Bismarck* steering northerly course." Really? Was Larcom right? Nine minutes later, a second aerial signal told him that the *Bismarck* was on a northerly course. Then a second report from the *Sheffield* confirmed the news.

If the *Bismarck* had not been damaged, why in the world would she steer this suicidal course towards the main body of his fleet? She must have been hit; indeed, she must be seriously damaged. No other explanation was possible. Now the opposing sides were coming to-

---

*An expression used in the Royal Navy when a 180–degree error is made in reporting a ship's course or bearing. It is easy to make such a mistake because, when a warship is lying almost bow-on or stern-on to the observer, her stern and bow are sometimes indistinguishable. Captain Charles Larcom was commanding officer of the *Sheffield.*

wards one another at a relative speed of almost 40 knots. That meant Tovey could force an action before it got dark. The *King George V* and the *Rodney* turned on a southerly course, towards the *Bismarck*.

It was somewhere about 2230 by the time the *Ark Royal* had recovered all her aircraft from the second attack. Captain Maund's debriefing of their crews revealed that a hit amidships on the *Bismarck* had been observed. Tovey was so advised but he was still mystified. If she really had been hit amidships, how could that have anything to do with her present course?

It being completely dark by this time, Tovey realized that the last reconnaissance planes would have returned to the *Ark Royal* and no more reports would be forthcoming from them. He consoled himself with the knowledge that Vian's destroyers would still be in contact with the *Bismarck* and, indeed, their subsequent reports convinced him that she was so seriously damaged that she could not change materially the course she was on. She was obviously compelled to run into the wind and, fortunately, towards Tovey's position.

His German opponent would not escape him now. But, not being absolutely certain of the positions of either Force H, to the south of him, or the *Bismarck*, he decided to delay any action until dawn rather than risk collisions on this pitch-black night. Around 2230 he and the *Rodney* turned to a north-northeasterly and, later, a northerly and westerly course. What he wanted to do was come out of the northwest the next morning, so that the *Bismarck* would be silhouetted against the glowing, eastern horizon and he would have the most favorable conditions possible for directing his guns.

Tovey had no sooner made his first change in course than a report from Somerville, in the *Renown*, informed him that the *Bismarck* had probably received a second hit—this one on her starboard quarter. That was what Tovey had been hoping for. It told him that the *Bismarck*'s rudders or propellers must have been damaged and she was therefore as good as incapable of maneuvering. Now nothing could prevent a fight in the morning. He dashed off a handwritten note to the commanding officer of his flagship, Captain W. R. Patterson: "To K.G.V. The sinking of the *Bismarck* may have an effect on the war as a whole out of all proportion to the loss to the enemy of one battleship. May God be with you and grant you victory. JT 26/5/41."

Tovey received the *Ark Royal*'s last reconnaissance report shortly before 0100 on 27 May. According to this message, immediately after the air attack the *Bismarck* turned two complete circles and came to rest on a northerly heading. If there was any lingering doubt about her inability to maneuver, it was now dispelled. After days and nights of almost unbearable tension, Tovey and his staff felt immeasurable relief. Only seven hours earlier, hope of stopping the *Bismarck* had been virtually abandoned. The odds against it were a thousand to one. Only a miracle could help, and a miracle had happened, one that allowed him not only to determine almost to the minute the time of the action but to choose his tactics against the crippled enemy.

Tovey was not the only one who, on 26 May, was making calculations that seemed to have only the slightest chance of being correct. His almost vanished hope corresponded with our remote fear that the *Bismarck*'s steering gear would be hit. How likely was it that that would happen? During our training period, we occasionally practiced the battle problem "hit in the steering gear." The drill was that two or three compartments were "flooded" and the men in them had to stay where they were. "How would it work in reality," they asked their training officer, "if a hit penetrated, would we all be dead?" "Well, yes," the officer replied, "and you should pretend to be dead. Put your caps on backwards and you'll be counted as dead." Then after a pause, he added, "But the chances of such a hit are a hundred thousand to one, practically nil."

Within a matter of seconds, a half-buried British hope became a miracle, and a piece of almost impossible German bad luck became a catastrophe!

Soon after he heard that the *Bismarck* had turned two complete circles, Tovey, wanting to be sure he didn't get too far away from the enemy, returned to a somewhat southerly course. He ordered Somerville to keep his task force at least twenty nautical miles away from the *Bismarck*, which would be close enough for air operations by the *Ark Royal* yet far enough to keep the *Renown* from being exposed to the *Bismarck*'s superior gunnery. About 0230 Tovey, as previously mentioned, instructed Vian to have his destroyers fire star shells periodically so that a better continuous watch could be kept over the position of the *Bismarck*. However, Tovey was not particularly chagrined when Vian decided some half-hour later that the firing of the shells was endangering his destroyers and ordered it to cease. Numerous rain squalls were reducing visibility to the point where hardly anyone in the *King George V* could see the flares, anyway.

At daybreak, still not sure of the exact position of the *Bismarck* and visibility being poor, Tovey decided to wait an hour or two after it had become completely light before beginning to fight. Thus, the *King George V* and the *Rodney* did not sight their enemy until 0843—0843 on 27 May.

It might be said that this was Tovey's fourth effort to bring about this encounter. The first, 0900 on 25 May, was missed because the *Suffolk*'s radar contact with the *Bismarck* had been broken a few hours earlier. The second, on the evening of 26 May, was missed because, by the time he knew the *Bismarck* had been hit, night had fallen. The third, dawn on 27 May, had had to be passed up because he did not have the *Bismarck*'s precise position and the weather was not favorable. It wasn't really a very long time since the evening of 26 May but it seemed to me then like eternity.

Besides the *King George V,* the *Rodney,* and Force H, two other British ships were trying to reach the scene of the coming battle on the morning of 27 May.

From the north came the ubiquitous *Norfolk*, our old "friend" from the Denmark Strait. Although she was running low on fuel, she had kept up the chase all day long on 26 May and, naturally, wanted to be in on the kill. As early as 0753 she sighted us to the southeast, at a distance of nine nautical miles. Assuming that we were the *Rodney,* Captain A. J. L. Phillips, the skipper of the *Norfolk*, ordered visual recognition signals to be made. He had no sooner done so than he realized that he was heading straight for the *Bismarck* at a speed of 20 knots. As he made an immediate, sharp turn to get his ship out of danger, he saw the *King George V* and the *Rodney* coming over the horizon and signaled Tovey, "*Bismarck* bearing 130°, range 16 nautical miles." Thereupon, recognizing that he was a bit too far to the north, Tovey turned southward.

From the west came the *Dorsetshire*, which had been escorting a northbound convoy. When, at about 1100 on 26 May, Captain Martin received the Admiralty's radio signal reporting that a Catalina had found the *Bismarck* again, he calculated that she was 360 nautical miles north of him. He immediately recognized that he had a good chance of intercepting her if it was true that she was making for the coast of France. On his own initiative, he decided to intervene and proceeded towards the *Bismarck* on an easterly course at high speed and with a following sea. When he appeared, unannounced and unexpected, at the scene of action, Tovey's forces took him to be the *Prince Eugen*, and he narrowly missed being fired on by the Home Fleet.

When Tovey, with the *King George V* and the *Rodney*, finally steered towards the *Bismarck*, he did so in the hope that the sight of his two battleships heading straight for them would unnerve the German range-finding and fire-control officers. After all, the four anxious days and nights through which they had lived must have taken their toll.*

---

*"Sinking of the German Battleship *Bismarck* on 27th May 1941." Dispatch by Admiral Sir John Tovey, Supplement to the *London Gazette*, 14 October 1947, Item No. 80.

33

The Last Battle

The alarm bells were still ringing when, returning from the bridge, I entered my action station. I picked up the control telephone and heard, "Two battleships port bow." I turned my director and saw two bulky silhouettes, unmistakably the *King George V* and *Rodney*, at a range of approximately 24,000 meters. As imperturbable as though they were on their way to an execution, they were coming directly towards us in line abreast, a good way apart, their course straight as a die. The seconds ticked by. Tension and anticipation mounted. But the effect was not what Tovey hoped for. The nerves of our gun directors, gun captains, and range-finding personnel were steady. After the utterly hopeless night they had just spent, any action could only be a release. The very first salvo would bring it. How many ships were approaching no longer meant anything; we could be shot to pieces only once.

Our eight 38-centimeter guns were now opposed to nine 40.6-centimeter and ten 35.6-centimeter guns; our twelve 15-centimeter guns by twenty-eight 15.2-centimeter and 13.3-centimeter guns. A single British broadside weighed 18,448 kilograms (20,306 kilograms, including the sixteen 20.3-centimeter guns on the heavy cruisers, *Norfolk* and *Dorsetshire*) against 6,904 kilograms for a German broadside.* In our foretop Schneider was giving orders in his usual calm voice. He announced that our target was the *Rodney*, which was

*The *Bismarck*'s main battery fired one round per barrel every twenty-five seconds; her secondary battery fired ten rounds per barrel per minute.

The battleship *Rodney* looses a salvo on the *Bismarck* during the action on 27 May. (Photograph from the Imperial War Museum, London.)

off our port bow and heading straight for us. Then, to the ship's command, "Main and secondary batteries ready, request permission to fire." But it was the *Rodney* that got off the first salvo, at 0847. The *King George V*'s first salvo followed one minute later.

The range had closed to less than 20,000 meters, at which distance the time of flight of the shells was less than one minute, but it seemed many times that long. Finally, white mushrooms, tons of water thrown up by heavy shells, rose seventy meters into the air. But they were still quite far from us. At 0849 the *Bismarck*'s fore turrets replied with a partial salvo at the *Rodney*. At this time, our after turrets could not be brought to bear on the target. Schneider observed his first three salvos as successively "short," "straddling," and "over," an extremely promising start that I only knew about from what I heard on the telephone because the swinging back and forth of the *Bismarck* allowed me only intermittent glimpses of the enemy. Obviously not considering dividing our fire, he continued to concentrate on the *Rodney*.

As the shells hurtled past one another in the air, I tried to distin-

The battleships *Rodney* and *Bismarck* in action on 27 May. (Photograph from the Imperial War Museum, London.)

guish incoming ones from those being discharged from our own guns. Suddenly I remembered wardroom conversations that I had had with British naval officers regarding range-finding techniques. They had high praise for their prismatic instruments while I praised our stereoscopic ones. Did we have the better principle? The *Rodney* seemed to need a lot of time to find our range.

I spent the first few minutes of the battle wondering why no enemy shells were landing on us, but that soon changed and there were more than enough of them. At 0854 the *Norfolk*, which was off the *Bismarck*'s starboard bow, began firing her 20.3-centimeter battery at a range of 20,000 meters forward of the starboard quarter. A few minutes later, the *Rodney* opened up with her secondary battery and, around 0902, she observed a spectacular hit on the forward part of the *Bismarck*. At 0904 the *Dorsetshire* began firing on us at a range of 18,000 meters from the starboard side, astern. The *Bismarck* was under fire from all directions, and the British were having what amounted to undisturbed target practice.

Not long after the action began the *King George V* and, a little later, the *Rodney* gradually turned to starboard onto a southerly course, where they maneuvered so as to stay on our port side. This tactic caused the range to diminish with extraordinary rapidity, which seemed to be exactly what Tovey wanted. Lindemann could no longer maneuver so as to direct, or at least influence, the tactical course of the battle. He could neither choose his course nor evade the enemy's fire. Tovey, on the other hand, could base his tactical decisions on the sure knowledge that our course would continue to be into the wind. We could not steer even this course to the best advantage of our

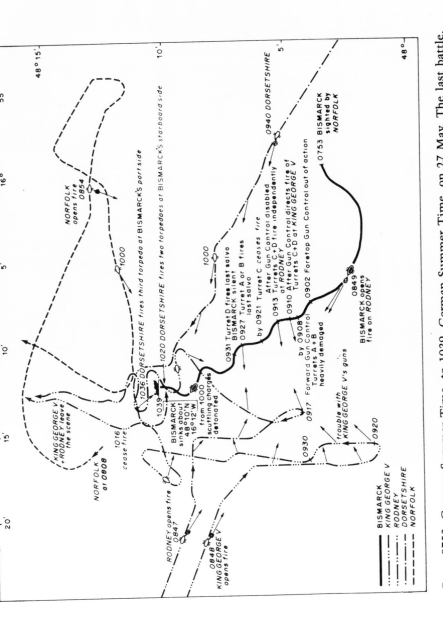

From 0753, German Summer Time, to 1039, German Summer Time, on 27 May. The last battle. (Diagram courtesy of Jürgen Rohwer.)

gunners, who were faced with great difficulty in correcting direction. Though I could not see what was going on around me from my completely enclosed, armored control station, it was not hard to picture how the scene outside was changing. As the range decreased, the more frequent became the *harrumphs* of incoming shells and the louder grew the noise of battle. Our secondary battery, as well as those of the enemy, had gone into action. Only our antiaircraft guns, which had no targets of their own and were useless in a close engagement between battleships, were silent. At first, their crews were held as replacements for casualties at other guns, and were stationed in protected rooms set aside for them. These "protected rooms," however, being on the main deck and not heavily armored, provided little protection even against shell splinters, let alone direct hits at the ranges this battle was fought.

When perhaps twenty minutes had passed since the firing of the first salvos, I searched the horizon through my starboard director for other hostile ships. Off our starboard bow, I made out a cruiser, the *Norfolk*, which by chance had just stopped firing. We had not fired on her because Schneider and Albrecht were still concentrating on the battleships, which were off our port bow and at that moment not visible from aft. No sooner had I begun to wonder whether, with so many enemies around us, our ship's command would decide to divide our fire, than I received an indirect answer. Cardinal came on the control telephone and said that the main fire-control station in the foretop was out of action or, at any rate, could not be contacted, that turrets Anton and Bruno were out of action, and that I was to take over control of turrets Caesar and Dora from aft. He said nothing about the forward fire-control station. I supposed that it would continue to direct the secondary battery, unless it had been disabled, which seemed not unlikely in view of the number of times the forward section of the ship had been hit. There was not time to ask long questions and, since I was not given a target, I had a completely free hand.

An observer in the *Norfolk* saw both barrels of turret Anton fall to maximum depression as though its elevating mechanism had been hit. The barrels of turret Bruno, he commented, were trained to port and pointing high into the air.

"Action circuit aft,"* I announced and, beginning forward, scanned

---

*"Action circuit aft" meant that the turrets were being directed by the after fire-control station through the after computer room. Then on duty in that computer room were the following men: Leutnant zur See Heinz Aengeneyndt and Stabsoberboots-

the horizon through my port director. Strangely enough, there was no trace of the *Rodney*, which I had not seen to starboard, either. She must have been in the dead space forward of my station. But there, steaming on a reciprocal course and now a bit abaft our beam, was the *King George V.* She was about 11,000 meters distant—near enough to touch, almost like a drill in the Baltic. "Passing fight to port, target is the battleship at 250°," I told the after computer room and, upon receiving the "ready" report from below, "One salvo." *Boom!* It went off and during the approximately twenty seconds that it was in the air, I added, "Battleship bow left, one point off, enemy speed 20 knots."

The excellent visibility would be a great help in finding the range quickly, I thought, which was particularly important because the target was rapidly passing astern of us. "Attention, fall," announced the computer room. "Two questionably right, two right wide, questionably over," I observed, then ordered, "Ten more left, down four, a salvo." *Boom!* . . . "Attention, fall" . . . "Middle over" . . . "Down four, a salvo" . . . "Attention, fall" . . . "Middle short" . . . and, full of anticipation, "Up two, good rapid!" Then again our shot fell and the four columns of water began to rise . . . quarter, half, three-quarters of the way, at which point they were useful for observation, "Three over, one short," I never did see the splashes reach their full height. Lieutenant Commander Hugh Guernsey, in the *King George V*, heard my fourth salvo whistle over and, wondering if the next one would be a hit, involuntarily took a step back behind a splinter shield.

My aft director gave a violent shudder, and my two petty officers and I had our heads bounced hard against the eyepieces. What did that? When I tried to get my target in view again, it wasn't there; all I could see was blue. I was looking at something one didn't normally see, the "blue layer" baked on the surface of the lenses and mirrors to make the picture clearer. My director had been shattered. Damn! I had just found the range of my target and now I was out of the battle. Though no one in the station was hurt, our instruments were ruined. Obviously, a heavy shell had passed low over our station and carried away anything that protruded. We tested all our optics and couldn't see our targets through any of them. I walked under the ladder to the

---

mann (Chief Warrant Officer) Friedrich Adams, order-transmission officers for the main and secondary battery, respectively; Bootsmaat (Boatswain Petty Officer) Paul Rudek, range-averager; Matrosenhauptgefreiter Herbert Langer, firing data compiler; Matrosengefreiter Adolf Eich, direction and elevation transmitter; Matrosengefreiter Hans Halke, firing signal transmitter; and Matrosenobergefreiter Heinz Jucknat.

The interior of one of the *Bismarck*'s armored fire-control stations, such as the author occupied at general quarters. The light-colored instrument mounted in the overhead is an observation periscope-telescope for the range-finder officer. Behind it, the darker, tall instrument is a gun director. (Photograph from Bundesarchiv, Koblenz.)

cupola and looked up towards our large range-finder and its operators. There was nothing there. Nothing at all. What only a moment before was a complete array had vanished without a trace. A heavy shell had ripped through the middle of the cupola, whose jagged ruin allowed a clear view of the cloudy sky. From the *Rodney*? The *King George V*? Who knows? It made no difference. My God, we said to ourselves, that was close. Two meters lower and it could have been the end of us. The armor of our station would not have been enough protection against a direct hit at that range.

Nothing could have been more devastating to me than being put out of action just when I had every hope of hitting the *King George V*. For our ship, that was the end of all central fire control. I called both computer rooms, but neither of them could get through to the forward fire-control station. The only thing to do was let turrets Caesar and Dora fire independently. My station being blind, I told their commanders that they were free to choose their targets.

At 0916, shortly after loosing six torpedoes from a distance of about 10,000 meters, all of which missed us, the *Rodney* turned to a northerly course and became the target chosen by our turret commanders. This choice was made apparently because the range to the *Rodney*, which did not go as far to the south as the *King George V*, had closed to 7,500 meters.* The last shots of our after turrets were not badly aimed; a few shells fell very near the *Rodney*. At 0927, one of our fore turrets, either Anton or Bruno, fired one more salvo, but the firing became irregular and finally petered out.† First turret Dora and then Caesar fell silent. At 0931 the *Bismarck*'s main battery fired its last salvo.

Our list to port had increased a bit while the firing was going on. Around 0930, gas and smoke began to drift through our station, causing us to put on gas masks from time to time. But it wasn't too bad.

Unable to leave our station because an inferno was raging outside, we knew little about what was going on elsewhere. Was the ship's command still in the forward command post? Was Lindemann still in

---

*After the turn to the north, the *Rodney*, which had been astern of the *King George V*, became the lead ship. Russell Grenfell in *The Bismarck Episode*, pp. 181–82, suggests that this was perhaps the reason for the *Bismarck* shifting her fire to the *Rodney*, but such was not the case.

†Russell Grenfell; *The Bismarck Episode*, says on page 182 that at 0927 our forward turrets fired a salvo together, which I consider extremely improbable. It would have been an extraordinary coincidence if the serious damage done to both turrets by hits they received shortly after 0900 had been repaired at so much the same pace that they were able to fire a last, joint salvo.

This exterior view of the *Bismarck*'s after fire-control station shows the optical range finder in its revolving cupola. Its lenses are pointing downward and have protective covers in place. Attached to the front of the cupola is a "mattress" radar antenna. To the left and behind the cupola base is the lens housing for one of the two directors in this station. (Photograph from Bundesarchiv, Koblenz.)

charge there? No reports came down to us nor were we asked what was happening in our area. We had not heard a single word from the forward part of the ship since the action began but, considering the large number of hits we had felt, there must have been some drastic changes. Suddenly I heard Albrecht's voice on the control telephone. "The forward fire-control station has to be evacuated because of gas and smoke," he said, and immediately rang off, precluding any questions. I was surprised. I had assumed that the reason for the fire control being turned over to me was that the forward station was out of action. Had Albrecht been directing the secondary battery from there? Was his own station serving only as a place of refuge? I would not learn the answers to those questions until many years later.

I was using all the telephone circuits and calling all over the place

Salvos falling near the *Bismarck* during her final action with the Home Fleet. (Photograph from the Imperial War Museum, London.)

in an effort to find out as much as possible about the condition of the ship. I got only one answer. I reached the messenger in the damage-control center, and asked: "Who has and where is the command of the ship? Are there new orders in effect?" The man was in a great hurry and said only that both the First Officer and the Damage-Control Engineer had had to abandon the damage-control center, adding that he was the last one in the room and had to get out. Then he hung up. That was my last contact with the forward part of the ship.

Before 1000, men who had had to abandon their own stations or protected rooms began arriving to take refuge in my station. Most of them came through the narrow emergency exit where a perpendicular companionway led down to the after gunnery reserve circuit space. They clambered up its iron rungs, the uninjured, the slightly wounded, and many so badly wounded that one could only marvel that they did it. We were lucky that my station was not hit. While heavy firing was still going on, I had the two small exit hatches carefully cranked open. I believed—and convinced the men—that it was better to take a chance on a few splinters than risk having the opening mechanism jammed by a hit. In fact, we were spared both shell splinters and fragments.

Around this time, the order was given to scuttle and abandon the ship, although I did not know it then. In fact, no such order ever reached me, but the situation on board compelled me to conclude that it must have been given. Nevertheless, I did not allow the men in my station to leave while shells were exploding all over the superstructure and main decks, and ready ammunition was blowing up. To do so would have been nothing less than suicide. I did not give the order to leave until long after our guns had fallen silent, the enemy stopped firing and, presumably, the shooting had come to an end.

By this time our list to port was heavier than ever and starboard was the lee side. I called to the men to look for a place aft and to starboard on the main deck. Forward, there was too much destruction and the smoke was unbearable. The quarterdeck was out of the question: the sinking ship was too far down by her stern and heavy breakers were rolling over her from her port quarter. Those who made the mistake of jumping from that side or who were washed overboard in that direction were thrown back against the ship by the sea, in most cases with fatal consequences.

The last one to leave the station, I went forward, towards the searchlight-control station or, rather, towards where it had been. The scene that lay before me was too much to take in at a glance and is very difficult to describe. It was chaos and desolation. The antiaircraft guns and searchlights that once surrounded the after station had disappeared without a trace. Where there had been guns, shields, and instruments, there was empty space. The superstructure decks were littered with scrap metal. There were holes in the stack, but it was still standing. Whitish smoke, like a ground fog, extended from the after fire-control station all the way to the tower mast, indicating where fires must be raging below. It obscured anything that was left on the superstructure. Out of the smoke rose the tower mast, seemingly undamaged. How good it looks in its gray paint, I thought, almost as if it had not been in the battle. The foretop and the upper antiaircraft station also looked intact, but I well knew that such was not the case. Men were running around up there—I wondered whether they would be able to save themselves, to find a way down inside the mast. The wreckage all around made it impossible for me to go any farther forward and I returned to my station, only to leave it again immediately and go aft. I had to clamber over all manner of debris and jump over holes in the deck. I saw the body of a fleet staff officer, lying there peacefully, without any sign of injury. He must have left his action station when the order was given to abandon ship, without waiting for the enemy fire to cease. Turret Caesar, its barrels at high elevation and trained towards our port bow, was apparently undamaged. The light, shining gray of its paint contrasted oddly with the surrounding devastation. Its commander, Leutnant zur See Günter Brückner, was forced to stop firing when his left gun barrel was disabled. Then Brückner directed the following words to his turret crew: "Comrades, we've loved life; now, if nothing changes, we'll die like good seamen," and ordered them to abandon the turret. From the upper deck I saw turret Dora, blackened by smoke, trained port side forward. A shell burst had shredded its right barrel, but the gun captain, Oberbootsmannsmaat Friedrich Helms, had still fired two shots from the left barrel. Then Mechanikersmaat Ernst Moog had climbed up from the interior of the turret, shouting that turret Dora was burning, and the whole crew, still uninjured, had to abandon it, so the turret fell completely silent. Later still a shell detonated, probably on the battery deck, and hurled the hatch to the munitions chamber high into the air. Helms and others suffered burns to their faces and hands through the jets of flame that shot up.

Moving on, I glanced across the water off our starboard quarter, and couldn't believe what I saw. There, only around 2,500 meters away, was the *Rodney*, her nine guns still pointing mistrustfully at us. I could look down their muzzles. If that was her range at the end of the battle, I thought, not a single round could have missed. But her guns were silent now and I didn't expect that they would go into action again.

The *King George V* and the *Rodney* had steered towards the scene of the coming battle on course 110° at a speed of 19 knots in line-abreast formation with a distance of 1,200 meters between them, the *Rodney* to port of the *King George V.* The *Rodney* had not attained her design speed of 22 knots for several years, but during the last three days she had nevertheless averaged between 20 and 21 knots. Through the consequent vibration she had lost some of the rivets in her hull, with the result that fuel oil was leaking into the sea and leaving a thin coating in her wake as far as the eye could see. At 0843 the sharp gray silhouette of the *Bismarck*, making an estimated 10 knots, appeared out of a dark rain squall 250 hectometers to the southeast and the *Rodney*'s Captain F. H. G. Dalrymple-Hamilton, a man of few words, spoke only five to his crew: "Going in now—good luck!" Then the *Rodney* had opened fire, followed a minute later by the *King George V.* Another minute thereafter the *Bismarck* had replied.

In the *Rodney* men realized that they were facing a German battleship which, while incapable of maneuvering, had all her guns fully intact and a gunnery officer who was probably hoping quickly to eliminate the heavy batteries mounted exclusively on the foreship of his principal opponent and therefore dangerously exposed by this bows-on approach to the *Bismarck*, and perhaps to need only a few salvos to do so, as against the *Hood* three days ago. For must not Schneider, well aware of the frightful penetrating power of the *Rodney*'s more than two thousand-pound shells, force a quick decision in order to survive? But he could attain such a success only if, despite the *Rodney*'s extremely small silhouette in the opening stage of the action, his observations enabled him to find his target right away.

To continue, in the words of an observer in the *Rodney:* "From about 0936 until cease firing at 1016 the *Rodney* steamed back and forth by the *Bismarck* at ranges between 2750 and about 4500 yards firing salvo after salvo of 16" and 6" during this entire period." The trajectories of the shells were nearly flat and the devastation of the *Bismarck* was readily visible to her enemies. Several fires were raging and the back of turret Bruno was missing. The superstructure had been destroyed, men were running back and forth on deck, vainly seeking shelter, their only escape from the hail of fire being over the side.

Around 1000 the *Bismarck* appeared to the British to be a wreck. Her gun barrels pointed every which way into the sky, and the wind drew black smoke out of her interior. The glow of fires on her lower decks shone through the holes in her main deck and upper citadel armor belt.

To Tovey it appeared almost incredible that the *Bismarck* was still afloat. The knowledge that German long-range bombers or German U-boats might appear at any moment made the urgency of sinking her ever more pressing. Moreover, his flagship and the *Rodney* were running alarmingly low on fuel. Repeatedly he urged Patterson, "Get closer, get closer—I can't see enough hits." In order to hasten the end of the *Bismarck*, the *Rodney* fired three full salvos with her 40.6-centimeter battery at full depression, scoring three or four hits per salvo. At a range of 2,700 meters, she released her last two torpedoes and the *Norfolk*, at a range of 3,600 meters, fired her last four torpedoes—the *Bismarck* remained afloat.

In the *Rodney*, senior Lieutenant and Air Defense Officer Donald C. Campbell had been able to observe the whole course of the engagement. The "highest man" aboard in his storm-tossed action station in the lofty, unarmored antiaircraft director, he had an unimpaired view, from which no German aircraft appeared to distract him. He saw the *Rodney*'s first salvo fall far ahead of the *Bismarck*, presumably the result of overestimating her speed. The second British salvo fell just a little closer and not until the third was one satisfactorily "short." From the beginning, the *Bismarck*'s shooting impressed him as excellent by any standards and almost aroused fears of a repetition of the *Hood* disaster. The first German salvo was around 180 meters short and drenched the *Rodney* with a spray of evil-smelling water. The second, roaring over like fifty express-trains, struck the water with a deafening detonation around 300 meters in her wake. Campbell could follow the flight of the British 40.6-centimeter shells with his naked eye: black dots growing smaller on their trajectory. As the five dots from the *Rodney*'s fourth salvo were on the point of vanishing he was horrified to see their number almost double as the *Bismarck*'s third salvo appeared on a reciprocal trajectory in a two-way race for seconds to shatter the enemy's armor and morale, a breathless duel that would decide life and death—and that the *Rodney* would win; for her five shells raised only three waterspouts and the *Bismarck*'s turret Bruno disappeared behind flame and smoke after the impact of two shells, while to Campbell the *Bismarck*'s onracing shells grew in size—he could even see a coppery gleam from their driving-bands, thought of the fate of the *Hood* and, in futile reaction, ducked his head. And then they hit, our third salvo, a straddle, a perfect straddle, port and starboard amidships, throwing great walls of dirty water over the *Rodney*, but not scoring a direct hit, missing her by a hairsbreadth. One of the many splinters flying around, a fist-sized chunk of red-hot iron, ripped into and around Campbell's directory, smashing instruments, gun-ready lamps, telescopes, and the master-trigger for the antiaircraft battery,, and finally came to rest with a thud, but, thank God, without harming a one of the five men in the station. Not until, that is, one of them, Hambly ("stupid boy"), picked up the three pounds of jagged metal to drop it with a yell, having badly burned his hand.

Campbell reported the director out of action, put his guns under local control and then gave his attention to how the *Rodney* steamed through the *Bismarck*'s frightfully near misses, ahead, astern, and alongside, without even taking a hit. At 6,000 meters he saw the *Bismarck*'s turret Anton explode into a blazing ruin, which meant that both the *Bismarck*'s fore turrets had ceased to exist and only her secondary battery continued to shoot. Then the *Rodney* could maneuver without any danger from the *Bismarck*'s defenseless bows.

Horrified, almost stunned, by the ongoing work of destruction, Campbell saw how the *Rodney*'s heavy shells crashed through the *Bismarck*'s armored sides, how a 15.2-centimeter shell burst against her bridge like an egg against a wall, how another sent the top of her main fire-control station spinning through the air like a giant trash-can lid—where a yellow-white flame like a scorching thunderbolt consumed its own smoke and incinerated living and dead. Through it all the *Bismarck*'s flag still waved, and Campbell cried out, "My God, why don't we stop?" And then, as if in answer, the cease-fire gongs rang. All that Campbell could hear then was the keening of the wind in the halyards and the wash of the sea against the ship's hull as the *Rodney*, the paint of her turrets blistered by ninety minutes of firing, her decks ripped by the tremendous blast of the guns, her guardrails bent by the same, withdrew from the scene of action, leaving the *Bismarck*, down by her smoke-shrouded stern, blazing fore and aft, a smashed but still beautiful ship.

The *Ark Royal*'s aircraft were anxious to get into the fight. Twelve Swordfish were launched at 0926 but, when they reached the scene of the action, they realized the risk they would be taking if they attacked. Four ships were firing simultaneously at the German battleship from several sides at very close range. That meant flat trajectories, and the Swordfish had to fly low to launch an attack. It was much better for them to forgo it.

Meanwhile, Tovey became increasingly irritated by the *Bismarck*'s refusal to sink. She endured a hail of shells, such as he could not have imagined. How much more would it take? How much more time would her obstinacy cost him? He had no more time. His fuel supply was almost exhausted; every additional half-hour he spent on the scene would make his return home that much more hazardous. Once again he examined the *Bismarck* through his binoculars. She lay deep and sluggish in the water; it now appeared certain that she could never reach port. And with that certainty he had to be content. At 1015 he ordered the *Rodney* to follow in the wake of the *King George V* on a northeasterly course at 19 knots. It was the course home.

At 1022, Admiral Somerville with Force H, out of sight to the south of where the action was, ordered the *Dorsetshire* to torpedo the *Bismarck*. Two minutes earlier, Captain Martin, acting on his own initiative, fired two torpedoes at the *Bismarck*'s starboard side at a range of 3,000 meters. One was observed to hit below her bridge, the other astern. Thereafter, the *Dorsetshire* went over to the battleship's port side and, at 1036, launched a third torpedo at 2,200 meters. This was the last of all the projectiles fired at the *Bismarck* on 27 May.

Suppressing a desire to retrieve a few personal belongings from my stateroom, which was not far away on the port side, I joined a little group of men assembled to starboard, forward of turret Dora, where they were waiting to jump overboard. For the moment, that seemed the best refuge. Many men were already in the water, and those with me were wondering whether this was the moment for them to jump. I told them to wait: "There's still time. We're sinking slowly. The sea is running high and we'll have to swim a long time, so it's best we jump as late as possible. I'll tell you when."

Before joining the group, I had seen the *King George V* and the *Rodney* steaming away to the north in line ahead and concluded that they would not take part in rescuing our survivors. But that other ships would do so, I was firmly convinced. "Some ship will surely come along and pick us up," I told my companions, but I had no idea which it would be. Had I given them false hope? Looking around us far and wide, I saw only empty ocean.

The ocean. Yes, it would soon accept us and, to all appearances, bring an end to us. Could this really be all there was—my death for Hitler and, as I saw it, against Germany—this merciless failure of my one-time expectation of someday being able to serve a normal state system? Was the closing balance of my life really to be the perversion of national life—the extinction of all one's own conceptions of the German way, the desiccation of Germany into a spiritual desert as a result of a dictator's insane excesses? I did not want to believe it. God would not allow it; he would still give me a chance not to have to see my life as a senseless waste. He would do it. And from that moment I had no doubt that I would be saved.

My thoughts also went back to Berlin once again. Hitler would be sitting in his Reich Chancellery and someone would give him a brief report on the sinking of the *Bismarck*. How angry he would be! Hadn't he told Raeder often enough that he would much prefer keeping his handful of big ships at home rather than baiting the superior British fleet on the world ocean, especially by sending them out on contemptible operations against merchant ships? But the grand admiral would not listen and thick-headedly kept biting off more than he could chew. And now this loss—moreover, of a ship bearing the name of the founder of the Reich, what a needless loss of prestige—it would make him absolutely furious. Two thousand men would die with the ship. Would anyone mention that to him? Would it interest him at all—interest him if fifty, five hundred, or five thousand men died at one stroke? I thought not.

Aside from Hitler's theatricals, Rauschning's conversations with Hitler, which had just been published, were still fresh in my mind.

"When I send the Germans in their prime of life into the storm of steel of the coming [!] war," as Rauschning recorded one of Hitler's remarks, "I will not feel the least regret over the precious German blood that will flow." Obviously, I felt, no human sacrifice would be too much for the maintenance of his personal power. "It's striking," Hitler's army adjutant, Major Gerhard Engel, recorded in his diary after some weeks, "how little, when he comes to speak of it, the fate of the *Bismarck* appears to affect F. [ührer]."

No, when I went overboard, it would definitely be without a "*Sieg Heil*," without a "Heil Hitler," without an arm upraised in the Nazi salute, without any sort of gesture in reminder of the worst enemy Germany ever had. My powerlessness prevented anything stronger than this unobserved quid pro quo.

Although we all must have heard many of the same terrifying sounds and must have shared a sense of incredible desolation that morning, we did not all have the same experiences or see the same things. Here, then, are accounts, in more or less their own words, of the events that stand out most vividly in the memories of some of the other survivors.

Soon after the battle started, water began pouring through the ventilator shafts into Junack's action station, the middle engine room, below the armored deck in Compartment VIII. It was clear that the enemy's shots were striking close to us. After a while, red-orange fumes coming through the ventilators forced the crew to put on gas masks. The bridge issued hardly any orders over the engine telegraph but, when the din of battle was reduced to an occasional explosion, Junack received the order through the engine-control station, "Clear ship for scuttling." That was the last order given aboard the *Bismarck*. At this moment, the entire communications system broke down; the central turbine room was cut off from the engine-control station and the bridge. When scuttling charges had been brought to the cooling-water intakes and things became quieter above, Junack sent his best petty officer to get further orders. The petty officer did not return, and Junack had no choice but to act on his own responsibility. He had all bulkhead doors to the shaft alleys opened, then sent his men to the main deck and ordered the chief machinist to set the charges with a nine-minute fuze. He was the last to leave the engine room, where the lights were still burning and the turbines turning in accordance with the last order, "Slow ahead."

Not until he reached the battery deck did Junack see the devastation of the battle. As he made his way through the wreckage, he heard the charges in the engine room exploding. There was no getting forward and, on his way aft, he ran into a crowd of men, scared because they found their passage blocked. Telling them not to panic, he pushed his way into the midst of them and, as soon as they realized he was an officer, they calmed down. They tried to shove their way through an armored hatch that was jammed half-open, but their gas masks and inflated life jackets made it a tight squeeze. Things went faster when, at Junack's suggestion, they took off their life jackets and jettisoned whatever other equipment they had. He had mastered the chaotic situation at a glance. Junack waited until last to climb through the hatch to the upper deck. There, five junior officers and several hundred men were gathered around the after turrets, getting ready to go over the side. By this time, the enemy was doing very little firing. A curtain of flame amidships hid from view what was forward of it. All he could see were some dead and wounded scattered about the deck. Our ensign still flew from the mainmast, but seawater was spilling over the quarterdeck in the brilliant sunshine and the ship was sinking ever deeper. There was no doubt that the *Bismarck* was slowly capsizing.

Far aft, the leader of Damage-Control Team No. 1, Stabsobermaschinist Wilhelm Schmidt, could tell whenever our guns fired by the shuddering of the ship. Five enemy shells penetrated the upper deck in the area of his responsibility and exploded on the battery and main decks. One landed in Compartment I and another in Compartment II, where it produced a huge flash. Nitrogen gas seeped through the closed armored hatch to the vicinity of the damage-control command post in Compartment III. Shell splinters from the third hit put the lighting and ventilator for the main deck out of action. All that was left was emergency lighting. Hits four and five were in Compartment IV where, among other things, they demolished the companionways. Fumes from fires penetrated everywhere. A messenger arrived from the damage-control center with an order to Schmidt to send some men to put out a fire on a superstructure deck aft. A party went, but none returned. Schmidt had already lost some of his people to shell splinters. A chief gunner rushed up with the news that there was fire in turret Dora, and Schmidt, reversing pump No. 2, flooded the ammunition spaces below the turret. Schmidt continued to receive reports of fires, some of them on the superstructure decks and in compartments on the battery and main decks.

Finally the order came from the bridge to all areas, "Scuttle ship."

Schmidt reversed whatever pumps were still in operation in his area and flooded the compartments. He heard the condenser intakes and the seacocks blowing up in the engine and boiler rooms. A messenger brought another order, "All hands on the upper deck." All the armored hatches on the main and battery decks were jammed and the companionways gone. The only way they could get to the upper deck was by using a narrow shell hoist. When they reached topside, Schmidt and his men joined the life-jacketed men waiting on the quarterdeck. The *Bismarck* was lying in heavy seas, fire and dark columns of smoke belching from her superstructure. There was no sign of the enemy near or far, only a few wheeled aircraft circling overhead.

Very soon after the firing started, most of the shells were landing forward in the ship, where fires raged and huge pieces of iron and steel flew through the air. The *Bismarck* was jolted particularly hard when, shortly after 0900, her fore turrets, forward fire-control station, and tower mast were hit. A little later, somewhat aft, a heavy shell went right through the superstructure deck in way of the aircraft catapult. The protected space it landed in was used for storing ready ammunition for the 10.5-centimeter guns, which blew up, killing the crews of the heavy antiaircraft guns who were taking shelter there. Around 0940 the backwall of turret Bruno, whose guns had jammed in a position pointing athwartships, was blown off and the turret was on fire. Shortly before the British ships stopped firing, bright flames burned briefly around turret Anton.

As a member of the ammunition-handling group assigned to the after antiaircraft control station for the heavy flak, Musikmaat* Josef Mahlberg was stationed in a powder chamber in Compartment IX. When the fight had been going on for some time, the door to the chamber opened and in stepped Bootsmaat Rolf Franke of the after antiaircraft computer room. He had a strange expression on his face. Mahlberg knew him well; the two of them always went most of the way to their stations together. Franke cried out, "The word's just come through, abandon ship, the ship's going to be scuttled!" Dropping everything, Mahlberg and his men scrambled to go through the auxiliary shell hoists to the superstructure. When that proved impossible, they turned back and went through the bulkhead door to the

*Petty Officer (Bandsman)

decks, where, in contrast to their well-lighted chamber, they were in darkness and soon lost sight of one another. Only flashlights made pools of light here and there.

Mahlberg's first stop was the battery deck in Compartment X, where hundreds of men were jostling one another in an effort to get to the upper deck. Suddenly he heard the familiar voice of the First Officer, sharp and incisive: "What's all this? Go forward and help put out the fire. We aren't lost, not by a long shot. Is there no officer here who can take command?" But none came forward. Whatever happened, Mahlberg somehow reached the starboard upper deck in the neighborhood of the aircraft crane. Only then did he fully grasp our plight. All that was left of the once-proud ship was ruin. He tried to get to the forecastle, but water flowing over the deck near the middle 15-centimeter turret blocked his way. He turned back towards the quarterdeck and when he passed turret Dora, he saw some of its badly burned crew sitting or lying on the upper deck. Because the quarterdeck was already partly under water, Mahlberg climbed up to the roof of the turret. "Just look at what's happened to my turret!" Oberstückmeister* Friedrich Alfred Schubert, one of the burned men, called to him. "Get away, it's going to blow up at any minute!" Mahlberg turned and went back to the main deck.

In the starboard turbine room Maschinenmaat† Wilhelm Generotzky was aware that our own guns were firing very irregularly and that we were being hit again and again, but not a single shell penetrated his area or anywhere else below the armored deck. He felt very proud of German naval architecture and German workmanship. He and his men had no idea what the upper decks looked like, but they could not fail to think that the end was at hand. The *Bismarck* seemed to have been transformed into a practice target for the enemy. The second mate of his watch, his face chalk-white, called to him in passing, "It's over, it's all over!" He knew the young mate well, knew he was happily married.

From the ventilator shafts that led to the diesel engines there came a sound like peas dancing on a drum. It was shell splinters falling on the main deck. A highly excited stoker came in and yelled, "Herr Maschinenmaat, transformer room No. 1 is on fire. You must go below!" Generotzky put on his respirator, grabbed a fire extinguisher,

---

*Chief Petty Officer (Ordnance)
†Petty Officer (Machinist)

and tumbled down the companionway. Below, he carefully opened the door to the transformer room—nothing, neither fire nor smoke greeted him. He went on to the door to the diesel room, but all was clear here, too. Still, while he was climbing down, he thought he smelled smoke. Where was it coming from? He checked all the spaces near the companionway and, as he opened the door to a 10.5-centimeter shell and powder chamber, acrid yellow fumes assailed him and he saw a reddish glare. Quick as a flash he closed the door and rushed back up on deck to where the flood-control valves were mounted on a bulkhead. Oh, God, how long it took, half a turn one way, half the other way—and beneath him the burning ammunition! At last, open. Quickly, open the seacocks, start the pumps. Open the flood-control valve more. Hold it, that won't work. Too much water pressure on the valve. Shut off the pumps, open the valve, let the pumps run again. Water was beginning to cover the burning ammunition! His hands were shaking, his knees trembling, and sweat was pouring down his face. Just as he was making his report to his leader, his division officer came from the engine-control station and gave orders to flood the rooms in flood group No. 4. But at the same moment, a petty officer from Damage-Control Team No. 4 reported that the rooms in flood groups Nos. 4 and 5 were already flooded. There had been fires in several ammunition chambers. Generotzky and his men did not know that all the 10.5-centimeter guns had been demolished or had their turrets shot away. They were also not aware that some of the 15-centimeter turrets had been hit and their armor penetrated on the port side by fragments or direct hits.

When "abandon ship" was ordered, Generotzky climbed to Compartment X of the battery deck, where some sixty men were already waiting to use the companionway to the upper deck. Hits landing above were clearly audible. In the passageway stood the First Officer and the commander of Division 11, Kapitänleutnant (Ingenieurwesen) Albert Hasselmeyer. Fregattenkapitän Oels said: "Don't go up there. It would be certain death. Better go to the forecastle and help put out the fires!" But that didn't make any sense. Fuzes had been set and the scuttling charges would go off at any moment.

Generotzky was standing about five meters from the companionway, with a wall of waiting comrades ahead of him. Suddenly there was a flash of light, a rumbling roar, and he was thrown into the air, landing hard on his back. A shell had hit the companionway. Men stumbled over him, one helped him up, and they both ran aft to Compartment VIII, where the companionway to the upper deck was a mass of men. Maschinenmaat Heinrich König unloaded the ammunition hoist from the trunk in the adjacent 10.5-centimeter shell and powder chamber, the one that Generotzky had flooded a few minutes earlier, so that it could be used to escape. Forty men, one behind the other, began to climb up the narrow shaft, only fifty centimeters wide. The lights had gone out and some of them held their flashlights in their mouths. Everyone waited his turn patiently. There was no pushing, no jostling. Each man was lifted by the ones behind so that he could grab the first rung of the ladder. Muffled explosions below encouraged them to make the greatest possible haste. Finally Generotzky's turn came. He was pushed up into the duct and, rung by rung, he pulled himself up. When he got a hold on the upper deck, his hands were in a pool of blood. He stood up inside the demolished superstructure and found himself surrounded by dead bodies, three and four deep, lying where they had fallen. But he was out, out of the frightening coffin the *Bismarck* had become. At least, there was light up there and the whitecaps on the water showed that there was life. The enemy was still firing, adding to the chaos, as corpses piled on top of one another. He made for the hangar, where, although it had a huge hole in one side, he hoped to find shelter, but when he got there he shrank back. Too many had already tried to find shelter there, in vain. He jumped down to the upper deck and ran aft, but so much water was already washing over it that he clambered back up. At last, the firing ceased.

On his way up from below deck, Maschinengefreiter Bruno Zickelbein of Damage-Control Team No. 6 saw the First Officer in Compartment XIII on the battery deck. "Comrades," Oels was shouting, "we can no longer fire our guns and anyway we have no more ammunition. Our hour has come. We must abandon ship. She will be scuttled. All hands to the upper deck." Oels then led Zickelbein and seven other men aft to Compartment IX and told them to carry four wounded men, who were waiting there, to the main deck. Carrying their burdens, the men went to the only companionway they could get up, the one near the catapult, amidships. When Zickelbein and his partner were halfway up with their load a shell struck and hurled them back to the battery deck. Another hit killed the wounded and a number of other men. Now, the companionway was wrecked and, through a huge hole in the battery deck, Zickelbein could see all the way down to the main deck. "Everyone here is dead," Maschinenmaat Erich Vogel told him, "we are the only ones alive." They gave up trying to get to the upper deck and went to Compartment X. Then came the order, "Maschinenmaat Silberling and his party report to the engine-control station immediately." Hans Silberling gave Zickelbein his hand and said: "We won't see each other again, this is the end! Say hello at home for me." They clasped hands for a moment and tears ran down their cheeks. Zickelbein was barely nineteen years old and the twenty-five-year-old Silberling had been a kind of fatherly friend to him. But there was nothing for it, and Silberling carried out his last order.

There were more hits and the lights went out. Holding handkerchiefs over their mouths and noses to protect themselves from the dense smoke, Zickelbein and his companions tried to get to the upper deck by way of the companionway near the enlisted men's mess. While they were waiting for wounded men to be carried up, they heard Marinestabsarzt* Arvid Thiele say, "Leave them, they'll sleep better here." Everyone knew what he meant. Hardly had the doctor spoken when a shell smashed the mess companionway, killing those closest to it. Fearing that none of the companionways forward was usable, the surviving men tried to climb the shattered one. So much water was pouring in from above that by the time Zickelbein reached it he was standing in water higher than his waist. Eventually he, too, escaped.

In power plant No. 2 in Compartment VIII of the lower platform deck Maschinenobergefreiter† Hans Springborn gave the generators and the diesel engines a final inspection shortly before the scuttling charges went off. He wanted to ensure that there would be light right up to the end, and there was.

Topside, the *Bismarck* looked like a heap of scrap metal, all on fire. Men were running back and forth, trying to find a way of saving themselves. However, the ship's boats, life preservers, and floats had all been long since destroyed. Amid all the devastation on the main deck, Springborn saw wounded men lying on stretchers. They were supposed to have been carried to the dressing station below but, because the continuing fall of shells made that impossible, the doctors were scurrying around giving them sedatives.

Maschinengefreiter Hermann Budich, the talker in action station "E" in Compartment IX of the lower platform deck, who around

---

*Lieutenant, Medical Corps
†Seaman (Machinist)

midnight had taken Maschinengefreiter Gerhard Böhnel's telephone report that the starboard rudder had at last been uncoupled, was wounded and brought to the action dressing station aft. Since he was not seriously hurt, he was laid on the deck outside. He had just heard one of the doctors say, "Only serious cases inside," when there was a frightful crash. A direct hit on the dressing station. Inside it nothing stirred.

It must have been between 0910 and 0915 that the mission Oels and Jahreis had been performing came to an end. The destruction on board and the growing mass of water in the ship made it senseless to record hits and try to limit their effects. The opposite had to be done: to destroy what could no longer be saved. Since 0915 at the latest the *Bismarck* had been mortally wounded, losses and lack of munitions had signaled the end. Now the two officers had to supervise the scuttling of the ship and devise ways for the men to get through the chaos of the main and battery decks to safety.

"Scuttling procedure, everyone overboard!" Oels ordered, and the transmission of this order to all stations was the last action of the personnel in the damage control center. That done, they formed a line to go through a bulkhead, and then into the communications shaft, which led vertically upwards and opened into the forward conning tower above the ship's bridge. "Come along!" Sagner summoned Maschinengast Statz, but the latter answered, "No, I'm staying here." Why he said that he doesn't know himself, probably out of fear, for the crackling of the hits outside was undiminished. Jahreis looked at Statz in surprise, shot his hand to his cap by way of farewell, and entered the connecting shaft. Oels went through the port bulkhead towards the stern, shouting as he went out, "We have nine or ten minutes' time!"

Followed by some of the men from his command center, Oels passed through Compartments XIII and X of the battery deck—where, as we know, he met Zickelbein, Mahlberg, and Generotzky—to Compartment VIII of this deck. There he found a surging mass of some three hundred men pushing and shoving towards the ladders. Acrid, yellowish green smoke swirled across the deck, and the men who didn't have gasmasks were wracked by choking coughs. The hatch at the top of one ladder was jammed halfway open. "Get out, get out," called Oels in an emotional, cracking voice, "everyone off the ship. She's being scuttled. You can't get through forward. Everything is burning forward." The words were barely out of his mouth when a green flash whizzed by, burst into a fireball, and exploded with a deafening crash. Men reeled, were hurled through the air, and fell hard on the deck; more than one hundred were killed, Oels among them. He was standing between the canteen and the companionway when the shell struck. The groans and whimpers of the wounded arose from every direction.

In the damage control center Statz remained standing at the table. His glance fell on the damage control board, which mercilessly revealed the bad situation of his ship. Red, the color for "taking water," covered almost the entire port side; green, for "flooded," showed for the port shell and powder chambers and nearly the entire starboard side—the outboard list-control tanks there had been filled for a long time. White, indicating "pumped," was lit up only for the engine rooms below the armored deck. First Statz emptied his pockets, there was an order about that, laid aside his machinist's action tool belt and his machinist's action hammer, which the men had christened "Junack's action hammer" after its designer. Junack was truly the father of damage control measures in the *Bismarck*, which, as Statz was reminding himself at this moment, made Junack's sudden transfer shortly before sailing to the post of turbine engineer in exchange for Jahreis all the more inexplicable. Then Statz put on his life jacket, unfastened, of course; but what to do next?

Statz was now completely alone in the command center; the electric light was burning as though nothing had happened. Nervousness gripped him. Should he, would he, go aft, as Oels had indicated? He tried it and stepped through the bulkhead out of the center, but he didn't get much farther. Pitch-black darkness and thick smoke made it impossible for him to see anything and soon he was standing in knee-deep water on the upper platform deck of the heavily listing ship. He stopped near the flood valves for the 15-centimeter munitions chambers. To think that barely thirty minutes earlier he and Sagner had opened them. The chambers had shown external temperatures of 80 degrees centigrade, and Sagner ordered for them all to be flooded. Statz objected, "But there are still people in there!" Yet after the chamber bulkheads could not be opened, Sagner stood firm: "For Führer, Folk, and Fatherland, it's got to be, otherwise we'll all go sky-high." My God, flashed through his head, are we really going to go sky-high now? Better get away from here, anyway, back to the familiar control center.

Once again Statz was alone in his still well-lit, accustomed surroundings, which he should have left long ago but in this almost incredible fashion could not. While he was considering what to do, the damage control telephone shrilled in the silence. Who can still be calling now, heavens, still now, after such an inferno? thought Statz. He picked up the receiver and heard my question from the after fire-control station: "Who has and where is the command of the ship? Are there new orders in effect?"

With Oels's last words spinning around in his head that barely ten minutes remained for the crew to save themselves—how many of them had already elapsed?—and thoroughly perplexed as he was, Statz pulled himself together and replied quickly and tersely: "First Officer and Damage Control Officer have left the control center together with the compartment personnel, I must follow." And from my call he realized: someone's still alive up there, there's still hope, but now I've got to get out of here fast!

Hardly had he hung up the receiver than suddenly two men entered the compartment, Maschinenobergefreiter Heinz Moritz and Erich Seifert—his messmate "Fietje." Two oldtimers from the building course who knew every nook and cranny in the ship, they had found their way from aft to the connecting shaft to the forward conning tower. But as Fietje—once so full of good advice—stood there barefoot, wearing only an undershirt, he had nothing at all to say and only stared at Statz without showing any sort of reaction. Turning to Moritz, Statz asked, "Should we try to go up seven decks through the cable shaft or communications tube and then four more below from there to the upper deck?" He had only a hazy recollection of that route. By way of answer, Fietje stepped smartly into the shaft, Moritz followed, and Statz—"I, the procrastinator"—came last.

Inside the narrow communications tube, the ascent was a true ordeal for the three men. The iron rungs were welded on the starboard side, but for some time the *Bismarck* had had a steadily increasing list to port, so that the men, hanging onto the rungs on the opposite side and repeatedly snagged by cable housings, had to expend three times the usual amount of energy to clamber up. This difficult climb, the hellish circumstances, and the worry constricting his throat as to how all of this would end completely confused Statz. Every time he glanced up past the men above him and saw light, he asked himself, "Is that the sky or is that water?" The higher he went—with the continuous battle noise becoming even more ear-splitting, the light ever brighter just where the forward conning tower should have cast everything in darkness—it became all the more clear to him that "something must have happened to the conning tower." And, in fact, on climbing out of the shaft, Statz found himself in the open, with apparently nothing left standing above the platform there.

Another direct hit struck the conning tower, demolishing its remains and spewing scraps of metal overboard. Now only the outline of the conning tower could very faintly be discerned in the short segments of upright armor plate on the deck, that was all. Its destruction had meant death for the many officers massed at their action stations there; they lay in their blue uniforms. Statz recognized Jahreis and Sagner, who had come from below shortly before, saw them not far from the mouth of the shaft, both dead, and thought, "Honor to their memories."

The last direct hit had also wounded Moritz, Seifert, and Statz, the latter with a twenty-centimeter-long gash in his left shoulder. Luckily, he was wearing leather clothing; the other two were not. Amid the glowing shell splinters he could only roll out of the shaft, and as he did so heard the familiar, Rhenish voice of his friend Oberleutnant Cardinal: "Well, Slim, did they get you?" My God, he thought, someone is still alive up here, too.

Then they were standing beside one another, Statz and Cardinal, just the two of them, for no one else was on his feet anywhere within their field of vision. It would have been impossible for the situation to have corresponded more completely to the battle problem at sea off Gotenhafen a month earlier. "Half bad with my wound," he told Cardinal, "but we must get below as quickly as we can." Then he saw Moritz lying terribly wounded on the deck with his whole chest torn open, and Statz and Cardinal pulled him gently behind the armored bridge bulwark, the only part of the ship that was still intact here above. How he could help his comrade, Statz was too excited to have any idea, and simply stroked his face, as one would a baby's. But Moritz smiled at him gratefully, gasped "Say hello to Cologne for me," and died.

The destruction round about was frightful. Everything up to the bridge bulwarks had been erased. Stumps indicated the columns on which nautical apparatus had once rested; the big binoculars in the middle of the ship on the bridge, remarkably enough, undamaged; on both sides, close to the wings of the bridge, the remains of antiaircraft guns identifiable only by the seats for the men who had directed them.

Cardinal and Statz now sought shelter behind the bulwark, but had to leap constantly from side to side, for shells continued to hit, mainly on the tower mast and below it. The heavy "trunks" could be seen clearly with the naked eye as they rushed through the air. After a leap to the starboard side Statz was surprised to glimpse another living being there. He was sitting on the bridge deck, immobilized by serious leg wounds, an officer with four stripes on his sleeve, a Fregattenkapitän. Bracing himself against the deck with his left hand, he sat completely upright—and around him only the dead! He was observing the bombardment with professional interest. What a fine, neatly styled haircut he had, thought Statz; what beautiful, lustrous white hair.

Then the hits had Cardinal and Statz on the run again, and Statz fervently hoped that the lieutenant would take the initiative and tell him the best way to get down from here. Yet he began to feel that it was he himself who had to lead now; Cardinal had changed. His previous question to Statz, "Well, Slim, did they get you?" were the last words he would ever speak; after them he kept silent—he, for Statz always "the officer," "example, expert, soldier, a man with whom one could move mountains." Statz no longer recognized him. From their position they had a completely unobstructed view of the flak control centers on both sides aft, standing like fingers in the sky, completely untouched, as though nothing had happened. Nearer, fires were swirling up to the more elevated admiral's bridge, the smoke coiling itself into dense swaths; the bridge itself appeared undamaged, the windscreen glass intact, but no one could be seen there.

Statz said, "I'm not going below to the starboard." Cardinal merely nodded. It really looked horribly high from up here; on the starboard side, the upper deck was already towering far above the sea. Several voices from below bawled "Gas!" and then a direct hit beneath the bridge silenced them. On with the gas mask, Statz told himself, and pulled it on, but immediately felt suffocated; in his excitement he had not unscrewed the microphone cover, so off with the mask, and by then the gas had blown away. Now he and Cardinal peered forward again, towards the main turrets, whose terrible condition brought tears to Cardinal's eyes. Then they saw a British cruiser approaching with guns blazing and the bridge deck again reverberated with impacts. But the little cruiser shells weren't so bad, not nearly so bad as the battleships' 40.6 and 35.6ers, which shattered everything beyond recognition wherever they hit. The Fregattenkapitän must have fallen victim to a direct hit, for the place where he had been sitting was no more.

Looking to port, Statz saw a rope ladder made fast forward of the flak control center and told Cardinal, "That's our chance!" Then suddenly, the firing ceased—what a blessing—and it became possible to walk upright again, diagonally across the bridge deck, where the conning tower had once stood, up to the bulwark. Statz helped Cardinal over; the latter climbed on the rope ladder and immediately fell like a stone—blissfully unhurt—to the lower bridge deck, for the belaying knots of the ladder had burned through. The fire was most intense here and somehow Statz managed to get down to the lower bridge deck, too. There, an absolute wasteland, nothing recognizable. Now, down again to the *Aufbaudeck* (equivalent to USN 01 level), dangle part of the way, jump the rest. And another leap to the middle port 15-centimeter turret, whose roof was intact, if in other respects it no longer resembled a gun turret. From there they saw some comrades who had sought shelter behind turret Dora, the first living men in an apparently endless time! They heard the national anthem sung and a triple *"Sieg heil"* and saw men leaping into the sea. Not a soul came from anywhere else in the forepart of the ship. Besides Cardinal and Statz, no one escaped the hell there.

Some men were trapped below. The hatches leading to the main deck (particularly on the port side) were either jammed shut or there was heavy wreckage lying on top of them—again more so on the port side where wreckage from the forward command tower including louvers to the boilers had been ripped away by direct shell hits. In Compartment XV near the forward mess on the battery deck, two hundred men were imprisoned behind jammed hatches. They were all killed by shell fire. Flames cut off the whole forward part of the ship. One of the starboard 15-centimeter turrets had been hit and its access hatch was jammed. No amount of effort from inside or out could pry it open. The turret became a coffin for its crew. Farther aft, two men who had managed to reach the main deck were blinded by the dense smoke and fell through holes in this deck back into the fire below. There were young sailors, petty officers, even men of the prize crews, experienced seamen, who decided it would be pointless to try to climb out.

With the silencing of our guns, one after the other, the doctors' and corpsmen's hour had come—and in what dimensions! Hundreds of wounded lay where they had been hit, in the foretop, on the bridge, in the control stations, at the guns, on the upper deck, and on the battery and main decks. Stretcher-bearers, including civilians, carried them from the upper deck amid a hail of shells, but the only thing that could be done for such numbers was relieve their pain by giving them morphine. None of those who really knew what feats were accomplished in the dressing stations and at the collection points lived to tell the story.

The task of the doctors and corpsmen became overwhelming as one action station after another was knocked out and the men who were no longer able to take part in the fight crowded the battle dressing stations. As the minutes passed and ever great numbers of wounded requiring ever more attention pressed into the stations, the possibility that our medical people would have a chance to save themselves became slimmer and slimmer. The armor of the battery and main decks within the citadel offered them no protection as they labored amid a stream of heavy hits, every casualty providing them with a preview of what lay in store for them. What they suffered was the epitome of what observers in two British ships preferred not to imagine: "What that ship was like inside did not bear thinking of; her guns smashed, the ship full of fire, her people hurt; and surely all men are much the same when hurt," "Pray God I may never know what those shells did as they exploded inside the hull."*

Referring to the forty-five minutes of relentless cannonading that followed the silencing of our guns, Captain Dalrymple-Hamilton said, "I can't say I enjoyed this part of the business much, but didn't see what else I could do."† Captain W. R. Patterson of the *King George V* would have stopped firing earlier had he been able to see what was happening on the *Bismarck*, but the wall of splashes from near misses obscured his view of her port side.‡

The doctors and the corpsmen endured the horror and helped the wounded until they themselves fell victim to a hit. When and where they died, I do not know. Only the direct hit in the action dressing station aft has been recorded. Marineoberstabsarzt§ Hans-Günther Busch, Marinestabsarzt Hans-Joachim Krüger, Marinestabsarzt Arvid Thiele, Marineassistenarzt der Reserve** Rolf Hinrichsen, and their corpsmen and assistants are here remembered with special respect.

This is as far as I can reconstruct the *Bismarck*'s last battle from my own experiences and from the testimony of others. The concen-

---

*Ludovic Kennedy, *Pursuit*, pp. 206, 208.
†Ludovic Kennedy, p. 207.
‡Russell Grenfell, *The Bismarck Episode*, p. 184.
§Lieutenant Commander, Medical Corps. Dr. Busch was posthumously promoted to Geschwaderarzt (Squadron Surgeon); Dr. Krüger, to Marineoberstabsarzt.
**Assistant Surgeon (Reserve)

tration of hits on the forward section of the ship in the opening stage of the battle explains why the *Bismarck*'s command system was crippled so early. Only afterwards did I understand why, once the battle had started, not one order or message from the bridge reached me in my after fire-control station. To us participants, each phase of the action seemed much, much longer than it actually was. By 0902, fifteen minutes after the first salvo was fired, the foretop, the forward fire-control station, and turrets Anton and Bruno had been disabled, which meant we had lost more than 50 percent of our firepower. No one who was in those forward action stations survived, and my report, from the perspective of a position aft, can only be a fragment.

No survivor saw the Fleet Commander during the last battle. I assume that Admiral Lütjens and his staff fell at their action stations.

34

The *Bismarck* Sinks

While the little group I was with was waiting to starboard, forward of turret Dora, the *Bismarck* sank still deeper by her stern and her list to port increased. The gradual emergence of more and more of her hull on the starboard side told me that the moment to jump was approaching. "It's that time," I said, "inflate your life jackets, prepare to jump." Just as earlier it was vital not to go over the side too soon, now, it was vital not to delay so long that we would be sucked down with the ship when she finally sank. "A salute to our fallen comrades," I called. We all snapped our hands to our caps, glanced at the flag, and jumped.

In the water we were pushed together in a bunch, as we bobbed up and down like corks. At first we swam away from the sinking ship as hard as we could to escape her suction. When I got clear by some 150 meters, I stopped and turned around for one last look and to take in everything I could about her.

What I saw was that the *Bismarck* was listing still more. She had no stability left. She was also deeper down by her stern, her bow rearing steeply out of the water. The whole starboard side of her hull, all the way to the keel, was out of the water. I scrutinized it for signs of battle damage and was surprised that I saw no trace of any. Her port side had borne the brunt of the battle, and that side of her hull may have told a different story.

When swimmers close to the bow of the ship looked back, they saw Lindemann standing on the forecastle in front of turret Anton. His messenger, a seaman, was with him. Soon, both men went forward and began climbing a steadily increasing slope. Lindemann's gestures showed that he was urging his companion to go overboard and save himself. The man refused and stayed with his commanding officer until they reached where the jackstaff had been.* Then Lindemann walked out on the starboard side of the stem which, though rising ever higher, was becoming more level as the ship lay over. There he stopped and raised his hand to his white cap.

The *Bismarck* now lay completely on her side. Then, slowly, slowly, she and the saluting Lindemann went down. Who among us knew that at this moment there was being fulfilled the demonically strange youthful yearning of a man who at the age of thirteen had conceived a passion for the navy and had then repeatedly told his brothers and his friends that his "greatest wish" was one day to command his own ship and to go down in her "with colors flying." Later a machinist wrote, "I always thought such things happened only in books, but I saw it with my own eyes." The time was 1039 and the battleship's position was approximately 48° 10′ north and 16° 12′ west.

At 1322 Group West radioed to Lütjens, "Reuter reports *Bismarck* sunk. Report situation immediately." But at the place where such messages had previously been received and answered there was now only empty sea.

The sight of the sinking *Bismarck* and the thought of my many comrades who had gone down with her cut deep into my heart.

It suddenly occurred to me that a Lenbach† portrait of Prince Bismarck had sunk with the ship. It hung where the guard outside the commanding officer's stateroom was posted. Three weeks earlier, when Hitler visited the ship. Lindemann pointed it out to him and was obviously concerned about the possibility of something happening to it during the war. Hitler shook his head. "If anything happens to the ship," he said, "the picture might as well be lost, too." Now it had come to pass.

And another thought came to me. Had the great ship that had just sunk before my eyes borne the name not only of a great statesman, but also of a convinced navalist, a supporter of mighty battleships, such as the *Bismarck* had been? Hardly! To the contrary, as I remembered from what I had learned in school, in Bismarck's day the policy

---

*The jackstaff itself along with the mooring and anchor casing had been shot away during the last battle.

†Franz von Lenbach was the leading German portraitist of the Imperial era.

of the German Empire had been determined by fundamentally Continental concepts; Bismarck had once even referred to the "nearly pathological naval enthusiasm of 1848," and when in 1897 the State Secretary of the Imperial Naval Office, Admiral Alfred von Tirpitz, visited him at Friedrichsruhe, Bismarck had refrained from giving his hoped-for blessing to the great German naval buildup, which was then beginning. He had told Tirpitz that he did not hold with big warships, many small ones were needed instead, and almost angrily rejected the idea that Germany could enhance its alliance value by a strong fleet. No, to the end of his life Bismarck had retained his reservations about the building of a great German battle fleet, true to his earlier idea that in regard to England it would be well, in conjunction with France, to maintain a certain counterweight at sea, but that war with England was never to be desired. A battleship as big as the *Bismarck* or even a bunch of them would certainly not have been his goal. He had declined an invitation that Tirpitz transmitted on the occasion of his visit to Friedrichsruhe to participate in the launching of the armored cruiser *Fürst Bismarck* on grounds of age and health.

For us in the water the scene changed quickly. We found ourselves being continuously swept from one cluster of men to another. In the distance I saw the familiar faces of Kapitänleutnant (W)* Werner Schock, commander of Division 12 and second damage-control officer, and Oberleutnant (Ing) Gerhard Hinz, commander of Division 8 and the ship's technical gunnery officer. I saw them briefly, then they were lost to sight, forever. All of a sudden I found myself next to the ordnanceman from my action station. "Careful, careful," he called out "don't get too close to me, I've lost a foot." "Listen," I replied, "we'll soon be aboard a Briton, and they'll take care of you." Shortly thereafter he, too, disappeared in the swells.

Like toys, we floated on the heaving Atlantic. Only when we topped the crests of waves did we catch glimpses of the horizon. Were there any British ships around? Would they come to our rescue? Although there were none in sight, I was quite sure they would come. Repeatedly, I called to the men near me, "Stay together, as soon as a ship comes we'll swim over and get aboard." It wasn't much encouragement but, I thought, better than none.

Even today, when I think about being out there in the Atlantic, it strikes me as remarkable that I was not conscious of the temperature

*Waffen (gunnery technology)

of the water. It was 13 degrees centigrade. Cool enough. But I was fully dressed, which helped keep me warm. And, still more important, the tension and excitement were such that external circumstances didn't matter. In our helplessness, all we thought about was what's going to happen, what's coming next. The minutes flew past, and the water temperature meant nothing to me.

One thing that was really horrible was the fuel oil from our sunken ship that was floating on the surface of the water in a wide, thick sheet. Its odor stung our noses. It blackened our faces and forced its way into our eyes, noses, and ears. What luck it's not burning, I thought, although I knew that was not much of a danger with heavy oil. My Tissot wristwatch stopped at 1031—salt water and fuel oil, the combination was too much for it. We continued to float in high swells. There were still no British ships to be seen.

When almost an hour had passed, from the crest of a wave I sighted a three-stack cruiser, her ensign stiff in the wind: the *Dorsetshire*. I urged my companions to hold on, "Cheer up, we'll soon be aboard her." The *Dorsetshire* steered for the thickest concentration of survivors and stopped shortly before reaching it. Soon she lay athwart the waves, drifting and rolling rather heavily. I had quite a long way to go to get to her. I told the men in my vicinity to be sure to head for the port, or lee, side of the ship and stay there.

The *Dorsetshire* threw lines over, a few of which had bowlines on the end. Lines and bowlines became so slippery from the oil in which they dangled that it was difficult to handle them, but it was that or nothing. I had a vision of a wide net up which a lot of men could climb at the same time, as they would up ratlines. But it was only a vision. At last, the *Dorsetshire* lowered a rectangular wooden raft (Carley float) for us to hold onto so that we could catch our breath.

Getting up those lines was not easy even for an experienced seaman. Not only were they slippery as eels but, because of the rolling of the ship, they were in the water one second and the next they were too far above our outstretched hands for us to grab. It was quite a trick to catch one at the right moment. Most of the men I saw were technicians, who had probably not had to use lines since they were in basic training, so I advised them to choose those that had bowlines. That, too, was easier said than done. I soon found that there was a limit to what the best-intentioned advice could accomplish. At some points men bunched up, all trying to grasp the same line, while lines nearby were ignored. Feeling that I was strong enough to do so, I decided to wait a while. Then I noticed that certain lines were almost always

Survivors from the *Bismarck* are pulled aboard the *Dorsetshire*. With the admiral's staff, prize crews, and war correspondents, the *Bismarck*'s complement numbered more than 2,200 men. Only 115 were saved. (Photograph from the Imperial War Museum, London.)

free. I called attention to this fact and swam to one with a bowline. I don't remember how many times I was within a few feet of the line for a fraction of a second only to have it jerk far out of reach. I almost gave up, but then I was lucky. Just as the ship was about to roll back up, I got one foot firmly in the bowline, closed both hands round the line, and gave the two British seamen above the signal to hoist. They did, and slowly, slowly, I went up the gray hull, past the portholes— how high can a ship be?—to the upper deck. I reached one hand out to grab the lifeline, intending to hold on to it as I climbed out of the bowline. But my reach was longer than my grasp was strong. One hand was not enough to hold the line, and I fell back into the water. Fortunately, I didn't land on anyone's head, nor did I hurt myself, but it was very disheartening. Had I so greatly overestimated my reserve of strength? I wouldn't wait long before I tried again. After getting my breath I looked for and found another line with a bowline. I glanced up and there were the same two seamen. Unwittingly, I had returned to the same line! They hoisted me up again. This time I kept both hands on the line and said, "Please, pull me on board." They did, and there I was standing on the upper deck, aft of the second port lifeboat, a prisoner of war, in an oil-stained uniform. The first thing I did was take a look over the side at my comrades still in the water. There were hundreds of them, hundreds of yellow life jackets. Perhaps eight hundred, I estimated. It would take a good while to get them all on board. That they would all be saved, I had no doubt, but I was not allowed to stay on deck for long. Others were now the masters of my time. Also, my two rescuers had to carry on with their humanitarian work.

One of them, Tom Wharam, a young telegraphist, obeyed an officer's order to take me below, to the midshipmen's quarters. Little did I know that barely a year later he would be among the survivors of the *Dorsetshire* when she was sunk in the Indian Ocean by Japanese dive-bombers. After the war he became a good friend of mine, in that unique brotherhood that, as he once wrote me, binds men who once fought on opposite sides.

Below I saw some of my shipmates in various stages of undress. They were being given dry, warm clothing. My allotment was the civilian suit of an obviously very large officer.

Stabsobermaschinist Wilhelm Schmidt went over the stern into the water, and found himself surrounded by three or four hundred men. From a distance of 100 meters he watched the *Bismarck* roll over, saw her keel uppermost and air bubbles rising from under her—

then she sank. After he'd been in the water a long time, he spied mast tips on the horizon. They belonged to the *Dorsetshire*, and, together with many others, Schmidt soon found himself on her port side, the lee side. Amidships he found a stout manila line with an eye at the end of it. Some of his companions had already been hoisted up when he succeeded in getting a grip on the line and was pulled up.

Musikmaat Josef Mahlberg was also 100 meters away from the *Bismarck* when she capsized. Just as I did, he looked for signs of torpedo hits or other damage to the starboard side of her hull and saw none.

Maschinenmaat Wilhelm Generotzky, who was standing on the superstructure deck, saw men jumping into the water, among them his best friend. He also saw Luftwaffe sergeants shoot themselves and heard a chief engineer say, "If I had a pistol, I'd do the same thing." Then there were shouts, "She's sinking!" and "Turret Dora's blowing up!" The deck was trying to slide out from under him. He and several others leapt down and went into the water from the starboard side of the upper deck. At almost the same moment that side of the ship rose completely out of the water. The jump must have brought a quick end to many of those men. Generotzky's leap took him to a considerable depth and, as he fought his way to the surface, he kept telling himself, "It'll get light any minute now." When that finally happened, he shot halfway out of the water and sucked precious air into his empty lungs. He saw the *Bismarck* some 100 meters away, floating keel-up. Hissing jets of water escaping from various apertures in her hull were soaring into the air. While he watched, her stern sank, her bow rose, as if in a last farewell, and, with a gurgling sound, the *Bismarck* slid below the waves.

All that was left were the men in the water, hundreds of them, fighting a desperate battle with the elements. Generotzky did not expect to be rescued. He had lost his socks and cold pressed ever deeper into his body. His legs became numb. Floating oil burned his face and hands and forced its repulsive way into his mouth. It took him about forty minutes to reach the *Dorsetshire* and the many lines that had been thrown over. He let himself be lifted up by a wave and grabbed hold of one of the lines. But in the trough of the wave he lost his hold and fell helplessly back into the cold bath. Several other times he tried, in vain. As more and more men reached the ship, a struggle for survival broke out. When two or three men would try to hang on the same line, none of them made it. In the scramble some-one stepped on Generotzky's head and while he was under water a wave threw him against the ship's hull, injuring his leg. Noticing that the British seamen aft were tying eyes in more lines, he floated in that direction, managed to get his foot through one of them, and clamped both hands on the line. Seamen pulled him on board.

The port middle 15-centimeter turret was already a third under water, the upper deck long out of sight. Cardinal and Statz looked at one another, then the lieutenant leaped into the sea. Statz, the pro-crastinator, hesitated until the appropriate moment had passed, let the big oncoming sea surge on and jumped as it subsided. Cardinal was swept away on the crest of a wave and when they were washed together again Statz saw that Cardinal's head was hanging slackly. The lieutenant had carried a pistol with him and used it on himself on the wave crest.

Statz now drifted parallel to the ship in the direction of her stern and was lucky not to be thrown back aboard by the sea. He saw the *Bismarck*'s heavy list and was barely past the ship before she rolled over. The entire starboard hull now lay before his eyes; unbelievable as it seemed, he could not detect the least damage, and not on the port side either, part of which he could see. Despite his nearness to the ship, he did not feel any suction and had no difficulty moving away from her. The *Bismarck* now lay keel upwards, her propellers still turning slowly and steadily; then she sank by the stern.

Now Statz was completely alone in the water; he did not even notice the cold, but the oil floating on the surface gave him trouble. For the first time, he noticed how good it was that he had kept on his leather clothes. The air pockets inside them, especially in the arms and knees, supported him wonderfully well, taking over the job of his life jacket, which had been completely shredded by shell splinters. Unfortunately, many others had not obeyed the ship's standing order, "Don't undress!"

Suddenly, Statz saw a ship coming towards him, very close, so that he had to swim hard to keep from being run over. In the end, he reached her starboard side. On the jack he saw an oversize British flag, on the upper deck men with steel helmets running back and forth, and recognized that this was the same cruiser he had last seen from the *Bismarck*'s bridge deck with all guns blazing. "Captivity," he thought, "my new lot," remembering a newsreel he had seen not long before of German soldiers in British captivity, wearing British

The *Bismarck* survivors in the water, as seen from the British cruiser *Dorsetshire*. Josef Statz declared that "this picture shows the view from the upper deck of the *Dorsetshire* as it will always remain in my memory." A total of 85 survivors were picked up by the *Dorsetshire* and 25 more by the British destroyer *Maori*. There had been 2,221 men embarked in the *Bismarck*. (Photograph courtesy of Josef Statz.)

uniforms with a colored square on the back. "We're not very well instructed about being prisoners of war," he reflected.

In the meanwhile, comrades had come swimming up from all directions. As Statz later determined, they had all gone overboard at the last moment; those who had jumped prematurely were carried hopelessly out of reach of the British rescue effort. Now Statz discovered lines hanging from the ship, with British seamen standing on deck ready to haul them up, and was urged on by the redeeming hope of finally being saved. But first came the struggle to get a hold on the oil-soaked, slippery rope-work—impossible to find it, his hands slipped off again and again. After definite eye contact with one of the rescuers, the latter threw him a rope ladder. Statz grasped it, held it in an iron grip, and was pulled up to the upper deck of the *Dorsetshire*. A last glance at the ocean showed him that there were still many swimmers in the water. "How easily Cardinal could be standing here beside me," he thought, "if he hadn't . . ."

Throughout the action Fähnrich (B) Hans-Georg Stiegler had performed his duties with two men inspecting the electrical cable circuits below deck on the starboard side aft. He and his men soon learned to distinguish between the recoil from the ship's guns (lateral shock), the impact of enemy shells (shock from above), and torpedo hits (shock from below). He had not seen an extreme situation in the course of the action; his equipment had been working perfectly and panic was nowhere evident before the order came to "Abandon ship!" He encountered a crowd of men for the first time on the main deck. Afterwards he could not say exactly which way he had taken to reach the starboard upper deck.

Above him Stiegler saw a burning launch; the smoke blocked his view and his way forward. Then the ship began to heel more and more to port. He observed some confusion among the men, kept them from jumping overboard too soon, and at a suitable moment slid down the starboard side of the ship's hull more-or-less amidships with them and entered the water without injury. He saw many heads in the heavy ocean swells, a lieutenant commander drifted past, then he took off his shoes—why, really?—with the unpleasant result that his legs bobbed up and he was left in an unsteady state for swimming. Not long thereafter, it seemed to him, the bow of the *Dorsetshire* appeared. He grasped the end of one of the ropes hanging from her and let himself be hauled up, but lost his strength and hold, and fell back into the sea. He tried again, winding the rope tightly around his thigh, held on desperately, and this time it worked; his rescuer hoisted him aboard.

Maschinenobergefreiter Hans Springborn saw many men dive overboard headfirst, hit the bilge keel, and fall into the water with broken necks. He wasn't going to let that happen to him, so he slid down the hull from the upper deck to the bilge keel and jumped into the water from there. When the *Bismarck* rolled over on her side, strong currents pulled him under and he was violently whirled around before he managed to regain the surface. That experience told him to get away from the ship as fast as he could.

After some time he saw the British destroyer *Maori* and had the luck to drift over to her. After several tries he got hold of a line, and was hoisted to safety by two seamen.

35

Survival

I was still changing my clothes when the *Dorsetshire* suddenly began to vibrate violently. What was happening? Was she leaving the area, and at a full power? Now, in the midst of the rescue? Was there some sudden danger? From what? There weren't any U-boats around, as we knew all too well. Only that morning, we had asked for one to pick up the War Diary and none had appeared. That was a sure sign that there were no U-boats in the vicinity. Also, neither during the night nor at dawn had any boat come to the aid of the *Bismarck*. No rumor even of any intended U-boat action had reached me in my after station. It couldn't be a U-boat that had caused this precipitate withdrawal. What could have? German planes? If that was it, the aircraft alarm would have been sounded. I racked my brain, but the only thing that registered was horror that our men in the water, hundreds of them, before whose eyes the *Dorsetshire* was moving away, were being sentenced to death just when safety seemed within reach. My God, what a narrow escape I had. There was nothing that I, a prisoner of war, could do.

After a while, we survivors were led to the wardroom, where we sat around a big table and were given hot tea. We were still numb and not very talkative, but the tea helped. When we had finished, Kapitän-leutnant (Ing) Junack, Fähnrich (B) Hans-Georg Stiegler, Nautischer Assistent* Lothar Balzer, and I—just four of the *Bismarck*'s ninety

*Nautical Assistant

officers—were taken aft to our allotted quarters. The eighty-one petty officers and men were taken forward.

That afternoon we rested. I lay on my bunk in a strange state between sleep and wakefulness. I could not take in all the terrible things that had happened in the last few hours. Did they really happen? Somehow, my mind rejected the thought; no one could have survived that devastating storm of steel. So many good men had been lost. Why they and not I? I knew only that God had heard me on the upper deck of the *Bismarck*.

As the senior-ranking survivor on board, I received the next morning a handwritten note from Captain B. C. S. Martin, the commanding officer of the *Dorsetshire*:

> I will be glad if you will visit your men this morning with my commander and then come to the bridge with him to see me.
>
> If there is anything you require for your personal needs please let me know.
>
> I hope you slept well and feel none the worse for your swim.

Escorted by the First Officer, Commander C. W. Byas, I went to see how our men were getting along. Everything was satisfactory; the ship's surgeon was taking care of the sick and injured, and they all felt they were being treated very well. They were getting five meals a day and eating the same excellent food as the crew. The smokers among them were being issued twenty cigarettes a day. I learned later that it was no different in the *Maori*, which picked up twenty-five men, bringing the number rescued by British ships to 110, about 5 percent of the more than 2,200 on board.

When Byas took me to the bridge, Captain Martin greeted me in a friendly enough manner and gave me a Scotch. The gesture was well meant but I was still too horrified at his leaving all those men in the water the day before to really appreciate it. "Why," I burst out, "did you suddenly break off the rescue and leave hundreds of our men to drown?" Martin replied that a U-boat had been sighted or at least reported, and he obviously could not endanger his ship by staying stopped any longer. The *Bismarck*'s experiences on the night of 26 May and the morning of the 27th, I told him, indicated that there were no U-boats in the vicinity. Farther away, perhaps, but certainly not within firing range of the *Dorsetshire*. I added that in war one often sees what one expects to see. And so we heaped our arguments against one another, uncompromisingly, beyond any possibility of agreement. Martin brought our discussion brusquely to a close with the words: "Just leave that to me. I'm older than you are and have been at sea longer. I'm a better judge." What more could I say? He was the captain and was responsible for his ship.*

Apparently some floating object had been mistaken for a periscope or a strip of foam on the water for the wake of a torpedo. No matter what it was, I am now convinced that, under the circumstances, Martin had to act as he did.†

At 1100 on 27 May Churchill informed the House of Commons of the final action against the *Bismarck*. "This morning," he said, "shortly after daylight the *Bismarck*, virtually at a standstill, far from

---

*In the first edition of his *Schlachtschiff Bismarck*, Brennecke writes on page 392: "In this connection [the *Dorsetshire*'s departure from the rescue scene], we have learned that it was one of the German survivors who, on the basis of his knowledge of the last radio signals, warned the British cruiser's captain of German U-boats. Did he do this out of nervousness? Out of fear? Or was it his intention to leave the rescue of the rest of the survivors to German U-boats?"

In his fourth edition, instead of saying "one of the German survivors" warned the captain of the *Dorsetshire*, Brennecke says "one of the ranking survivors," to which statement he attaches note 361a, "It was not the now-retired Kapitän zur See Junack." I cannot imagine to what radio signals he refers. Furthermore, when we got aboard the *Dorsetshire*, none of us could have warned the captain, who was high up on the bridge, about anything. Upon coming on board, every survivor was immediately taken below. That applied to me also and, as I have recounted, I did not see Captain Martin until the morning of 28 May, twenty-four hours after the rescue operation. My repeated requests for documentation on the alleged warning have not been answered by Herr Brennecke. Needless to say, I flatly reject the insinuation that, since "it was not Kapitän Junack," it could have been I, the senior-ranking survivor.

Captain Martin's official report leaves no doubt as to who warned him: "When about 80 survivors had been picked up and I was on the port wing of the bridge directing operations in that vicinity, I received a report from LtCdr. Durant that a suspicious smoking discharge was seen to starboard, or leeward beam about two miles away. I went to the compass platform and saw this myself. It appeared to me that it could have been caused by a submarine, and in view of this and other indications that enemy aircraft and submarines were most likely operating at the scene of the action I was reluctantly compelled to leave some hundreds of the enemy personnel to their fate."

†The presence of a U-boat in range to attack the *Dorsetshire* at around noon on 27 May has never been proved. I did not know it at the time, but the *U-556* (Wohlfarth) and the *U-74* (Kentrat) may have been *relatively* near the *Bismarck*. However, Wohlfarth, who did not see even the *Bismarck* on 26 or 27 May, wrote me in February 1978, "I don't believe that a German U-boat was in the vicinity of the *Dorsetshire*, for, as all the boats [those in the ocean area around the *Bismarck*] were on the way home, it would have been reported somehow and be known today." Kentrat, having received the radio order, "Search for survivors, the sinking of the *Bismarck* is to be expected," spent the whole day in a fruitless search.

H.M.S. DORSETSHIRE.

28/5.

Dear Von Mullenheim,

I will be glad if you will visit your men This morning with my commander and Then Come To The bridge with him to See me.

If There is any Thing you require for your personal needs please let me Know.

I hope you Slept well and feel none The worse for your swim.

Yours Sincerely

B. Martin.

help, was attacked by the British pursuing battleships. I do not know what were the results of the bombardment. It appears, however, that the *Bismarck* was not sunk by gunfire, and she will now be dispatched by torpedo. It is thought that this is now proceeding, and it is also thought that there cannot be any lengthy delay in disposing of this vessel. Great as is our loss in the *Hood*, the *Bismarck* must be regarded as the most powerful, as she is the newest, battleship in the world." Scarcely had Churchill sat down when a note was passed to him. He rose again and announced to the members that the *Bismarck* had been sunk. "They seemed content," he wrote.*

A day later he telegraphed Roosevelt: "I will send you later the inside story of the fighting with the *Bismarck*. She was a terrific ship, and a masterpiece of naval construction. Her removal eases our battleship situation, as we should have had to keep *King George V*, *Prince of Wales*, and the two *Nelsons* practically tied to Scapa Flow to guard against a sortie of *Bismarck* and *Tirpitz*, as they could choose their moment and we should have to allow for one of our ships refitting. Now it is a different story."†

After my talk with Captain Martin I remained on the bridge of the *Dorsetshire* for a while.‡ When I asked if I could see the chart in the navigation room, permission was readily granted. Alone with my thoughts, I gazed for a moment at the mark showing where the *Bismarck* had gone down. Then I asked and was given Martin's permission to visit our men in their quarters once every day and to concern myself with their wishes.

As Fähnrich (B) Stiegler later expressed it, after coming on board he had "for the first time stood defenseless in the presence of the enemy." His thoughts were difficult to describe but were "different from those of his comrades, for, in contrast to them, he had already seen action in the Polish campaign." After he was led below, the British must have noticed his Fähnrich's piping, for a doctor whose

---

*Winston Churchill, *The Second World War*, Vol. III, p. 283.

†Winston Churchill, *The Second World War*, Vol. III, p. 286.

‡Russell Grenfell, *The Bismarck Episode*, mentions in a footnote on page 180 that a survivor is alleged to have told Captain Martin that it was a shell from the *Dorsetshire* that disabled the *Bismarck*'s fire-control station. He supposes that the survivor did this because he wanted to ingratiate himself with his captor. Grenfell is referring to me, but how this theory could have arisen is a mystery to me. I did not even know that the *Dorsetshire* was present. A shell that came in shortly after 0910 left my station blind. Therefore, I could not have said anything to Captain Martin about it.

words the other survivors could not understand came to him. The German seamen called out, "Herr Fähnrich, they want to poison us with their injections. But we're delighted to be saved and would like only a cigarette." Stiegler played the interpreter and some of the men accepted the sedative injections. Then Stiegler grew weak. Soon he found himself back in an officer's cabin, where he could bathe and sleep, and was given dry, warm clothes. He received his first meal from the ship's midshipmen's mess. Later, Captain Martin called him to the bridge. "What is the story on the dummy second stack you had?" he asked. But Stiegler could answer, "with a clear conscience," that he had heard about it on board but had never seen it. He had performed his duty below deck and had not come on the upper deck until after the end of the action on 27 May.

"Why did you have to leave so many of our seamen behind?" Statz asked his interrogating officer shortly after coming on board the *Dorsetshire*. The latter replied, "Just be happy that you were rescued, we've picked up enough for interrogation." Statz felt that "this interrogation officer was no seaman." The British seamen had helped him undress and had brought him to a compartment in which several of his comrades were lying, covered with blankets. But then they had turned him out again, carefully, and signaled for him to come with them—Statz had no idea why—into the sick bay. They had noticed his wound and helped him onto the operating table, where the cut in his shoulder was sewn up.

Among the survivors was Maschinengefreiter Gerhard Lüttich. He had lost an arm and was so badly burned that none of us could understand how he managed to get aboard. He was being cared for in the ship's sick bay, but he died on 28 May. The following day the ship's chaplain officiated at the military rites accorded him and, after the firing of three salvos by an honor guard, his body was solemnly committed to the deep. In the late sixties, when I was consul general of the Federal Republic of Germany in Toronto, an extraordinary thing happened. I was approached at a social gathering by Philip Mathias, assistant editor of the *Financial Post*. Conveying friendly greetings from his father, Arthur, who, as master-at-arms in the *Dorsetshire*, was in charge of the prisoners of war, he handed me the identity tag that Arthur Mathias had removed from Lüttich's dead body.

While the *Dorsetshire* and the *Maori* were steaming north, far to the south of us a dinghy was floating in the Atlantic. Its occupants were three seamen, Herbert Manthey, Otto Höntzch, and Georg Herzog, who, towards the end of the firing, took cover behind turret Dora. Nearby they saw a rubber dinghy and, with the help of shipmates, dragged it behind the turret. Soon thereafter, as they stated later, they and the dinghy were washed overboard by the splash of a near miss. Although the dinghy floated away from them, they were able to reach it in about fifteen minutes and climb in. Very close by they saw a rubber raft with two men on it, one of them wounded, but they could not bring their drifting dinghy alongside and it was soon lost to sight. About the time the sun reached its zenith, they sighted a Focke-Wulf 200 Condor and tried to attract its attention by waving at it. Exhausted as they were, their hope of being rescued sank lower and lower as the day wore on until, around 1930, they became aware that there was a U-boat nearby.

As already recounted, Kapitänleutnant Kentrat in the *U-74* was alerted on the evening of 26 May to go to the assistance of the *Bismarck*. Between 0000 and 0400 the next day, he saw gunfire and star shells on the horizon. He tried to approach the *Bismarck* but, with a freshening wind and rising seas, it was very difficult for him to make any headway and waves constantly washing over his bridge made it virtually impossible for him to see what was going on. Around 0430, however, on the opposite side of the *Bismarck*, he saw the end-on silhouette of what he took to be a heavy cruiser or a battleship at a range of approximately 10,000 meters. He turned towards it, but visibility was so poor that he promptly lost sight of it. In his War Diary, he remarked: "It's an abominable night. No torpedo could run through these swells."

At about the same time as he sighted the silhouette, he heard three explosions, one of them particularly loud. Some two hours later, he made visual contact with Wohlfarth's *U-556* and, as we already know, Wohlfarth transferred to him the mission of maintaining contact with the *Bismarck*. Around 0730, a cruiser and a destroyer suddenly emerged from a rain squall directly ahead of him at a range of 5,000 meters and he was forced to submerge. From 0900 on, Kentrat heard one explosion after another, but when he surfaced at 0922 there was nothing to be seen. At first, he assumed that what he was hearing was the scheduled Luftwaffe bomber attack. However, he wrote in his War Diary, "It must have been the *Bismarck*'s last battle."

For 1200, the *U-74*'s War Diary contains the entry, "The pick-up of the *Bismarck*'s War Diary could not be carried out." Thereafter, in accordance with a radio directive from Commander in Chief, U-Boats, Kentrat began looking for survivors from the *Bismarck*. After about seven hours of searching, the *U-74* sighted three men in a rubber dinghy. With considerable difficulty because of high seas, Kentrat took them aboard. Scarcely had Herzog, Höntzsch, and Manthey gone down the hatch of the conning tower when an aircraft was seen to starboard. Kentrat waited until it had disappeared astern, before resuming his search. His objective was the spot where the *Bismarck* had gone down and, in order to be there at dawn on 28 May, he maintained a northerly course and traveled at low speed.

At about 0100 Kentrat's men became aware of a strong smell of oil, and a couple of hours later the watch officer saw a red star below the horizon to the southeast. In the War Diary, Kentrat noted: "I was so exhausted I did not take in this report. A pity, perhaps we could still have saved a few comrades." The *U-48* and the *U-73* joined the *U-74* to form a line of search but, other than oil fumes in the air, they found no trace of the *Bismarck*'s sinking. Kentrat thought he had missed the position where she sank. In the afternoon, however, he saw floating corpses and debris. He kept up his search for survivors until 2400, then headed for Lorient. His War Diary entry for 2400 on 28 May states:

> The weather has abated, the seas are getting progressively calmer. As though nature were content with her work of destruction.
> The 27 and 28 May will always be bitter memories for me. There we were, powerless, our hands tied, against the unleashed forces of nature. We could not help our brave *Bismarck*.

At Lorient, representatives of Group West awaited Herzog, Höntzsch, and Manthey. They were taken to Paris and there gave the first eyewitness account of the end of the *Bismarck*.

While the *U-74* was looking for survivors, the German weather ship *Sachsenwald* was doing the same thing to the south of her. On 27 May this ship, under the command of Leutnant zur See (S)* Wilhelm Schütte, was en route home after fifty days at sea. At 0200 that day she received a radio signal ordering her to proceed immediately to the *Bismarck*'s position. That meant steaming directly into the seas against a north–northwest wind of Force 6 or 7. At 0600, she was

---

*The "S" stood for Sonderführer, which signified an officer assigned to specialist duties.

ordered to stay where she was. Between 1100 and 1200 she sighted German planes and shortly after 1400 an order came to steer for another position. The weather was deteriorating. At 2010 a Bristol Blenheim that suddenly appeared to starboard fired at the *Sachsenwald* with her machine guns at a range of 11,000 meters, but did not hit her.

Schütte spent the morning of 28 May in a fruitless search for survivors. Around 1300 he picked up some thin streaks of oil and followed them to the north. Before long the lead case of a German gas mask was seen on the water and, minutes later, numerous corpses in life jackets, empty life jackets, and wreckage came into view. The *Sachsenwald* cruised back and forth through the debris, but saw nobody. After darkness fell, around 2230, three red flares suddenly shot up into the sky nearby. The *Sachsenwald* turned towards them and, through his night glasses, Schütte made out a rubber raft with two men on board. When he was close enough, he yelled, "Are you German?" and got the resounding reply, "Ja, hurrah!" By 2245 the ship and the raft were alongside one another and two exhausted men were hauled up a Jacob's ladder. They were Matrosengefreiter Otto Maus and Maschinengefreiter Walter Lorenzen.

The men told Schütte that there was another raft in the vicinity, so he searched the area throughout the twenty-ninth. He made wide swings to the east and west, every turn taking him five nautical miles to the south, following the wind and seas. An empty rubber dinghy that Maus recognized as belonging to the *Bismarck* was taken on board that evening.

Around 0100 on 30 May Schütte, still in the search area, saw the *Canarias*, the Spanish cruiser that Group West had asked to go to the *Bismarck*'s assistance, and the two ships exchanged recognition signals. Immediately thereafter Schütte, his provisions almost spent and his search being unproductive, headed for home. When, on 1 June, the *Sachsenwald* entered the Gironde, Maus and Lorenzen disembarked and were taken to Paris where they reported to Group West.

After her encounter with the *Sachsenwald*, the *Canarias* picked up two dead bodies which, through their tags and uniforms, were identified as Musikgefreiter* Walter Grasczak and Marinesignalgast† Heinrich Neuschwander. At 1000 the next day, covered with the Ger-

---

*Seaman Apprentice (Bandsman)
†Signalman

man flag and accorded full military honors, both bodies were buried at 43° 46' north and 08° 34' west.

The time in the *Dorsetshire* passed quickly and on our fourth day, 30 May, she arrived at Newcastle. The *Maori* had separated from her at sea and gone into the Clyde.

The last time I talked with Commander Byas, he warned me that the army, which would take us into custody at Newcastle, would not treat us as well as the *Dorsetshire* had. Naturally, he was right. From many peacetime associations, I was aware of the bond between our two navies. Although we were then at war, this feeling came to the surface under certain circumstances. The fight that the *Bismarck* put up to the bitter end earned the admiration of British seamen, which probably accounts for the good accommodations we were given and the way we were treated on board ship. The fact that Captain Martin was well treated as a prisoner of war in Germany in World War One may also have had something to do with this. When he made his rounds among our men he always told them, "As long as you are here with me, you'll have it just as good." And the attitude of his crew was the same. The British seamen were always pleasant and helpful. "You today, us tomorrow," they said. Their tomorrow was not long in coming. On 4 April 1942 the *Dorsetshire*, under a new commanding officer, Captain A. W. S. Agar, was sunk by Japanese bombs southeast of Ceylon.

On the morning of 31 May, the petty officers and men were the first to disembark. We officers followed and were piped over the side as the ship's watch presented arms, a ceremony usually reserved for peacetime.

Our journey to the prisoner-of-war camps had begun.

36

Exercise Rhine in Retrospect

The battleship *Bismarck* owes her place in naval history primarily to the gunnery actions in which she engaged on 24 and 27 May 1941.

On 24 May she demonstrated her exceptional striking power. At an average range of 16,000 meters, it took her only six minutes and the expenditure of only ninety-three heavy shells to sink the largest and most famous British battle cruiser of the day. This lightning success exceeded the most sanguine expectations and showed the *Bismarck* to represent a high point in German naval gunnery.

On 27 May the *Bismarck* displayed an almost unbelievable staying power. She was also a high point in German shipbuilding. It required the collective efforts of a British fleet of five battleships, three battle cruisers, two aircraft carriers, four heavy and seven light cruisers, and twenty-one destroyers to find and destroy her. In addition, more than fifty aircraft of the RAF's Coastal Command participated in her destruction.

At ranges that diminished to 2,500 meters and brought a proportionately high rate of hits, the following ordnance was fired at the *Bismarck* after the action off Iceland:

Shells
380 40.6-centimeter (16-inch), *Rodney*, 27 May
716 15.2-centimeter (6-inch), *Rodney*, 27 May
339 35.6-centimeter (14-inch), *King George V*, 27 May
660 13.3-centimeter (5.25-inch), *King George V*, 27 May

527 20.3-centimeter (8-inch), *Norfolk*, 27 May
254 20.3-centimeter (8-inch), *Dorsetshire*, 27 May

A total, therefore, of 2,876 shells in the course of an action that lasted ninety minutes.

Torpedoes
8, aircraft from the *Victorious*, 1 hit, 24–25 May
13, aircraft from the *Ark Royal*, 2 hits and possibly a third, 26 May
3, *Cossack*, no hits, 0140, 27 May
1, *Cossack*, no hit, 0335, 27 May
2, *Maori*, no hits, 0137, 27 May
2, *Maori*, no hits, 0656, 27 May
4, *Zulu*, no hits, 0121, 27 May
4, *Sikh*, no hits, 0128, 27 May
12, *Rodney*, 1 hit claimed, 27 May
8, *Norfolk*, 1 possible hit, 27 May
3, *Dorsetshire*, 2 hits and possibly a third, 27 May

On 27 May there were a few penetrations of the 320-millimeter main belt, particularly near the port forward 15-centimeter turret. The latter, according to Josef Statz, started a fire in its magazine. Because of the range of the action many of the shells struck the *Bismarck* in her superstructure. As the *King George V* and *Rodney* left the scene of the action, Tovey signaled Somerville, "Cannot get her to sink with guns."

There has been a great deal of discussion as to whether the *Bismarck* sank as a result of the three torpedoes fired by the *Dorsetshire* in the concluding phase of the action or whether she was scuttled. Although I was still on board when the *Dorsetshire* fired her first two torpedoes, around 1020, I was not aware of the explosions they produced. That fact, however, has no bearing on the question of what damage, if any, they did. I certainly was aware as I left the after fire-control station at about 1020, that the *Bismarck* was very, very slowly sinking. Heavily down by her stern, she was behaving as though one compartment after the other was flooding, gradually but irresistibly. She showed all the effects to be expected after the scuttling charges had been fired and the seacocks opened somewhere about 1000. The settling, the sinking by the stern, and the heel to port increased more rapidly after 1030, so it may be that, with the battleship already extremely unstable, the *Dorsetshire*'s third torpedo hastened her end, but it was not responsible for it. I am morally certain that the *Bismarck* would have sunk without this torpedo hit, only perhaps somewhat more slowly.*

In his final report on Exercise Rhine, Tovey wrote: "She [the *Bismarck*] put up a most gallant fight against impossible odds, worthy of the old days of the Imperial German Navy, and she went down with her colours flying."

How effective was German gunnery, at least at the beginning of the *Bismarck's* last battle? "No casualties or damage to any of our ships during the action on 27 May," wrote Tovey in the above-mentioned report. This outcome may seem surprising in view of Schneider's incredibly accurate straddling fire in the first few minutes of the action, between 0850 and 0900. But it must be remembered that the crippled *Bismarck* could not steer a straight course. She kept on heeling to port and turning unpredictably, whereas the *Rodney*, being maneuverable, could take action to avoid the *Bismarck's* registering salvos while the latter was adjusting her fire. And then at 0902, less than fifteen minutes after we opened fire, Schneider's control station in the foretop and our two forward main turrets, Anton and Bruno, were put out of action. Apparently, Albrecht's forward fire-control station was also put out of action, at least temporarily, at about the same time. This meant that we had been in the fight only a quarter of an hour when two of our four main batteries and, with the foretop, the "brain" of our gunnery were knocked out. The *Bismarck's* main fire-control station was not well enough protected, a defect common to foretop control stations on all battleships of the time: in the interest of stability, heavy armor could not be installed at that height.

After 0910 I was able to fire only four salvos from the after turrets, Caesar and Dora, before my own control station was put out of action. That happened just as I had registered on my target, the *King George V.* Thereafter Caesar and Dora went on firing under local control, lay well on target, but without the help of a fire-control apparatus could not score any hits.

*Patrick Beesly, *Very Special Intelligence*, says in a note on page 85: "There seems little doubt that scuttling charges were fired but whether they actually caused *Bismarck* to sink is doubtful. It would have been a remarkable coincidence if they [the charges] had taken effect at exactly the same moment as *Dorsetshire's* torpedoes." I do not see that any meaningful coincidence would have been involved even if steps to scuttle the ship had been taken at the same moment the *Dorsetshire's* torpedoes arrived. After all, the scuttling actions did not produce instantaneous results, and by the time the torpedoes arrived, some twenty minutes later, the *Bismarck* was irretrievably sinking.

There is no doubt that the *Bismarck* had an outstanding gunnery system, and it was very efficiently directed by Schneider and Albrecht. But, because of the number of ships she was up against, their threefold superiority in weight of shells, and the constantly closing range, the decisive blows she suffered were delivered quickly and almost simultaneously.

To be sure, Tovey's formulation "no damage to our ships" hid the fact that the *Rodney* suffered not inconsiderable damage from her own fire. The blast pressure from her 40.6-centimeter guns, which were at maximum depression for the concluding portion of the cannonade, severely damaged deck structures and several guns jumped their cradles. Her guns were depressed to maximum depression at times because the ship's command wished to score hits at or below the *Bismarck's* waterline (these experiences soon led to improvements in the construction of British battleships). A further indication of the condition of the *Rodney* after the battle reached me through a U.S. citizen, George C. Seybolt, who wrote to me in July 1982. As a lieutenant (junior grade), USNR, Seybolt was assigned in 1943 to the Intelligence Volunteer Special Service in London, where he heard that as a result of her sustained firing of full salvos, the *Rodney* was badly racked and even her keel had been driven out of alignment. It was understood that either the *Rodney* was not designed to fire broadsides or had failed under that punishment. As Seybolt's statement has never been confirmed by another source, however, I am inclined to regard it with considerable doubt. In any case, in June 1941 the *Rodney* entered the U.S. Navy yard in Boston, Massachusetts, for an overhaul and repairs. Her arrival there was observed by a then sixteen-year-old American, John Love, who wrote to me in 1983 that, although apparently the ship had not sustained a direct hit, she showed what appeared to him to be battle damage on her starboard side, presumably from the blast of her guns firing at full depression.

If any questions remain on our troubled conscience, it is the reason why Lütjens did not attempt to end the terrible and ultimately futile slaughter of the final battle by signaling Tovey, Cease fire, the *Bismarck* is scuttling herself, save our survivors. How Tovey would have reacted, I must leave open. To understand the conduct of a German warship captain or task force commander in battle it is necessary to recall the edict issued by Raeder on 22 December 1939 in reaction to the scuttling of the battle-damaged pocket battleship *Admiral Graf Spee* off Montevideo. This read in part: "A German warship will fight with utmost force until she is victorious or goes down with colors flying." Such wording virtually precluded showing the white flag, as the light cruiser *Emden* had done at the end of her engagement with the Australian cruiser *Sydney* in November 1914 without diminishing her historical renown. And it was wording to which Lütjen's signal of 2140 on 26 May corresponded almost exactly. In principle, Raeder's directive was as binding as it reads, but, in the final analysis, whether or not it was carried out to the letter depended upon the personality of the on-scene commander. I incline to the assumption that Lütjens was not the man to rise above it, but I cannot and will not say so for certain. In the absence of information about the exact time that the fleet commander was killed or possibly wounded, I do not know whether he was physically in condition to have contributed to ending the battle in this manner. Furthermore, if the fleet commander was incapacitated, I do not know how quickly Lindemann learned of it so that he could take over. Viewed as a whole, too many aspects of this complex question remain factually unclear, so I must let it pass.

The enemy's detection of the beginning of Exercise Rhine and his almost continuous contact with our task force thereafter resulted in all our encounters being with heavy British warships, in the *Bismarck*'s spectacular sea fights, her lightning victory over the *Hood* on 24 May, and her lonely, tormented death on 27 May. Given the drama of what took place, it is easy to lose sight of the fact that the destruction of enemy warships was not the primary aim of German surface forces in the Atlantic, and that, viewed strategically, Exercise Rhine was a failure from the moment we left Norway. The *Bismarck* did not even come close on one single occasion to carrying out her principal mission of commerce warfare.

It is worth taking a look at the overall risk the Seekriegsleitung took in sending the *Bismarck* out and the individual risks Lütjens took in the course of the operation.

Concerning the former, the best source is the highest professional witness, Grossadmiral Raeder, commander in chief of the Kriegsmarine, who wrote:

> Whether or not to send the *Bismarck* out presented me with an extraordinarily difficult decision. Some of the conditions on which the Seekriegsleitung based its original thinking on the subject no longer pertained. The sortie of the *Bismarck* was to have been part of a broad operational plan, but now, if she went out, it would be an individual undertaking and there was the possibility that the enemy would concentrate all his forces against her. That seriously increased the risk. On

the other hand, the military situation was such that we could not afford simply to conserve such a powerful combatant. Postponing the operation until the *Scharnhorst* and *Gneisenau* were again ready for sea, might mean that we would never be able to use the new battleships for offensive operations in the Atlantic. It was almost impossible to predict when the *Scharnhorst* and *Gneisenau*, which were in port in northern France and constantly exposed to attacks by the Royal Air Force, would be combat-ready. In fact, neither ship got to sea until they both escaped in February 1942. Postponing the operation still further, until the *Tirpitz* was operational, would result in at least half a year of inactivity—a period during which the enemy would not be inactive and the situation in the Atlantic would probably deteriorate because of the attitude of the United States, if for no other reason.

An extremely strong psychological ground for my decision was the confidence I had in the leadership of Admiral Lütjens, an officer who understood sea warfare and its tactics inside and out. Even as a young officer in the First World War he commanded a half-flotilla of torpedo boats off Flanders. He later became a flotilla chief, cruiser commander, and Commander in Chief, Torpedo Boats, and was for a long time engaged in staff work. It was when he served as my chief of personnel that he won my special confidence. At one time during the Norwegian campaign he replaced the ailing Fleet Commander in command of the heavy striking forces, and finally demonstrated his great ability during the Atlantic sortie of the *Scharnhorst* and *Gneisenau*.

The decision to give the final order to execute the operation was made very much more difficult for me by Hitler's attitude. When I informed him of my plans, he did not reject them, but it was evident that he was not in complete agreement with them. However, he left the decision up to me. At the beginning of May he had a long conversation in Gotenhafen with Admiral Lütjens, who described his experiences during the Atlantic cruises of the *Scharnhorst* and *Gneisenau* and explained his intentions regarding the tactical deployment of the *Bismarck*. The Fleet Commander also pointed out that enemy aircraft carriers could be a serious danger for the battleship.

After carefully weighing all the circumstances, I gave the order to execute.*

It was undoubtedly his awareness that the risks would be far greater if the *Bismarck* were sent out alone that led Lütjens to express certain reservations to Raeder in Berlin on 26 April. At that time he suggested that it might be better to postpone the operation until the *Scharnhorst* had been restored to combat-readiness or even until the

---

*Erich Raeder, *Mein Leben*, Vol. II, p. 266 ff.

Tirpitz was operational. Granted, he reverted on his own to the original idea of Exercise Rhine, that the sortie of the *Bismarck* and *Prinz Eugen* should not be delayed. Both of his immediate predecessors as Fleet Commander were relieved of that command because of disgreements with the Seekriegsleitung.* So I think his desire to be in accord with Raeder and the Seekriegsleitung was responsible for his reversal because that was so very obviously what they were striving for. As I interpret Lütjens's conduct, he was going against his better judgment in agreeing to immediate "teaspoon" deployment of our battleships, which could only diminish their chances of accomplishing anything in the Atlantic. Later, the British saw it just as he had. Russell Grenfell wrote: "But happily for us, the Germans decided to expend their capital ships in penny packets."†

Reader continued: "I bear responsibility for the deployment of the newest German battleship, just as I do for all naval deployments made during my time as commander in chief of the Kriegsmarine. I alone bear it. No one forced me to carry out the operation. My decision was based solely on the necessity to fight the enemy in war with every available means and according to all the rules of the military art, and that entails committing one's own forces." To be sure, Raeder had not drawn a personal lesson from this so keenly felt responsibility.

In chronological order, the risks that Lütjens accepted or could not avoid are detailed below.

At the end of April 1941 British intelligence learned that the *Bismarck* had requested Fleet Headquarters to forward charts—not available in Gotenhafen—for the prize crews she carried. This news strengthened the suspicion that the *Bismarck* was about to undertake an operation in the Atlantic.

British intelligence obtained this information by decoding the radio signal by which the *Bismarck* requested the charts. It had recently gained the ability to do so when, during a raid on the Lofoten Islands, the British disabled and captured the German armed steam trawler *Krebs*, aboard which was a German Enigma cipher machine and supporting material. As a result, British intelligence was able to decode a number of previously intercepted German signals, including this one.

*Jochen Brennecke, *Schlachtschiff Bismarck*, p. 15.
†Russell Grenfell, *The Bismarck Episode*, p. 196.

The transmission of an Enigma-encoded radio signal from a ship at sea was a normal occurrence. That in this case, owing to the capture of the *Krebs*'s code material, the British could read the signal requesting the charts was an exceptionally unfortunate development which Lütjens could hardly have anticipated. Therefore he could not avert the risks it involved.

In the second week of May 1941 the British noticed a significant increase in German aerial reconnaissance over Scapa Flow and as far west as the Denmark Strait. They also deduced from a few Luftwaffe radio signals that they decoded that a breakout by the *Bismarck* was imminent. Admiral Tovey directed the cruisers *Suffolk* and *Norfolk* to conduct intensive surveillance of the Denmark Strait.

This was an unavoidable risk, and the Seekriegsleitung had to live with it unless it was prepared to give up the idea of breaking out into the Atlantic. Lütjens must have been aware that our intensified aerial reconnaissance would not go unnoticed by the British, who therefore had some warning.

The Seekriegsleitung had known since at least the middle of April that by March 1941 the British naval attaché in Stockholm, Captain Henry W. Denham, had built up an organization to monitor the traffic passing through the Great Belt.

Whether Lütjens knew of this risk, I cannot say. So far as I know, nothing that might prejudice our chances of conducting war at sea happened during our passage through the Great Belt on the night of 19 May. Either we were lucky or the enemy's organization was not foolproof.

The heavy traffic in the Kattegat on 20 May made it obvious that there was a danger of enemy agents learning about the movement of our task force. That risk increased when the *Gotland* came into view.

I do not know how Lütjens evaluated the danger we faced from agents in Scandinavian waters, but we do know from his radio report that he had misgivings about having been seen by the *Gotland*. That he did not take that risk more seriously may be attributed to the response his radio report brought from Generaladmiral Carls. As it turned out, the *Gotland*'s report and its transmission to London led to the loss of the *Bismarck* on 27 May. On 28 May, the Admiralty wired Denham in Stockholm: "Your 2058 of 20th May initiated the first of a series of operations which culminated yesterday in the sinking of the *Bismarck*. Well done."

On the evening of 20 May Viggo Axelsen saw our task force off the coast, near Kristiansand. His ensuing radio message confirmed for the Admiralty Denham's earlier report.

Whether Lütjens took a risk of this nature into account is beyond my knowledge. Even though Axelsen's message did not tell the Admiralty anything new, it was extremely valuable confirmation.

After entering the fjords near Bergen, we spent a whole day within reach of British short-range aerial reconnaissance. Tovey wrote later: "The *Bismarck* and the *Prinz Eugen* were contemplating a raid on the ocean trade routes, though, if this was so, it seemed unlikely that they would stop at a place so convenient for air reconnaissance."*

This was a risk that Lütjens did accept. Consequently, British aerial reconnaissance identified the *Bismarck* and an *Admiral Hipper*-class cruiser around noon on 21 May. Further aerial reconnaissance on the evening of 22 May ascertained that the task force had left Norway.

Upon leaving the fjords on the evening of 21 May Lütjens learned that a British radio message had instructed the Royal Air Force to be on the lookout for two German battleships and three destroyers that had been reported on a northerly course the day before.

Lütjens, apparently unperturbed, continued on his way. He thereby accepted the risk that the enemy, once alerted, would extend his search to the latitudes through which the task force was to pass.

On the evening of 23 May, when he first met the *Suffolk*, Lütjens did not turn away. After the subsequent appearance of the *Norfolk*, he continued to hold his course, followed by both cruisers.

During the commanders' conference in the *Bismarck* on 18 May Lütjens had indeed said that, should he encounter enemy cruisers, he

*"Sinking of the German Battleship *Bismarck* on 27th May 1941." Dispatch by Admiral Sir John Tovey, Supplement No. 3 to the *London Gazette*, 14 October 1947.

would attack them if the circumstances were favorable, but that his highest priority would be to preserve the *Bismarck* and the *Prinz Eugen*, so that they could continue their operation for as long as possible. In the above instance, he applied the principle of preserving his ships by pressing on without engaging. In so doing he may have hoped, not unreasonably in the light of experience, to shake off the *Suffolk* and the *Norfolk* during the night. Yet, he thereby unavoidably accepted the risk that he would not succeed and that instead, the cruisers would call up heavier ships.*

Lütjens was poorly served by German aerial reconnaissance, misinformed about the ships at Scapa Flow in the decisive days, and encouraged by Group North to continue an apparently unendangered operation. He did not realize it, but he was in fact operating with his task force in a goldfish bowl.

The battle of Iceland deprived Lütjens of the freedom of tactical decision he had had before he encountered the *Suffolk* and the *Norfolk* the previous evening. Thereafter, the damage that the *Prince of Wales* had inflicted on the *Bismarck* determined the course of Exercise Rhine. It forced Lütjens to head for the west coast of France through an ocean area that could be covered by British long-range aerial reconnaissance. The pursuit of the *Bismarck* which began on her 1,700-mile run for St. Nazaire, was fraught with almost unbearable suspense on both sides. It led to exciting changes of fortune, hopes alternately rising and falling, and continuous fluctuations between high optimism and profound disappointment. The enemy lost contact with the *Bismarck* and regained it. We suffered from the hits scored by the *Prince of Wales* and from our failure to take on fuel in Norway or from the *Weissenburg*, which prevented us from steaming at higher speeds and thus, perhaps, saving ourselves. Then, there was the rudder hit that crippled our ship and led to her destruction—the end of a journey nearly 3,000 nautical miles in length which, since

---

*In the corresponding phase of his operation with the *Gneisenau* and *Scharnhorst*, on 28 January 1941, Lütjens did turn away when he encountered cruisers of the British Home Fleet in the ocean area between Iceland and the Faeroes. He then postponed the operation until the beginning of February, at which time he broke out unseen through the Denmark Strait. Presumably, the Denmark Strait was his first choice for Exercise Rhine because he knew that visibility in that area was usually poor—indeed, he had found it so before—and therefore he would minimize the chance of being discovered. Moreover, in the Denmark Strait he would not have to worry about running into British battleship squadrons as soon as would be the case in the ocean area around the Faeroes, which was much nearer to Scapa Flow.

her discovery in Norway, had brought the *Bismarck* nine-tenths of the way to her destination in France.

The loss of the ship and most of her crew was a bitter, heartrending blow. But it remains to be said, and in the interest of historical truth it must be said, that in view of the risks that the Seekriegsleitung and Lütjens knowingly accepted, the loss could not be ascribed to an unforeseeable fate, nor was it tragic in the classic sense, because it was not the result of a fatal flaw in the character of the Fleet Commander.

The sinking of the *Bismarck* had a decisive effect on the war at sea. Shortly thereafter, British forces sank six of the steamers belonging to the resupply organization for the conduct of the war in the Atlantic, thereby dealing that force a devastating blow. It was no longer possible for our surface forces to undertake large-scale operations of any duration in the Atlantic. Tovey's words of 26 May came true: "The sinking of the *Bismarck* may have an effect on the war as a whole out of all proportion to the loss to the enemy of one battleship."

It has been nearly fifty years since the *Bismarck* sank at 1039 on 27 May 1941. She lies at 48° 10′ north and 16° 12′ west, not very far out in the North Atlantic, and yet the distance of an eternity from the shores of France. The end of her brief career foreshadowed the passing of the battleship era, of which she was a technological triumph and upon which she and her brave, fallen crew left an indelible mark.

37

Cockfosters

The way into captivity began by leading Junack and me from Newcastle to London. After a train ride in a pleasantly outfitted first-class compartment purposely secluded from the traveling public, we reached the "London District Cage" in the Kensington district, which served as a sort of shuttle station for newly arriving prisoners of war. The cage was located on Kensington Palace Gardens Road, otherwise known as Millionaires' Row, which ran along the west side of Hyde Park; no one could have foreseen that today it would serve as the chancellery of the Soviet embassy.

The cage was operated by the British Army for the initial confinement of prisoners of war. Its commander was a major of Boer origin, a thickset, gray-haired, hard-boiled and taciturn man with a thin mustache, who spoke a very good, guttural German. The major himself was not authorized to interrogate prisoners, but he willfully disregarded this restriction from the start. The Royal Navy and the Air Force repeatedly had to complain that the major was present at initial interrogations by their representatives. He noted what had not been answered and afterwards grilled the prisoners with sledgehammer tactics. Some prisoners were manhandled and even beaten. By this method, the major certainly succeeded in obtaining one answer or another, but it was very frequently false. In any case, prisoners who had been treated in this manner were "spoiled" for further interrogations, so the major became involved in many discussions with the navy and air force over his methods.

In the case of captured naval personnel, representatives of the Royal Navy decided whether these should be transferred to a regular camp immediately or first subjected to an examination. During their visits to the cage, they did not actually interrogate the prisoners and never in the least intensively. They merely noted the naturally talkative, the former holders of important commands, and those who openly declared themselves ready to cooperate. The latter were without exception enlisted men; some of them had come from the merchant navy and remained Communists at heart. Members of these three categories were candidates for dispatch to the Combined Services' Detailed Interrogation Center (CSDIC) in the Cockfosters district. From the beginning, as the *Bismarck*'s senior surviving officer and as one of the ship's gunnery officers, I scarcely doubted that I would be questioned at the interrogation center.

This center, which we always referred to simply as Cockfosters, lay inside Trent Park, opposite the northernmost station of the Picadilly underground line. It was a majestic eighteenth-century mansion, whose magnificent, gently rolling grounds, then closed to the public, included a wood, a lake, a golf course, and tennis courts. Converted into an interrogation center after the beginning of the war, the estate had formerly belonged to Sir Philip Sassoon, the art connoisseur, who had filled the house with choice furniture and paintings, which the army had replaced with simple government-issue furnishings. But it was still evident that in time of peace, the "Upper Ten Thousand" had gathered here for romantic parties at which the guests, well shielded from the eyes of the uninvited, had frolicked in the garb of eighteenth-century shepherds and shepherdesses. Now the British navy, army, and air force had their respective offices on the ground floor; the interrogation rooms were on the second floor; and the prisoners' cells on the third.

"One hundred eighty centimeters tall, slender, high-domed forehead." After my arrival at Cockfosters I heard these and other descriptive phrases applying to me being said in a loud voice. It belonged to a powerful man in his late fifties with bristling hair and a distinctly Teutonic appearance, who obviously made quick work of routine. I soon found myself alone and, as it turned out—following policy to isolate new arrivals—separated for three months from the other *Bismarck* survivors in a rather roomy cell on the top floor. Its barred windows provided an extensive view of lawns, lake, and forest—a seeming island of idyllic peace in a warring world. Of course, on the

The former Combined Services Detailed Interrogation Centre (CSDIC), the interrogation camp for newly captured German prisoners of war, lay inside Trent Park at Cockfosters in northern London. (Photograph by the author from the 1960s.)

far horizon the barrage balloons tethered over London recalled reality. In my cell, however, there was only me and time—time in an apparently endless perspective.

In the hall outside the cell there was a little lending library with German and English books. It was very mixed—I saw Max Brod's *Tycho Brahes Weg zu Gott*,* Pittigrillis's *Jungfrau von 18 Karat*,† and more of the like. I read constantly whatever interested me; but soon I was brought out for interrogation, for which, after all, the Cockfosters camp was chiefly equipped.

By May 1941 the British had developed three methods for pumping prisoners of war. The first and the most frequently employed—and also favored at Cockfosters—was direct questioning. If the prisoner was cooperative, either from the start or because of a degree of pressure, this was the most effective method. Its success depended to a

* "Tycho Brahe's Way to God."
† "18–Carat Virgin."

large extent on the amount of information already available to the interrogator, his experience, and his skill in handling the prisoner. As a rule, he was already familiar with the latter's unit, its leading personalities, and state of technical development. Such information was available mainly from the questioning of other prisoners or from secret sources.

At Cockfosters since the beginning of the war the British had through the interrogation of captured crewmen gained considerable knowledge of the German U-boat arm and had developed a routine in regard to interrogating its members. But no one there had a glimmering about German battleships, and the shock at the sudden prospect of examining one or two thousand *Bismarck* survivors was substantial. What, in God's name, should one ask them? It was therefore, a "deliverance" when only a few more than one hundred men appeared.

I myself was interrogated by two periodically alternating interpreters. One was Lieutenant Commander Bertram Cope, a sturdy man in his late fifties who had drawn up my "warrant" upon my arrival at Cockfosters. He had learned his German in the Thomas Cook travel service and was a little rough around the edges, yet not unpleasant upon acquaintance.

The other was Dick Weatherby, about twenty-four years old but older-seeming, of average height, thin, with pitch-black, shiny hair. He came from a good Wiltshire family, which, as the hereditary keepers of the *Stud Book*—the register of English thoroughbred racing horses—had a name in society. His background included an academic schooling in German and an extended prewar visit to Germany. Without a profession at the outbreak of war, he had joined the Royal Naval Volunteer Reserve and completed a six-month sea-training course for junior officers. He did not go to sea, however, but was attached to the staff of the Naval Intelligence Department, which had a desperate need for German speakers knowledgeable in naval matters. Like the other interrogating officers, he had never been trained for this activity, but was assigned to it at random. It may well be that his rather threatening exterior, his character, and temperament helped him with his assignment—"head and neck like a cobra," many said; yet friendly, super-persuasive, occasionally furious, but without actually feeling the anger he displayed. As an interrogator he was a natural talent, probably the best in Cockfosters.

I no longer recall in detail the questions put to me by Cope or

Weatherby in repeated sessions. From the beginning, there was something different in the case of the *Bismarck* from that of most of the U-boats whose crews had been lost or captured. The invisibility that characterized their operations often made their missions a puzzle; therefore, the British focused their relentless curiosity on the where and when; but the great battleship had been pinpointed by the British almost continuously—from her arrival in the Kattegat on the morning of 20 May until her sinking 400 nautical miles west of Brest on 27 May. The position and course of the *Bismarck* thus lay more or less open to view. The answer to the question of the ship's mission, I kept to myself. At any rate, it was not hard for the British to figure it out.

So the questions concentrated on the *Bismarck*'s technical characteristics. Two of them were repeated with great regularity. The first: "How large was the *Bismarck*?"—which I always answered with "35,000 tons." The second: "Is it true that some of our torpedoes bounced off ineffectually on hitting the *Bismarck*?"—to which I replied, "No idea." The latter question arose from the worry that over the course of time an apparatus might have been developed in Germany that made British torpedoes harmless. In any event, we hadn't had it in the *Bismarck*. Our interrogators' interest in the technical aspects of the *Bismarck* was, no doubt, also inspired by the wish on the part of the Admiralty to gain knowledge about her sister ship the *Tirpitz*. Winston Churchill was quite concerned with her too, and my knowledge of the *Bismarck* would have been invaluable to any attack the Royal Navy would launch against the *Tirpitz*. However, I did not see myself in a position to oblige.

The second method of pumping prisoners consisted of bugging their cells with a hidden microphone. Thus it was possible, for example, to overhear conversations between members of the same German unit before they were directly interrogated for the first time. This method proved especially productive for the British. On the one hand, through the factual knowledge gained. And on the other, for the helpful starting point it provided for direct questioning. The disadvantage was that the conversations could not be steered from outside. Yet in certain ways the conversations could be prepared, sometimes already in the "London Cage." There, the interrogators would address the interesting points that could not be clarified immediately in an energetic but not unduly pressing manner. They expected that these would stick in the prisoners' minds and later be raised in conversations between cellmates.

In Cockfosters, as well, these methods brought the British by far the richest results, although at this time only two or three cells there were bugged. This low number was imposed by the relatively large number of army personnel needed to cover each cell twenty-four hours a day: listener, transcriber, and translator. Their work was bothersome and tiring. They were not expected to do it for longer than two consecutive hours.

According to Donald McLachlan's *Room 39*, prisoners had already been warned of the risks of being overheard before entering their cells. This was in no way the case with me personally. I took it as a given, however, and my assumption was reinforced by my experience in the time to come. Days of isolation alternated with those in the company of other prisoners of war. For a while Wohlfarth was quartered with me. He had lost his *U-556* to the depth charges of a British corvette a month after the sinking of the *Bismarck*. What a surprise and joy it was to see our "Sir Parsifal" again, our "sponsor," who in the last desperate hours of 26 May had been so completely helpless to aid his "protégé" *Bismarck*. "We two together—wow!—they'd really like to listen in on us," I said to him upon his arrival. "We'll keep completely mum!" We played skat—*the* German card game—continously.

After Wohlfarth came an officer from a German auxiliary vessel that had been lost in the Atlantic, then a fighter pilot. For me this remained a variegated and not unwelcome change. Each time, we were supposed to be stimulated to conversations that would be profitable to our listeners. Always I warned my new companions of this danger. And I don't believe that we ever served as a source of secret information to our warders.

The third method of pumping prisoners consisted of the planting of so-called decoys. Originally recruited from emigrant circles and later from prisoners of war, they were carefully prepared for their role, in which they would win the confidence of prisoners to be tapped and lead them into conversations. Trained by the British army—there were forty-nine during the course of the war—they proved themselves thoroughly successful. However, they never posed as members of the same branch of service as the prisoners being pumped—that would have made the risk of discovery too great. I personally was never confronted with this method at Cockfosters.

All the information elicited from German prisoners was relayed to the subsection "German Prisoners of War" in the "Germany" section of the Naval Intelligence Department in London. The head of this subsection was Colonel B. F. Trench of the Royal Marines, who in 1910—it may be of some interest—had been sentenced to four years' fortress confinment* in Germany after he had been caught in too close an inspection of the guns in the fortress of Borkum. Trench for his part forwarded the information gathered from the prisoners of war, properly worked up, to the chief of the German section. From him, after it had been checked against other sources, the information went to the chief of the department, the Director of Naval Intelligence, Rear Admiral John Godfrey, in the Room 39 destined for historical fame. A sharp-witted, energetic man, Godfrey placed great demands on his subordinates and could be obnoxiously impatient but spared himself least of all.

The crème of the British intelligence service was assembled in and around Room 39. Naval specialists, civil experts from the naval reserve, university professors, scientists, attorneys. Here the entering information was definitively analyzed, accepted or rejected, and a decision made about what to send the operations section "for further action" and what not to send.

Two examples illustrate the successes Cockfosters brought Room 39, and three the reverses when Room 39 discounted information from Cockfosters.

The successes. My interrogators' questions concerning the suspected ineffectiveness of British torpedoes "bouncing off" the *Bismarck*, answered by my "No idea," had its origins, unknown to me at the time, in the area of German torpedo failures. The first U-boat personnel captured by the British had complained bitterly among themselves about the numerous failures of *their* torpedoes to detonate. Mutually, they had consoled themselves in the expectation of new acoustic torpedoes that would follow the target vessel's propeller noises, with which German U-boats would soon be armed.

Cockfosters forwarded this bugged self-exposure to Room 39. In consequence, the British developed a protective device against the future threat, the so-called "Foxer." This consisted of nothing more than two steel rods towed behind the British ship at an appropriate distance. The metallic noise produced by their banging together would attract the acoustic torpedo away from the ship's propeller to the rods, and it would detonate at a safe distance from the vessel. The

---

*Confinement in a military installation was considered more honorable than in a civilian jail. Trench did not actually serve time, however; the Kaiser commuted his sentence and he was merely expelled from Germany.

"Foxer" was ready before the Germans had their acoustic torpedoes at the front. Despite the technical deficiencies connected with it, for a while it contributed to saving many an Allied ship.

In routinely censoring captured German naval officers' mail, the Naval Intelligence Department noticed at an early date that in their letters U-boat officers were using a simple code based on the symbols of the Morse Code. The dashes and dots of the Morse alphabet, as well as the separation marks between these letter symbols, were reproduced through three groups of letters into which the alphabet had been divided for this purpose. The secret information was concealed in the first letters of the words in the text of the letter. Of course, this type of code limited the writer's freedom of expression, but it still left him enough to compose a sufficiently natural-seeming text which did not openly betray the encoding of a very different sort of message than the one that was outwardly evident. In this manner U-boat personnel were to report to their commander how, among other things, they had lost their boats and been made prisoner. Initially, Cockfosters let all this information go through uncensored—in the hopes of catching a bigger fish. And that was on the way.

In the summer of 1943 a German U-boat officer in the Bowmanville camp in Canada used the letter code to request the Commander, U-boats,* to send a boat to the country's east coast. There it would pick up several officers who were to have participated in a mass breakout from the camp and carry them back to Germany to rejoin the undersea war.

This letter was no masterpiece of apparently innocent phraseology and had a number of artificially arranged substantives, striking enough; but the representative of the Naval Intelligence Department in Ottawa noticed nothing—despite years of indoctrination in the code by way of London! So the letter, completely unnoticed by Ottawa, reached its goal and was rewarded by a letter from the commander agreeing to the operation and transmitting the organizational details.

In contrast to the request, the commander's reply was extremely adept in its choice of words, completely natural-seeming and absolutely innocent. No wonder that Ottawa did not notice anything or even subject it to a cursory scrutiny. Then by pure accident the British came to the rescue.

Since 1942, Ralph Izzard, a lieutenant commander in the Royal

*Admiral Karl Dönitz

Naval Volunteer Reserve and member of the Naval Intelligence Department in London, had been in Washington as a visiting instructor training American officers in the examination of German prisoners of war. As the reply had come from Dönitz personally, for this and no other reason Ottawa reproduced it as an object of presumably general interest for its postal distribution list and also sent a copy to Izzard in Washington. The latter, who had just thoroughly explained this very letter code to his students, immediately began to decode the letter, purely out of routine as a teaching aid, in view of the apparently harmless contents without special expectations, in the self-evident certainty that Ottawa, technically competent, had long before gone over the ground for him.

But what a surprise! Peeled away, there it stood in black and white, that the *U-536* would appear in Chaleur Bay to pick up German U-boat officers after a breakout from camp. The exact date would follow. Izzard's congratulations to Ottawa: "That was well done"—but in Ottawa nothing at all had been "well done"; the content of the letter had been overlooked. Izzard's congratulations informed the authorities of the alarming situation for the first time!

Now it was up to the Allied planners to build a trap in which to catch the expected escapees and to ensnare, to destroy, better yet to capture the *U-536*. The Naval Intelligence Department and the Canadian army and navy went to work. They chose to let the German plan unfold without hindrance while they secretly readied their countermeasures, and then strike at the last possible moment with the maximum chance of success. For the Germans, who continued to believe themselves unwatched, everything seemed to click—even if in the end only a single officer, Wolfgang Heyda, succeeded in breaking out on 24 September. But when he reached the rendezvous point on the coast—awaited with anxious satisfaction by the British and Canadian authorities—where he was to give the prearranged light signals to the *U-536* to send a rubber boat to the beach, the heavy hand of a Canadian coast guardsman came down on his shoulder.

"You're under arrest!"

A completely independent organization, the coast guard had known nothing of the operation in progress, nothing of the trap that the Canadian army and navy, together with the British, had readied for the Germans—the trap which, in ignorance of the planned course of events, it had just ruined. Ottawa had neglected to inform it. Under the circumstances, what else could the lone-wolf Heyda be for the coast guardsman than a suspicious stranger in a prohibited area?

And so it came about that the *U-536*, punctually entering Chaleur Bay, never received the prearranged light signals. Instead it received the radio request "*Komm! Komm!*"* from the British naval officer who, with the help of a whole group of destroyers, was directing the entire operation against the *U-536* and the escapees from the shore. The stir caused by Heyda's arrest had drawn his attention, and he had already greeted the would-be escaper with the question: "Well, now, are you the gentleman who was to be picked up here by a German U-boat?" Astonished, Heyda realized that it was "over" for him.

"*Komm, Komm?*" Rolf Schauenburg, the captain of the *U-536* asked himself. That was by no means the agreed-upon radio message and furthermore, it was on the wrong wavelength! The secret radio transmitter at Bowmanville was supposed to have reported the successful breakout on an entirely different wavelength. But nothing had been received from it, and now there was no light signal from the beach, either.

Growing suspicious, Schauenberg halted, turned about, and for fear of surprises submerged to the bottom and lay there, waiting. No sound must come from the boat now! And then the submarine chasers burst into action, their propellers churning nauseatingly near, depth charges crashing. But in the end, with much patience and skill Schauenberg escaped back to the open sea, with a practically undamaged boat, ready for new operations in another area. But why, he kept asking himself, had the object of his operation so mysteriously avoided him? Why?

Yet for the British, too, the operation had finally failed, at the last moment, through the Canadians neglecting to notify their coast guard. Red faces in Ottawa! For London and Ottawa the situation would appear somewhat less disreputable when shortly thereafter the *U-536* was sunk by British and Canadian destroyers while attacking an Allied convoy northeast of the Azores on 20 November 1943.

Room 39 had wanted to let the breach of the German letter code, which it made at the beginning of the U-boat war, ripen into a fruit that would count. Except for the breakdown in Ottawa, presumably it would have so ripened. Had Heyda been able to exchange the prearranged light signals with the *U-536* in Chaleur Bay, the Allied action against the boat and the escapee would have succeeded. The basic British plan had certainly proven sound; it had brought a great success almost over the threshold: the capture of a U-boat. It was sheer

* "Come! Come!"

bad luck that at the decisive moment an ally's omission had spoiled it. At least the subsequent sinking of the U-536 near the Azores was a retroactive consolation.

The reverses. Soon after the beginning of the war Cockfosters had learned through interrogations that German U-boats could dive deeper than 185 meters. The British submarine staff and British submarine constructors dismissed this information as unrealistic, however, and British depth charges continued to be set for depths of up to 185 meters. German U-boats profited from that and could evade depth charges set too shallow.

Then in August 1941, an unhoped-for stroke of luck came to the assistance of the British. They unexpectedly captured the U-570, which saw service from 1941–1944 as HMS *Graph* in the Royal Navy.* Its hull was composed of steel of a strength whose utilization in submarine construction had previously been thought impossible. Now, hoping to make up for lost time, the Admiralty acted upon the information received earlier from Cockfosters and had depth charges set to depths of more than 200 meters.

How right this was later emerged from a report by the Anti U-Boat Division, Naval Staff, of 5 July 1943, in which the destruction of U-202 was described. It says in part: "It should be noted that U-202 was probably of similar construction to HMS *Graph*, being built at approximately the same time and under the same conditions of mass production and prefabrication. *Graph* could dive to 800 feet [266 meters] in an emergency but examination of her hull has shown that this depth is dangerously near the collapsing point for strength. Furthermore, her pumps were only designed to work to a pressure head of 400 feet of water."†

Another instance of the Admiralty's disbelief of information from Cockfosters concerned the guns of our *Narvik*-class destroyers. Ger-

---

*The U-570 was so renamed in February 1942 when she went to the Clyde for trials. She became fully operational at the end of September 1942, leaving Holy Loch for patrols in the Bay of Biscay early in October 1942. At the end of that year she was reallocated to patrols in northern waters, still attached to the Third Submarine Flotilla, to cover the passage of Russian convoys. On 1 January 1943 she sighted two destroyers and fired a salvo of four torpedoes, but without success. She went into refit in June at Chatham, which lasted until January 1944. On 16 March she left Aberdeen in tow. Early on the 18th the tow parted, and on the 19th the vessel was reported still adrift with no crew on board at 55° 55' north and 06° 33' west. On the morning of 20 March she was sighted aground on a rocky coast at 55° 48.8' north and 06° 27' west, on the west coast of Islay.

†"Observations of the Hunt," p. 59.

man prisoners had spoken of their carrying guns of 15 centimeters rather than 12.7 centimeters, which had been customary for destroyers until then. However, the Admiralty held that this would be completely impossible for a ship of only 2,400 tons and did not even notify the Home Fleet. In 1944 a destroyer of the *Narvik*-class fell into British hands. Inspection revealed that the British experts had been wrong to doubt.

In the third case, Cockfosters overheard a sensationally strange-sounding piece of information while bugging some of the *Bismarck's* enlisted crewmen as they were talking among themselves—that the Seekriegsleitung originally intended to bring the *Bismarck* back to Germany through the English Channel after her repairs in a port in western France. Cockfosters speculated: the knowledge possessed by these enlisted men must be based on things that had been spoken of on board. Certainly, there was no more *Bismarck*—but could not such a train of thought, presumably the fruit of long and serious consideration, be put into practice someday with other German ships? However, Room 39 found the idea to be absurd and did not forward it. Except for such oversight, the British operations section might have made dispositions that would have stood in the way of the subsequent Channel Dash by our ships *Scharnhorst, Gneisenau* and *Prinz Eugen.**

"Good morning. How are you today?" The greeting, spoken in German, came from a tall, slim figure of easy elegance and cosmopolitan bearing, who entered my cell one day in early June. It was Ralph Izzard—whom we have already met at his subsequent work in Washington—lieutenant commander in the Royal Naval Volunteer Reserve. Prewar correspondent of the *Daily Mail* in Germany and an expert on Berlin and its society, he had developed friendly personal relations even with our former crown prince; the latter once invited him to Cortina for the winter sport. Izzard knew how to chat fascinatingly; one quickly felt at ease in his company. I soon grew accustomed to him and was always glad when he came.

Every now and then he appeared during the German night air raids on London to see how his prisoners reacted when they had their own Luftwaffe up against them. On his first visit of this sort he said:

---

*In February 1942 these vessels succeeded in returning to Germany from Brest by an audacious dash through the English Channel. The London *Times* complained that "Nothing more mortifying . . . has happened in Home waters since the 17th century."

"Your Italian allies are already cowering in the corners of their cells and doing their beads." Then for a while we listened together to the noise of the action outside. But in that summer of 1941 I never had the impression that any air raid was really threatening Cockfosters.

Another time Izzard talked about my prior service as an assistant to our naval attaché in London. "Well, do you still remember your motor trip to northern England and Scotland in spring 1939?" he said meaningfully. "We knew exactly where you were staying and what you were doing at all times."

"I certainly would not have expected anything else," I growled, without going into it any deeper, also without having to feel a prick of conscience about my outwardly altogether correct information-gathering trip in April 1939. It had taken me, for the purpose of getting to know the country, to Manchester, Glasgow, and Edinburgh, among other places. Naturally, I had also visited our consulate in Glasgow. I will never forget a remark made by our acting consul there. "You could do a good deed," he opined, "by persuading as many as possible young Luftwaffe officers to spend their leaves in and around Glasgow. That way they could themselves pick out their bombing targets in this important industrial region. I would be glad to help them with it."

"Bombs on England!"—At the time these words were spoken, Hitler had yet to renounce the Anglo-German Naval Agreement of 1935, and the Second World War staged by him still lay nearly five months in the future. Yet several years of a regime of violence in the Reich and its practice of foreign-policy ultimatums had long since demolished the intellectual barriers against war, even all-out war, among some of its diplomatic representatives.

So far, Izzard had obtained his only experience at sea in the role of an able seaman gunlayer 2nd class in an Atlantic tanker. The personal intervention of Troubridge, the former British naval attaché in Berlin, had released him from this position. His knowledge of German had then immediately landed him an officer's assignment in the Naval Intelligence Department. From there he was assigned to Room 39 and ordered to Cockfosters. Here he belonged to the staff responsible for naval interrogations, but he seldom took part in them himself. As a former journalist, it was incumbent upon him to compose the evaluation reports destined for the Naval Intelligence Department.

I did not learn to know him by his family name then—he went about as Lieutenant Daly, a cover name which he bore, like the other interrogating officers in Cockfosters. The thought was that this would protect them personally in the event of a successful German invasion. The German prisoners of war could not then facilitate the identification of their interrogating officers through knowing their real names. For the British government strongly reckoned on such an invasion from the end of the French campaign until Hitler's attack on the Soviet Union. And in view of the constant concentration of our captured U-boat and air aces in Cockfosters, this camp was regarded as a primary German operational objective—when these aces would immediately be set free. Therefore the British army, which adminis-tered all prisoner-of-war camps, stationed an especially strong force at Cockfosters.

For me, only now and again did the army step out of the camp administration that it accomplished in the background to make a direct and, I am glad to say, agreeable appearance. As a rule on Sunday evenings, a welfare officer brought cigarettes, chocolate, and, the most important to me, newspapers! I recall the first *Times* that reached me in this manner—it contained an obituary of the German ex-Kaiser, who had died the day before in Doorn. A major sometimes took me for walks through the great park around the house. He was an expert on British literature, which we chiefly discussed. His great favorite was the Scottish poet Robert Burns, whose social criticism on behalf of the poor and whose nature lyrics he praised. He always said that Burns was read much too little.

It was 22 June 1941, around 1000 hours in my cell. My glance fell on Izzard and I heard him say, "Well, do you know that you're at war with Russia now?"

His words made me feel numb. But that really can't be true, I thought, I won't believe it. Not, of course, that Hitler would shrink from brushing aside and violating a nonaggression pact that he him-self had concluded; no, pacts and treaties meant nothing to this man. That had been made clear, at latest, by the occupation of Prague in March 1939 in violation of the Munich Agreement of 30 September 1938. And mentally I excluded the possibility that Hitler had struck preemptively, for until now the Russians had remained faithful to the pact. The experience of Napoleon and the course of the First World War had not held him back from beginning a two-front war on the Continent! For in the final analysis, the war in the west was still not over. His hunger for land, his craving to conquer "living space" in the east, had overpoweringly, relentlessly, swept him along.

"No," I said finally, "how could I?"

"Yes," Izzard continued, "today Goebbels had to get up very early again and tell the German people that the Russians are still utter swine."

If at best the war in the east reaches a stalemate, thought I, but the war in the west continues, there are a good ten to fifteen years behind barbed wire ahead of me—the self-absorbed vision of the future of a prisoner of war in solitary confinement immediately entered my mind.

Over the next days the British press brought the details. In a special broadcast over the "Great German Radio" at 0530 hours on 22 June Goebbels had read the "Führer's" proclamation to the German people, in which he "unveiled" Moscow's "treacherous machinations" since signing the nonaggression pact on 23 August 1939 and reported the advance of German, Finnish, and Romanian armies on a front from the North Cape to the Black Sea. The whole blame, according to Hitler, belonged to the "Jewish-Bolshevistic rulers." By the threatening deployment of Russian strength on our eastern frontier and incessant violations of our border they had impeded the radical ending of the war in the west. They had blackmailed him and threatened "European culture and civilization." Now, however, the hour had come to stand up to this plot of the Jewish-Anglo-Saxon warmongers and the equally Jewish rulers of the Bolshevist Moscow control center. The defense against this "Russo-English plot" against the Reich, indeed, against all Europe, was the—unbelievable—kernel of Hitler's otherwise painfully long-winded proclamation on 22 June 1941. And he had then without any declaration of war attacked in the east.

The reason for this attack had indeed been clarified by Goebbels in his speech to the Blohm & Voss personnel in Hamburg on 17 December 1940, "to make good the mistakes of 400 years of German history to obtain a just share of the world's riches." And from whom did Goebbels get the political score other than his master Hitler? There is no need for us to go back once more to the latter's words to high-ranking officers in Berlin in 1935: "Yes, gentlemen, I still need to wage a European war." We clearly hear Hitler say the same thing to the commanders in chief of the three branches of the Wehrmacht who had been summoned to the Reich Chancellery on 23 May 1939. I had learned of it during a brief visit to Berlin in June 1939, but only peripherally and without details. Hitler to the commanders in chief:

> The mass of 80 millions [the Germans] has solved the ideological problem. The economic problem must also be solved. . . . The solution to the problem will require courage. It must not be approached with the

idea of avoiding a solution by adapting to circumstances. Rather, it must be a matter of adapting circumstances to needs. This is not possible without the invasion of foreign states and the seizure of foreign territories. . . . Danzig is not the object around which it revolves. For us it is a question of the expansion of living space to the East and the guarantee of the food supply. . . . The question of whether to spare Poland is therefore eliminated and the decision remains to attack Poland at the first suitable opportunity. A repetition of Czechoslovakia is not to be expected. It will come to a fight. The mission is to isolate Poland. The success of the isolation is decisive. . . . It must not come to a simultaneous confrontation with the West. . . . Principle: confrontation with Poland is a success only if the West stays out of the game. If that is not possible, then it is better to attack the West and thereby dispose of Poland at the same time. The war with France and Britain will be a war of life and death. . . . We will not be dragged into a war, but we cannot get around it.*

How did Grossadmiral Raeder, my commander in chief, choose to describe this address of Hitler's, at which he was present? On pages 163–64 of Volume II of *Mein Leben*,† we read:

On 23 May Hitler gave an address to a small gathering in which he expressed remarkably contradictory ideas about the Polish problem [The address] had according to my impression only one definite purpose, namely, the establishment of a small study group outside the General Staff. The final conclusion, which, moreover, Hitler himself drew, was that the ship-building program should be continued in its existing format and that the other armament programs. . . . would be put off until the year 1943–44. No change in Hitler's intentions in regard to England [the previous intention had been "avoid war"] was evident on this occasion. After the end of his address, Hitler had [further] explained to me personally that politically he had a good grip on things. He was convinced that war with England was not to be expected on account of his latest demand for the revision of the Polish Corridor. . . . After these assurances, I had no hesitation in sending the battleship *Gneisenau* into the Atlantic in June 1939. . . . Despite the events that had taken place in the spring [the German entry into Prague, Hitler's renunciation of the German-Polish Non-aggression Pact and the Anglo-German Naval Agreement] and despite the proclamation of the Franco-

*Joachim Fest, *Hitler*, p. 802f., on the basis of the International Military Tribunal, XXXVII, 546ff.
†A slightly abridged English translation, entitled *My Life*, was published by the Naval Institute in 1960.

British guarantee of Poland, the international political situation did not appear to me to be threatening in the summer [of 1939].

It is hard for me to comprehend that Raeder so simply accepted Hitler's assurances about the international situation. To "have a good grip" on the unfolding of international politics? War with England "is" not to be expected? So simple, so easily ascertained as all that? Now, to be sure, Raeder's memoirs show him in general to have been a political innocent of the first water. But his interpretation of Hitler's address of 23 May reveals a bloodcurdling lack of political perceptivity in a commander in chief that should have distinguished him from a mere departmental administrator. Moreover, had not the navy always prided itself on its superior knowledge of the outside world and its inhabitants? Was not the navy often envied by members of the other armed services for the greater possibilities it possessed of gathering information abroad? And must not that apply in especial measure to Great Britain, which lay so near and was traditionally associated with us in seafaring? Should not Raeder as a result of his long professional experience have been capable of forming a realistic estimate of British reaction to Hitler's recent violence in Europe, which was now repeating itself against Poland? Did he allow this estimate simply to be prescribed to him by Hitler, who, as was well known, had never understood the British mentality? With him, Raeder, Hitler truly had an easy game. How far ahead of him in the political view of the world was the army officer Ludwig Beck.

And it was, characteristically, another striking error of judgment that led Hitler to sound the trumpet of the "long-desired crusade" and "holy war" against Bolshevism to Great Britain, The German press and the German radio emphasized these themes. I now saw the outcome in the London daily papers. Hitler desired in this way to bring the Anglo-Saxon powers to ally with Germany as the saviour from Bolshevism. Winston Churchill answered him over the British radio on the evening of 22 June 1941 in a speech that has become famous.

At four o'clock this morning Hitler attacked and invaded Russia. All his usual formalities of perfidy were observed with scrupulous technique. A non-aggression treaty had been solemnly signed. . . . No complaint had been made by Germany of its non-fulfillment. . . . Hitler is a monster of wickedness, insatiable in his lust for blood and plunder. . . . The terrible military machine, which we and the rest of the civilized world so foolishly, so supinely, so insensately allowed the Nazi gangsters to build up year by year from almost nothing, cannot stand idle lest it rust or fall to pieces. . . . The Nazi regime is indistinguishable from the worst features of Communism. It is devoid of all theme and principle except appetite and racial domination. . . . We have but one aim and one single, irrevocable purpose. We are resolved to destroy Hitler and every vestige of the Nazi regime. From this nothing will turn us—nothing. We will never parley, we will never negotiate with Hitler or any of his gang. We shall fight him by land, we shall fight him by sea, we shall fight him in the air, until with God's help we have rid the earth of his shadow and liberated its people from his yoke. Any man or state who fights on against Nazidom will have our aid. Any man or state who marches with Hitler is our foe.

But herewith Churchill had not only answered Hitler's idea of a "common crusade against Bolshevism." He had also rejected in advance the idea of those Germans in the Reich who in April 1945 clung to the hope of a last-minute reversal in the alliances: the Western powers henceforth on the side of Germany against the Soviet Union! Germany, which through the unreliability and international aggression of the Nazi regime had long since come to be regarded as a pariah by all sides? A soap bubble, identifiable as such since 22 June 1941 at the latest.

From now on, the war in Russia hung like a shadow over my cell in Cockfosters. It defied any estimate of its length or its outcome. It posed new puzzles to a patriot concerned for Germany.

38

An Outing in London

"If you'd like," I heard Izzard's now-familiar voice, "this afternoon we can go out together, have a look at London, and visit some pubs. Of course, you must give your word of honor not to make any attempt to escape. You'll be provided with suitable civilian clothing. To keep you from feeling 'nationally' alone, a second German officer can join the party."

At first I thought that I hadn't heard correctly. Then I did some quick calculating: the welcome change of scene against the risk that I would make a slip of the tongue in the course of such a tour. How expertly, how intensively, would I be pumped? A wrong word, a wrong gesture, could be critical. Would I get through it? What to do? Better not, then? But my curiosity about London and the wish to see it again won out. And I felt sure of myself. "Agreed," I said.

And that same afternoon Izzard, Dick Weatherby, another German naval officer, and I—the two of us in borrowed civilian clothing—rode in a chauffeur-driven government car to the center of the city. Through familiar streets, past spots and scenes with minimal bomb damage—everything seemed so unchanged. Berkeley Hotel, the bar there, was our first destination. The British public surrounded us, many in uniforms—which I had scarcely ever seen there in peacetime—also de Gaulle's "Free French," proud of their status, naturally all the more in uniform. One, two drinks, chats about times past, harmless, not military. The same scene an hour later in the bar at the Ritz in Piccadilly. In this street I still knew the contours of the great houses which in 1938–39 I had passed daily on the way from my apartment in Belgrave Square to the embassy in Carlton House Terrace. An indescribable feeling, to be here in the scenes of faded, happy peacetime days and—if only the damned war didn't lie like a lump in the way—to be able to walk through them again freely. If ever again? That could only be a vague hope.

"Gentlemen," Izzard suggested after a while, "we should go to dinner now, just around the corner from here." The Écu de France, another familiar place from past years. Uniforms here, too, as before, including Free French, these at the very next table. First-class food, good wine, nothing indicating wartime shortages, and more light, neutral conversation.

From there we continued on through London, which in the meantime had grown pitch-black, to an unnamed destination in a basement somewhere in Chelsea. Uniformed British naval officers, nearly enough to take one's breath away, stood dispersed throughout the room, as though at a drinks party. I had not imagined that the coming attack would be altogether so massive. All the red lights went on in my head. For heaven's sake, be careful!

In a casual manner, also as at a drinks party, outwardly relatively unobtrusive but damned purposefully, they opened a conversation with me. The questioners were, of course, a collection of specialists: ship constructors, engineers, gunners, range-finding officers, signals officers.

"What was the highest speed, what was the radius of action of the Bismarck?"

"Twenty-eight knots certainly, perhaps even a little more, didn't we keep pace with your fast formation in the Denmark Strait?"

"The thickness of your armor, outboard, below decks, at the guns and control stations?

"I'm very sorry, I don't know. All this is secret. Anyway, the thickness of armor usually corresponds more or less to the caliber of one's own guns—you know that, too."

"Muzzle velocity, weight and range of your largest calibers?"

"Sorry; as for range, well, we had two major actions with your ships, the shooting always began at a range of around twenty kilometers—the maximum range is certainly in excess of that, but how can one then accurately observe the fall of shot without the help of an aircraft?"

"Rangefinding, still your stereoscopic system, nothing beyond that, no radar for the guns?"

"I discussed your co-incidental and our stereoscopic system with your comrades aboard the station ship of the Royal Naval Volunteer Reserve in London, HMS *President*, in 1936. They believed in their system and we in ours, which is probably still the case today. The battle in the Denmark Strait may have proven us correct; during the final action on 27 May your preponderance in gunnery was too great. And radar for the guns? I'm sorry to say that I know nothing about that."

The conversation ran on like this for an hour until our departure to return to Cockfosters.

We had had something to drink in the course of the evening, but we felt clearheaded enough throughout. Nevertheless, had we got through the voluntarily accepted challenge without doing any military harm to the Kriegsmarine or the Reich? Had we said one word too many anywhere? I thought not. But it would be impossible to go through such an experience without being left in the end with a residue of doubt, however small. Later, after the close of the investigation of the *Bismarck*, the Naval Intelligence Department would determine that all the survivors had been extremely closemouthed when questioned about things that were meant to remain secret.

"You seemed so familiar to me when we were introduced; I thought right away that I'd seen you before." These words were spoken to me in the early 1960s by retired British Rear Admiral Keith McNeil Campbell-Walter on the manicured lawn of King's House in Kingston, Jamaica, at a reception being given by the governor-general, Sir Kenneth Blackburne. As a former father-in-law of the industrialist Heinrich von Thyssen-Bornemisza—who had married Campbell's beautiful daughter, the ex-model Fiona—Campbell-Walter's name had long been a familiar one in the society columns. At the moment he and his wife were taking a short vacation on the enchanting Caribbean island, where they were staying in an expensive property belonging to the industrialist on Jamaica's north coast. Sir Kenneth and Lady Blackburne had invited my wife and me this time not only as the German ambassadorial couple—I was then the German Ambassador to Jamaica, with consular jurisdiction in the British Caribbean— but also so that two former officers of once warring navies could meet one another. Sir Kenneth himself loved the sea and seafaring, was an enthusiastic and successful sailor and commodore of the Royal Yacht Club in Jamaica, and was interested in naval history. In 1960 he had insisted that I go with him to see the film *Sink the Bismarck* in Kingston. He was one of the those who encouraged me to write some day about the German battleship.

I now looked closely at Campbell-Walter. "I'm sorry, Admiral, unfortunately I can't say the same."

"Do you still remember," he continued, "the drinks party in Chelsea in 1941? I tried to sound you out there about the *Bismarck*'s radio equipment and transmissions. I had a microphone under my lapel; the receiver was in the cellar. But you didn't say anything."

And who had thought up this outing to London and planned its details in the first place? None other than Ian Fleming, later the creator of James Bond. Admiral Godfrey had taken him, a former stockbroker, bright and shrewd, to be his personal assistant after entering the post of director of naval intelligence in 1939. Fleming—quick-witted, good looking, and sophisticated—had earlier considered and prepared himself for entry into the army or the diplomatic service. Now, as a lieutenant in the Royal Naval Volunteer Reserve, he was assigned to Room 39, where he acted as the "ideas man." Without any experience at sea, he, through his flexibility, broke up—or relaxed—many of the naval orthodoxies around Godfrey and enlivened the department with his brainstorms, usable or not. Two may be selected from the number that bore fruit; one in 1941, with the aim of capturing secret materials from a German weather-reporting ship in the Atlantic, was later carried out successfully; the other, copied from the example of the German paratroopers who seized secret British materials in Crete in 1941, was accomplished three years thereafter in Germany by a commando team that captured from the German Kriegsmarine tons of archival material of inestimable value to the British Admiralty.

While I was sitting in Cockfosters, someone may well have recalled my activity on the staff of the naval attaché at our London Embassy in 1938–39, and have regarded my "ideological conversion" to the British side as conceivable, and so given Fleming the idea for the outing. Fleming then turned its planning over to the deputy chief of the "German Prisoners of War" subsection, his friend Eddie Croghan. The latter—around thirty-five years old, plump and black haired, fluent in German, and previously a much sought-after interior decorator in London—had taken over the arrangements for the evening. Croghan had obtained his position as deputy subsection chief through Fleming's initiative. He was for his chief, Trench, what Fleming was for Godfrey—"the ideas man." To be sure, Trench was sharp-witted, but he was also conventional and simple hearted; his hobby was knitting. Therefore, as Fleming saw it, Trench, too, needed a "spark-plug." This role was now played by Croghan, who prior to Izzard's arrival at Cockfosters had composed the written reports of the interrogations of prisoners. He himself never took part in them on a regular basis and only came to Cockfosters now and then, when some point had to be cleared up.

Our London outing had not been cheap. The Admiralty paid for it. For no other German prisoners would it ever again spend so much money for such a reason. The "standard outing" for prisoners "giving reason for ideological hopes" led to the fixed-price menu at Simpson's on the Strand, the quantity and quality of which were surprisingly good for the price; and afterwards to a part of the city upon which the Luftwaffe liked to claim it had inflicted extensive damage. It did not fail to leave an impression, for example, to see St. Paul's standing intact in the midst of ruins.

To my knowledge, however, a very different kind of special treatment was extended to a nephew of Martin Niemöller, a U-boat officer. He was deeply religious and had repeatedly told his interrogating officer of his desire to participate in a divine service. Accordingly, orders came from London to take him to church. On three Sundays two interrogating officers escorted Niemöller's nephew and another German officer to various churches: St. Alban's Abbey, Stokes Page Church (where in 1750 Thomas Gray wrote "Elegy in a Country Churchyard"), and St. George's Chapel in Windsor Castle. Each time the German officers knew all the hymns in the service and, to the embarrassment of their British escorts, loudly joined in singing the words—in German.

And the results, as regards an "ideological conversion," of special treatment in Niemöller's case and mine: nil. Churchill was always after the Naval Intelligence Department to designate a German officer whom he could present to the British public as a symbol of crumbling morale in the Reich. But Cockfosters always had to report that the Germans' discipline remained very high. A suitable German officer was not found in Great Britain until the beginning of 1944—somewhat earlier in the U.S.A.—and only a few enlisted men had come forward before that.

And what would an invitation to an "ideological conversion," which was at no time substantively addressed to me, have really meant to me personally? Since 1937–38 I had recognized the inevitability of our national ruin under the Brown tyranny and the urgent necessity of Hitler's disappearance in our national political interest, but of course I had regarded this as a purely internal political problem. Certainly, it had increased the spiritual torment to be compelled to see more clearly from year to year that, in view of the Germans' political apathy, this goal would never be attained internally, but now through war, or, at any rate, through its outcome. The millions of deaths throughout the world constricted in its meaning to a change of government in one's own country? It was a cruel dilemma. But it could never serve as a bridge for an "ideological conversion." "Ideologically," in terms of my basic political and constitutional persuasions, there had been for a long time nothing to "convert." I had never allowed myself to be infected with the poison of the so-called "National Socialism." And from the beginning I had firmly rejected a "conversion" on the grounds of possibly betraying military secrets. Also under prisoner-of-war conditions nothing remained but to continue withdrawing into myself and further to await the day of the internal decay of the "Brown system." It was indeed in its nature to overextend itself internally and externally, and one day it would collapse under the boundlessness of its military aggression. Gradually I came no longer to have the shadow of a doubt of that.

"I'm afraid I can't help you at the moment," said the station doctor at Cockfosters. "The best thing would be for you to wait a while, and if it doesn't get any better we can always take another look." It was a late summer morning in 1941 and the day had not begun very pleasantly for me. Quite suddenly I had felt indeterminate stomach pains and had to vomit repeatedly without evident cause; I couldn't make rhyme or reason of it. As the trouble wouldn't go away, I finally asked the floor sentry if I could see the doctor. After the latter's words I looked at him, rather at a loss, and then he was gone. When the afternoon brought no improvement, I asked to see the doctor again. This time he didn't come in person, but only sent a message: "If you have pain, you must put up with it."

How to describe my surprise when, shortly before midnight, my cell door burst open and a doctor and his staff, no less than five people, walked in briskly! "Pack right away, you're going to a hospital and will be operated on tomorrow morning," I heard, before I had any idea for what I was to be operated on. And at noon the next day a surgeon in a white smock leaned over my bed: "Well, that was high time, you really had a roaring appendix." I thanked him, "It's a good thing that I came into your hands while there was still time."

By degrees I discovered where I now found myself: in Hatfield House, a manor house about thirty kilometers north of London built at the beginning of the seventeenth century by Robert Cecil, the first earl of Salisbury and prime minister under King James I, and in the possession of the Cecil family for nearly four centuries now. It was surrounded by a great park and built according to a plan beloved since the time of Queen Elizabeth I, two wings joined by a central element which formed the outline of an E, the first letter of the great queen's name. Its exquisite interiors included marvelous paintings, choice furniture, rare Gobelin tapestries, historical arms and armor, and, in the chapel, an original Flemish stained glass window of biblical themes. Now this castle had been converted into a military hospital for the duration of the war. As a German prisoner of war I lay, separated from the Allied patients, on the upper floor of the west wing. The windows of my spacious room provided a charming view of the Elizabethan garden, which I was repeatedly assured still looked exactly as it had in the time of Elizabeth I when a predecessor of the present building had stood here.

In such beautiful surroundings, cared for by two pretty nurses, I could get along very well, even if at first I let all the food offered me pass unenjoyed for lack of appetite.

When I began feeling better and the days seemed longer, at my request a friendly auxiliary brought me a copy of Erskine Childers's *The Riddle of the Sands* from the house library. The novel had appeared in 1903 and made use of the author's observations on a voyage along the German North Sea and Baltic coasts in 1897. At the time he had felt that the German activity there portended an invasion threat for England, an incredible thesis, which the London Admiralty later declared to be absurd. Nevertheless, Childers developed it in such an absorbing manner that the book immediately became a great success. His descriptions of everyday life in a small sailboat were fascinating in themselves. I had first become entwined in the book following a suggestion from my gunnery instructor at the Mürwik Naval School in 1931, Kapitän zur See a.D.* Günther Paschen. Paschen was a good judge of English literature. All at once I had to think of him as one of the strongest and most independent-minded characters I had ever encountered. At the time I had no foreboding of his cruel fate.

Günther Paschen was born in 1880, the son of a vice admiral and a mother of Danish origin. During the Battle of Jutland on 31 May 1916 he was the chief gunnery officer in the battlecruiser *Lützow*, which sank early on the day after the action as a result of the damage she had sustained. He had shot rapidly and with great success at the British

*Ausser Dienst (Retired)

Kapitän zur See a.D. Günther Paschen, the accomplished first gunnery officer in the battlecruiser *Lützow* at the Battle of Jutland on 31 May 1916 and gunnery instructor at the Mürwik Naval School 1929–36, rejected National Socialism at an early date and was murdered by "People's Court" in 1943. (Photograph courtesy of Ruth Paschen.)

capital ships *Princess Royal, Black Prince, Indefatigable,* and *Warspite.* Later he wrote, "Jutland Day on the *Lützow*"—the flagship of the commander of the Scouting Forces, Vice Admiral Hipper— "represents the high point of my career as a naval and gunnery officer; memories of a great and fine work in the service of the cherished weapon bind me to the ship and her crew. Into the battleworthiness of this ship I put all the knowledge and ability that service and study had given me."

A recipient of the Iron Cross I. Class, Paschen had been discharged in 1919 and taught as an instructor at the Mürwik Naval School from 1926 to 1936. In my mind's eye his tall figure now stood again before me there, his face aglow with intelligence and determination—deeply absorbed during instruction in his favorite weapon or at ballistic demonstrations on the grounds of the naval school. Married to an Englishwoman, he had a complete mastery of the English language, shunning the American slang that was becoming increasingly current in Germany, and in his manner cultivating an English charm. He had seen through the mendacity of National Socialism from the beginning; his opposition to the regime was widely known, for on occasion he had spoken his mind—imprudent in a police state.

At the end of August 1943 Paschen opened his home to two unknown Danes who supposedly wished to rent a room, but were actually Nazi agents-provocateurs who had come to involve him in compromising conversations. They succeeded in short order. Paschen said that he did not believe in a German victory and that the Führer's "secret weapons" were just a bluff. As his mother was a Dane, he spoke her language, went hunting in northern Schleswig, and spent a good deal of time in Denmark. He also believed that this country had been wronged in 1864 and that the Reich should give Schleswig back to Denmark.* One of the two Danes later repeated these remarks to a female naval auxiliary with whom he had relations. That was enough for the "People's Court" to condemn Paschen: in private conversation in his own home with citizens of an occupied country the accused had made a public attack on the German military potential and that of an allied people. On 8 November 1943 Günther Paschen was murdered in Brandenburg Prison by Hitler's henchmen. He had refused to appeal for mercy. Raeder, who on private occasions used to stress the strength of his Christian convictions, did not intercede with Hitler in favor of Paschen even after the latter's daughter Ruth implored him by letter to do so. He did not even answer Ruth Paschen's letter. Nor did any of the doomed officer's crewmates step forward to offer a helping hand. Everyone seemed frozen in fear of the "Führer."

In 1951 Professor Dr. Karl Römer, ship's surgeon on the *Lützow* in Paschen's day, wrote a friend of the family:

> Your friendly card continues to move me greatly. Oh, that the noble Paschen was put to death! But it seems thoroughly fitting for that upright man. Already on SMS *Lützow* he was the strong character. You

---

*The border province of Schleswig, whose population was predominantly Danish, had been incorporated into Germany following Denmark's defeat in the War of 1864.

know that of all the officers he was always the one for whom I really had respect. You had to know him, this tall man with a thinker's forehead and a face full of character, who spoke little, and impressed us surgeons as kind and courtly . . . . Everyone spoke of him with respect. Everyone knew that he was really the one who got things done. When he came to the table—frequently late—you knew that he came from work. In humanity and character, he was, in fact, the best . . . . You probably know that he scored a hit with the first shot from the *Lützow*. Furthermore, he impressed me in a most exceptional way: it was probably in April 1916, in a disagreement with other officers, that he remarked that British reports were accurate, while ours were—well, I'll say—colored. He was the only one who saw that at the time; and from then on, I was certain that we would lose the war. And from then on, I felt silently bound to him by the knowledge that the struggle was hopeless. Please give his wife my heartfelt and respectful regards, from one in whose memory her husband remains in death a shining example.

A shining example, a clear-sighted, perceptive patriot, Günther Paschen—honor to his memory!

Amid more reading and conversations with the medical personnel, the time in Hatfield House flew swiftly past. One day I discovered the attraction of the delicious food and decided to help myself well enough to make up for lost time. I also explained this to my physician. O woe! It was an injudicious remark. "If the food tastes so good to you," said the doctor, "you're completely well again and can go back to your camp at once." And straightaway it was farewell to the meat dishes in Hatfield House and back again to my cell in Cockfosters.

39

Shap Wells

My new stay at Cockfosters following my return from Hatfield House would be of only brief duration. My time there had run out. And soon I was on another journey, this time to the north, to my first regular prisoner-of-war camp. This was Camp Number 15, Shap Wells Hotel, near Penrith, Cumberland, a camp allocated solely to the reception of captured German officers.

The hotel, a rectangular building of weathered, local stone, lay as though hidden in a swale about three kilometers from the London-Carlisle road. Its situation in the landscape gave promise of an agreeable coolness during the hot summers, and in winter protection from the sharp winds and often penetrating fogs of these northern latitudes. Its isolated location made it appear an ideal place for quartering prisoners of war.

The hotel was before the war—and is again today—a famous starting point for tours of the in parts majestic, in parts monotonous landscape of the Lake District and the Yorkshire valleys. Its history is remarkable. The present building was always operated as a hotel and was already opened as such in 1833. It had throughout belonged to the earls of Lonsdale. One of them—the one who on account of the color he preferred on his conveyances, the color of his servants' livery, and the yellow carnation that was always in his buttonhole was called "The Yellow Earl"—had the German emperor as a hunting guest at his ancestral seat, Lowther Castle, not far from Shap, in 1910 and 1911. Today, the memory of these visits by Wilhelm II still lives on in the names "Emperor's Lodge" for a row of guest residences

The former Prisoner-of-War Camp No. 15 near Penrith in Cumberland. Today it is again, as it was before the war, the Shap Wells Hotel. (Photograph courtesy of Shap Wells Hotel, Ltd.)

there and "Emperor's Drive" for one of the approaches to the castle. Into the twenties, members of the British royal house had as hunting guests of the Earl of Lonsdale repeatedly visited Shap Wells, which until the Second World War was known as a hotel for the rich and famous.

Shaps Wells Hotel was transformed into a prisoner-of-war camp in February 1941 and Major G. A. I. Dury, M.C., Grenadier Guards, was appointed its first commandant.

There was a great hello upon my arrival there, where among the camp's seventy inmates I encountered many personal acquaintances. In the first place stood the German camp leader, a Korvettenkapitän with whom I was acquainted from prior service. Officers of all three branches of the Wehrmacht were present: among the naval officers, mostly submariners who had lost their boats; Luftwaffe officers who had been downed during the preceding years' air battle over England; and—only a few—army officers who had fallen into British hands after the invasion of the west in May 1940. Whoever had been captured in September–October 1939, like a few of the submariners, already considered themselves expert "old prisoners"; for the newcomers towards the end of 1941 there was, in view of what almost everyone still expected to be a short war, no more "room" for a long stay in British custody. "What! You've come now—it isn't worthwhile anymore!" No wonder—the quick victories from 1939 to the summer of 1941 were still fresh memories; things would certainly continue to move just as fast!

I cannot complain of the accommodations in the camp. Of course, it was less roomy than in my spacious cell at Cockfosters, but I shared my room with nice comrades on one of the upper floors reserved for prisoners. There was a great deal to tell and to ask and a little less space soon lost its significance. The hotel furnishings, including bed linens, were completely at our disposal. At night searchlights, which had been set up around the camp, slid over the iron bars mounted outside the windows. They were supposed to frustrate attempts to escape under cover of darkness. Of the rooms on the ground floor, the big dining room served us prisoners; the rest were claimed by the British camp authorities. The garden adjoining the building we found very pleasant. We could go walking in it and sometimes also plant flowers or vegetables. Two rings of barbed wire ran around the building and garden, an obstacle against escape to be taken seriously by prisoners of war.

It was customary for every newcomer to give a talk to the camp inmates on the circumstances of his capture as soon as possible. Naturally, mine concerned the action and end of the battleship *Bismarck*. After fulfilling this duty one was, so to say completely, accepted into the camp community.

The prisoners' daily life was determined by an unvarying uniformity. The external discipline followed a fixed schedule: wake up, to the roll call that ascertained we were all present; meal times; in the evenings "lights out." Variations in our existence came about mainly through the occasional arrival of "new ones," the coming and going of the seasons, and the impressions of political and military changes in the world. Soon it became a crucial question of keeping ourselves physically and mentally fit for an indefinite period. At Shap Wells, praise God, we had the freedom to do both in sufficient measure.

Of our food, always a sensitive point, I personally had no complaints. If in quantity it often seemed scanty, it was still adequate and of good quality. Time and again, however, comrades suffered from serious indigestion, apparently a result of the fact that the cooks, formerly assistant cooks from U-boat crews, were not completely the masters of their craft. These cooks had to process, altogether on their own, the raw materials the British provided, which corresponded to the rations of second-line British troops. But the kitchen's performance never became optimal and the shortcomings in food preparation did not cease.

In the end, one of the camp inmates especially concerned about this matter, Oberleutant (Luftwaffe) der Reserve Franz Schad, seized the initiative on his own responsibility. With the aid of P. Eduard Griffith* of the London Oratorium, who often visited the camp, he gained the understanding of the fundamentally well-meaning British camp commandant, who was well acquainted with the priest. Major Dury consented to Schad's proposal to engage interned civilian cooks from German merchant ships on a voluntary basis to work at Shap Wells. With their arrival in November 1941 the food became magnificent; the chronic indigestion that a few inmates had gradually developed disappeared.

Whoever wished could do gymnastics in the garden or care for plants or occupy himself with handicrafts. Here our Austrian comrades were especially resourceful. The necessary tools were available, a pleasant peculiarity of this camp. Those interested could borrow saws, files, hammers, drills, etc., from the hotel's supply. These objects were issued against a receipt and had to be returned by 1600 hours at the latest—strictly for hobby use was understood. In fact, no "misuse" became known, which would have brought this practice to an early end.

Physically bracing walks outside the camp were also possible. Major Dury, a well-meaning and good man as we have already seen—a school director before the war—had no objection to that. "The participants must, of course," he emphasized to the German camp leader, "give their word of honor not to attempt to escape while outside the camp." And whoever agreed to that could move through the open landscape two or three afternoons a week. Not always to the undivided joy of the British escort officers, who were already older men. For it was nothing for the young German officers quickly to cover kilometer after kilometer of the hilly terrain.

A camp library was available for intellectual interests and occupation. It was also possible to buy books. The officer prisoners received a monthly allowance according to rank, with which books could be

---

*Born on 1 May 1909, Griffith was elected general procurator of the worldwide community of the Oratorium of St. Philip Neri in Rome in 1948 and elected its first visitator in 1958. He died in Livorno on 14 June 1959.

purchased through the canteen. I personally obtained a series of Oxford University Press grammars and dictionaries, as well as historical and constitutional literature on the "host country," Britain and the Commonwealth. In his book, *The Government of England*, the author A. Lawrence Lowell, former president of Harvard University, first called my attention to the presently well-known political prognosticator Alexis de Toqueville and the latter's standard work, *La Démocratie en l'Amérique*, his comparison of national constitutions.

However, a minority in camp wished to create a more far-reaching intellectual life. The foremost was Franz Schad, by civilian profession a counselor to the government of Württemberg and an attorney experienced in state administration. Intellectually at home in the Catholic youth- and student-movements, he proposed the immediate formation of intellectual- and scientific-study groups. Although the appropriate interest was present, Schad could not carry through with his idea. His drive for an organized study program was defeated by the opposition of the German camp leadership and, in the final analysis, by the anti-intellectual reflex that was then so widespread in German lands. For a long time, infectious Nazi slogans such as "You are nothing, your Folk is everything," "Führer command, we obey," "The Führer is always right," and similar slogans had reached the level of an intellectual epidemic and led to a submissive self-surrender of the individual to Hitler, who was identified with the "State." No wonder that such surrenders made themselves evident chiefly in the life of communities, including such a one as Shap Wells: all young officers who had experienced nothing but the explosive victories of 1939–40 and would live to see more like them until the "final victory" and Hitler's "New Order" for Europe. Must not someone or other's sudden turn to civilian studies in the midst of the war appear to them a sign of "defeatism"?

Whoever wished to acquire technical school or university-level learning in Shap Wells, therefore, had to find an avenue for himself. Franz Schad, learned and extremely well read—known and renowned as the "Crown Jurist" and the "Academic Yeast Germ"—and others, who were qualified engineers and mathematicians, were ready to help any way they could. So those who were interested could study seriously and profitably, even in the absence of a formal program.

Of course, artistic activity also flowered in Shap Wells. In the camp, tiny in comparison with those of the later war years, some officers showed themselves to be talented painters and drawers, ac-

Oberleutnant (Luftwaffe) der Reserve Franz Schad, an attorney experienced in government administration, intellectually at home in the Catholic youth- and student-movements, was renowned in various prisoner-of-war camps as the "Crown Jurist" and the "Academic Yeast Germ." He is shown here at the prisoner-of-war camp at Grande Ligne, Quebec. (Photograph courtesy of Franz Schad.)

tors and instrumentalists. Musical recitals and theatrical productions brought a highly welcome diversion and delight to many an evening. I especially recall an Austrian Luftwaffe officer who had played the violin very well before the war. In Shap Wells he took it up again with energy and consistency. Soon he regained all the ground that he obviously had mastered before. Later, in the big camps in Canada he became the concert-master and celebrated soloist of the symphony orchestras organized there. It is also worthy of grateful note that throughout the years of captivity he gave coaching in the violin to those who requested his assistance.

It is almost superfluous to say how important the opportunity of maintaining contact with relatives at home was to the prisoners.

Every month the officers were allowed three letters of twenty-four lines each and four postcards of seven lines, on paper that had been treated to frustrate the use of invisible ink. The censors on both sides deleted the passages they found objectionable with black ink. For the most part, this postal system worked. Naturally, every now and again wartime conditions led to great delays in delivery.

There was scarcely a German prisoner-of-war camp that over the course of the years did not have its "breakers out," and Shap Wells was no exception. It was November 1941 and two young Luftwaffe officers, Karl Wappler and Heinz Schnabel, decided to break out. I learned of their plan when they asked if I would help them in one respect. "Gladly," I said, "what's it about?"

"Well," they explained, "we want to pose as Dutch pilots who have been detailed to train airfield personnel to defend against a possible German airborne invasion. We gained plenty of the appropriate experience after the beginning of the campaign in the west in May 1940—and this must appear on our identity papers, which will be in English. Can you provide us with the text? We can prepare the papers themselves." "But certainly," I said, "no problem."

After the German camp leader, to whom naturally the plan for such an escape had to be submitted, had approved it, Wappler and Schnabel made ready to carry it out. They studied British illustrated magazines that somehow came to hand, noting the pattern, color, buttons, and badges of the Dutch uniforms pictured, then tailored their own outfits. At a tactically suitable moment, they supplied themselves with blank identity papers from the office of the British camp commandant, and immersed themselves in maps and meteorological charts, as well as wind atlases. For it was their intention to proceed to a training field not far from Shap Wells, steal an aircraft, and disappear for good in the direction of the Continent. The adventurous details of their successful escape from camp have since been described in the literature of the war and will be merely sketched here. As neither Wappler nor Schnabel are still alive, I have followed the publications of British authors in describing their experiences outside camp.

On Sunday, 23 November, everything was ready. On the afternoon of that day Wappler and Schnabel concealed themselves in a hollow space as high as a man, inside a pile of firewood that had been collected on walks outside the camp and stacked in the garden for use during the winter. After nightfall, they left their hiding place and crawled along a shallow ditch screened on both sides by rhododendrons to the boundary wire. The origin of the ditch had been explained to the British camp authorities as a means of garden "beauti-fication," but had actually been planned from the start to facilitate this operation. Moving only in the intervals of darkness between the sweeps of the searchlights circling the camp, they reached the barbed wire, whose individual strands they pried apart with a wooden double-lever they had fashioned for themselves. And then nothing but go through and get out of there—perfect work!

Then they proceeded—they knew the lay of the land from previous outings—to an especially steep cut of the London, Midland, and Scot-land Railway, which ran near Shap Wells. There they sprang from the slope onto a freight train wheezing its way north. Upon reaching the freight yard at Carlisle, they left the train, took off the overalls that until then they had worn over their "uniforms," and sought refuge in a nearby cinema. After the film, they attached themselves to some Allied members of the RAF, in whose company, unchallenged, they reached their goal, the Kingstown airfield, only around three kilome-ters away. At its entrance they were blinded by the dazzling flashlight of a sentry, who, however, excused himself with a "Sorry, sir," as soon as he recognized the "Dutch officers." Wappler and Schnabel passed completely for what, on the strength of their "identity pa-pers," they now were—Wappler, "Flight Lieutenant Harry Graven"; Schnabel, "Pilot Officer George Henry David." They spent the night behind a hangar.

Morning came and now it became a question of finding a little aircraft, fueled up as fully as possible and ready for immediate use. Upon carefully patrolling the airfield they saw something that struck them both as advantageous: there were crowds of Poles, Czechs, Dutch, and Norwegians in training, which meant that rudimentary English would scarcely be noticed among the jumble of languages. But, it suddenly occurred to Wappler, perhaps there are too many Poles, from whom there is nothing good to expect. Yet we won't let ourselves be discouraged, no, not at this pont, he consoled himself.

It was a foggy morning. Flight operations had yet to begin, but aircraft inspection was under way. They walked on, to the edge of the field, where they had spied two Miles Magisters, little monoplanes that the RAF used for training purposes. "Good morning," Wappler said to the younger of the mechanics working there, "the base com-mander has ordered that one of these two machines take off on a weather reconnaissance. Prepare one for take off!" Wondering about the choice of such a small training plane for this purpose, the me-chanic was ready to challenge it until Wappler roughly reminded him that there was "never any accounting for" the base commander's choices, after which the man gave him a plane. Wappler and Schnabel cast a quick glance over the cockpit fittings, nodded: "We'll soon be through with that"—and clambered into the two seats. It was approximately 1130 hours on this 24th of November.

"Engine on!" Wappler ordered the mechanic, who obeyed; the motor coughed once, twice, came on, and revved up to full power. And the way was clear—to the runway and into the air. The mechanic's shout didn't carry to the two passengers in the plane: "Those two chaps don't even have one parachute, despite the regulations! They probably can't even read English yet. Oh, these Poles!"

Above the clouds the Germans had no idea of the confusion of the airfield commander, Wing Commander Francis S. Homersham, upon learning of their flight. They were concerned solely with the correct course to Germany and their supply of gas—would it suffice? That the range of the Magister was 367 miles they did not know exactly, only that the shortest way over the North Sea led to Holland and that was about 365 miles. If the fuel was dropping visibly before they reached the sea, they would land in England and trust to their well-tested nerve to have the plane fueled up again.

It was a day of nasty weather; unpleasant clouds hung to sixty meters, the ground could seldom be seen, and visibility forward was only about two miles, which greatly complicated navigation. The air temperature at their altitude was only a little above zero; they were miserably cold, and the air stream finally ripped off Wappler's head covering. From a little map they had carried along he believed that he could confirm flying over Leeds and then following The Wash to the coast near Norfolk, where the decision of whether to cross the North Sea would have to be made. There, however, came a warning signal from the fuel indicator; its needle was already near the red danger zone. And so it would have been sheer suicide to begin the crossing now, without any life-preserving equipment on board in case they had to ditch in the sea. After only a few minutes over the water they decided to turn back to England and make an emergency landing somewhere, with the aim of refueling.

It was 1450 hours and they had flown approximately 325 miles when Wappler set the Magister down cleanly in a meadow at Scratby, north of Great Yarmouth. To the curious villagers who assembled, he served up his "history": "We're Dutch pilots on a training flight to Croydon. Unfortunately, we've run out of fuel. Can we get some here?" The local policeman, who seemed to be impressed by the RAF markings on the aircraft and the two men's papers, put through a call for Wappler to the duty officer at the nearby RAF airfield at Horsham St. Faith. But, as by then it was growing late in the day, the latter could not comply with Wappler's request for assistance in making an immediate take off. Instead, he sent a car to pick them up. And carry them to the RAF airfield—into the heart of the enemy air arm. The prospect could bring anyone in their place to the verge of panic. But what good would that do? This wasn't the moment to give up the bluff—not yet!

"Give these Dutch officers some tea!" said the duty officer at Horsham St. Faith to a sergeant, after he had heard and believed the Germans' "history." He also gave them quarters for the night. But he was the last British officer to be taken in. In the meanwhile, the Magister's "departure" from the Kingstown airfield had become a subject of discussion and had buzzed through the circuits to southern England. And Wappler and Schnabel's hot bath was ended prematurely when a group of officers armed with pistols entered their room and the airfield commander, Group Captain James N. D. Anderson, OBE, said in a friendly manner, "I am sorry, gentlemen, you deserved better luck. We shall have dinner together but after that I shall have to hand you over to the PoW authorities." Indeed, there was no help for it now, Wappler and Schnabel had to own up to their identities. The military police brought them back to Shap Wells, where they were sentenced to twenty-eight days' confinement, the standard penalty for attempted escapes.

"One really has to take off one's hat to them," Major Dury said privately. "I really regret having to lock them up." And, like him, the British public was impressed by the pair's audacity and cold-blooded nerve. Admiration for their imagination and courage appeared in the press. Wappler and Schnabel's undertaking may be counted among the coolest and most imaginative attempted escapes by German prisoners of war in the Second World War.

At Shap Wells one German officer lived apart from the camp community, hermetically secluded. He had his own quarters, was served his meals separately, and went walking alone. All the officers were instructed by the German camp leadership not to speak to him and to avoid any contact with him. This officer had been ostracized and was to spend his entire captivity, in different camps and continents, in this sort of bleak isolation. He was Kapitänleutnant Hans Rahmlow, former captain of the *U-570*, the boat whose capture by the British in

August 1941 I have already mentioned. I was completely in the dark as to the exact circumstances of the loss of the U-boat and his being taken prisoner; what his side of the story might be, I had no idea. Inwardly, I felt the impulse to ask him to tell me about it. Personally, I felt no inhibitions at all about showing sympathy for him. But I abstained, in the interest of keeping peace in camp.

It was known that in another camp an "Honor Council" composed of U-boat officers had sat in judgment of Rahmlow's first watch officer, Oberleutnant zur See Bernhard Berndt. This board, acting as an "Honor Court," had found Berndt guilty of "cowardice in the face of the enemy," as Rahmlow's deputy sharing responsibility for the loss and British capture of the *U-570* and ostracized him in the camp. Among officers "cowardice in the face of the enemy," if in fact it had occurred here, was viewed as a shameful offense. And since this was a question of such an offense, a conversation with Rahmlow—an arbitrary breaking of the ban—would have only inflamed the atmosphere in camp and created a tempest in a teapot which in the end would have accomplished nothing. So it was simply more sensible to give up the thought of talking with Rahmlow. And indeed it was conceivable that he himself would not have welcomed it, so *coram populo*.

Whenever, in those days, I pondered over Rahmlow, the shamefulness of the conduct held against him, and the guiding concept of "Officers' Honor" formed by centuries of monarchical tradition—in terms of which the ostracism of Rahmlow appeared explicable if not obligatory—I could on the other hand think only with the greatest bitterness of the grave wounds that the "Führer," very personally and in the absence of an appropriate rejoinder, had long since inflicted on the Wehrmacht's honor code. Hitler's murder of Generals von Schleicher and von Bredow* in July 1934 and his unprecedented insult to the Wehrmacht in the shamelessly conducted dismissal of the army's commander in chief, Generaloberst Baron von Fritsch, in 1938 came to mind.† Blinded by the succession of Hitler's sham successes, inwardly weakened and made unsure by the ceaseless cascade of Brown

*General Kurt von Schleicher, who had served briefly as chancellor in late 1932 and early 1933, his wife, and his closest collaborator, General Ferdinand von Bredow, were among the victims of the Blood Purge (please see note, p. 22).

†Early in 1938 Hitler dismissed Werner Baron von Fritsch as commander in chief of the army on account of what were later proven to be fabricated accusations of homosexuality. Although subsequently Fritsch was officially "rehabilitated," he was not restored to his post. He found a soldier's death while accompanying the regiment of which he was honorary colonel during the Polish campaign of 1939.

propaganda, the Wehrmacht had been unable to mobilize its honor code as an effective defense. Insofar as the code was still intact and useful in the conduct of the war, Hitler would make use of it, to be sure. But basically he had long since taken leave of those whom with a view to the officers he once ridiculed as "antiquated knights with a dust-covered conception of honor."

Increasingly Hitler's hypocritical ideology had penetrated the erstwhile apolitical preserve called the Wehrmacht and had introduced there, among other things, a new "standard of honor." It stipulated, for the first time, that a married officer also bore full responsibility for defamatory conduct on the part of his wife—an anticipation, initially little remarked, of the barbarity of *Sippenhaft.** New formulas also appeared for the public aspect of the honor code. One motto read: "My honor is my loyalty." Loyalty to whom? Well, to the "Führer" alone, who dictatorially and without responsibility to anything or anyone, had started to destroy civilization in Europe to the extent that the Wehrmacht's territorial conquests enabled him to do so. And later he developed such a frenzy to retain the conquered territories that he not only ordered them to be held, under *all* circumstances, *whatever* the cost, without regard to the strategic situation, but on account of his inflexible demands even introduced a new "Honor Concept" for the "German officer." He subsequently formulated it: "May it some day belong to the Honor Concept of German officers . . . that the surrender of a district or city is unthinkable and that above all the military leaders will have to set a shining example of the most faithful performance of duty unto death." "Honor à la Hitler" instead of strategy and tactics, to hold territory in every case, without regard to *anything*, "performance of duty" for Hitler's interests— which were not the German interests—total obedience! A thousand worlds removed from the intelligent obedience understood by a Tauroggen-Yorck,† a Hubertusburg-Marwitz, who "chose disgrace where obedience did not bring honor," a Colonel Buchholz in the First World War: "I don't command arsonists, this order will not be carried out." Here now were slaves to command.

But of course every German retreat, however slight or however

*A law promulated in 1944 which made an entire family liable for an act committed by any of its members.

†General Ludwig Yorck von Wartenburg commanded the Prussian corps assigned to support Napoleon's army in the Russian campaign of 1812. Acting without orders, on 30 December he concluded the Convention of Tauroggen, an agreement with Russia whereby his forces assumed a neutral status. This bold initiative encouraged his country's ensuing switch from reluctant ally to ardent enemy of France.

substantial in individual cases, signified a Soviet advance to the west, a thrust forward by the "ultimate avengers," which they would indeed be, towards Herr Hitler's own precious skin, more precious than the Reich. And the nearer the avengers thrust, the deeper he buried himself in personal security, against war and assassination until the end in Berlin, where he let half-grown boys be slaughtered for him. If only the destroyer of the Reich lived on! One must never lose sight of it: he was such an egomaniac and nihilist, despiser of the officer corps and its "dust-covered conception of honor," for whom in the final analysis Rahmlow had to suffer long years of isolation in the camps and bear the brunt of a life thus ruined.

Newspapers and magazines were not available to individual prisoners at Shap Wells, but the German camp leadership received a selection. The latter also had access to British radio broadcasts. The camp leader could periodically give a comprehensive report on the progress of the war at our common mealtimes. The terminology of such newscasts was, understandably, in keeping with the Brown spirit of the time, which included the obligatory anti-Christian accent. Whenever it was necessary to speak about Winston Churchill, and in England that could not be avoided every now and again, his name changed itself, unforgettably, into "Church-evil."

In any event, we could follow the situation on the many fronts. The stagnation of the German offensive on Moscow at the beginning of winter in 1941, the serious defeat there in December, the Japanese attack on Pearl Harbor on 7 December, Hitler's declaration of war on the U.S.A. on 11 December—we learned of all this almost immediately. Declaration of war *on*, not *by* America, that was a long way from the Hitler who on board the *Bismarck* on 5 May had said, "I consider American intervention in this war to be out of the question!" But I cannot claim, even in retrospect, that at the time the significance of the failure of our Moscow offensive to the entire course of the Russian campaign fully dawned on us.

Also in December, the British radio reported the loss of the capital ships *Repulse* and *Prince of Wales* to Japanese aerial torpedoes in the Far East. At our table the news was greeted with long-lasting rejoicing. The *Prince of Wales* had stood opposite the *Bismarck* in the battle southwest of Iceland half a year earlier; my memory of it was still so fresh. But so, too, were the gruesome scenes on the decks of the *Bismarck* a few days later. Similar scenes might now have played themselves out in the *Prince of Wales*. The mere thought of them choked any feeling of rejoicing in me.

40

Transport to Canada

In March 1942, a delegation of British officers from London visited Shap Wells and spoke with Major Dury. At once rumors, which soon congealed into certainty, arose that we prisoners were to be moved—but where? To Canada.

In imminent expectation of a German invasion, Great Britain had shipped most German prisoners of war, numbering around three thousand, to Canada in 1940. What awaited us was a seaborne transfer of approximately one thousand men, including two hundred officers, after whose departure only about two hundred German prisoners would remain in England. No other power participating in the Second World War dispersed its prisoners so far around the world as Great Britain: besides the British Isles themselves, in Australia, Canada, the U.S.A., Egypt, Tunisia, Algeria, France, Belgium, Italy, Austria, Norway, Cyprus, Malta, Gibraltar and, at times, still other places. By the end of 1942 more than ten thousand German prisoners were to be brought to Canada from camps in the Near East. The remote expanses of this enormous land afforded the necessary space.

At the end of March we left Shap Wells to travel to the port of Greenock. Here a veritable armada of ships, defended against air attack by countless barrage balloons, was being organized into a convoy. Our quarters for the coming days and nights was the transport *Rangitiki* (16,755 BRT, 15 knots, employed as a troop transport since February 1941). On boarding the ship we stepped onto decks strung with barbed wire that left room for a daily walk for exercise on the upper deck. Following the convoy's zigzag course as a precaution against U-boats, the *Rangitiki* brought us to Halifax, Nova Scotia.

The voyage passed without special incident, even if occasionally we were in somewhat "precarious" spirits. For as much as one wished his U-boats success, one nevertheless hoped that they would not torpedo the very ship in which a person himself was traveling.

After a railway trip of several days, repeatedly interrupted by halts, the train stopped in an open field that for all we knew might have been anywhere in Canada. However, we were still well within the eastern part of the country. "This is it," the word came, "everybody out." So, carrying our baggage, we tramped cross-country to the entrance gate of our new "hostel," whose name we now learned: Bowmanville, established as a prisoner-of-war camp in 1941 and in the meantime occupied by hundreds of German officers. More than one hundred German enlisted men looked after the cleanliness of the quarters and worked as barbers, tailors, cobblers, carpenters, and cooks. After the mild weather in England and during the ocean voyage, the snow that was falling upon our arrival made such an impression that I noted the date. It was 9 April 1942.

The first glimpse was highly agreeable. We saw pleasant, low houses and one or another higher, utilitarian structures, all built of solid stone, with pretty grounds planted in between with trees and shrubs. As a senior Kapitänleutnant—together with a Luftwaffe major—I enjoyed the advantage of being able to take possession of a double room in a long building. Besides a bed, we each had a table and, for the two of us, a separate bathroom with tub and sink, all centrally heated, and with hot water out of the tap. In fact, we were living in one of the teachers' residences of a former country school of the Province of Ontario for handicapped boys, about sixty kilometers east of Toronto. The province had to put it at the disposal of the federal government in Ottawa after the previously defective accommodations of German prisoners had led to sharp exchanges between the German and Canadian governments and to threats of reprisals on the German side. I knew right away that I now found myself in a camp which later and quite justifiably came to be known as "unquestionably the finest on this or that side of the ocean." And as long as I was a prisoner in Canada I would not voluntarily consent to being transferred to any other camp. The test of my resolution came quickly. A number of officers, among which I was included, were to be transferred to another camp in Ontario. I asked the German camp leadership to intervene with the Canadians on my behalf, as in the meanwhile I had been making progress in an academic course of instruction. The Canadians had no objections. Only the number of

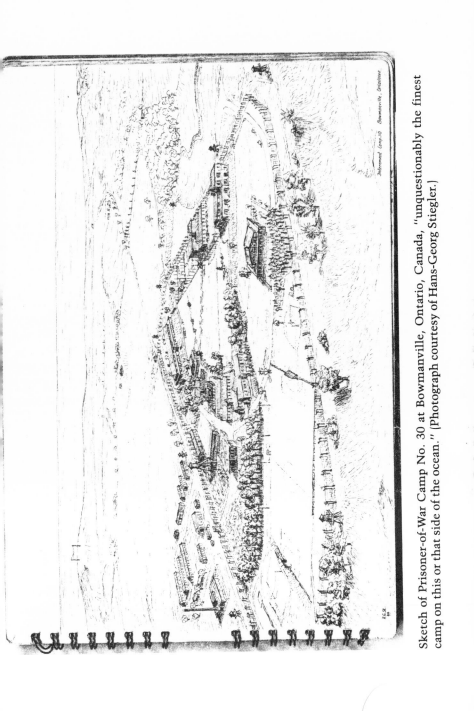

Sketch of Prisoner-of-War Camp No. 30 at Bowmanville, Ontario, Canada, "unquestionably the finest camp on this or that side of the ocean." (Photograph courtesy of Hans-Georg Stiegler.)

men transferred mattered. In such cases there were always volunteers.

The truly comfortable accommodations—although for junior officers extremely cramped in interior space—were matched by the other camp facilities: reading and work rooms in the houses (later wooden barracks were built for classrooms); an auditorium for assemblies; a large gymnasium and beside it a heated swimming hall; a large kitchen next to the dining room; a dispensary; handball and volleyball courts, tennis courts that in winter were converted for ice hockey and figure-skating, football fields, a track, fields for gymnastics, medicine ball, etc.; land for laying out little gardens of vegetables or ornamental plants; a hothouse for tropical plants. In exchange for one's word of honor not to escape, it was possible to take supervised walks outside the camp, to swim in nearby Lake Ontario and, in winter, to ski and toboggan. On their word of honor, those interested could also work on the adjacent camp farm. This produced extra potatoes, vegetables, and kitchen herbs. In the course of time, horses, cows, chickens, and pigs were also obtained. Inside the camp there was even a little zoo, consisting of two rhesus monkeys, three raccoons, a little crocodile, and two tame ravens and tortoises. The contents of the camp library were already imposing upon my arrival and increased significantly in the years to come.

Thus Bowmanville offered ample employment for mind and body and adequate freedom in the choice of activities.

The camp proper was enclosed by two barbed wire fences, each four meters high, with a knee-high warning wire on the inside. Outside stood tall watchtowers for the Canadian warders, the so-called Veteran Guards, who impressed us as older, calm and decent men. At night this security zone was illuminated by searchlights and ground lights and, understandably, as a rule we were not allowed to leave the houses.

At Bowmanville, as at Shap Wells, it was obligatory to make a presentation to the inmates of the camp on the circumstances in which one had been taken prisoner. As there were already about five hundred officers in camp, the number of listeners was substantial. When my turn came, before me there sat a representative part of our nation's military bloodline, young men in the spring of life, navy, air force, and army officers, many of them daredevils, decorated, a few highly decorated—they all had been snatched out of the air, off the sea, or from the war on land in the years from 1939 to 1941.

We soon became accustomed to the daily routine of the camp. A complete roll call was held at 0700 and 1800, and the meal times were at fixed hours. We ate in sections, as the dining hall would not seat everyone at once. The food was good, also in its variety, and abundant. Furthermore, we received a monthly allowance according to rank; for me as a Kapitänleutant it was $28.00, and later, as a Korvettenkapitän, $32.00. With this we could buy additional foodstuffs in the canteen and order personal articles and commodities of every sort, even such things as athletic equipment and lawn chairs from the mail-order catalog of the Eaton department store in Toronto. Rationed quantities of cigarettes and beer were also available. Naturally, the purchase of stronger alcohol was prohibited.

Our transfer to Canada could only confirm the suspicion I had harbored since Hitler's attack on the Soviet Union that the war would be a very long one. In any case, I wanted to use the time to come for a serious course of study and hoped to find an opportunity to do so in such a generously equipped camp as Bowmanville. It came soon and was due especially to the preliminary work of two men. On the *Rangitiki* Franz Schad, who has already been mentioned several times, had met another open-minded jurist: Dr. Walter Seeburg, a reserve major in the Luftwaffe, in civil life justice of the Hanseatic Provincial Court and deputy president of the Reich Higher Admiralty Court. Seeburg was a restrained but decided democrat—he and Schad had understood one another from the start. In many conversations below the barbed wire entanglement on the upper deck, walking back and forth near the ship's bridge, they decided to start a program of study in the New World. From the experience in England they knew that passive resistance was to be expected from the German camp leadership, but this time, they resolved, they would overcome it. In Bowmanville this resistance was broken by a threat from Seeburg, the idea for which came from Schad: if necessary, Seeburg would denounce the anti-intellectualism in the officers' camps in a letter to the state secretary in the Reich Ministry of Justice, Dr. Rothenberger, his former superior. This worked and the ice melted. The German camp leadership assigned a lecture room, as well as a library-workroom, to the two men for their course. The faculty of law was born.

On Ascension Day 1942 Franz Schad opened the Bowmanville law course with a lecture in a side room of the dining hall on the necessity and significance of the study of the history of law, which was also a prerequisite to understanding the various legal systems. I had enrolled as a student for the entire course in jurisprudence. While Schad spoke, the dining hall rang with an "anti-intellectual" protest as plates and utensils were banged against one another. But such protests soon disappeared; people get used to anything.

While Seeburg was the "dean" of our faculty of law and Schad a founding lecturer, now it was necessary to recruit other teachers for the many-sided study of jurisprudence. They were found among the camp's reserve and even, in part, regular officers; later accessions of prisoners brought increasing numbers of reserve officers, including lawyers. As lecturers there came into consideration especially officers who had qualified for the bench or the higher civil service. But those who had taken their first bar examination and had been appointed Assesoren (K)* during the war also in part proved to be outstanding lecturers. Gradually the program of instruction was broadened and deepened and it became possible to study almost every aspect of an ordinary law course. Lectures, study, exercises, seminars, examinations, and homework were all included in the methodology. In September 1942, the second semester at Bowmanville opened with more than forty students. Altogether, the studies there lasted six semesters, until the end of 1944, when transfers to other regions of Canada heralded the closing of the Bowmanville camp in April 1945.

There is no need to emphasize how important the supply of teaching materials was for these studies. It was, continually, acceptable to good. Law codes, textbooks, and commentaries were not only available but so abundant per capita that as a student at the University of Frankfurt-am-Main in the years 1947–49 I often thought longingly of the law library in Bowmanville. Specialized journals and Reich law statutes were also available. We owed this supply to the charitable and humanitarian organizations legitimatized by the Geneva Convention for the protection of prisoners of war, especially the International Educational Office, Geneva—Department for Mental Assistance to Prisoners of War, the International Committee of the Red Cross, the German and the Swiss Red Cross, the German Caritas Union, and the Young Men's Christian Association. Here I think warmly and gratefully of the Director for Canada of the War Prisoners' Aid of the Young Men's Christian Association, the deceased Swiss citizen Hermann Boeschenstein. He frequently visited the

*Probationary attorney (wartime). This term was used to designate candidates for admission to the bar who, as a result of wartime exigencies, had been advanced to the "probationary" grade sooner than was customary in peace.

camp and occupied himself with the innumerable requests of the German prisoners. His activities were recognized in 1970 when, as consul general in Toronto, I presented him with the Grand Merit Cross of the Order of Merit which he had been awarded by the president of the Federal Republic.

Learning materials could also be acquired through private channels. In this connection hardly anyone was busier than the indefatigable Schad, who from the beginning of his captivity had made requests for literature from personal friends and from official sources in Germany and Switzerland and received it continuously. Engaged as he now was in research and teaching, he gradually accumulated seven hundredweight (350 kilograms) of professional publications in his baggage and was allowed to carry them along in his intermittent transfers from camp to camp, undisturbed by the British and Canadian authorities, although according to international agreement they were obliged to allow a total of only one hundredweight per officer. Oh yes, Schad and his books: when in 1946, coming from Canada with twenty-eight boxes from the last Canadian camp library in his baggage, he entered a British camp his comrades there greeted him with the words: "Oh no, here comes the Canuck, and he's bringing twenty-eight boxes of democracy!" Unforgettable. But the British always had a soft spot for him. Upon his own repatriation, he left his store of books at the last camp in England. After it was closed the British government sent them to his home address in Württemberg, free of charge and postage paid!

One of the prerequisites for my admission to continue law studies at the University of Frankfurt-am-Main in April 1947 was proof of the six semesters of studies that I had completed at Bowmanville. The university gave me four semesters' credit for them and, for the purpose of the first state law examination, certification of at least three consecutive semesters' study in a German university. The credit for Bowmanville studies was optimal and I could be content. I took the first state law exam in Frankfurt in May 1949. Gratitude filled me then and fills me today to our teachers in Canada, who took it upon themselves to perform years of selfless labor to help those who were interested to prepare for the future. Very special thanks are due to program-founder Schad and to the memory of our Bowmanville "dean," Dr. Walter Seeburg, who unfortunately died early.

The studies in Bowmanville gave me, a professional naval officer, the first direct insight into the devastation that Hitler had wrought and continued to wreak on the legal system in order to carry through his dictatorship over our national life. This is an area about which a great deal has since been published and about which, writing from an autobiographical perspective, I can mention only a few points from my own experience. The course of study at Bowmanville began at a time when the Allied press was reporting a spectacular and apparently new attack by Hitler on the German judicature. The background lay in his speech to the "Greater German Reichstag"—which assembled for the last time on this occasion—in the Kroll Opera House in Berlin on 26 April 1942. At its end, the so-called Full Powers Act, later interpreted as the Supreme Enabling Act, proposed by Hermann Göring was "unanimously" accepted. Naturally, the details, text, or official significance of this law were not immediately available to prisoners of war in far-off Canada. As a rule, we could obtain so complete a picture only over a long period of time, often months, by various means: the Canadian radio, Allied news publications, secretly received radio broadcasts from Germany, the gradual receipt of statutes, specialized journals, and the like. And so now it was some time until we really understood this Reichstag session, about which the available extracts from Hitler's speech had only shown his usual violent rhetoric and dark threats. What did it mean?

Among other things—I restrict myself to the field of law—Hitler had himself proclaimed "Supreme Magistrate," and this "without being bound by existing legal formulas." The public acceptance of the explanation he had given the Reichstag on 13 July 1934 after the murders in the Röhm affair,* in which he had said—"In this hour I was responsible for the destiny of the German nation and therefore the German people's Supreme Magistrate"—no longer satisfied him; henceforth, he would no longer publicly need a spectacular, special motive to commit murder. From now on, therefore, murder at any time, murder enemies of the regime, critics of the regime, with or without the law—what was new about that, what was new about the long-established, absolute abrogation of the separation of powers?

In the first part of his April 1942 speech, Hitler once again and vehemently denounced the "Jewish element also responsible for this war," attacking over and over again the "Jewish world-pest," in the style of his speech of 30 January 1941, which I had had to listen to on board the *Bismarck*. His fury towards the Jews now appeared to reach a new height and, as I learned after the war, he had in fact just signed a decree "concerning the systematic intellectual fight against Jews

---

*Captain Ernst Röhm, commander of the SA, was the most prominent Nazi leader killed in the Blood Purge.

. . . as a duty required by the war." Among other things, it regulated the state's right to confiscate Jewish cultural properties that "are ownerless or not of incontestably clear provenance." How might they have become truly "ownerless"? Well, scarcely otherwise than by physical force, of which I had observed a small sample on the Kurfürstendamm on 9 November 1938. Only now and in the darkness of wartime disorders such physical force would be exercised even more limitlessly and fiercely. In his aims Hitler was extremism itself, and he knew he would easily drag the Germans, as he understood them, down his path. Anyone who was an eyewitness to and perceived the meaning of the 1938 pogrom already had Auschwitz before his eyes: not by name, not by number of victims, not by technique of murder. But as one of the terrible scenes from the vision of the unbounded expansion of power that his manias seemed to have burned into Hitler.

In 1938 most Germans still had not grasped that it was Hitler himself who wanted all this. In his memoirs Raeder wrote, "Hitler assured me . . . most earnestly that the entire action [of 9 November 1938], which had come to a head as a spontaneous reaction to the murder of a member of the German legation in Paris, contradicted . . . his policy in every respect. It had happened without his knowledge or consent; the Gauleiter [of Berlin, Goebbels] had let go the helm on him. . . ." Even today, there are historians who deny Hitler's personal authorship of the murder of the Jews. They claim that no written order can be traced to him. These historians either did not live through that period in Germany or did not do so with an observant intelligence. For Hitler's long arm reached into (almost) every corner of the country; it was easy for him inconspicuously to give signals, and the starting point of his orders could be hidden without trace in the mazes of the apparatus of power, covering up responsibilities, when that was indicated.

But a foreigner who saw through Hitler at an early date was Sir Horace Rumbold, the British ambassador to Berlin. On 11 May 1933, the day of his first conversation with Hitler, he wired his foreign minister, expressing his conviction "that Herr Hitler is himself responsible for the anti-Jewish policy of the German Government and that it would be a mistake to believe that it is the policy of his wilder men, whom he has difficulty in controlling. Anybody who has had the opportunity of listening to his remarks on the subject of Jews could not have failed, like myself, to realize that he is a fanatic on the subject. He is also convinced of his mission to fight Communism and destroy Marxism, which term embraces all his political adversaries."

After three months of Hitler's regime Rumbold, a foreigner, had already grasped what still had not dawned on Raeder after five and a half years under the regime in a leading position in Berlin.

During the program of study I could almost smile at the allusions in the Reich Supreme Court's decisions to the universally acknowledged competence of the NSDAP in private lawsuits—the Reich Supreme Court: "The concepts of the community of housing and the responsibilities of owner and tenant are in no way in conflict if in a dispute one party turns to the NSDAP: the Party is always competent!"—almost amusing—yet the "Brown"-sprinkled doctrines of some professors in the Reich caused anger and anguish.

Otto Koellreutter, professor of law, Munich: "The political genius of Adolf Hitler . . . the new political élite as symbolizing the new political leadership preemptively excludes political organizations which represent other political ideas. . . . Absolute conformity and uniformity of fundamental spiritual-political posture . . . the defense of the Folk in its racial quality . . . the necessity of legislation to defend the Folk against the influx of alien racial elements . . . degenerate liberalism."

Reinhard Höhn, professor of law, Berlin: "National Socialism establishes a living community . . . of racially equal Folk comrades . . . self-government has again become a vital process of the Folk."

Hans Erich Feine, professor of law, Heidelberg: "Adolf Hitler . . . the great Leader . . . purification of public life of racially and hereditarily alien elements . . . the Leader Principle as the formative principle of German state and communal life."

Theodor Maunz, professor of law, Freiburg-im-Breisgau: "Law is the plan formed by the Führer. . . . The plan formed by the Führer is the highest order of law. . . . As the Führer above all others is called upon to decide, proclaim and administer the law, the law is a decision concerning the content of Folk law, against which there can be no appeal to a higher authority of Folk order . . . the powers are combined in the Führer's person . . . to a truly total power, the Führer-power . . . a kind of protective custody serves the preservation of the Community of the Folk . . . a Folk comrade who disturbs the community will be removed from his political and social environment . . . protective custody as a defense against all actions which disturb the National Socialist edifice . . . the protective custody will be carried out . . . in concentration camps. . . . The actions of the policy according to the Leader Principle are 'rule-free' but not 'law-free' . . . it signifies a complete subversion of our constitutional life the moment that police practice deviates from the Führer's will."

Law professor Maunz in the service of the rule of illegality, ad libitum.

Carl Schmitt, constitutional lawyer, appointed to the Prussian State Council by Hermann Göring in 1933, in his evalution of Hitler's murders on and after 30 June 1934: "The Führer defends the law"; and "An act in the Führer's legitimate jurisdiction." "This suffices, Herr Schmitt," I muttered to myself.

In such a manner did these professors, once pledged to preserve the laws of Western civilization, assist Hitler in consolidating his criminal state—these representatives of the legal profession, over whom the "Führer" repeatedly poured his scorn for their "defective personalities," their "legal hair-splitting" that only stood in the way of his political frenzy and by whom to be "supported" he basically thought laughable. Whether they acted from coercion, stupidity, or opportunism, what did it matter? I considered it a deplorable spectacle. Hopefully, after the war these gentlemen would never again be heard from the teacher's chair. This was a vain hope.

In postwar conversations the lack of resistance by the German military to the initiation of the Hitler dictatorship has often been held up to me. It is quite true that, corresponding to the division of power in the state, after the middle or end of 1933 only the Reichswehr could have curbed Hitler. "But," I am accustomed to answer, "you can't expect military men—of all people—to pass a democratic litmus test. You must realize that their traditions made them, at least at first, especially susceptible to the Prussian values that the Nazis put out like flypaper: discipline, training, duty and obedience, national greatness, the subordination of the individual to the 'community.' To check the Hitler movement, the military would have had to be motivated by democratic, Christian, and legal-minded civilian circles; by politicians, churches, universities, and the judicial system, for example. No impulse came from there when it could still have borne fruit. And according to the doctrines I know to have been held by the leading jurists of the time, nothing was to be expected from there."

During our studies at Bowmanville there were indications that after the war the civil law code would be replaced by a "people's law code." The authors of the former, stemming from the nineteenth century, had long been showered with abuse by the Brownshirts. They were denounced as "individualists," "liberals" and "capitalists." In the new legal system, the "healthy instincts of the people" à la Hitler would be the baseline of the judicial process. It happened otherwise. The military defeat of May 1945 allowed the good old civil law code to survive.

41

The Battle of
Bowmanville

". . . and the Canadian government, in response to the
proceedings of the Oberkommando der Wehrmacht,*
has ordered that henceforth designated officers and men of the German army in this camp will be handcuffed."

A part of the hurried, English-inflected German sentences of the
Canadian camp interpreter had been blown away by the often strong
wind in Bowmanville. The background and origin of the announcement by the interpreter, who assembled us to hear it after a routine
muster one evening in October 1942, remained in the dark. Amaze-
ment reigned, indignation was widespread. The following day the
Canadian camp commandant gave the German camp leader a list of
the army members concerned. Until further notice, the latter were to
present themselves at the camp gate in the morning to be handcuffed
and in the evening to have the handcuffs removed. The excitement in
the camp increased, the German camp leader protested to the Canadian commandant against this violation of international law. But the
latter stood firm and set a deadline for carrying out his government's
orders, failing which he threatened to use appropriate force. The
camp leader also stood firm: "Commandant, our resistance is
assured."

The chain of events which would transplant the military scenario
molded in Europe to Bowmanville had begun in August of that year at
Dieppe on the Channel coast. Two Canadian brigades and a group of
British Commandos had undertaken a landing there in preparation

*Supreme Command of the Armed Forces

for the subsequent Allied invasion of France. Their objectives were partly achieved, but mostly not, and after a bloody engagement both sides had taken prisoners. The Canadians had handcuffed the German prisoners; supposedly so that they could not destroy their papers after being captured. The Oberkommando der Wehrmacht and the British War Office had entered a public altercation over such a violation of international law, threats of reprisals were exchanged, and a chain reaction was unleashed. Its development rolled along until the Oberkommando der Wehrmacht ordered that beginning on 8 October 4,000 British prisoners in German custody would be handcuffed each day from 8:00 in the morning until 9:00 at night. The British reacted immediately and among other things ordered that, with Ottawa's agreement, 1,100 German army members in Canadian custody should be handcuffed. This was the command that the Canadian camp interpreter had intended to make clear after the evening muster.

On the day on which our army comrades were to have been handcuffed for the first time, we all refused to turn out for the roll call, stayed inside our living quarters, and barricaded ourselves there. It was open rebellion, a direct challenge to our Canadian warders. Would these, the Veteran Guards—they were indeed all older men—suffice to overcome our resistance? After tension-filled hours the answer to that question came with the arrival, easily observed through the fence, of a company of younger, frontline soldiers. They formed up outside, where they were required to turn in their live ammunition and were armed instead with billy clubs, baseball bats, and the like. "The prisoners are to be made prisoner again and to be disciplined until they acquiesce in the handcuffing of their army comrades, but no more than that, not killed!"—thus ran the orders of the Canadian camp commandant. The "armament" was in keeping with these aims. And then they came inside to reconquer the camp. Thus began what will live on in the annals of prisoners of war as "The Battle of Bowmanville."

The Canadians' first objective was the cook house, which stood nearest to the camp gate and also contained the big dining hall. In this stone structure our enlisted men, whose wooden barracks would have been too flimsy for the approaching "operations," had barricaded themselves. They had placed upended tables against the windows and posted themselves behind them, armed with hockey sticks, chair legs, and soup ladles; as projectiles they had readied crockery, cutlery, and marmalade jars.

And then the Canadians attacked. They broke the window mullions with battering rams and stuck their heads cautiously into the cook house, but the defenders' blows on their steel helmets checked their initial élan. Then one of them made a daring leap into the house. The superior force inside quickly put him out of action and was delighted to have his helmet as booty. But soon fighting broke out at every window, blows landed on heads and shoulders, marmalade jars and other projectiles flew, soon there were injuries and on both sides bloody and in part marmalade-smeared faces, which were easy to confuse. The fight swayed back and forth, but in the end the Canadians, with their superior numbers, succeeded in making a decisive breakthrough into the cook house and overwhelming its occupants, the "conquest" of their operational objective. Among the occupants of the cook house were the army enlisted men whom the Canadians sought to handcuff, but they had not yet found a single officer. The army officers would still have to be hauled out of the other houses, one house after the other to be stormed. The next operational objective that presented itself was House VI, which was right beside the cook house. As it served as the hospital, however, it was spared from the "prosecution of war."

Instead, the Canadians attacked House V, an officers' quarters on the other side of House VI. Its occupants had withdrawn into the cellar and barricaded themselves there. The Canadians thereupon decided upon a different tactic. From outside, they used fire hoses to flood the cellar. And as only a few Canadians were needed for this operation, many of them had the unexpected, welcome opportunity to look through the rooms on the ground floor. And there were so many things to discover: beer, cigarettes, German medals, rank badges, cockades, valuable objects of every sort. Stimulated by the beer, they took these "souvenirs" home in their pockets.

In the meanwhile, the water had nearly filled the cellar and done its job; the German officers climbed out, dripping wet, with "hands up," the way the Canadians had shouted at them to do. Their captors, whom the alcohol had gotten out of control, greeted them with blows, shoves, and kicks, readying a regular gauntlet for the Germans to run, with the aim of avenging the injuries their comrades had received during the conquest of the cook house—it was not a very sporting conclusion to the capitulation of House V. The Canadian camp technical officer, Captain Brent, especially aroused the Germans' anger. In an absurd victor's pose, he let his swagger stick dance indiscriminately on the heads of the German officers as they came up.

And thus the first day of the Battle of Bowmanville came to an end. The Canadians sought out the army officers who were on their list from House V and handcuffed them. Yet this was only a portion of the total to be handcuffed and the battle itself was still in no way decided.

The next day, the Canadian camp commandant for the first time proposed a deal to the German camp leader. If all the army officers on the list would voluntarily report to be handcuffed, some of the officers from House V who were being held outside the camp as security could return to their quarters. Yet Captain Brent's swagger stick had left bad blood. To their "Nein" to the Canadian's proposal, the Germans joined the recommendation that the captain had better not let himself be seen near them again. And insofar as the other army officers were concerned, the Canadians could haul them out for themselves. The situation remained at this stalemate, even after the visit of a representative of the Swiss protecting power, who rushed to the scene from Ottawa. The latter's attempts at mediation also failed, for by now passions were running high.

Under the circumstances, it was only a question of time until "war" would resume. First, however, the Canadians had to bring in reinforcements from another garrison to make up for the personnel losses they had suffered through injuries. In their absence, the second day of the battle would have passed uneventfully—had it not been for the fact that Captain Brent deemed it necessary to disregard the Germans' warning and inspect the camp. Of course, he had to view the damage to the buildings. Naturally, his swagger stick was not forgotten and his movements were closely watched by the Germans. And at a suitable point, out of the field of vision of the nearest guard tower, the fist of a German officer laid him low—"This, Captain, is for your swagger stick!" Surrounded by a group of Germans, Brent was bound with ropes and paraded through the camp. But this was too much for the guards in the towers and they fired live rounds. Sand spurted up near the edge of the still-intact group. Now, however, there was nothing for it but back into the building, with bullets striking close behind. In the end, one German was tagged. Three shots had already hit near him, in the building's window frames and masonry work. Before he could vanish inside came the fourth, right through the thigh. Admission to the hospital withdrew him from the struggle. The Veteran Guards now freed Captain Brent from his bonds. And for him the incident was now all over. In succeeding days he showed no desire for further retribution.

The third day of the Battle of Bowmanville would be decisive in the Handcuff War. An active Canadian battalion appeared, turned in its ammunition, as before, readied itself for the assault, helmets on, with bayonets and baseball bats, as usual. Three buildings had still to be stormed, Numbers I, II, and IV. Soon the struggle broke out around them. Barricaded they had been for days, with tables and beds up-ended against doors and windows; and behind them the defenders, pillows tied on their heads for lack of helmets, bearing as small arms fire axes and tent stakes, as projectiles jars of marmalade. Where the Canadians could not break through the doors and windows, they climbed to the roofs, cut holes in them, and dropped through into hand-to-hand combat; it was a marvelous brawl. Stones, jars, vases flew, water spurted from fire hoses, bayonets stabbed, wooden clubs struck bodies, indiscriminately, blood flowed, unconscious men lay all around, flooded cupboards spit their water back out, glass splintered and tinkled.

Inevitably, the Canadians emerged the victors. "Wasn't it a wonderful fight?"

The German officer, wounded by a bayonet, looked up at the Canadian who had posed the question. He saw only a single eye in a red waste that once had been a face. "It was quite all right," he replied.

The total wounded of the "Battle of Bowmanville" numbered forty-four German prisoners and thirty-eight Canadians.

Even though in the end we lost, we had at least shown our spirit and made the handcuffing of our army comrades not so easy. And this turned out not to be so bad, after all. The ritual required those concerned to appear in the morning to have handcuffs put on and in the evening to have them removed. And so they did. Except that, with the resourcefulness that prisoners of war cultivated, they quickly discovered how they could remove them for themselves: for example, slide the handcuffs' connecting chain along the edge of an iron bedstead, give a gentle twist of the wrist, a strong tug, and the chain sprang apart. This procedure caught on and soon the Canadians had to use another type of handcuff. But these, too, could be slipped off and lay around uselessly all day long. In the evening they were fastened on again in time to be officially removed.

In the meanwhile, efforts to negotiate an end to the Handcuff War were keeping the international wires hot. The belligerents involved, their protecting powers, and the president of the International Committee of the Red Cross, Carl J. Burckhardt, made one proposal after another, to no avail. Finally, on 12 December, the British lifted the handcuff order. Thus the handcuffing era at Bowmanville ended at 1300 on 12 December. However, the German government for its part held stubbornly to the handcuffing of the originally selected British prisoners of war. And it would be a long time until it declared its readiness to reach a similar understanding with Burckhardt. At last, on 20 November 1943, Reich Foreign Minister Joachim von Ribbentrop consented to the ending of the handcuffing episode on the German side, under the prerequisite of strict discretion: German prestige must not suffer in consequence!

In Bowmanville the Handcuff War had a bureaucratic epilogue. The Canadians charged the Germans damages for the government property destroyed in the "battle." They wrote the German camp leadership: "$80,000 from you, payable from the current allowances of the officers." The Germans countered: "And from you $80,000 for damages to German property and 'missing souvenirs.'" This went on, back and forth, for a while. In the end, both sides renounced all financial claims from the Battle of Bowmanville, ratifying the agreement with all due formalities.

For the time being what remained were holes in windows and doors, traces of the battle of past days. Icy Canadian winter storms blew into the quarters, driving snow onto tables and beds. We patched things up the best we could. But the major repairs could be accomplished only by the Canadian camp administration. It did so, if more than slowly. Not until the spring of 1943 were the last damages resulting from the Battle of Bowmanville made good.

In the meanwhile, suddenly and without a transition period, the sunny autumn weather that still prevailed in the days of the Battle of Bowmanville had come to an end. As fitting for a Canadian winter, our camp was soon buried in snow. Outdoor activities gave way to occupations in our quarters, to instruction and studies.

Contributing to this was the fact that the year 1942 did not appear to have brought a decision in the German campaign in Russia or an end to the war any closer. All estimates of the length of our captivity were lost in uncertainty. It was therefore no wonder that more and more officers devoted themselves to studies of long duration and that new study- and interest-groups took form. Besides our law we soon had an economics "faculty." Other subjects also found their fanciers: mathematics, medicine, botany, history, philosophy, foreign languages and literature, music, graphology and shorthand, to name only a few. Such tendencies increased from then on and a year later, in the winter of 1943–44, the German camp leadership directed every occupant of the camp to take part in a winter study group or else to submit an independently prepared academic treatment of a subject of one's own choosing the following spring.

I restricted myself to my law studies, which sufficed to fill my days, but soon added shorthand to them. The reason was to be able to write faster during lectures. Later, interested linguistically, I also learned English stenography, the so-called Pitman System. This phonetically constructed method rewarded me with the additional advantage of perfect instruction in pronunciation. For the reproduction of an English word according to Pitman also indicates its correct pronunciation. And thereby one can correct himself in individual cases.

All of this did not detract from our athletic activities; quite the contrary. In the big gymnasium men did acrobatics on the equipment, climbed ropes, bounced on trampolines, performed gymnastics with and without medicine balls, and played fast-paced basketball. What a sweat that can work up! In an adjoining building was the heated swimming hall, with shower room, ready for use all day long. Swimming competitions were held from time to time. Outside the courts used for tennis during warm weather were converted for ice sports and carefully kept in condition for them. A vigorous hockey game was the rule, but a place was reserved for figure skaters. To be on the ice on a still, sunny day with a temperature of minus 5°C—truly heavenly! We could also skate at night under artificial illumination. Skiers made long runs over the hilly terrain outside the camp; there were even little slopes. Indeed, we could keep ourselves in good condition, physically and mentally, at the Bowmanville camp. There were scarcely grounds to complain over the living conditions.

Through the intercession of our international patrons, our intellectual life was soon enriched by weeks'-long lecture series and individual presentations by foreign guest professors. They came mostly from the university at Toronto, only sixty kilometers away. Their subjects: "The American Revolution," "The Constitution and History of the U.S.A. from 1800 to 1850," "Characteristics of French Canada," "Indians of Canada," "History of Canadian Transportation," "The English Novel from Defoe to Dickens," "Great English Authors." After the lectures there was sometimes an opportunity to ask questions.

Participation in these events was generally lively; I attended nearly all of them, then enjoyed reading up for myself on the subjects treated. If we were rich in anything, it was time. Yet no other professor left so deep and long-lasting an impression on me as Professor D.

J. McDougall, an historian at the University of Toronto who had been blinded in the First World War. His knowledge was immense and profound; when he spoke, man and message were the same. He lectured, not only at Bowmanville but at other camps as well, on "Characteristics of the British Constitution and its Reforms in the Nineteenth Century," "The British Government and the Cabinet System," "The Labor Party," "Cromwell and the Problem of Military Dictatorship," "British Rule in India," "Constitutional Principles of the Commonwealth"—all viewed from the perspective of a constitutional historian and sociologist. Time and again he cited what he perceived as the fundamental principle of government: "That which concerns all should be determined by all"; I told myself that as long as I lived I would never forget this theorem, so far removed from the reality of the Reich, where such constitutional postulates had been extinguished, at the latest, by the public book burning of 10 May 1933.

McDougall always closed his presentations with an hour for questions and increasingly lively discussion. It was on such an occasion that in private conversation with Franz Schad, McDougall made respectful mention of the German historian Franz Schnabel. He knew many of the works of this native of Mannheim, above all of course, his *Deutsche Geschichte im 19. Jahrhundert,** esteemed the liberal traditions of western Germany alive in the author of these works, his firm support of the Weimar Republic, his early independence of historical judgment. It had fascinated him that Schnabel wrote German history, not in purely national terms, but in a European context—Germany as a European nation, before the background of European events. Sooner than many historians on the North American continent, McDougall had recognized Schnabel's wisdom and political maturity and regarded him as a man of the stature of Leopold von Ranke, the nineteenth-century German historian who is regarded as the founder of modern historical methodology. The deeply humanistic way of thought evident throughout Schnabel's works had made a strong impression on McDougall the humanist, just as had the accuracy with which Schnabel described and evaluated English historical phenomena on McDougall the Anglo-Saxon. That Schnabel's fears for the freedom of the individual in the approaching age of the masses had not met the approval of the Brown authorities, that indeed his "whole direction" led in 1936 to his dismissal from the position of

---

*"German History in the 19th Century."

full professor at the Technical College in Karlsruhe, raised him still higher in McDougall's eyes. He believed that through his works Schnabel had saved the honor of German historians. Schnabel's tenets were also his: "The true value of the past can temporarily be obscured, but never destroyed. For whoever lives must die; but the great bearers of the German state and the German spirit have done more than merely live; in the 19th century, too, they have concerned themselves with eternal values."*

Personally, McDougall was refined and charming; he cast his spell even over men who were rather remote to his subjects or themes. After I assumed my office as consul general of the Federal Republic in Toronto in April 1968, I was moved to seek him out to thank him again, also in the name of the countless other prisoners of war whose lives he had enriched. In his unassuming way, the professor brushed it off—he had only done the obvious.

Despite all our studies and sports, we would hardly have been able to endure year after year at Bowmanville without access to the fine arts. The camp's occupants included musicians and soon a symphony orchestra about fifty men strong was formed. We obtained musical instruments and scores through the aid of the Red Cross in various countries, the YMCA, and the representatives of our protecting power. The latter even went to the trouble of having some privately owned instruments shipped from the homeland. In June 1943, I was delighted to take delivery of my violin, which had been sent from Germany at the beginning of March. When at times scores became difficult to obtain, the Toronto Symphony Orchestra helped out in individual cases. Our orchestra's regular conductor and instructor was a concert pianist, who also composed; the concert master was the Austrian who had been at Shap Wells, who had made many public appearances at home before the war. I remembered the distant violin of my school days, and now played it and later also the viola in the orchestra. The cells of the camp guard house stood at the disposal of those who wished to practice—unless the chance presence of a delinquent precluded such usage. Every day from one to three hours of practice, the scale, the technique of bowing, then from étude to étude. "I should have practiced with this consistency and the understanding that age brings in my younger years," I told myself again and again when I found how hard it is for a man in his thirties to get

---

*In the foreword to the second volume of *Deutsche Geschichte im 19. Jahrhundert*, Freiburg/Br., 1933.

anything new out of his fingers and wrists. But the only thing that mattered was to enjoy making music. Thus many evening rehearsals in the orchestra rolled by; the big gymnasium was the place for them, as well as for public performances. We played symphonies by Haydn, Mozart, Beethoven, one or another movement by Brahms, works of Bach and Handel, and also compositions by our conductor. The latter and our concert master gave solos. There were also request concerts. Besides the big orchestra, we formed a smaller one for pop music and dance music; the best instrumentalists united in a chamber music group; a rich musical life came into being. The performances brought never-ending joy; many may have counted them among the happiest hours of their prison life. I certainly did, with the advantage, even during rehearsals, of allowing myself to be enveloped in and carried away to the world of our classical and romantic composers.

Special enthusiasts could also enjoy recorded music of the highest international renown. Gramophones and records could be purchased through the camp canteen. I often heard the foremost solo violinists, cellists and pianists of that day: Adolf Busch, Bronislaw Hubermann, Mischa Elman, Yehudi Menuhin, Jascha Heifetz, Joseph Szigeti, Emanuel Feuermann, Gregor Piatigorsky, Vladimir Horowitz, Artur Rubinstein, and Robert Casadesus, to name only a few.

We also put on plays. The performances included dramas, comedies, farces, and puppet shows. Curtains, costumes, wigs and all the requisites were conjured from next to nothing; the resourcefulness and craftsmanship of some individuals achieved true triumphs. The actors, all amateurs, played their roles with insight and dedication; all the female parts were necessarily filled by men, which in general caused no problem and sometimes even added to the charm. I remember *The Piccolomini, Wallenstein's Death, The Seven Years War, The Spanish Fly, The Muzzle, Hocus-pocus, The Emperor of America*, and puppet shows such as *Aladdin and the Magic Lantern* and *The Canterville Ghost*. The evenings were a great success before an audience that hungered for any sort of diversion. Recitations and readings also found their visitors.

As a rule, we could see German and American films two or three times a week; the German ones often gave us a chance to revisit familiar scenes. The American ones acquainted us with practically the entire modern U.S. film production—which until now had been virtually closed to us—social, adventure, mystery, musical, and war films. Their style of English might make understanding difficult in some cases, but this was not a serious obstacle. The quality of the film varied greatly, from masterpieces of scriptwriting, directing and acting to absolute nonsense. Unforgettable to me remain the war film *The Sullivans*—which told the story of five brothers who were assigned to the light cruiser *Juneau* and were all lost when the ship was sunk in the Pacific in 1942—and the dance films with Fred Astaire. Up to then only little known in Germany, the master dancer with the unique style was at the peak of his career. I never let pass an opportunity to admire his elegantly aesthetic movements, perfected to the last detail by relentlessly disciplined practice. Linguistically a delight were the films of George Sanders. His appearance of elegant corruption and his marvelously cultivated English made him one of the most sought-after Hollywood stars of the thirties and forties.

Many highly talented men engaged in painting and arts and crafts. Brilliant works of art and craftsmanship were created and could be viewed in exhibitions.

Never cramped, especially not in summer, was the time for the already mentioned sports. Many different kinds could be practiced on Bowmanville's spacious grounds: handball, football, volleyball, and hockey (bruising as always), tennis, athletics, gymnastics. Day in, day out there was a flourishing athletic life, which was stimulated by competitions, such as footraces. Amateur gardeners had the chance to combine physical activity with the joy of growing things in the outdoors, as their carefully tended flower and vegetable gardens announced. In the greenhouse they could work the whole year through. Anyone who wanted to swim in Lake Ontario could do so upon giving his word of honor not to try to escape. On one's word of honor it was also possible to go on long walks through the thinly settled neighborhood of the camp. Of course, all activities outside camp were under Canadian surveillance.

We found the Canadian climate, with its long winters and correspondingly short summers, to be quite extreme. In summer the often intense heat sometimes provoked monstrous thunderstorms. The sky would grow dark and dismal, the most dazzling lighting would flash through it, and hailstones the size of hens' eggs would beat down. On many such occasions the ground was covered by a foot of ice. In winter the country was frequented by blizzards and raging snowstorms. Yet in our "feudal" Bowmanville quarters we were relatively well protected from such extremes. On many evenings the northern lights appeared in the sky. Strange, glowing beams and bundles, like changing stage-curtains, played across the sky. This spectacle always captivated us. The most beautiful of all Canadian seasons was the autumn, the "Indian summer" that began punctually in the first half of October. The deciduous forest that surrounded the camp, maples and still more maples, glowed to the edge of the horizon in red and gold. The radiant sun was alluring in its taciturn splendor.

Were there escapes, as had taken place earlier at Shap Wells and were indeed the order of the day in every prisoner-of-war camp? Of course there were, cleverly staged, one of which I have sketched in connection with the British surveillance methods at Cockfosters. But like it, none of them achieved the aim of reaching Germany, of returning to the battlefront. I will not record them here, for they have been described at length, in detail and very suspensefully in Reinhard Stallmann's *Die Ausbrecherkönige von Kanada* * and also in part in Paul Carell's *Die Gefangenen.*†

As a result of the distance and the Battle of the Atlantic, the delivery of our personal mail took much more time than it had in England. To this was added the usual delay of censorship. Letters from Germany needed two or three months to reach Canada; they moved faster in the opposite direction. Towards the end of the war, the delivery time increased greatly. Mail did not arrive for a year or more; the connection was largely or completely broken. Then the flight of much of the German population and the chaos and destruction in the homeland led to an eloquent silence.

---

* *The Breakout Kings of Canada.*
† *The Prisoners.*

42

Crisis in Camp

Our opportunities to follow the events of the ever-widening war and political changes around the globe were excellent—if one used them. Of course, German government reports could not officially be obtained. The forwarding of German newspapers and the like was prohibited; the only thing left was to listen in illegally on shortwave transmissions from the Reich. To receive them, soon after the opening of the camp skillful hands had conjured up a radio set, built from next to nothing and concealed in the hollow leg of a table the prisoners had made. The electricity for it was taken from the Canadian system by means of a converter. Replacement tubes were obtained as needed by mobilizing the kindness of our Canadian guards by—*stets paraten*—plausible pretexts and with the help of little gifts. This information gathering was extremely delicate; the radio was also capable of transmitting, and every such contact with the outside world was a dangerous undertaking for prisoners of war; one must never be caught off guard. Keeping the radio secret was of utmost importance and the daily tuning-in was done only with the strictest security against unwelcome surprises, with lookouts at the door. The news received served as the camp's quasi-official "newscast," which was read out after the noon meal.

But whoever wished to inform himself beyond this "something for everybody" information that mirrored the officialese of the Reich could do this, too. On the outside of the living quarters hung loudspeakers from which one could listen to public radio programs, news, and entertainment, to which the Canadian camp administration tuned in. It was possible to take subscriptions to Allied newspapers and magazines, which were easily paid for from our monthly allowances. Of course, some prisoners could not stand such media. "All purely enemy propaganda, we don't want it." They rejected information from Allied sources *a limine*. Others subscribed, however. I took the conservative Toronto daily paper, *The Globe and Mail*, the British weekly *Daily Mail Overseas*, the U.S. business magazine *Fortune* and later, in place of the latter, the British political monthly magazine *The Nineteenth Century and After*. *The Globe and Mail* also regularly carried syndicated columns by two of the most important American journalists, the great international commentator Walter Lippmann and that German expert and humanist, the unforgettable Dorothy Thompson. With the help of these publications I felt that I was broadly and for the most part accurately informed about the course of the war and world politics.

Of course, as a subject of conversation in camp, world politics and—as a congruent to the subject of Hitler—politics in general were for me as good as taboo. The monstrous spectacle of the dictatorship in the Reich and the hopelessness of helping the victims who had become addicted to the propaganda of the Brown state to gain reasonable national perspective had long since closed my mouth. On Hitler, there was a parting of minds; opposing attitudes towards him lacked any common ground. For our camp community was fundamentally nothing else than a miniature German "Community of the Folk," as though viewed through a reducing lens with a power of five hundred. Its center was formed by the overwhelming majority of Hitler-believing fellow travellers. On the opposing ends of the spectrum were the representatives of more pronounced viewpoints; on one side, the extreme, fanatical Nazis, the so-called 150 percenters, and on the other, insignificant in numbers, the confirmed opponents of the regime. And did it make sense to heat up raw emotions in conversations with those who thought differently, without the release of purposeful activity, indeed without any possibility of it, behind barbed wire in the middle of a war? Very dangerous. The consequences could not be controlled. Politically motivated murder and manslaughter had already occurred in other camps. Better, then, to keep one's mouth shut and to work. On a still very distant day one would again be free to say what one wished. Hitler could not hold the Germans in chains forever. To be sure, he might have nothing to fear from inside. But now the military might of almost the entire world was threatening him. He himself had set it in motion against him. He was his own worst enemy.

Of course, to keep my mouth closed under any and every circumstance, uninterruptedly, so to say, was more than I could manage. The most violent agitation gripped me whenever I read a report in the Allied press, often half hidden, by way of suggestion and unconfirmed conjecture, of killings and atrocities behind the German battlefronts. Before the background of the racial madness loose in Germany—with the crackling Kurfürstendamm of 9 November 1938 always in mind— such press notices sprang to horrifying reality

"Who are we, that we set ourselves up as judges over other people, that we feel called upon to decide on the 'worth and worthlessness' of foreign life, to legitimatize our elimination of 'inferior beings'?"—I spit out the words, as it were, on one of my walks with one of the two or three officers in camp to whom I could say such things at all. "The German reputation, our right to self-respect, they will be lost for an eternity, we are pulling ourselves down—for every single day of the Hitler regime, it will take a year to rehabilitate Germany among the community of nations—and even that may not suffice. The outlook is becoming worse and worse." My uncontradicted monologue had relieved me somewhat; I couldn't expect that it would do more. Then again, the day came when abruptly and for no apparent reason, the blinders fell. "We are basically still not a nation at all," I announced to one of my trusted friends. "For what was jammed together and tied up with so much pressure and force from above, can hardly have grown into it organically. After a thousand years of German history, still not grown into it, still no true nation!" At that time, in the tenth year of the Hitler regime, I found this a disturbing realization.

One other time also I was unable to contain myself: on the morning of 21 July 1944, the day after the unsuccessful attempt to assassinate Hitler. In the camp street, otherwise empty at that early hour, I met, of us inmates, *the* officer with whom I could talk more openly than with any other. "Damn!" we called to one another, "it didn't work!" And immediately after, again almost simultaneously, "Have we gone crazy, to shout that out here? Let's clear out!" The first excitement and the chill despair that fate had again so cruelly decided against Germany had swept over us. Yet out of the initial surge of emotion I could not form a lasting view of the consequences of the failure. In the end, it was necessary to distinguish and inwardly to choose between two evils. Either Hitler lived, as had happened, and only our adversaries' victory would bring the frightful killing and destruction to an end. Or, to enter into speculation, suppose the attempt had succeeded. Then, in my opinion—with the "stab in the back" legend following the First World War, my own initial gullibility in the face of it, and the striking susceptibility of my countrymen to political legends always in mind—another consequence would have become inevitable. The new legend would have freed Hitler from responsibility for the defeat and fastened it on the assassins, the "traitors." The prospect of the devastation of Germany to be expected from the living Hitler had to be weighed against, in the other case, the politically ruinous way of thought to be feared among subsequent generations who believed the legend. Each person may assess these alternatives, now historical, for himself.

The news of Count Claus Schenk von Stauffenberg's assassination attempt reached us through the secret radio station the day that it occurred and shook the camp like an earthquake. Everyone was speedily informed of the events in the Wolf's Lair.* Uneasiness and the paralysis of all emotion were the first reaction; the events in the Reich were spoken of only in whispers and undertones. Soon we also learned of the execution of Stauffenberg and others in the Bendlerstrasse and—to me the most tormenting—the appointment of Himmler as commander in chief of the Home Army. Then the possibility that the conspirators had symphathizers in Bowmanville arose, was dragged forward, and bruited about. Suspicion of certain individuals spread throughout the camp. The waves of excitement grew ever higher; if and the extent to which they would die down appeared increasingly questionable. During those days National Socialist fanatics in another officers' camp shouted, "String up the Catholics and the nobility!" And some people in Bowmanville may not have viewed matters very differently. The senior officer in camp acted at once. Generalleutnant† Arthur Schmitt, a veteran of the *Deutsches Afrika Korps* and above all suspicion as a supporter of Hitler and suitably certified by his annual address on 9 November, the anniversary of Hitler's unsuccessful Munich Putch in 1923, assembled us at a muster on the evening of 21 July. He damned the conspirators and called on us to close ranks behind Hitler. And in fact camp life returned to normal. At least outwardly; emotional residues and potentially explosive attitudes remained in existence.

It was on 14 August 1944 that one of our officers, a Luftwaffe captain whom we will call X, went over to the Canadians. He had taken advantage of a stay outside the compound not to return and placed himself at the disposition of the custodial power. A wild wave

*Hitler's East Prussian military headquarters
†Lieutenant General

of excitement gripped the camp; attitudes still heated from the attempt on Hitler reached the boiling point; for days the air seemed to lie on us all heavy as lead, thick enough to cut, unwilling to lift, suffocating. A self-appointed drumhead court-martial condemned X, in absentia, "to death on account of desertion" and declared him an "outlaw."Any occupant of the camp who encountered him anywhere would be entitled to kill him. "Absolute nonsense," Seeburg growled to me at a favorable occasion, "no one here has jurisdiction."

The extreme Nazis in the camp then raised additional questions: "Who will desert next? Who knew of X's plan? With whom was X most often seen together? And what kind of people are they, inside and out?" They "found" that Schmitt had not conducted the previous investigations aggressively enough and wanted to "investigate" for themselves. Camp discipline fell into the shadows. Advocates of vigilante action were undermining the primacy of the military hierarchy, but before things got dangerously out of hand Schmitt did the only correct thing and undercut the competition by undertaking the interrogations and making the decisions himself.

For my part I now expected to be questioned by Schmitt at any moment, as in the past months I had occasionally talked with X on walks. In the complete rejection of the so-called National Socialism I had found myself at one with him, although our motives were very different. But our exchange of thoughts always remained purely academic; through no syllable, no sign, could I have become aware of his intention to desert. Besides, he must have regarded the creation of initiates as a danger to his secret plan. My fundamental attitude to such changes of sides had long been clear: To have emigrated on political grounds before the war in the conviction that one would be unable to lessen the national catastrophe under Hitler and, to the contrary, would personally have to collaborate with it—that I can understand. But to desert in 1944, during the war—no, never!

"You know the monstrous thing which has taken place, Müllenheim, and I have to get to the bottom of your possible complicity in the desertion of Captain X," Schmitt told me when he summoned me on 17 August. "As you were repeatedly seen together with X, the possibility cannot be dismissed that you had been initiated into his plans and improperly kept silent." He continued, "You also know that, in violation of military conventions, I have been attacked by some hyperactive officers as supposedly too indecisive in the investigation of Captain X. I am personally conducting this investigation and according to the standards that duty dictates. I will announce the results at a camp assembly, at which I will also give my opinion of the gentlemen who have personally pressed me too closely. What do you have to say?"

"It is quite true, Herr General," I replied, "that I have spoken with Captain X on occasion. But I never heard anything about his intention to desert or even any such ideas. I myself most definitely condemn his step and have absolutely nothing to do with it. Of this I assure you, and there is nothing more that I can say."

"I will take that under serious consideration," Schmitt said, "but, Müllenheim, there is something more. Your continually critical remarks about our government are known, and indeed have been for a long time, and, because of the present atmosphere in the camp alone, I do not see how I can avoid publicly naming your name."

This was a damnably unwelcome revelation and I had to reflect before replying. Certainly, as I've said before, over the years I had been reserved in political conversations or avoided them altogether. But one could scarcely conceal his inner self completely for long in such a crowded, communal society. Gestures and the unspoken word counted in it. Hadn't just recently an officer newly assigned to the camp told me of his first question to a friend he encountered there: "With whom can one speak openly in this Cloud-Cuckoo-Land?" and hadn't the latter answered, "With Korvettenkapitän von Müllenheim of the *Bismarck*." And soon thereafter hadn't we had a conversation that he characterized as "an oasis in the desert"? Hadn't I long been to many the "objective one," the "citizen of the world"? To attempt to deny my critical remarks about "our government" to Schmitt would therefore have been more than merely tactically a false move.

"Herr General," I finally formulated it, "your announcement is not agreeable to me and I would much prefer it if you left me unmentioned. With the case that is the only thing being debated here I have nothing to do, absolutely nothing at all."

Schmitt seemed to hesitate. "I will see and you will hear further," he said before the door closed behind me. Then he continued his investigation, sounding out people about me and interrogating others. When he summoned me again on 24 August he had dropped the point of my "complicity in the desertion," but not my "criticism of our government." Apparently he was under enormous pressure from the camp extremists. Yet I could only repeat my previous statements. He once again withheld his final decision. More days had to pass in agonizing suspense before the morning of 28 August, the day of the assembly, when I once more stood before the general.

"No, Müllenheim," Schmitt told me, "I'm sorry, but I can't leave you out of my address this evening. I have made inquiries, very many, very precise inquiries, and you appear too heavily compromised by your critical remarks. But at first and for the most part I will settle accounts with those gentlemen who have laid their hands on military discipline and have seriously wronged and insulted me. Your turn will come later."

"If you believe that you must act in this manner, Herr General, I must understand; besides, I can't stop you," I replied, and my last interview was over.

Schmitt acted on his words. After condemning the deserter and justifying the verdict of the drumhead court-martial, he devoted the main portion of his eighty-minute-long address to reprimanding the officers who, although in an ever-so-well-meant excess of zeal, had forgotten military conventions. He did not come to me—politically the other extreme, so to speak—until the very end and then very briefly. He deplored my repeated criticisms and advised me to lay aside my uniform after the war and leave the armed forces. Curiously, the thought that came to mind was, "The outcome of the war, Herr General, will be such that you may have to lay aside the uniform before I do." But I was in anything other than high spirits. A deep silence lay over the hall and when at the end of the address I returned to my quarters like everyone else, with the usual camp stool tucked under my arm, it was as though I did so inside a glass jar of isolation. A new era of communal life might have begun for me. I would find out; but I certainly would not change my views of Hitler.

"Cheer up, it's been publicly certified that you've thought otherwise"—these surprising words were as welcome as they were unexpected a greeting the next morning. Out on an early walk through the camp, I had encountered Generalleutnant Hans von Ravenstein and it was he who had spoken to me in such a friendly way. I looked at him gratefully but avoided involving him in a longer conversation in public, which in view of the still ticklish mood in camp could have unpleasant consequences for him. He was the last person I would have wished them on. Moreover, although much remained unsaid, to me we appeared to be completely in agreement. After the war—that was how I summed up his message to me—we would have a politically "sanitary" government without a Brown residue. At the time we certainly did not visualize a Globke-

Oberländer state,* a state of conservative restoration and lacking political hygiene.

Generalleutnant von Ravenstein, a Silesian from a military family dating from before the wars of Frederick the Great, slender, with the finely chiselled features of an aristocrat, even a little reminiscent of the Hohenzollerns, had come to our camp in 1943 after being captured while commanding the 21st Panzer Division in Libya. Soon after his arrival he had proven himself to be a speaker who could figuratively tear his listeners our of their seats; his fiery words, his repeated *"In Afrika wird ge-Rommelt,"*† seemed to have truly transferred the battlefield into the auditorium—if anyone was able to fire up soldiers, he was definitely the man. But to listen to him most carefully was absolutely necessary. For what he left unsaid was as important for an understanding of his evaluations and judgments as were his spoken words. Repeatedly decorated for bravery during the First World War and awarded the Order Pour le Mérite as a captain in May 1918 for an outstanding feat of arms, after the war he was for many years active in a high position in the communal service in the Ruhr. Becoming a soldier again in 1934, during the Second World War he had fought in Poland, France, the Balkans, and Africa, receiving the Knight's Cross in June 1940. His charming, charismatic personal-

*Globke, Hans, state attorney, born 1898. From 1929 to 1945 in the Reich Ministry of the Interior. As a ministerial councillor and expert advisor on questions of nationality, among other things he collaborated on the edition of a commentary on the Nuremberg Racial Laws (1935). From 1953 to 1963 under Konrad Adenauer he headed the administration of the Federal Chancellor's Office, initially as ministerial director and then as state secretary. On account of his activity in the Reich Ministry of the Interior, he was attacked with increasing sharpness. (Brockhaus 1969)

Oberländer, Theodor, political economist and politician, born 1905. In the NSDAP since 1933, from 1939 to 1945 he was Reich Leader of the "League of the German East." From 1953 to 1960 he was Federal Minister for Displaced Persons, Refugees, and Disabled Veterans. In 1960 he retired from ministerial office because the accusation was made that as a member of the "Nightingale" unit he had participated in the shooting of Jews and Poles. In 1960 Oberländer was juridically rehabilitated. (Quoted from Brockhaus 1971)

Author's comment: Both Globke and Oberländer were too deeply intertwined with and had held places of too much prominence under the criminal National Socialist system to have been again employed in high positions without a thorough investigation of their unsavory past. Their occupation of high offices in the postwar years remains for me the perfect example of the deplorable lack of political hygiene since the Adenauer period.

†An untranslatable pun on the name of Field Marshal Rommel and the verb *rummeln* (to rumble or jolt), signifying "In Africa, Rommel shook things up."

Generalleutnant Hans von Ravenstein, captured in Libya while commanding the 21st Panzer Division, was held in great esteem by both Germans and Canadians as camp leader at Grande Ligne, Quebec. (Photograph courtesy of Franz Schad.)

ity and his innate diplomacy, refined amid the changing scenes of his life, would later make him in another place a camp leader who was equally well respected by the Germans and the Canadians.

On 29 August, the day after Schmitt's speech, there was a general sports day in camp. Everyone had to take part; it was not to be a championship competition since participation was all that mattered—a good thing. I refused to give in to a fleeting impulse, born of the bitterness of the past days, not to turn out. Nothing would have been more wrongheaded. I did all the required exercises, even if doing so was still a little like being under glass. It rapidly became clear that on the whole Schnitt's words had purified the atmosphere and helped restore camp discipline to what it should be. How many hard feelings remained on an individual level after all the turbulence was something that would become evident, eventually.

And it did. Difficulties were placed against my continuing membership in the law class. A few in attendance wished to expel a "politically unreliable." As the pressure continued to mount, I considered the situation from all angles and discussed it with a few friends. From the very beginning, Seeburg supported my inclination to continue, and the attitude of our dean was decisive. "Give in to the pressure," I said to myself, "only because I hold politically sound opinions? I won't think of it." On 5 September, the beginning of our sixth semester, I appeared in the lecture hall as usual. In an atmosphere of icy rejection and, to counter it, of defiance, I took my customary place. The lecture began. Many more lectures began. And time overtook the rest. It carted my difficulties away. Already we were not far distant from the dissolution of the Bowmanville camp and our transfer to another part of Canada.

And otherwise? Some men with whom I had become personally close over the years showed themselves unwilling to be seen with me and sealed themselves off. Some friends became only "friends." I must and could live with that.

In the outside world our defeat at Stalingrad and the collapse of our U-boat war already lay more than a year—and the Allied invasion of Normandy a few months—in the past. In the Soviet Union our armies appeared to be flowing back to the frontiers of the Reich almost without a halt. Whenever the decisive turning point of the war had actually occurred, for a long time now it had not taken a prophet, even behind barbed wire, to foresee our defeat. And for how long now I had gone to bed and gotten up with the vision of an apocalypse—the consummation of the German catastrophe that was taking place before our eyes: the mere military course of events, the quaking of the decaying Reich under the blows administered by the world coalition, the desparate mobilization of imaginary reserves provided their own depressing commentary. The tension often drove me outdoors, for it became increasingly difficult to bear all this in silence.

"You, too, certainly see," I said at the end of 1944 to someone who could hold his tongue, "that the moment for an attempt to save diplomatically whatever of Germany can be saved, to enter into negotiations, has long since passed. But the 'Führer' will not negotiate; besides, who would negotiate with him? The only thing that matters to him is the prolongation of his rule, a prolongation of days, hours—

what it costs in life and material values is immaterial to him. And if at the time of his exit, nothing is left of Germany except ashes, he can't imagine anything finer. You remember his speech of 8 November 1943—just seven months ago?"

My companion did not know of it. "Well now," I continued, "in his traditional speech on the anniversary of his Putsch in the Bürgerbräukeller in Munich he said something, I heard it over the radio or read it in the press at the time, that immediately caught my attention. 'I would not be sorry if the German people go under, for in that case it would have deserved nothing better.' He is living out this resolution now," I went on, "the battlefronts tell it to you—yes, whoever surrenders himself to that charlatan doesn't need his own supply of cynicism."

Degrading, insulting attacks by Hitler on his German listeners were nothing new, nor did they disturb them, but, to the contrary, increased the exultation of the masses. Thus Hitler could make such pronouncements without risk to himself and apparently delighted in doing so. He said something similar—I learned of it later, however— to the *Reichleiter* and *Gauleiter* at the Wolf's Lair in August 1944— that if the German people should be defeated in this struggle, then it has been too weak, has failed its test before history, and would therefore be destined for nothing other than destruction. With only slightly different words he had expressed himself to a foreigner as early as the setback outside Moscow in November 1941, saying that he would shed no tears for the German people.

True, in order to understand that Hitler thought this way, it is not at all necessary to know of such remarks. They were clearly evident in his policy. At the end of 1944, with the "rubbing out" of Germany that Hitler had so publicly accepted before our eyes, I now thought that even our enemies might have something more merciful in mind for us.

But how did millions unflinchingly allow themselves to be led senselessly to the slaughterhouse by one single individual? If I viewed the years 1933 to 1944 as a whole, they taught me something. State philosophers and historians long ago crystallized that something into historical experience. And I don't know who ever expressed it more clearly than the French parliamentarian and author Étienne La Boétie more than four hundred years ago in his treatise *On Voluntary Servitude:* "It is the people themselves who mistreat themselves through their tyrants, they are the helper's helpers of the thieves who rob them, and they encourage the murderer who kills them; they are traitors to their own cause." In twentieth-century Germany, nothing had changed.

Others in the camp showed perplexity, naturally. One said: "We must become still more fanatical, more Japanese than the Japanese." He was thinking of the kamikazes and had a very fixed look in his eye. Another: "Well now, the retreat in Russia, to me it appears to be nothing more than the reaction to the action—billiard balls roll back on rebounding. It certainly looks bad at the moment, but that's exactly why we have the 'Führer.' I believe in him." Nothing could have been falser than the suggestion that even a billiard ball could roll back to its starting point. Everyone was permitted his sort of consolation.

43

Whites, Grays, and Blacks

The turn of the year 1944–45 was accompanied by the first rumors of imminent transfer and the dissolution of the Bowmanville camp. One heard of the "categorization" of prisoners of war on the basis of their political attitude—read, attitude towards National Socialism—according to the Canadians' knowledge, estimation, or suspicion of it. The majority were assigned to Group B, the so-called "grays," which signified the average fellow-travelers. Group C would consist of the "blacks," the seemingly fanatical, incorrigible Nazis, and Group A of the "whites," the so-called anti-Nazis and democrats. Where the Canadians found the criteria for categorizing individuals, we did not know. The course of previous interrogations, the tenor of letters, the observations of guards and perhaps also winks from one or another German must have been the basis for it.

At the beginning of February 1945 matters had progressed so far that 162 officers, the obvious "blacks," were transferred to the See-bee camp in Alberta. The "blacks" in the far west, the "grays" in the midwest, and the "whites" in the eastern part of the country—such was roughly the geographical distribution. That some—in individual cases very serious—errors were made in categorization will be no surprise. Our "grays," 187 in number, were transferred to Wainwright in the midwest at the beginning of April and the remainder, the "whites," 174 officers and other ranks, myself among them, to the Grande Ligne camp in the Province of Quebec. At noon, while we were waiting for our train at the Bowmanville station, the news arrived of the death of Franklin Delano Roosevelt. I have never forgotten that day.

As our captivity would indeed continue, I left Bowmanville with mixed feelings. On the positive side was the time spent there that would be useful in so many respects in later life. I really had not wasted my time there. The facilities and living conditions of this camp, even outwardly so beautiful, I also felt to be positive. So far as all that was concerned, henceforth with each new camp—and there would still be some—a progressive deterioration in quality was to be expected. But in the final analysis that was only natural. When I thought of the misery and want in the homeland in April 1945, my comfortable life put me to shame. On the other hand, in the past months an almost unbearable psychological pressure had weighed on me. A "pause for breath" would be welcome. Certainly, my comrades were fundamentally pleasant and decent, and as members of the military profession we had very much in common. But patriotism is not the same for everyone. And so far that is concerned, Germany remains a difficult Fatherland.

That many years later I would have the opportunity to recall before a public forum in Bowmanville my days as a prisoner of war there—that certainly lay beyond all imagining upon departing from the station in April 1945. The Rotary Club of Bowmanville invited me—consul general in Toronto since April 1968—to be its guest speaker for World Understanding Week in November of that year. The resulting press coverage was detailed and positive. From hated enemy to respected NATO ally, what a way we had traveled since then. We had also received the spiritual equipment for it in the Bowmanville. No, there was really nothing to complain of in this camp.

And what had the Canadians themselves to say about the background of our "categorization"? How did the Germans behind barbed wire strike them as political beings? The Canadian archives, recently opened to the public, do not reveal much quantitatively, but nevertheless they cast a ray of light. And since they indicate typical phenomena, I will quote a few, not just from the Bowmanville camp.

Excerpts from the monthly reports of Canadian camp commandants to Ottawa:

Fort Henry, Ontario, 1942:
Count 'A' and others requested separation from Nazi elements in view of their anti-Nazi views in 1941. This request was not taken seriously at the time and 'A' was regarded as a mere troublemaker.

Grande Ligne, Quebec, 1942:

(a) Commander 'B,' quiet but seems to be forced into "agitation" by more aggressive elements. Lt. Commander 'C' is a fanatical Nazi.

(b) A Luftwaffe major in camp is continually challenging others to duels.

(c) [Curiously] Canadian officers of 2nd Lieutenant rank were to be admonished for chewing gum in the presence of senior German officers and for sloppy saluting.

The entry from the Fort Henry camp—which was closed in 1942—may justify a slight digression. If, as a German, one can easily imagine the nature of the differences—that do not matter here—between Count 'A' and his adherents and his Nazi camp comrades, the Canadian evaluation of Count 'A' as a mere troublemaker reflects an almost laughable absence of any inkling of the reality of National Socialism. But in the final analysis what could the latter be to Canadians and many others, too, than a practically unknown transatlantic phenomenon? We can scarcely wonder that peoples who never experienced fascism themselves could have no idea at all of the circumstances under which it attained and asserted power. And had that not even been the case with England in 1939, when, in the face of the highly advanced German rearmament, she remained far too weak, unready for war, and still intensely absorbed in the idea of the League of Nations? Had not Chamberlain himself clung to his dream of "peace in our time" even *after* the Munich Agreement and *after* Hitler's craving for territorial expansion in Europe had become so obvious? For much too long, England had viewed Hitler—granted, not much differently from many circles in Germany itself—as a figure, albeit a curious one, of German politics in the traditional national interest, and not as the sadist in power, the apostle of conquest and the destroyer of freedom, which he was above all else. For too long the British had not paid heed, had not wanted to pay heed, to the protests of those Germans who saw Hitler as the beginning of a national catastrophe. What had Fritz Günther von Tschirschky, a patriot whom conscience drove from the diplomatic service and his homeland after Hitler's mass murders in the summer of 1934, learned as an emigrant in London of British opinion of Nazi Germany late in the decade? "In conversations with important persons in British political and social life, I was repeatedly pained that I was given to understand: 'You and your group have failed with your politics. Now you are only attempting to disseminate a completely negative impression, indeed, hatred of the regime ruling in Germany.' I must . . .

repeat: It pained and shook me to the core, how in England at that time most people stuck their heads in the sand; they did not want to see, they did not want to believe, what really happened in Hitler Germany."

And how much less were such insights to be expected in far distant Canada! And then to recognize, to understand the nature of political differences between the Germans through the additional filter of barbed wire? Hardly conceivable. Yet all this was really no wonder in a world that had long been accustomed to see, in place of statesmen conscious of their responsibilities, only partisan politicians at work. So it really had to take proportionately longer to discover a Hybris there where she was to be found—to understand the revolt against her there, where she showed herself.

Seemingly cast into oblivion, lost, was what one Briton had at an early date recognized and expressed: Sir Horace Rumbold; we have already met him, British ambassador to Berlin from 1928 to 1933. He had read *Mein Kampf*, in good time and very closely. On 26 April 1933, after only three months of Hitler rule, in his 5,000-word "Mein Kampf Dispatch" he had reported on Hitler and the Germans, compared book and reality, and analyzed them:

The parliamentary regime has been replaced by a regime of brute force. . . . The prospect is disquieting . . . revival of militarism. . . . The new regime is . . . determined to . . . entrench itself in power for all time. . . . Hitler himself is, with good reason, a profound believer in human, and particularly German credulity. . . . The outlook for Europe is far from peaceful. . . . Hitler's thesis is extremely simple. . . . Only brute force can ensure the survival of the race. . . . Intellectualism is undesirable. . . . What Germany needs is an increase in territory in Europe. . . . Germany must look for expansion to Russia. . . . Colonel Hierl is (or rather was, in 1929) surprisingly candid.* "The abandonment . . . of the policy of submission (to the Allies) . . . does not involve war at a moment's notice, though it does mean war in the long run." . . . There is something oddly reminiscent of the Tirpitz period in the present state of things. The problem before the naive exponents of National

---

*Konstantin Hierl (1875–1955), a professional officer, was teaching at the War College in Munich in 1911. During the First World War, he served on the General Staff. In 1919, as a Freikorps leader on assignment from the Reichswehr Ministry, he played a leading part in the suppression of the Soviet government in Augsburg. Retiring from the army in 1924 as a colonel, he was active in Ludendorff's Tannenbergbund, 1925–27. He joined the NSDAP in 1927 and became *Reichsorganisationsleiter II* in 1929 (from Brockhaus's *Enzyklopädie*, Wiesbaden, 1969).

Socialism is even more difficult than that which confronted Admiral von Tirpitz. The problem of 1905 . . . was the construction of a fleet sufficiently powerful to challenge Great Britain at sea without being "caught out" before that task was completed. . . . The task of the present German government is more complicated. They have to rearm on land, and . . . they have to lull their adversaries into . . . a state of coma. . . .

However, from the first Rumbold's realistic appraisal of the Nazi regime had not met with the corresponding understanding of his government and among the British press and public. After the conclusion of the Reich Concordat with the Holy See in July 1933 *The Times* wrote: "Herr Hitler is certainly not devoid of ideals. . . . He undoubtedly desires to re-inculcate the old German virtues of loyalty, self-discipline, and service to the State. . . . Herr Hitler will win support which may be very valuable to him if he will genuinely devote himself to the moral and economic resurrection of his country." More and more, Rumbold's warnings were put aside. After his death in 1940, Anthony Eden wrote his widow: "I have always deplored, and always shall, the decision that moved Sir Horace from Berlin, where he was doing such wonderful service. No one ever had a clearer perspective of the dangers and his dispassionate but far-seeing analysis of things to come should have earned the reward of a fuller understanding at home."

Now back again to the impressions and reports of the Canadian camp commandants, from the files in Ottawa:

General summary, 1943–44:
For the continuous surveillance of the prisoners of war, intelligence officers were attached to each camp's security staff. Their monthly reports contain numerous extracts from letters sent to the prisoners from Germany. The reports placed great weight on the regularity with which the prisoners attended camp church services—which were held about every three weeks. The Canadians repeatedly expressed concern at the irregularity and lack of German participation in these services. "Grande Ligne" and "Sorel"—both in the Province of Quebec—come into the foreground as camps to which at the appropriate time the prisoners classified as "white" or "light grey" would be moved; the "Seebee" (Alberta) and "Wainwright" (Saskatchewan) camps are designated for the reception of the "blacks," alias incorrigible Nazis.

Bowmanville, 23 May 1944:
The camp commandant: A German prisoner is being ostracized. It was unknown if a sort of Gestapo existed in the camp, but he enclosed a

list—which cannot be located today—of the political firebrands. The following are designated "ardent Nazis": Lieutenant General 'C,' Lieutenant Colonel 'D,' Commander 'E,' Lieutenant Colonel 'F,' and Majors 'G,' 'H,' and 'I.'

The Ottawa archive also indicates that the Canadians had apparently obtained a copy of the "Secret Guidelines" of the senior officer at Bowmanville concerning "Conduct and Discipline." The separation of the so-called "whites" from the "blacks" was decided on in the fall of 1944: the "black" officers were sent to Seebee (Alberta), the other "black" ranks to Gravenhurst (Ontario). According to one report, in February 1945 the "blacks" were transported from Grande Ligne to Seebee and two hundred "whites," including General von Ravenstein, moved from Bowmanville to Grand Ligne. Canadian correspondence suggests that the "whites" would be repatriated before the "blacks."

Grande Ligne, October 1944–February 1945:
The intelligence officer: "Hari-kari Clubs" have been formed in camp. Lieutenant Colonel 'K,' Major 'L' and Captain 'M' intend to murder the "whites" and commit suicide after the German defeat.

Bowmanville, April 1945:
Subject: PoW Security Bowmanville, DND-Army-Inter-office correspondence Secret.—Transfer of 174 PoW Officers and 32 other ranks on 12 April 1945.

According to this report, some prisoners had gone to great pains to be regarded as "gray" or "white." The "grays" in particular did all they could to maintain or improve their status. For example, large numbers of diaries were encountered from which many pages had been ripped out.

Several German officers took advantage [on the day of the transfer, 12 April 1945] to converse with [Canadian] officer personnel. . . . The latter were particularly impressed with the sincerity and "whiteness" of four PW officers. It is suggested that psychological warfare might give consideration to the employment of the following [who are named].

It was in the year 1955 that as a member of the German delegation to NATO in Paris I met a Canadian who belonged to the international staff of that organization. He said, "Müllenheim—Müllenheim, I remember your name very well. You know, during the war I was assigned to the Central Prisoner of War Administration in Ottawa when you were at Bowmanville. We thought that you were personally in danger and considered individually transferring you from the camp. But then we backed off—maybe it wasn't such a good idea and could be harmful to you in the long run." I replied, "Your restraint was correct. I would not have accepted the offer of a protective transfer. Such things must be borne inside the barbed wire."

Gray on gray was what we saw on the day of our arrival at Grande Ligne, our new camp near Montreal. Its buildings: a three-story stone structure with a central section and wings on both sides and a little brick building had once served as a boarding school; a separate, typically Canadian wooden house as the headmaster's residence. There were many rooms in the center section: on the ground floor, former offices and classrooms, a little library, a workroom, a big auditorium, and a still bigger living room (called "The Red Ox"), plus dining room and kitchen. The center and the wings each had a staircase. On every floor were little rooms provided with numbers, in which either two field-grade officers, three captains, or four lieutenants lived. Each officer had a camp bed, a little worktable and a chair at his disposal. There were washrooms, showers, and toilets on each floor. Everything was clean and well arranged. The windows, which received a second pane of glass in winter, gave a view over wide fields and open meadows, with hills and forests in the distance. The beautiful panorama reminded some of the Münsterland in Germany. Senior officers, generals and colonels lived in the separate wooden house, in which I was also accommodated; noncommissioned officers and men, in barracks behind one of the wings of the central building. Nearby was a canteen, handicraft rooms, a laundry, steam rooms, sick rooms, the big gymnasium, which could be reached by a covered way from the main house, and the disciplinary cells. Between the buildings were lawns, a basketball court, and a tennis court. Outside the enclosure was an athletic field accessible by a wooden bridge. Through the camp gate it was possible to reach a field two or three hectares in extent where inmates could farm or keep little gardens.

"Generalleutnant von Ravenstein now camp leader—thank God!" ran in a letter sent from Grande Ligne to Germany in April 1945, and I shared that feeling. What would he have to say to the inmates of the camp when he assembled them in the gymnasium on 20 April, the "Führer's" birthday and obviously the last that would be celebrated?

His address ranks among the most memorable of my life. The occasion and Hitler's name did not come up at all. Von Ravenstein spoke of the military situation, commented carefully, exhorted us to stick together, opened future perspectives, and connected them with his experiences in the Weimar period, which proved that whatever happened in the coming days, Germany could still live on. We listened silently, almost breathlessly—the hall stayed quiet even as we were leaving. Certainly, it was generally quieter in camp since the "political" transfers of February 1945. But the last days of the war and the personal fate of Hitler, now at the sticking point, left their mark as seeds of discord. Ravenstein had to walk a rhetorical tightrope, and he accomplished it brilliantly. His address of 20 April 1945 was a diplomatic masterpiece.

The following weeks (after surgery for varicose veins) I spent, unfortunately, in the Montreal Military Hospital, where I learned of Hitler's suicide on 30 April and the German capitulation on 8 May. The two words, GERMANY QUITS, in huge headlines on the papers being sold on the streets could be read from a great distance, even from my hospital window. But their content meant nothing more to me than that, simply that—over the course of the years I had long since outlived inner shuddering over Germany's fate. At Grande Ligne, von Ravenstein reflected on the occasion before the camp's inmates assembled in the auditorium. Even a defeated people has its chances, he said. What matters is to use them and now to make every effort to get home soon. And Franz Schad noted: "Hard times are ahead for us all. Once again in the history of humankind, as perceptive, right-thinking men . . . feared from the start, the attempt to re-erect the Tower of Babel has failed. Of the inexpressible, millionfold suffering and misery, I will keep silent . . . if they lead us men to genuine contemplation and a just self-determination . . . but already new dark clouds show themselves."

In those weeks confined to bed, with much time to read, I fastened upon an article on the Yalta Conference appearing in *The Nineteenth Century and After* for March 1945.* It was a uniquely passionate condemnation of the "Declaration" issued there, its content and its language. According to the author, it aimed at a "dictated" peace for the whole of Europe and a fundamentally anti-European order that could be upheld only by force. The concepts of "democracy" and

---

*F. A. Voigt, "Yalta," pp. 97–107.

 391

"democratic" were most shamefully misused. If the conference of the "Big Three" (Roosevelt, Churchill, and Stalin) at Tehran in November 1943 had already led to the misfortune of the projected division of Europe into occupation zones, the new declaration sealed its destruction as a cultural unit. The author was most especially moved by the fate that it set forth for Poland: "Poland has been sacrificed . . . the Anglo-Polish Treaty of Alliance was violated." An urgent warning followed of the dangers to a democratic Poland of the "Lublin Committee," already designated the "Provisional Government of Poland," which had been founded under Soviet pressure at the end of 1944 with the aim of squeezing out the Polish exile government in London. Under the latter's aegis, it suddenly came back to me—the destroyer *Piorun* had certainly not fought the *Bismarck* in 1941 for a Poland geographically shifted to the west, and a Communist one at that. The rousing indictment, which I read in complete agreement, ended with a demand "To undo the work done at Yalta." That a journalist could fearlessly make such a massive attack on his own government in wartime was a wonder to me.

The article had been written by the long-standing editor of the magazine, F. A. Voigt, who had attracted my attention in the past months by his unsparing analyses of the actual political situation in the countries of southeastern Europe. Voigt had outstanding credentials for his assessments, having come to know the Continent, especially Germany, well in the course of his long career. Already in the twenties and early thirties he had written reports for the *Manchester Guardian* on German topics, on the SA's Storm troops in Brunswick in 1932, the Nazi terror in Germany in March 1933, the position of the Jews in Germany in January 1934—to name only a few. He had also carried out lengthy assignments in Germany later. Very well educated, firmly convinced of the underlying unity of European culture and, as a result, that the Continental countries should always be viewed in a European context, in the thirties Voigt became the *Manchester Guardian*'s key European correspondent. At home in the intellectual and artistic life of Weimar Germany, a regular at the legendary Romanisches Café near Berlin's Memorial Church, a close friend of the artist and social critic Georg Grosz—he ripened into an authority on European problems, who presented his views with great civil courage. But his attack on Yalta immediately revealed itself as the product of an ideal still based on the old, already historically defunct Europe—overtaken by the new constellation of great powers, a dream from the world of yesterday, the world of the European balance of power once so dear to England. Voigt still knew nothing, many still knew nothing, of the determination with which the advancing Soviets carried Stalin's postwar concept of a Communist eastern Europe in their knapsacks. The Western Allies not only had none of their own, so far they had still not even understood Stalin and would only later comprehend him. For the United States, some illusions would end in 1947. Arthur Bliss Lane withdrew from his post as the first postwar U.S. ambassador to Warsaw after recognizing the true character of the so-called "free" Polish parliamentary elections in January of that year. In his book, *I Saw Poland Betrayed*, he later expressed his deep disappointment in Roosevelt's submissive policy towards Stalin.

Unfortunately, my sojourn in the Montreal Military Hospital lasted longer than originally expected. Happily, the regular and regularly changing company of comrades from the camp kept boredom from setting in. Among them were tellers of tales, anecdotes, and jokes, but most especially one, a true natural talent in depicting "happenings" from life; true or false, that was immaterial. He had merely to purse his lips and a roomful of people would wait in amused anticipation of what was coming next. They were never disappointed. In this way and with the help of a gramophone obtained somehow and records ranging from the classics to boogie-woogie, the time flew by. At the beginning of July, I returned to Grande Ligne, but only for two weeks. In the middle of the month, together with eight other officers, I was transferred to the Sorel camp.

The new, so-called "democratic" camp at Sorel, on the St. Lawrence at the mouth of the Richelieu River, was, so to say, a political experiment. In its composition it could hardly have been more heterogenous. Here colonels in the general staff, officers of all grades, noncommissioned officers, enlisted men, reservists of all ranks, academics, foreign legionnaires, railway men, locomotive engineers from the highest staffs found themselves together. The camp, used in the past for very different purposes, now served for the quartering and "democratic" schooling of prisoners of war. The living conditions were not bad. I was able to establish myself comfortably in a relatively large room in one of the many quite solid wooden barracks. Even the winter cold was no problem. Potbellied stoves provided adequate warmth in the living quarters, dining room, and classroom barracks.

Whereas in former camps decisions regarding internal problems and controversial matters were more or less militarily made from above, in Sorel a "camp council" organized according to democratic principles sat and decided. Its speaker represented the camp to the Canadian commandant. One of his first successes was to persuade the commandant, an enthusiastic baseball fan, to increase the supply of inexpensive foodstuffs sold by the camp canteen at the earliest possible moment. For immediately after the day of the German capitulation, Ottawa had drastically reduced the prisoners' ration level to 1,000 calories a day, a sudden drop from the previous 4,000. Some of our comrades were nearly floored by it and became quite apathetic. So in August 1945 the first abundant edibles from the canteen, fruit and sausage, were greeted with a happy hello. Our daily ration allowance also improved gradually.

From the beginning the camp council, occasionally supplemented by the entire camp assembly, strove to develop training and educational programs for the forthcoming winter. Classes of all sorts down to the smallest study groups were formed. Of subjects and sections there were English interpreting; a legal study circle for special areas such as corporate law; questions of Christianity; an Evangelical study circle; principles of democracy; constitutional questions for Germany; cultural history. Foreign guest professors also gave lectures on historical subjects as well as on the international organizations then being formed. Franz Schad, whom I had been delighted to encounter again upon my arrival here, once more engaged himself as a high-performance motor for the intellectual work. Convinced that so dissimilar a group of camp inmates could be held on a firm course only by intellectual "torch bearers," he ceaselessly occupied himself with the organization of the educational program, including the library—a true missionary endeavor, as he himself once called it, in the face of the religious intolerance and ideological narrow-mindedness of the time, the inner need, and the deep insecurity of the individual with regard to the ultimate, decisive things.

Despite all this, sports and outdoor activities did not suffer. Ball games of every kind were played on the camp fields. Long walks through the extensive forests in the area alternated with bathing in the nearby Richelieu. I retain an adventurous mental picture from one of these walks. Our group, escorted by an Anglo-Canadian officer, approached a group of houses half hidden in the woods to the left and right of the path. All at once an extraordinary commotion appeared to be taking place in them. And it was. Out of the houses streamed men armed with every possible sort of clubbing and stabbing instrument and perhaps with firearms, too; at that distance, it was hard to tell. Hello—we lived in and were now wandering through French Canada, with its ethnically tight-knit population that had not experienced an emigration from France since 1763 and whose rural regions had since then lived in almost airtight isolation from the outside world. And the latter had now produced something surprising. Our stroll, of which this settlement had received wind, was interpreted there as an "attack of the Teutons," against which naturally the men had to defend. But as soon as our escort officer recognized the situation he reversed the direction of our march and the "Battle in the Forest" did not take place; the French Canadians remained behind as "victors." A moldy scent of European history; France's defensive attitude towards the growing power of Prussia in the eighteenth century, petrified and perserved in Quebec, had been stumbled upon by twentieth-century Germans in the forests of eastern Canada.

In camp, the coming and going was continuous. We witnessed new arrivals as well as the relegation of some individuals to "gray" or "black" camps and the early repatriation of groups with privileged status under international law. From the first, I was content to regard the stay in Sorel basically as a preliminary to the return to Germany and did not undertake any studies of long duration. I enjoyed devoting myself to a few selected areas. The level offered by our teaching staff was high, its substance fascinating. My violin also came into its own again. To be sure, I had to wait longer than I originally expected to say farewell to Canada, but a signal, at least, came in February 1946. We learned that all prisoners of war in Canada would soon—we at Sorel in the beginning of March—be transported to Great Britain, although to remain there until further notice. Nevertheless, it was a step in the desired direction. The pleasurable anticipation ruled our succeeding days.

At the beginning of March, it really came to pass. Packing, baggage inspection, chief baggage inspection, and after thirty hours on the train we reached Halifax on the evening of 5 March. We proceeded immediately to the *Letitia*,* upon reaching which we received an impressive boarding card: "Deck D, Cabin 3" stood on mine, but the accommodations were terribly crowded, nonetheless. We remained

---

*The *Letitia*, 13,475 BRT, 15 knots, was placed under the Ministry of Transport in 1946. (She was a sister ship of the *Athenia*, torpedoed by the *U-30* on 3 September 1939.)

in harbor until the ship finally sailed early on 10 March. The silhouette of the busy city and the contours of the New World, where we had been involuntary lodgers for four long years, slowly sank behind us. I accepted it as a small consolation that the time there had not been completely wasted. Memories returned of my voyage to it from England in the spring of 1942, the time-consuming zigzagging, the escorts to guard against German U-boats. Of all that, there would be no more—Hitler's war was already almost a year at an end. Now new uncertainties occupied me, hopes for Germany . . .

44

Featherstone Park Camp

An only moderately heaving Atlantic seemed to grant comrades without sea legs a merciful opportunity to escape seasickness. But it did not all go as they wished and in the following days a heavy blow came up.

After such a long intermission, I enjoyed the rough voyage immensely; it couldn't be stormy enough for me. As was proper, we also practiced lifesaving drills, *"Schiffsrollen,"* as the seamen called them. We had to appear with life belts put on near the life boats on the upper deck. And it was on one such occasion that the storm claimed my old blue cap as a personal sacrifice to the Atlantic. A gust seized it and let it coast along at eye level, but already overboard, for a second before it slid away, as though under sail with a following wind. It was a painful but dignified leave-taking. On the fourth day of the voyage we received an unexpected passenger. A snow owl, evidently injured, lit high up on the mast. The object of universal sympathy, it remained there for a day before vanishing as mysteriously as it had appeared. And after a crossing spent mainly in reading and playing cards, on 18 March we reached Liverpool and, after midnight, a transit camp near Nottingham.

There followed days of rather monotonous routine, of the obligation to kill time; nothing else was to be expected in a transit camp, where men did not make preparations for a long stay. A few were interrogated again by a British intelligence officer, politically "shaken out." Indeed, it was of concern to the British to pass the German prisoners of war sent from Canada to the main camps according to their criteria and, as far as possible, without too great error, the "blacks" and the "dark grays" to Camp 17 near Sheffield, the "whites" and the "light grays" to Camp 18 in Northumberland.

When, as a member of a large group, I first glimpsed Camp 18, the Featherstone Park Camp near Haltwhistle in Northumberland late in March 1946 something unusual was immediately evident. There was no barbed wire; no watchtowers; British guards were nowhere in sight. I saw German prisoners leisurely strolling outside the camp area, completely without British "supervision"; their simple word of honor sufficed now. Immense in its extent, the camp then housed around 2,500 inmates, and over the course of time a total of 4,000 officers and 20,000 noncommissioned officers and men would pass through Featherstone Park. The accommodations were not exactly comfortable in the long, low, slope-ceilinged and not always rainproof—and a mass of rain would fall in this summer of 1946— Nissen huts, which supposedly had served as quarters for part of the U.S. Army before the invasion of Normandy in June 1944. What a comedown from Bowmanville, I could not help thinking, but what did it matter; now, so close to going home, I could put up with (almost) anything. I found lodging in a hut occupied exclusively by naval officers, the "Navy Barracks." In it lived ranks from Kapitän zur See to Fähnrich. New and old captives were now together, not just in my hut, but, in keeping with the arrival of transports from overseas, throughout the entire camp: prisoners of war from the years 1939 through 1945. What impression did the "Germans from Canada," the men who had been captured between 1939 and 1942, make on their British interrogators? Between February 1946 and February 1947, 33,400 German PoWs arrived from Canada. Of all the PoWs who came to Britain after the war, they were the most steeped in the Nazi outlook. Let us read the screeners' report:

The vast majority are young men in the 20's and 30's who fought with the Africa Korps and have been prisoners from as early as 1941/42. A certain number were captured in 1939/40 in Holland and on the high seas. All these men picture Europe and Germany as they were before the war and cannot appreciate the vast material changes and the alteration in the mental outlook of Europeans which have taken place since that time.

PW camps in Canada were very large and more intensively Nazi than Germany itself. The German camp staffs were all senior NCOs and former Party members, fanatically imbued with the Nazi philosophy. Even the slightest criticism or expression of doubt as to the eventual

German victory was suppressed with all the ruthlessness of Nazi terrorism. That this is no overstatement is shown by the fact that in Camp 123 (Medicine Hat) two anti-Nazis were tried in secret and subsequently brutally murdered. The second of these political murders took place as late as September 1944.

All the PW lived in a political vacuum up to the end of the war and the types of men who would have been "greys" a long time ago in the camps in this country are today still "blacks." They only lost faith in Hitler after the war.

One encouraging factor is the "A-plus" and "A" categories. All these men were persecuted for their courageous opposition and most of them had to be transferred to a special protection camp in order that their lives should be safeguarded. . . .

Of the 1,200 officers screened most had been captured early from the Afrika Korps. In part they have become quite different people and ascribe the change to the influence of re-education in Canada, contact with civilians and the writings of Dorothy Thompson.*

And an impression of how the arrival of the "Canadians" affected other German prisoners, this time in a British work camp:

The new intakes from USA and Canada, totalling over 50% of the strength, have adversely affected the political complexion. 95% of the Ps/W from Canada and 60% of Ps/W from USA are said to be ardent Nazis. On arrival many of them gave the Hitler salute and discarded very reluctantly the Nazi insignia. The white element in the camp was shocked and bewildered, realising that their reeducational efforts had to be started anew.†

Did these British observations of a more differentiating political outlook, particularly among the Germans captured towards the end of the war, also hold true of the naval officers concentrated in Featherstone Park? Would not the shock of the atrocities of the Hitler regime, which became visible to everybody after the total military defeat, have driven them, too, to a fundamental reappraisal and reevaluation of the last twelve years? I myself was extremely anxious to see it happen: for example, the admission that for more than a decade one had erred disastrously—had served a false idol and mass murderer, a regime of the crudest cynicism and most revolting immorality. In the last few weeks, hadn't everyone had the opportunity to let

*Henry Faulk, *Group Captives*, pp. 178–79.
†Faulk, p. 179.

his eyes be opened by the exceptionally extensive sources of information at Featherstone Park?

To pose all these questions means to answer them in the negative, aside from a very few exceptions. In the vast majority of cases, the officers persisted in a sort of last-ditch obstinacy. And the individual naval officer really "couldn't help" that this was so. "Unity" of thought in the officer corps, whose self-image was still affected by the 1918 mutiny,* the all the more absolute "toeing the line" of prescribed standards, the "Unity of the Navy" from inside and out which was advertised by the especially authoritarian naval leadership under Raeder—all these belonged to the cardinal demands that the navy made upon its officers. Binding "rules on what to say and what not to say" promoted such an homogenous outward appearance—the navy was and remained "united" until the end and afterwards, "united" on the wrong course, to be sure, Hitler's course, but nevertheless "united," for Hitler was the Ver-Führer† of the nation and unity the trademark of the navy. A tight social circle quickly imprinted the individual with its approved views, ensnared him in Hitler's criminal system (which was not recognized as such), and the German spirit of subordination and a misunderstood oath of allegiance impelled him to the end along a course directly contrary to the well-understood interests and needs of his nation. How had Grossadmiral Raeder still formulated the political requirements of the day in his address to the officers of the Oberkommando der Kriegsmarine on 30 January 1943 upon the occasion of laying down his supreme command?

I believe you will agree with me that in the year 1933 I succeeded in leading the navy unitedly and smoothly behind the Führer into the Third Reich. That was made easy by the fact that, in spite of all outside influences, the whole education of the navy during the time of the "System"‡ aimed at an attitude that of itself produced a truly National Socialistic outlook. For this reason we ourselves had nothing to change and could with sincere hearts become true adherents of the Führer from the first. It has filled me with special satisfaction that the Führer has always valued this highly and I would like to ask you all to work to see that the navy remains a firm and reliable support for the Führer in this respect, as well.

---

*The German revolution of November 1918 was sparked by a mutiny in the heavy surface units of the High Seas Fleet.

†Mis-Leader

‡Term used contemptuously for the period of the Weimar Republic by its enemies of the political right.

To simply ignore such postulates, to let such words glance off, deservedly—under the conditions of naval training, not many would be given to doing that. Still deeply depressed by the shocking films of Auschwitz and Bergen-Belsen, in Featherstone Park I told a naval officer who seemed to me relatively tolerant: "I regard the outcome of the war as a divine judgment." He did not agree with me, he replied, remaining quite calm. "Well, everyone is entitled to his own opinion," I said. "It is already a gain, in comparison to time past, that someone can say something like that without immediately setting off an explosion."

Of course, it was a completely different matter to see navy comrades again in Featherstone Park on a purely personal basis. They lived not only in the "Navy Barracks," but also in other huts scattered throughout the immense camp, collectively a substantial number. And so there were many reunions, with friends, acquaintances, participants in the same operations and peacetime cruises. And there was so much to tell; it was always as though no more than a day had passed since we parted. The intimacy seemed so complete that it brought out the finest aspects of navy fellowship. The profession of naval officer was indeed a very attractive one on the whole; life in the navy had a singular charm—had not Hitler's evil shadow fallen over each and all.

The freedom of activities in Featherstone Park entirely accorded with the readiness of the British administration to provide any reasonable assistance to the German prisoners. Soon after the camp's opening, a university, academic and other study groups, a theater, a "church" converted from a barracks for both denominations, and a symphony orchestra were established. The university offered a complete lecture program in law, political science, economics, history, philosophy, and philology. The faculty was recruited from the large numbers of reservists in camp. The study groups, led by former college professors and journalists, concerned themselves primarily with the German political past. Foreign university professors also taught and debated and gave lecture series in camp. Once the British assembled a "Brain Trust" to exercise us: "You ask, we answer—How can Germany solve the social problem?" On this topic spoke radical socialists, a young man with good common sense, an advocate of state-controlled private enterprise, an objective-minded economist, a socialist worker, an intellectual Social Democrat, and a Christian social thinker. All this was highly interesting, not the least for the technique, the method of discussion, offered by representatives of a nation with centuries of experience in it.

For the theater, two groups were formed, one for serious pieces, the other for sketches and merrier things. The serious played, among others, *The Death of Danton*, *William Tell*, *The Broken Pitcher*, and *The Captain from Köpenick*. The most splendid costumes were conjured from old sacks and dyes, armaments from tin cans. The inmates of the camp included a writer's son who functioned as head producer, helping to select and work up pieces. Women's roles were deleted, with a single exception—for Shakespeare's *Troilus and Cressida*, men had to step forward. Many professional musicians played in the symphony orchestra; we enjoyed grand evenings of music and occasionally even the performance of an operetta.

From the beginning, the British had allowed the German leadership of this camp, established in 1945 and kept free of "incorrigible Nazis," access to the country's press. A German "press officer" gave newscasts from a selection of newspapers. Later the supply became more generous. Each barracks could receive its own newspapers; *The Times*, *The Manchester Guardian*, and *The Spectator*—a weekly magazine—were read, for example. From them newscasts were put together and periodically announced. I myself did this for the "Navy Barracks" for a while. In time, the British also permitted the publication of an uncensored German camp newspaper. It appeared under the title *Die Zeit am Tyne* ("The Time on the Tyne"). The first political voices from Germany reached us through a central press office. None was more passionate and moving than that of Kurt Schumacher, who with only a brief interruption had been tormented in Hitler's concentration camps from 1933 to 1945. A fiery anti-Communist, rejecting any collaboration with Communists anywhere, he vehemently called for the reunification of Germany and the integration of a free, complete Germany into a free Europe. He proclaimed a political concept that was very agreeable to me; as national minded as ever, I was still disconsolate over the loss of the unity of the Reich.

For the generosity extended to us during this last camp life, on the British side we had to thank first of all the commandant of Featherstone Park, Lieutenant Colonel Vickers. He was the worthy exponent of an honorable ex-enemy's readiness to effect a reconciliation. At his side stood the British Foreign Office Representative for PoW camps in Northern England, Colonel Henry Faulk. Faulk had been recommended for his difficult mission of the "re-education" of German prisoners by his knowledge of group psychology; he later wrote about it. At the time he saw his task as follows: "According to the Yalta agreements the Germans were to be demilitarized, deNazified and democratized. Great Britain had promptly begun that in 1945. It was up to me to carry out the appropriate work in the German prisoner-of-war camps. Up to then the German prisoner was not a man but a 'Nazi,' a concept that inspired revulsion and fright. But my experience showed me that the German prisoner was a man. And so the original 're-education' ended in an enthusiastic collaboration for our common future in a new Europe."

In his daily work, Faulk quickly recognized that the purely political thrust of "re-education" envisioned at Yalta was misdirected. To re-educate a National Socialist into a "democrat" without prejudice to his relationship to the German people? In practice, he soon came to view this sort of task as unrealistic.

The problem was a human one. Every man must feel that he has a right to belong to a group. Until the German capitulation, the rejection of National Socialism meant that one would be cast out of the group. Only a very few Germans dared to expose themselves to that danger. For this reason, the prisoners of war almost exclusively professed National Socialism until the end of the war. After the capitulation Nazism was dead and the prisoners, like all other Germans, needed a new group system. And at this time the British began the attempt to place humanity, human rights and human dignity in the forefront of the efforts being made with the prisoners. The prisoner should re-think about human life, but not about the political system. It was a disadvantage for this new attempt that the prisoner still viewed "re-education" as a political symbol. He embraced, accordingly encouraged, democratic organizational forms, but only very superficially, even purely organizationally. The actual political influence of this area of "re-education" remained small. On the other hand, almost all prisoners were influenced by the new attempt to place the whole problem on the human level, in connection with which they did not perceive that this spirit, too, could not take effect without organizational forms. In the confined camp life, even the most intelligent among them often lacked perspective and they tended to judge the big picture on the basis of local circumstances and personal relationships. At any rate, the most important thing was to bring the prisoners as much as possible into contact with the best British examples. Unfortunately, there were not enough of these and in some instances they were complete failures. But everyone was full of good will, which led to the end result that "different men" left the camp than had entered it.

And Colonel Faulk it was who helped so many German prisoners to a new start in life. He lives on in the grateful memory of many of them.

Most of all to be remembered in this regard, however, is a captain in the British Army, Herbert Sulzbach, who performed exceptional, indeed quite extraordinary service as Interpreter Officer, Featherstone Park Camp. For his mission in this camp, then viewed by the British as especially important, he had, as the saying goes, won his spurs in previous assignments, first as a staff sergeant, and then a lieutenant at the prisoner-of-war camp at Comrie, Scotland. At the beginning of 1945 around four thousand men found themselves there, among them fanatical Nazis and even members of the Waffen-SS. Sulzbach undertook his task of "re-education" in countless individual conversations and thought of something special for 11 November, the Armistice Day of the First World War. After he had proposed to the four thousand that they should honor the dead of *all* nations on this day, he administered the following oath to those assembled on the camp's football field:

> Never again shall such murder take place! It is the last time that we will allow ourselves to be so deceived and betrayed. It is not true that we Germans are a superior race; we have no right to believe that we are better than others. We are all equal before God, whatever race or religion. Endless misery has come to us, and we have realized where arrogance leads . . . . In this minute of silence, at 11 A.M. on this November 11, 1945, we swear to return to Germany as good Europeans, and to take part as long as we live in the reconciliation of all peoples and the maintenance of peace. . . .*

Only around a dozen of the prisoners sulked in the huts, while the majority stood motionless outside intoning the salute to the fallen. Herbert Sulzbach's commentary: "Nazism could be fought, and beaten as early as 1945." Who was this unusual man?

Sulzbach was born of Jewish parents in Frankfurt-am-Main in 1894. His grandfather had founded the private Sulzbach Brothers Bank there in 1855; his father later inherited it. Herbert had reported as a wartime volunteer in 1914 and was posted to the 63d Field Artillery Regiment in August. He served four years on the Western Front, rising to the rank of lieutenant and earning the Iron Cross I. and II. Class and the Front Fighters' Honor Cross. In 1935 he published his war diary, *Zwei lebende Mauern*.† It received warm reviews, even in

---

*Terence Prittie, "Herbert Sulzbach: A Memoir," in Herbert Sulzbach, *With the German Guns*, trans. Richard Thonger, p. 13.

†"Two Living Walls," for whose English translation see the preceding note.

the Brown press, which apparently had not noted its author's "Jew-ishness." But just two years later, with the Nazi persecution of the Jews in full swing, Herbert Sulzbach had to emigrate. The destination of his choice was England, where a paper products factory that he had founded as a filial of his Berlin firm would provide a modest standard of living. In 1938 he had to accept the high risk of a journey to Germany, through the search lists of the Reichssicherheitshaup-tamt.* He still had to bring his wife, Beate, a niece of the great conductor Otto Klemperer, and her sister to England. The atmo-sphere was filled with tension on both border crossings, but every-thing clicked. In the following period, German citizenship was with-drawn from him and his wife; they became stateless and, upon the outbreak of war in 1939, "enemy aliens" in England.

An ensuing internment on the Isle of Man, with Nazis and anti-Nazis, a nightmare for them, ended in 1940, after Sulzbach, upon his application, was accepted into the British Army. Various assignments with the pioneers followed until 1944, when an army order came to his attention: "German speakers are urgently sought!" The number of German prisoners of war in the country was growing by leaps and bounds. He talked it over with his wife. On one hand, he wanted to make himself as useful as possible; on the other, he recoiled from coming back into contact with the swastika, which the Germans all wore on their breasts! Sulzbach: "It was actually my wife who per-suaded me and told me: 'You can do it!' " And then he had begun it, the great task which would engage him for years and fill the rest of his life, the task of understanding and reconciliation between German and Briton.

The German prisoners in England between 1944 and 1945, so Sulz-bach reported later, were for the most part still fanatical Nazis and still under the illusion that Hitler would win the war. "But of course there was also a row of doubters, indeed anti-Nazis. There was the frightful murder of a Hitler opponent, a sergeant, who was beaten to death and then hanged by fanatical comrades because he had made anti-Nazi entries in his diary, which they had gone through while he slept. Incidentally, the murderers were hanged in the summer of 1945. Then there were doubters and fellow travellers, who were natu-rally the easiest to convert."

And what did Sulzbach have to say about Featherstone Park?

*Reich Chief Security Office

At first I let everything come my way. Prisoners entered my office with every imaginable question and concern. Then it was always up to me to bring the conversation around to England and Nazi Germany, and I tried in a few words to point out the difference between freedom and tyranny. The Germans became trusting and reported on their talks with me in the barracks. More and more, I came to be a spiritual counselor or helper rather than anything else that I could or would be. There were hardly any difficulties from the British side in this regard. I had the great luck to have understanding camp commandants, who left me a free hand, then that great man Henry Faulk, and, not least, equally understanding gentlemen in the War Office in London. It wasn't hard for me to tell stubborn Nazis, fellow travellers and anti-Nazis from one another. Of course, as a born optimist, I may at times have been too easily taken in. But I would rather send someone who did not deserve it home early than do the opposite. On the other hand, as I was also responsible for political classification, I often quite consciously put young men who were still Nazis in levels which stamped them as anti-Nazis and the success was all the greater. After the war's end it was naturally easier to make doubters and Nazis into normal men. I never actually worked out methods for myself; for I spoke with everybody individually. Perhaps there is still something to emphasize: I have, as a German emigrant, never pretended to be British or changed my name, and in most cases that inspired trust.*

When I myself visited Sulzbach for the first time, we had a special topic of conversation: the fate of my prewar London possessions. A member of the staff of our naval attaché there in 1938–39, I had not been able to have my personal belongings forwarded to Germany before war broke out. Of course, as a footloose young bachelor I did not have any too much to leave behind. Everything was confiscated, placed in official custody, and eventually auctioned off, and the small proceeds were credited to me. It was orderly enough in its way. In our general conversation Sulzbach weighed a typical finding from his many conversations with other prisoners of war. The Germans needed to "loosen up, loosen up . . ." I could not contradict him.

The sun was smiling down, a lovely landscape in the young green of early May rushed past, and a warm wind blew in the open windows of the express train from Newcastle to London. In the compartment sat a little group from Featherstone, on a fast ride to the south, itchy with the anticipation of an imminent change in the still somewhat

*West German Radio, "Stärker als Stacheldraht," transcript of a broadcast, 1963.

monotonous life of a prisoner of war. Only three days earlier Sulzbach had informed me and the others of a transfer to a Documentation Center. What we were to do there, he did not explain very exactly, but we would find out immediately upon our arrival. And after leaving the camp at an ungodly hour we reached King's Cross in London at noon and continued on to Charing Cross and from there to Tonbridge in the county of Kent. An auto brought us to our destination, Prisoner of War Camp 40, Halstead Exploiting Center, built like a youth hostel in the midst of a beautiful scenic panorama. By then it was around 2100, but still light, and we recognized German military equipment captured by the British, apparently naval ordnance—what's this? we thought; a big question mark immediately took form.

The next day a British officer explained our new assignment. To the booty assembled there belonged countless classified directives, such as descriptions, instructions for use, illustrations, etc., all highly technical and very difficult to put into English—which was precisely what was expected of us. It would surely take a long time, but we already knew that we could not be repatriated before October, in any event.

We Featherstoners looked at each other in surprise. That we would not accept this task was at once clear to most. Officially, however, we asked for time to think it over. The following morning we came forward with our "No" to this task. That afternoon the camp commandant personally tried to change our minds, unsuccessfully. The day thereafter a major from the War Office made a special trip from London to win us over to the project, equally unsuccessfully. "Now that you have taken all this material as booty," was and remained our reply, "its use is exclusively your affair. We will have nothing to do with it." Period. This caused no bad blood with the British; they accepted it. The opposing viewpoints were again aired in individual conversations with them in the following days, but nothing changed. Inevitably, we were transferred back to Featherstone Park, which we reentered in the middle of May. After barely two weeks, the Halstead intermezzo was over and we resumed the customary camp life.

The coming months seemed to me to be no more than a transition to the return home to Germany. I attended selected lectures; gave some myself; visited the theater, films, and musical performances in the evening; and hauled out my violin again. A professor of Russian animated me to take a beginning course in that difficult language, so that together with further study of English, again by means of the Pitman shorthand, my days were full enough. Now and again I made use of the possibility, which had existed at Featherstone Park since the summer of 1945, of working outside camp and without guards, chiefly in agriculture, after signing a promise to return. Volunteers were sent daily to about 250 farms and 18 drainage sites, and already by October 1945 the number of Germans engaged in such outside work reached a total of 850 per day. In 1945 more than 9,000 tons of potatoes were harvested in the vicinity and a large portion thereof was sent to provision the British occupation zone in Germany! Some officers were already living on farms and others in Camp 18's newly established outside facilities ("hostels"). The results of a year's drainage work were 450 kilometers of ditches dug or improved and more than 2,500 hectares of waste- or swamp-land converted into productive farmland. I myself went to the farms, undertaking piecework such as whitewashing stalls, but had the greatest pleasure in the drainage of the peat bogs of Sewing Shields, a workplace of the Women's Land Army. It was a lot of fun to be around those jolly, sturdy girls. There was never the least pressure from the German or British camp authorities to participate in these labors. Many personal relationships sprung up between the Germans and the English population, and the German name still has a good reputation in Northumberland. The ancient Romans had also left occasional projects behind for us. Near Featherstone Park ran the wall built by and named after the emperor Hadrian (117–138 A.D.) as a frontier fortification of the Roman province of Britannia, 120 kilometers in length, originally with 17 citadels, 80 gateways and 320 towers. The centuries had gnawed at it and it needed restoration everywhere. Also, it was regularly being excavated at some point. Once we were able to visit the thoroughly impressive cathedral in Durham and take part in a divine service there.

Early in October 1946, the first little group left us to return home. At the beginning of November, I learned that my own repatriation was imminent. And early on 5 November, I was put under way as a member of a new group of the homeward bound, intermediate destination: Camp 23, near Sudbury, where we still had to spend a few days as a preliminary to being embarked for Germany. They were days of dreary routine and pure waiting. But eager anticipation arose when, after four days, the names for the first transport home were read out. Transports to the British occupation zone alternated with those to the American. My group departed from Sudbury on 20 November, reached the coastal city of Hull at midday, and was embarked in the afternoon on the *Empire Spearhead*—what a great name, I thought, it could really befit a large ocean liner! But I was more than satisfied with our modest freighter as the sun shone down on us while she slowly slipped out of harbor.

During the night aboard the *Empire Spearhead*, the last before we saw Germany again, sleep would not come to many. We spent it in conversation or in thought. Some of us could at least return to our former homes, to familiar surroundings, perhaps even to circles of friends—those from the east, myself from Silesia, could not do that. In 1943, on account of increasingly heavy bombing raids, my mother had given up her residence in Berlin and returned to Silesia—not to Hirschberg, the scene of my childhood, but to Bad Schwarzbach in the Isergebirge. In Silesia, outwardly so peaceful, the full gravity of the military situation had not really dawned on her until January 1945; the Reich radio had certainly not suggested it. But when one January day she asked the station master about the state of rail traffic, he had looked at her wonderingly. "Well, if you want to get out of here at all, the next and last train is leaving in an hour." And she managed to make it, in a great rush, with a little suitcase in hand and otherwise only what she was wearing, not exactly her best things— these she would not expose to the rigors of a wartime evacuation! And so after stopping at a relative's in Bad Harzburg, with whom, however, she could not stay, she proceeded further into Hanover, where she was now living as a refugee in a small room in a farmhouse at Leeseringen an der Weser. Therefore I belonged to the transport to the British zone.

The *Empire Spearhead* entered Cuxhaven at 1730 on 21 November. We climbed into a train standing ready near the quays and, after a locomotive breakdown lasting three hours, we reached Münster Camp between three and four o'clock in the morning. The halt there lasted only two days altogether. "Paper war"—discharge certificate, rubber stamp, pocket money for the cost of the journey home. All had been made ready for our entry into postwar civil life.

On the morning of 23 November, we traveled by truck to the main railway station in the city of Hanover, the point of departure for everyone discharged in the British zone. Jump down, grab the baggage, and keep going—God in heaven, what didn't I have in all that stuff: suitcase, duffel bag, packet of books, violin, an almost incredible mass, to haul through the crowded station, up the long line to the ticket window, across a platform black with people, and into a train, already filled to the seams, for Nienburg. Alone, I would never manage it—but helping hands presented themselves, some inspiring confidence and others that appeared less so. Especially imploring was the look of a young disabled man; with his crutch, he hardly seemed able to last through the job, but his, "I'd really like to help you, I can do it, believe me," was welcome. Up on the platform, I could write off any attempt to get into a compartment together with all my baggage. So give up on this train and wait for the next one? Wait, wasn't that an empty brakeman's cabin at the end of one car? It was. "Hey!" I shouted to my companion over the hubbub, "Up here!" Hurriedly we shoved piece after piece up the small stairs. In the cramped space above, half crushed by my things, I fumbled for my cigarettes, threw twenty to my helper: Thanks, thanks, and good luck! And already the train was rolling out of the station, my friend below vanished from sight—it was really a close shave!

It was five and a half years, almost to the day, since the last time I had left Germany, on board the powerful battleship *Bismarck* from Gotenhafen in May 1941. At that time there had been no bomb damage in the eastern Reich and the night raids I had experienced in Hamburg in the winter of 1940–41 had hardly scarred the Hanseatic City. Now for the first time I saw the awful effects of the air war with my own eyes. I felt a morbid curiosity mixed with deep anguish as my train rolled past the destruction on the horizon, a literal fulfillment of Daladier's words in the late summer of 1939—"Destruction and barbarism will most certainly triumph"—ruins to the right, ruins to the left. The depressing sight of them dredged up that sentence from the historical ruins of the last twelve years: "Give me four years and you will not recognize Germany!" Four years!—He had received them three times over, the great "Führer." And he had paid for them with 50 million dead, the loss of the German East, ruins everywhere, and the flight from any responsibility. Even from that which rhetorically he had worn out, "before history."

45

End of a Nightmare

For a German damned by his perceptions to recognize the creeping poison of so-called National Socialism (which seemed to me neither nationally oriented nor socialistic), the years under Hitler had to appear a veritable nightmare, a purgatory for insightful patriots. Such a German could not fail to perceive the reality of the years 1933–39 as a period in which, after the murderous elimination of effective opposition, Germany was irresistibly transformed into an intellectual, moral, and cultural wasteland, a collecting ground for warlike aggression; and the years 1939–45 as a period of naked assertion of physical force, of painful realization that the enemy in front of the guns was only technically the enemy—that in reality Germany's enemy was the man in the Reich Chancellery.

To be sure, on 8 May 1945 such a German felt no less than any other German the deepest grief at the abrupt fall of his country into seeming nothingness. But one great consolation was granted him: that Germany's liberation from Hitler and his clique at last gave his people the opportunity to turn away from the political aberration of the past twelve years, the shame of a millenium. And he may have had the feeling that Germany couldn't sink any lower; it could only rise.

From now on, I knew, that everything I do in my walk of life will, after all, have a sense of civic purpose and contribute to a rational community. For the first time since 1933! It was an indescribable sensation!

A great hope, perhaps too great? Since after all, we had not freed ourselves from Hitler by our own exertions, but owed our freedom wholly to the victors of the Second World War? And after years of observing that National Socialism was anything but an "historical accident," but that to the contrary it seemed to be written all over the Germans—with its cunning appeal to the instincts and habits ingrained in German subjects by centuries of German authorities: order and discipline, authoritarian rule, and the subordination of the individual to the state, to the "whole," now formulated into a pithy slogan ("You are nothing, your Folk is everything")! And had not such claims upon the quasi-hierarchial structure of the people also exerted a special attraction on military circles and the navy? The mobilization of mystical feelings slumbering in the people, dark, muddled beliefs, books like those of the English racist Houston Stewart Chamberlain, Nazi ideologue Alfred Rosenberg's still worse *Myth of the Twentieth Century*—all had made their contribution to confusing the mind of a people who needed clarity and rationality more than anything else in politics.

A diabolical state stage-production showed the Germans a future under Hitler in a radiant light. The never-ending parades, wild victory celebrations, tributes to the dead—above all the glorification of death itself—were the inducement of the accentuation of the emotional, the irrational, the sensual, the delirious.

It was really no wonder that in place of a dispassionate analysis of national policy there emerged a blind faith in the "Führer" and his "teachings"—a faith, and this was the most dreadful thing, that held itself to be "enlightenment." "Führer, command—we obey," became its everyday currency in political discourse, the attestation of a nation's intellectual abdication. And it was equally understandable that the mass of people was taken in or lacked the antennae to pick up what was going on in the background. Anyone who saw acts of "spontaneous vengeance" taking place in public, as on the day of the Jewish pogrom of 9 November 1938, no longer perceived the even worse horrors that must be raging in subterranean secrecy!

I cannot claim that I myself, stemming from an archconservative family, was granted an early insight into the nature of the Hitler regime at its start. The standard by which I first judged Hitler was nothing more than his face, which I found repulsive. I could never read a sense of statesmanlike responsibility into him and even his rhetorical mimicry did not enable him to supply what I missed. To expect good things for Germany from the possessor of such a miserable face, the countenance of a psychopath?—instinctively, I never could. Personally regarding Hitler's accession to the office of chief of government with disgust, I lived through his decisive acts in the destruction of our legal and constitutional state in 1933–34 without—professional soldier and non-lawyer that I was—fully grasping their magnitude. However, I perceived an ominous signal, a terrible impulse to reflection, for the first time in the political murders instituted by Hitler on and after 30 June 1934. Not that I knew more about the bloody business than most people. But the public "justification" that Hitler offered afterwards seemed to me to leave much too much unclear, did not satisfy me. Too many dark things were obviously being skipped over. All it communicated to me was mistrust, a panicky mistrust ready to swell at any moment.

This was the impression that Herr Hitler, who was so warmly regarded by the conservatives on my mental horizons, had made on me up to 1934. Immediately upon the formation of the Weimar Republic an uncle of mine who mourned for the monarchy, a government lawyer and veteran of the 1914–18 war, not yet fifty years old, told the family that "I cannot serve this state" (but whose retirement pension he did not mind accepting). Towards the end of the twenties an aunt informed me, "Your grandparents are going to vote for Hitler from now on. I've persuaded them to. Only from him can Germany expect improvement." Only with clenched teeth did the navy celebrate 11 August as Weimar's Constitution Day until 1932— "disreputable things" were associated with it; one didn't need to talk much about it, everyone understood one another on the subject of this miserable Weimar.

I had observed all of these standpoints in my early years, without really accepting them, but I also had not fully understood them. For politics then remained a far too distant field for me; as a boarding school student and then as a naval officer I had yet to develop a basic outlook on them. With the passage of time, I categorized Hitler politically as neither "right" nor "left," but as a phenomenon to be understood only in its own terms—with, no doubt, a special allure to conservatives, who did not hesitate to flock to his camp. Had not one of the Nazis' first public acts, the book burning in Berlin, Munich, Cologne, and Koenigsberg on 10 May 1933, raised one of the right's own ideas to a new height? Had not a family friend once told me during my school days in the early twenties of the intellectual currents of the militant academic right? The friend had spoken rapturously, but at the age of sixteen I did not perceive the political background of his words. In 1923 one of the basic documents of the antirepublican right had already prepared for the book pyres of 1933 by asserting:

> We are fighting with every available means the bearers of the Jewish spirit, whose effects destroy German racial consciousness, sap German strength, contaminate German art, and stifle German idealism in the slime of materialism. We are fighting the most pernicious chimera of our era, self-emasculating pacifism, and, because of its ruinous effect on the strength of the Folk, branding it as high treason to our nation. We will ceaselessly expose the true nature of the so-called democracy. . . . We are making an assault on the un-German parliamentarianism that has done everything possible to shatter the German Reich and will never summon the strength needed for the rebuilding of the Reich.*

The conservative novelist Ernst Jünger of 1930 even lent a hand, writing that "in the same measure . . . in which the German spirit gains focus and strength, for the Jew the faintest illusion of being able to be a German in Germany will become untenable and he will see himself confronted with his final alternative: in Germany either to be a Jew or not to be."† What a parallel existed between the targets of the right and of the Nazis then gathering strength! I had a very different recollection of people of "leftist" political tendencies, a few teachers from my school days, rational critics distanced from all mass illusions. They had often spoken contemptuously of the hurrah-patriotism they had witnessed during the First World War—and this was only a decade before the new breed of *"Sieg heilers"* appeared in the forums of the Third Reich. A more discriminating patriotism was permitted on the left.

I myself, in continuous self-doubt and inner antipathy to the figure of Hitler, could simply not convince myself that Hitler's "revolution" was a revolution at all. If from today's perspective the decisive effects of his regime on Germany—the displacement of the old Prussian upper class and the necessity for its replacement by another, the dissolution of Prussia, the disappearance of the capital from Berlin, and the division of Germany—may appear as the result of a deliberately initiated revolutionary process, I could not discover a corresponding serious start in Hitler. A man like Otto Strasser may have

---

*Walter Jens, *Die alten Zeiten niemals zu verwinden* (Address on the 50th anniversary of the book burning of 10 May 1933), Akademie der Künste, Anmerkungen zur Zeit, Nr. 20 (Berlin 1983).

†Ibid.

aimed at a truly socialistic reformation of German society, but Hitler? What did he do other than for tyrannical (only outwardly glorified as messianic) aims to collect all those dissatisfied with the republic into militant organizations in which, with the help of a mystical-racial ideology, to bind a narcoticized people to a pseudoreligious mass illusion and to transform Germany into a circus of fanatical frenzy and ruthless inquisition and the Germans into political St. Vitus's dancers? Did not his public appearances and those of his rhetorical stand-ins mask the fact that everything was undertaken only to keep Hitler and themselves at the levers of power, even at the cost of the nation's welfare, that Hitler's "revolution" was a revolution in disguise—one that was in fact an archaic, shameless, brutalizing reaction? Only the dynamic of his power, his "coordination" (gleichschaltung) which flattened out the social groups and classes into a "Community of the Folk" and of the war he unleashed could, in their totality, transmit the impression of a consciously contrived social revolution to his posterity.

Even after the serial murders in the summer of 1934, my progress along the path of growing recognition of the depravity of the National Socialist regime was by no means straightforward and untroubled. For a young man, politically uninformed, fundamentally immature, in surroundings in which devotion and loyalty to Hitler were the order of the day, such a development would have been very difficult. Over and over, beside my doubts about Hitler, I felt doubts about myself. Could it really be that so many Germans viewed him wrongly and so terribly few rightly? And then there were always Hitler's radio broadcasts. Whether I listened to them by order or was magnetized by the mere sound: what rhetorical cascades fell over me, what dizzying eloquence! What achievements could he not endlessly enumerate: the chaos in Germany overcome and order restored, unemployment conquered and millions of jobless reintegrated into the productive process, the dictate of Versailles dismantled step by step, German military sovereignty reestablished—a persuasive, incontrovertible presentation.

Once, in the beginning of 1936, he particularly praised the German soldier as the support of his state, as the armsbearer of the nation, flattering the German officer—how gullibly did we take the bait! Even the ceaseless repetition of such recitals was not wearisome, but allowed the glow of persistent past successes to light up the future, in which things would most definitely continue to improve. Like the beating of a powerful surf, Hitler's speeches repeatedly swept me off the ground of seemingly unshakable skepticism and aversion, and I found myself swimming against doubt: wasn't I in error, musn't I reorient my basic outlook? But, remarkably, such agonizing uncertainty never lasted more than two or three days and then I was myself again: No, his venomous speech, his burning fanaticism, his irrational outbursts of anger appeared somehow fraudulent, intellectually questionable, the man wasn't right; instinct more than understanding told me these things. And so I could never fully explain myself rationally, could never "prove it." It was a spectral existence, as if between two worlds.

"My God, why are you so dejected?" A girlfriend asked me that question when in the summer of 1937 I returned to Berlin after a long absence.

"If you're thinking that something happened recently to depress me," I replied, "it's not that. I can't think of anything of the sort this year, or even in 1936. No, it's something else entirely, apparently insignificant, for a long time now even commonplace. I believe that today was the day I sat down once too often in a restaurant near some of those loud-mouthed, as you well know, black-uniformed people who consider bodily measurements and the color of one's hair and eyes as valuable instruments of national policy. These physically trained, weltanschauung-indoctrinated,* nationalistically supercharged men regard the Aryan as the measure of all things and as such entitled to rule the world and eliminate everyone not of their kind. When I come to think that such criminal nonsense has been stuffed into young people's heads since 1933, that this will continue, and that it will never be possible to set things right in this state, then only some sort of historical catastrophe can put an end to such nonsense. When and how it will come, I can't say. But it hangs over us, like eternity."

That was only a year before the murderous Jewish pogrom, the public performance of racial madness. "Of course, where wood is planed, shavings fall"—someone applied this, which gradually became the most absurd of all sayings, to that outrage. Hermann Göring had used it once, in a speech at Essen in March 1933. The Jewish department stores there had then been shut down by the state and completely innocent people arrested and mistreated. The latter were the "shavings." Thereafter the saying became very fashionable and was always thought suitable when referring to the victims of the

---

*A comprehensive perception of the world from a specific point of view

Brown tyranny. The "planing" went on, according to the "Führer's" recipe, for twelve years. And when in 1945 the plane fell, the "shavings" included four million German war dead, the unity of the Reich, a thousand years of German territorial history, and ruins spread over the country. If only the great planer had tasted his testament.

Others who made their way through the Third Reich but felt budding doubts about its course engraved themselves in my memory with the words that they had to participate or remain at their posts in order to prevent "worse" from happening. No doubt many of them did individual good, meritoriously, even nobly. But, from a national perspective, did they prevent "worse"? If indeed so, then, unfortunately, it was only to the benefit of the "worst."

If Hitler said any one thing that continually outraged me over the years, it was that he bore the responsibility for his policies "before history." From his mouth, nothing more than a big, empty aphorism. For a head of government must face the constitutional judges of his time. If, like Hitler, he does not admit, or even eliminates them at the start of his regime, then in truth he permits no criticism and must therefore fear it, and the phrase "responsibility before history" turns out to be hollow nonsense. When does this "history" begin, who defines and evaluates it, and who sits on the judge's bench? One of the subsequent "historical schools," or a subsequent government *qua* "historical institute," according to the demands of the day? As long as the frustrated politician who refers to history is alive, for him it will not have begun—a convenient court, namely, none at all. And does one who feels absolutely no official responsibility have need of even such a court?

My outer life until 1945—*Abitur,** naval officer, war, victory and defeat—can truly be seen as the regulation sort for a man of my origins and upbringing, the internal and external challenges in perfect harmony. But the appearance is deceptive, for the harmony was broken as of 1934. Inwardly shaken to the core to see Hitler misusing the idealism of German youth and the patriotism of the mature generations more and more from year to year; gradually to recognize him as the gravedigger of civilized Germany, in the execution of the "Führer's will" myself a servant of the state who would have to lay hands on the Reich; to have to assist in maintaining the defensive wall behind which Hitler could commit murder the more undisturbed; to be nothing other than one of the Führer's "assistant undertakers of

---

*School-leaving examination qualifying the student for admission to a university

the Reich"; to perform nationalistic "duties" instead of real duties; to pursue civic "values" instead of real values—in all of them I beheld the suffocating, crushing challenges of my time. But the insight upon which I did not act, which did not keep me from being among the "participants," establishes guilt, personal guilt. Hitler's ruthless tyranny, his deadly security apparatus, the senselessness of isolated resistance, a resistance without a chance, lessen the guilt. But a residue will remain until the end of my days. I cannot amortize it, too much is irretrievably past. It will live on only as shame and mourning—and as the life-long forfeiture of the claim ever again to step before a German youth.

I have spoken of hope for Germany, hope after 1945, perhaps too great a one? No, until now, at any rate, it has not shown itself to be too great—the twelve-year wait has been rewarded and apparently continues to be rewarded. In a sadly reduced area, to be sure—a cost of Hitler—and painfully separated from my beloved Silesia, the land of my childhood, for decades now I have been a citizen under the most liberal constitution that I have been politically conscious of experiencing in Germany. Until now our citizens have on the whole made good use of it. But a constitution is nothing more than an instrument of the intellect. And in the presence of the authoritarian tendencies deeply imbedded in the German mind, in the end it will only be the citizen himself who develops it into the instrument of a lasting democracy—or does not.

Afterword

"National Socialism" was identical to the greatest mass movement Germany ever brought forth. Its historical roots were deep and abundant. They made it easy for Hitler immediately to transform his initially "legal" government into a diabolical regime such as even the most authority-enamored among us would never have believed possible. It was a mentality formed by centuries that the great demagogue manipulated—but it was a mentality, and these grow and change only slowly. So it would be a wonder if National Socialism should have disappeared as abruptly and totally as the battleship *Bismarck* and our surface strategy did in the Atlantic on 27 May 1941 or as abruptly as the succession of outward phenomena since 8 May 1945 might indicate. And, indeed, such a wonder neither occurred nor is to be expected around the next corner. The dark past a closed chapter, dead and buried by authority of a democratic constitution? No, unfortunately not. What takes long to ripen takes long to wither.

The preamble for such a speedy burial would have been lacking when the time came for it. What was the situation at the beginning of the democracy? The generation responsible for reckoning with the results of the vile regime continually suppressed the past and withdrew into a stony silence. Neither the school teachers nor the parents at home enlightened the children properly, surely out of shame or cowardice. An immediately inaugurated age of political restoration brought former leading Nazis to the highest positions in the Federal Republic. The democratically imperative need to square accounts with the "perpetrators" of the vanquished regime, including its legal aspects, was pursued hesitantly, half-heartedly, or not at all, as Jörg Friedrich has given us another convincing proof in his book, *Die Kalte Amnestie*. Judges who sat on the murderous "People's Court" and on the more than twenty "Special Courts" supposedly responsible for "criminal and political offenses" but in reality serving to suppress the political opposition, were seldom if ever held to account and for the most part escaped due expiation for their misdeeds—they and other merciless persecutors of members of the opposition and enlightened patriots have often experienced undeserved clemency under the jurisdiction of the Federal Republic.

Of course, for a long time there has been talk that we must "overpower" (*bewältigen*) the past. But what does this miserable word really mean? Its phonetics alone indicate an unnatural act of force, a sweeping-under-the-carpet of all the horrors and, if this succeeds, please don't bring them up again. Only, a large enough carpet has not been found and never will be. Therefore why not, in place of fits of overpowering, a simple, honest assessment of the past, a true self-examination? It would be the proper, until now neglected step on the path to a self-ordained instead of decreed democracy. So many unhealthy symptoms are appearing ever more unmistakably: the again increasingly evident anti-Semitism; the necessity to resist the "Auschwitz Lie" with a penal law—which in its part was diluted by a mentality of setting off the post-war expulsions of Germans against the Auschwitz horrors; the scandalous conduct of neo-Nazi groups; the belittling of the victims of the resistance to Hitler; a recent glaring attempt on the part of members of the ruling conservative Bonn coalition to bend the course of justice in a social democratically governed state to its wishes, in other words, to make, as it were, the legal system the "whore of politics." Citizens who saw through this political game being played for the preservation of political power and to the detriment of the administration of justice and who had lived through Nazism could immediately recall Goebbels's dictum, "The legal system must not be the master, but the servant of state policy." This dictum of March 1942 was the prelude to the resolution of the "Great German Reichstag" of 26 April which officially made Hitler the "Supreme Magistrate" of the Reich. And whoever remembers that also remembers Winston Churchill's words that vigilance is the price of freedom. It always will be.

Epilogue

The news of the discovery of the *Bismarck* wreck by Robert Ballard on 8 June 1989 gave me a great emotional shock. There should have been no such shock because I had previously known of the intended search for the battleship by Dr. Robert Ballard, the discoverer of the wreck of the *Titanic*. Ballard had given me the first hint of his *Bismarck* plan when we met in Frankfurt/Main in October 1987 at a luncheon given during the Book Fair by a publisher for whom both of us had written works. And hearing of such a project from a man with a reputation for high competence and determination was to me almost tantamount to the success of that search once it was undertaken. The subsequent failure of Ballard's initial search for the *Bismarck* in 1988 had not diminished my conviction that he would not be deterred but would once again try harder—and succeed. Thus, no shock should have resulted from a discovery I had expected.

And yet, there the shock was. During the decades since the loss of the ship in May 1941, the operation of the *Bismarck* had been described in many books and press articles, as well as in films. I had written two books on the subject—the second, an expanded version of the first, in which I tried to solve or at least shed light on some of the questions that had not yet been answered concerning Exercise Rhine.

And after all that had been said or done, *Bismarck* to my mind had come to be thought of as a naval cemetery on the bottom of the ocean, a grave of fallen seamen that no human would possibly ever see again—a place to be held in respectful memory.

The discovery changed all this, for the moment. There sprang to life once again all the dramatic details of that world-famous operation, and I relived them in spirit, from the departure from Gotenhafen on 19 May 1941 to the end in the Gulf of Biscay on 27 May. Robert Ballard's photography made it possible to see much more clearly than had been possible at the time, the final state of the sunken giant, enabling experts to partly revise their conclusions about how the *Bismarck*'s last battle had run. Splendid underwater pictures of the *Bismarck* have been shown in magazines such as the U.S. *National Geographic* and the German *GEO*.

However, the next-of-kin of the fallen *Bismarck* men as well as others have expressed fears that the next step might be intruding into the wreck to collect loose objects or even raising the entire wreck to the surface. No such serious intention by the explorer is known to me, nor would any such action be favored by the government of the Federal Republic of Germany, which regards itself as the proprietor of the battleship. Eventually, I feel, the *Bismarck* will return to what she has been for so long: a remote seamen's grave to be held in all due respect.

 **A**

The Seekriegsleitung's Operation Order for Exercise Rhine

Commander-in-Chief of the Navy   Berlin, 2.IV.1941
and Chief of the Seekriegsleitung
B. Nr. 1. Skl. I Op. 410/41 Gkdos Chefs.*

COMMANDERS' EYES ONLY!   SECRET—COMMANDS ONLY
OFFICER COURIER ONLY!

I.) Copies to: Group West
                 Group North
                 Fleet Commander
                 Commander-in-Chief, U-Boats
   Subj.: Directives for Future Operations by Surface Forces
   No direct references
   I. During the past winter the conduct of the war was fundamentally in accord with the Seekriegsleitung's directives for the war in the winter 40/41 (Seekriegsleitung I. Op. 2270/41 Chefs.) and closed with the first extended battleship operation in the open Atlantic.
        Besides achieving important tactical results, this battleship operation, as well as the operations of the cruiser *Hipper*,

---

*Seekriegsleitung Operations Section, Chief Operations Officer, Order Number 410/41, Commands Only, Commanders' Eyes Only.

showed what important strategic effects a similar sortie could have. They would reach beyond the immediate area of operations to other theaters of war (Mediterranean, South Atlantic).

The goal of the war at sea must be to maintain and increase these effects by repeating such operations as often as possible. To accomplish this, the experience already gained must be exploited and the operations themselves expanded.

We must not lose sight of the fact that the decisive objective in our struggle with England is to destroy her trade. This can be most effectively accomplished in the North Atlantic, where all her supply lines come together and where, even in case of interruption in more distant seas, supplies can still get through on the direct route from North America. The employment and operational area of our battleships and cruisers must take this viewpoint into account.

Gaining command of the sea in the North Atlantic is the best solution to this problem, but this is not possible with the forces that at this moment we can commit to this purpose, and given the constraint that we must preserve our numerically inferior forces. Nevertheless, we must strive for local and temporary command of the sea in this area and gradually, methodically, and systematically extend it.

During the first battleship operation in the Atlantic the enemy was able always to deploy one battleship against our two on both the main supply lines. However, it became clear that providing this defense of his convoys brought him to the limit of the possibilities open to him, and the only way he can significantly strengthen his escort forces is by weakening positions important to him (Mediterranean, home waters) or by reducing convoy traffic. (Escort by American warships or active intervention by the USA would necessitate new decisions.)

What we need to do is, on the one hand, cause the enemy to disperse his strength by continually changing both our operational methods and our area of operations, and, on the other hand, attack with concentrated forces the weak points thus created.

As soon as the two battleships of the *Bismarck* class are ready for deployment, we will be able to seek engagement with the forces escorting enemy convoys and, when they have been eliminated, destroy the convoy itself. As of now, we cannot follow that course, but it will soon be possible, as an intermediate step, for us to use the battleship *Bismarck* to distract the hostile escorting forces, in order to enable the other units engaged to operate against the convoy itself. In the beginning, we will have the advantage of surprise, because some of the ships involved will be making their first appearance and, based on his experience in the previous battleship operations, the enemy will assume that *one* battleship will be enough to defend a convoy.

II. The main features of the conduct of the war in the summer of 1941 will be determined by their connection to Operation Barbarossa.* The relevant general directives are set out in Seekriegsleitung I op 262/41 Chefs. of 6.3.41.

The regions of emphasis and the assignment in broad outline of forces and missions in the group command areas will be according to that directive.

The following directive, therefore, deals only with the next deployment of battleships and cruisers to the Atlantic.

III. *Directive for the Deployment of the Battleships* Bismarck *and* Gneisenau *and the Cruiser* Prinz Eugen *in the North Atlantic at the End of April*
  1) At the earliest possible date, which it is hoped will be during the new-moon period of April, *Bismarck* and *Prinz Eugen*, led by the Fleet Commander, are to be deployed as commerce-raiders in the Atlantic.

  At a time that will depend on the completion of the repairs she is currently undergoing, *Gneisenau* will also be sent into the Atlantic.
  2) The lessons learned in the last battleship operation indicate that *Gneisenau* should join up with the *Bismarck* group, but a diversionary sweep by the *Gneisenau* in the area between Cape Verde and the Azores may be planned before this happens.
  3) The heavy cruiser is to spend most of her time operating tactically with *Bismarck* or *Bismarck* and *Gneisenau*.

  The disadvantage that is accepted by bringing along the cruiser, with her lesser radius of action, will be offset by the

*The invasion of the Soviet Union

advantages of greater search capability, availability of a ship suitable for operations against light forces and shadowers, and her powerful torpedo armament, which could be useful in attacking strongly defended convoys as well as disengaging from superior enemy covering forces.

The difficulties created by her lesser operational radius must be surmounted by the appropriate disposition of tankers, by periodically releasing her to fuel, or in emergencies, by transferring fuel to her from *Bismarck*.

The release of dispatch of the cruiser on special missions remains the option of the operational command or, while at sea, of the Fleet Commander.

4) In contrast to previous directives to the *Gneisenau-Scharnhorst* task force, it is the mission of this task force to also attack escorted convoys. However, the objective of the battleship *Bismarck* should not be to *defeat, in an all-out engagement*, enemies of equal strength, but to tie them down in a delaying action, while preserving her own combat capability as much as possible, so as to allow the other ships to get at the merchant vessels in the convoy.

The primary mission of this operation also is the destruction of the enemy's merchant shipping; enemy warships will be engaged only when that primary mission makes it necessary and it can be done without excessive risk.

5) The operational area will be defined as the entire North Atlantic north of the equator, with the exception of the territorial waters (3-nautical-mile limit) of neutral states.

In all probability, respect for the American Neutrality Zone will no longer need to be taken into account at the time of the operation. Because of the danger of shadowing by U.S. forces, however, it does not appear expedient to station supply ships or tankers in the part of the existing Neutrality Zone that lies in the sphere of the USA.

6) Previous experiences have shown that, contrary to what might be expected, we do not have enough knowledge of convoy routes and schedules to determine the time and place in the vast area involved where convoys might be intercepted. One major difficulty is posed by the weather conditions in the Atlantic, which often restrict visibility and prevent the use of embarked aircraft.

The effectiveness of the operation must therefore be improved by every conceivable form of reconnaissance. For this, there come into question:
a) *U-Boats*

The last battleship operation showed that cooperation between surface forces and U-boats in the same area can have advantages for both. For this, there must be a means of direct communication between the surface forces and the U-boats and there will be. The U-boat short-signal book is to be enlarged and copies placed on board the ships.

In general it would not be advisable to have battleships cruise in a line of search with U-boats that are deployed as scouts for surface forces, because such positioning would make it more difficult for them to respond. It would be better to deploy the U-boats in the designated area of operations in a scout line and to charge them with reporting targets to the battleships and subsequent shadowing or attack.

Conversely, the Fleet Commander, either by shadowing reports or direct order, will be able to advise the U-boats of any sighted convoy.

As a further test of this collaboration, the following orders will—provided the discussions held in preparation for this operation do not produce more promising possibilities—apply to the proposed operation:

1) There will be at least two boats in the U-boats' Operations Area South (Freetown area) throughout the operation, and they will be under the command of the Commander-in-Chief, U-Boats. Should the opportunity arise for direct cooperation with the fleet forces, however, the Fleet Commander has the right to give the boats operational orders.

2) On the Halifax convoy route, two or more boats of the northern group will be deployed far enough to the west to support, by reconnaissance or attack, an operation of the Fleet Commander between 30° and 45° west.
   Command and control as under paragraph 1) above.

3) The supplying of these U-boats with fuel, provisions, and munitions is to be provided for by outfitting more

store and escort ships. Allocation of supplies by Commander-in-Chief, U-Boats, or Fleet Commander.

b) *Scouts*

Besides the deployment of U-boats, camouflaged ships could be deployed as scouts for the fleet formation.

This deployment might be in tactical association with the task force or in specially designated, remote scouting areas. For the former type of deployment, the ships, preferably oil-burners, should have adequate operational range and a cruising speed of at least 12 knots. Ships that do not have these characteristics are not suitable for tactical association with the fleet, but can be used in the latter type of deployment.

An effort will be made to deploy two suitable ships for use in the former capacity. Prizes taken during the operation may also be used for this purpose.

Moreover, Group West will be charged with examining the captured whalers and, if satisfactory, providing one of them for use in the former capacity and *Schiff 13* and *24* in the latter.

The severe shortage of shipping tonnage caused by newly arisen transport missions will make it scarcely possible to prepare other, special ships for this purpose, but the question will be examined by the Oberkommando der Kriegsmarine, as will the deployment of *Schiff 23* and *Togo* for scouting purposes.

c) *Aircraft Mother Ships*

The question of deploying such ships (catapult; two to three aircraft, landing mat) will be examined by the Oberkommando der Kriegsmarine. The existing catapult ships *Friesenland* and *Schwabenland* are not suitable.

d) *Supply Ships*

During the last operation the deployment of supply ships for tactical cooperation with the fleet formation proved extremely useful. Nevertheless, these ships should be used for this mission only if all other possibilities fail, as their loss would have critical consequences, not only for this operation but also for subsequent ones with large formations. Moreover valuable cargoes (munitions) would be in jeopardy. With this warning, however, their deployment is left up to the Fleet Commander.

The same applies to fleet oilers.

7) *Ermland* is available as a supply ship, *Heide, Weissenburg, Brehme, Esso, Ill, Spichern,* and *Lothringen* as fleet oilers.

Care is to be taken that the requisite readiness dates are not upset by modifications or the installation of equipment. If necessary, ships undergoing such work and unable to meet the schedule must be deployed as reserve tankers.

Thorn and *Egerland*, which have been prepared for other uses, will not be available at first.

Uckermark probably cannot be made available because she is deployed with the cruiser *Lützow*; other supply ships (*Dithmarschen, Kärnten, Passat*) probably will not be operational until a later date (1.7, 1.9, 1.10).

8) The group commands have operational control in their zones. The Fleet Commander has control at sea, the U-boat groups attached to him will be under his tactical command for the duration of the joint operations (the Commander-in-Chief, U-Boats, will detail a U-boat officer to the Fleet Commander's staff for the duration of the operation).

9) The groups will contact as soon as possible the Fleet Command and the Commander-in-Chief, U-Boats, regarding the execution of the operation and will report the result from such contact to the Seekriegsleitung at least fourteen days before the operation begins.

IV. As already indicated under I, the objective must be to confront the enemy with new situations created by wide-ranging changes of the areas of operations.

Upon further confirmation of the manner of conduct of the war up to now, consideration may be given to extending the next-following operation as far as the South Atlantic.

When the need to respect the PanAmerican Neutrality Zone has passed, the intersection of the route from North and Central America to Freetown and Central Africa (important military supplies) with the La Plata route, and also with the Cape-Freetown route, will offer promising operational possibilities.

The prerequisite for the execution of such a distant operation is the deployment of the greatest possible number of auxiliaries. The Seekriegsleitung will initiate appropriate measures.

Such a shift in the area of operations may prove necessary if, as a consequence of the next operation and those past, the North Atlantic routes that we have been attacking become more strongly defended by the enemy.

Until *Tirpitz* becomes operational, attacks against strongly defended convoys on the main supply lines in the North Atlantic will not have good prospects for success.

The time for extending operations to the south must remain open at the moment. The reason for announcing the intention is that it will enable Group Command West and the fleet to evaluate their experiences with regard to this new area of operations.

/s/ RAEDER
Commander-in-Chief of the Kriegsmarine

/s/ SCHNIEWIND
Chief of the Seekriegsleitung

/s/ FRICKE
Chief of the Seekriegsleitung Operations Section

 **B**

General Orders for the Atlantic Operation

(Annex I to "Operations Order of the Fleet Commander for the Atlantic Operation with *Bismarck* and *Prinz Eugen*—Exercise Rhine," Fleet Order 100/41 A1, Secret—Commands Only, Commanders' Eyes Only, 22 April 1941.)

1. *The object of the operation* is to do the greatest possible damage to the enemy by destroying his merchant shipping, especially that proceeding *towards* England.

2. The operation conducted with the battleships *Gneisenau* and *Scharnhorst* from January until mid-March 1941 showed that, in spite of information provided by the B-Dienst regarding the sailing dates and routes of convoys, it is extremely difficult to intercept a convoy in the vast ocean spaces with the few units available for this purpose, and it depends on coincidence and luck.

   Therefore, I do not intend to restrict the deployment of the ships exclusively for attacking convoys, but also from the outset for capturing or destroying ships steaming independently. However, as far as time permits, they will be deployed in the area of operations in such a manner that there is a prospect of intercepting a convoy.

3. *Attacks on Convoys*
   Some of the convoys encountered by the battleships during the operation were escorted by a battleship and, in one case, by two cruisers and two destroyers also. Escorts of comparable strength must be anticipated in the future. The operational directives of the See-

kriegsleitung and Group West allow *Bismarck* only to *tie down* a battleship escorting a convoy, insofar as that is possible without fully engaging, and that only in the event such action gives *Prinz Eugen* the possibility of success against the rest of the escort or against the convoy.

Accordingly, when *Bismarck* and *Prinz Eugen* attack a convoy, they must do so from opposite sides. In every case, tactical and attack orders will come from the Fleet Commander.

Without coming in battle contact, the exact strength of a convoy's escort can usually be determined only by shipboard aircraft. This deployment is, however, dependent upon the tactical situation and the weather and therefore rarely possible on the Halifax-England route. It must, therefore, be anticipated that, in making an attack, *Prinz Eugen* will encounter escorting cruisers even if *Bismarck* succeeds in drawing off the big ship. In this event, the cruiser's attack on the convoy is to be broken off and an immediate report made. But even when only one big ship is escorting the convoy, the enemy, if he follows good tactics, will stay in the immediate vicinity of the convoy and *protect it from all sides*. In this case there can be no question of an attack by the cruiser; that may occur only if the big ship allows the *Bismarck* to draw her so far from her charges that the cruiser has a chance of getting within effective shooting range of the convoy.

If the ships are in search sectors and *Prinz Eugen* sights a convoy, she should report it by short signal at close range and stay at the extreme edge of visibility (smokeless). With respect to the necessity for *later surprise attacks*, it cannot be the task of the cruiser to ascertain the strength of the escort. That must be left to the *Bismarck*. In an attack on a convoy, the main objective must be to sink as many steamers as possible. When a *weakly* escorted convoy is attacked, the convoy commander will certainly disperse his charges. In this case, the first objective must be to disable the largest possible number of steamers by gunfire. (They can be sunk later.) For this, all batteries are to open up with exact firing directions and at the lowest possible range appropriate to the caliber. (Main and secondary batteries with nose-fuzed and base-fuzed projectiles, heavy flak nose-fuzed.) Steamers that have been disabled by gunfire are not to be sunk until there is not one steamer still moving within sight of the ship concerned. *To conserve ammunition, the heavy flak is to be nose-fuzed and used in the following manner: close within 300–500 meters of the ship, then have the best gunners fire individual shots into the waterline. Fire only when the ship is on the up-roll. Shoot holes in all of the steam-*

er's compartments (the largest room is the engine room). With 3.7–centimeter ammunition, shoot holes in the upper part of the steamer, so that during the flooding of the rooms, air can escape upwards.

Prinz Eugen will also use her torpedoes in an *attack on a convoy*. Against a *strongly defended* convoy, there will be only a short time, if any, available for the cruiser's attack. This must be exploited as fully as possible. In *this case* especially, everything will depend on speedy action. The steamers are therefore to be sunk *primarily with torpedoes*.

The work of destruction may not be delayed by rescue operations.

The rescue of survivors, especially those from a convoy that has been attacked, can expose our own ships to serious danger from enemy submarines and surface forces. In such cases, concern for our ships must take precedence over the rescue of survivors. If necessary, a small steamer is to be spared for the purpose of rescuing survivors.

4. Ships Steaming Independently

In the absence of orders to the contrary, all lone steamers encountered will be captured or destroyed. When weather conditions permit boats to be lowered, the steamers will be searched and, if they themselves are valuable or have valuable cargoes and they can get under way, *brought home* (examine fuel supply, provisions, etc.). In principle, tankers that can make more than 10 knots, refrigerator ships and fast motor ships, if they can get under way—whether they are laden or not—are to be captured and brought by a prize crew over the designated course into the mouth of the Gironde.

Experience has shown that it is best not to bring prizes immediately into the Bay of Biscay, especially those that have transmitted radio signals, but to wait a few weeks in a remote ocean area, then to set out for the Gironde at intervals so as to prevent the enemy from capturing them as they enter the Bay of Biscay. For this, in some circumstances it will be necessary to equip the prizes with extra provisions and send them to an escort tanker so that they can replenish. The start of the prizes' return voyage is to be reported by short signal.

Prizes must not fall into enemy hands under any circumstances. In every case, therefore, as soon as it boards, the prize crew must make preparations for scuttling at short notice.

For searching steamers, a boarding party is to be organized. Each ship has three prize crews and must organize two others from its company. Equipment is to be stored within easy reach. Prize crews must be instructed on the mission they are to discharge on board the steamers. All books, code instruments, tables, and notes found on the bridge, in the charthouse, in the radio room, in the captain's pockets, and elsewhere are to be seized and examined on board the ship by officers qualified in the language.

On approaching a ship sailing independently, fly the British ensign and keep the turrets at zero degrees to avoid arousing suspicion. Signal her to stop and forbid her to use her radio. The transmission or completion of a radio warning signal must be prevented if possible. For this, the following measures are to be taken:

a. If the steamer is radioing before the ship gets within firing range, the message must be interrupted by the sending of a prepared radio message (in the English language) or a radio weather report. As soon as the steamer is in effective range, open fire. Whenever possible take the *bridge superstructure* under fire. (On most steamers the radio room is behind or below the bridge.)

b. If the steamer is radioing within the effective range of the heavy flak, open fire immediately and destroy her radio installation as in paragraph a.

So that tankers and valuable ships come into our hands as intact as possible, do not fire any longer than is necessary to prevent the transmission of signals. Establish good connections between the radio room and the bridge.

Approach a steamer so that one side is to leeward, quickly bring the ship to a stop, and lower a boat immediately.

The boarding party will take over all important points (bridge, charthouse, radio room, engine room) and have the crew of the steamer assemble immediately on the upper deck.

British Forces Deployed Against the *Bismarck* During Exercise Rhine

Note: The right-hand column shows where the ships were before the
pursuit of the *Bismarck* began.

HOME FLEET AND SHIPS ATTACHED

Battleship	*King George V*	Scapa Flow
Battleship	*Prince of Wales*	Scapa Flow
Battleship	*Rodney*	En route from Clyde to Boston with the troop transport *Britannic*
Battle Cruiser	*Repulse*	Clyde, assigned to troop convoy WS-8B
Battle Cruiser	*Hood*	Scapa Flow
Aircraft Carrier	*Victorious*	Scapa Flow, assigned to troop convoy WS-8B
Cruiser	*Norfolk*	Denmark Strait, on patrol
Cruiser	*Suffolk*	Refueling at Reykjavik, Iceland
Cruiser	*Galatea*	Scapa Flow
Cruiser	*Aurora*	Scapa Flow
Cruiser	*Kenya*	Scapa Flow
Cruiser	*Neptune*	Scapa Flow
Cruiser	*Arethusa*	En route to Reykjavik, Iceland
Cruiser	*Edinburgh*	Off the Azores, on patrol
Cruiser	*Manchester*	Faeroe Islands passage, on patrol
Cruiser	*Birmingham*	Faeroe Islands passage, on patrol

Destroyer	*Inglefield*	En route to Scapa Flow
Destroyer	*Intrepid*	En route to Scapa Flow
Destroyer	*Active*	Scapa Flow
Destroyer	*Antelope*	Scapa Flow
Destroyer	*Achates*	Scapa Flow
Destroyer	*Anthony*	Scapa Flow
Destroyer	*Electra*	Scapa Flow
Destroyer	*Echo*	Scapa Flow
Destroyer	*Somali*	At sea with *Rodney* and *Britannic*
Destroyer	*Tartar*	At sea with *Rodney* and *Britannic*
Destroyer	*Mashona*	At sea with *Rodney* and *Britannic*
Destroyer	*Eskimo*	At sea with *Rodney* and *Britannic*
Destroyer	*Punjabi*	Scapa Flow
Destroyer	*Icarus*	Scapa Flow
Destroyer	*Nestor*	Scapa Flow
Destroyer	*Jupiter*	Londonderry

WESTERN APPROACHES COMMAND

Cruiser	*Hermione*	En route to Scapa Flow
Destroyer	*Lance*	Scapa Flow
Destroyer	*Legion*	Clyde, with battle cruiser *Repulse*
Destroyer	*Saguenay*	Clyde, with battle cruiser *Repulse*
Destroyer	*Assiniboine*	Clyde, with battle cruiser *Repulse*
Destroyer	*Columbia*	Londonderry

PLYMOUTH COMMAND, 4TH DESTROYER FLOTILLA

Destroyer	*Cossack*	Clyde, assigned to troop convoy WS-8B
Destroyer	*Sikh*	Clyde, assigned to troop convoy WS-8B
Destroyer	*Zulu*	Clyde, assigned to troop convoy WS-8B
Destroyer	*Maori*	Clyde, assigned to troop convoy W S-8B
Destroyer	*Piorun*	Clyde, assigned to troop convoy W S-8B

NORE COMMAND

Destroyer	*Windsor*	Scapa Flow

British Forces Deployed During Exercise Rhine

Force H

Battle Cruiser	*Renown*	Gibraltar
Aircraft Carrier	*Ark Royal*	Gibraltar
Cruiser	*Sheffield*	Gibraltar
Destroyer	*Faulknor*	Gibraltar
Destroyer	*Foresight*	Gibraltar
Destroyer	*Forester*	Gibraltar
Destroyer	*Foxhound*	Gibraltar
Destroyer	*Fury*	Gibraltar
Destroyer	*Hesperus*	Gibraltar

America and West Indies Station

Battleship	*Ramillies*	At sea, escorting convoy HX-127
Battleship	*Revenge*	Halifax, Nova Scotia

South Atlantic Command

Cruiser	*Dorsetshire*	At sea, escorting convoy SL-74

The following submarines were also deployed:

Minerva	On patrol off southwestern Norway
P-31	Scapa Flow
Sealion	English Channel
Seawolf	English Channel
Sturgeon	English Channel
Pandora	En route from Gibraltar to Great Britain
Tigris	Clyde
H-44	Rothesay

 **D**

The Rudder Damage: Were All Possibilities of Repair Exhausted?

The existing literature on the *Bismarck* poses a question that I have been asked repeatedly: whether or not everything possible was done to repair the damage to her rudder. I want to deal with this matter, anyway, but the many questions make me feel obliged to do so.

Kapitänleutnant (Ingenieurwesen) Gerhard Junack, who not only participated in some of the attempts at repair but whose station was closer to what was going on than was mine, has said: "I cannot help wondering whether everything was really done that night, every possibility exhausted, to save the battleship *Bismarck* in spite of everything. Would it have helped if, contrary to naval custom, the officer of the watch had conned the ship from the engine-control station or the chief engineer had stood beside the captain on the bridge and been in direct contact with the turbine operators? Full-power orders relayed through the engine telegraph certainly weren't going to work. What if a charge had been set in the stern, regardless of what it might have done to the propellers? So long as the rudders were jammed, it wasn't much use having the propellers in working order, anyway. Suppose a U-boat had been taken in tow as a course stabilizer or a stern anchor had been suspended from a float and dragged behind? With three propellers capable of 28 knots still serviceable, was there really nothing she could do but head towards the enemy at low speed? Who's to say what would have been possible with an unbroken fighting spirit?" These points will be examined in sequence.

Junack did not say what good it might have done to have the officer of the watch conn the ship from the engine-control station, and I cannot imagine. I believe that the officer of the watch must be on the bridge. If he were below, it would be impossible for him to carry out his most important task, conning the ship by the view that is available only topside. What could he have done better in the engine-control station than on the bridge?

Similarly, Junack did not say what the advantage would have been in having the chief engineer stand beside the captain on the bridge in direct contact with the turbine operators. Orders could undoubtedly have been transmitted to the engines just as quickly by telephone as by engine telegraph but, without being told more, I cannot see how this would have helped.

As for setting a charge in the stern without regard for the propellers, we have seen that after the rudder rooms flooded, attempts to enter them and do repairs were defeated by the force of the water. For the same reason, no one could work in the after steering rooms, either. If none of the spaces in the steering plant could be entered, how could a charge be attached to the rudder shafts? Such a relatively simple task as disengaging a coupling took a diver hours of exhausting work. Has Junack given any valid reason for thinking that, despite everything, it would have been possible for anyone to force his way into a rudder room and place a charge there? As a concerned investigator, he would have surely tracked down any such possibility and provided a persuasive argument to show it could have been done. But he didn't do that. The proof is lacking, even the probability.

Let us assume, for the sake of discussion, that it would have been possible to force a way into the after steering room and there set a charge, "regardless of what it might have done to the propellers." It seems to me that to recommend taking the risk of losing the propellers and perhaps of more flooding simply in order to get rid of jammed rudders would have been a counsel of despair. Without her propellers, the Bismarck would have been dead in the water and at the mercy of every vagary in the enemy-infested ocean area around her. Reduce to impotence a propulsion plant still capable of 28 knots? Would that have been a responsible course of action?

On the other hand, since the propellers were forward of and below the rudder shafts, a correctly measured charge might not have damaged them at all or at least to a lesser extent. The explosive charge is instantly changed into a gas jet that tends to rise towards the surface. However, since water is incompressible, the shock wave associated with that explosion could still damage the propellers.

I do not know how precisely demolition charges could be measured on board but, assuming that a charge commensurate with the need could have been prepared, did the *Bismarck*'s command neglect to do something that might have improved her situation? Only if there were solid prospects of achieving the desired result. And what were the prospects? During our shake-down cruises in the Baltic we found that it was very difficult to steer the *Bismarck* with her propellers alone. Obviously, it would have been even more difficult to do so in the raging Atlantic on 26 May and it would have been virtually impossible to hold the giant ship on a course for St. Nazaire with a following sea. Therefore, even if it was technically possible to blow the rudders away, the objective in doing so would not have been achieved.

Take a U-boat in tow to stabilize our course? First of all, a U-boat would have to have been available. We now know that none was available. And had there been, how could the *Bismarck* have taken and kept it in tow? If even the *Bismarck* was laboring heavily in the stormy seas, how much more tumultuous would it have been for a U-boat. The U-boat's men were to handle the heavy hawsers on a very small deck, while the boat itself was being maneuvered? And, so that all this could be done at night, should Lindemann have illuminated the area of the deck where it was going on, and perhaps have turned on a searchlight as well, thereby helping the enemy to pinpoint our position and giving him precise firing data, particularly for his torpedoes?

Moreover, it would have been necessary to post a detail on the *Bismarck*'s quarterdeck to maintain continuous surveillance of the tow connection. Had the enemy suddenly appeared, which he was expected to do momentarily, the presence of these men might very well have delayed the immediate employment of our main after turrets. Anyway, we would not have been able to fire astern without endangering the U-boat there. In other words, we might have been forced partly or completely to forgo the use of our after turrets. Such a limitation could have been put on our fighting power only with the most serious reservations and could scarcely have been maintained. Even had the tow been managed, the *Bismarck*, more than 50,000 tons of her, running before a northwester that became a storm, could hardly have been held on course by a U-boat of, let us say, 500 tons. If the sea had been calm and there had been no enemy ships around, perhaps, but, given the circumstances, I consider the idea unrealistic. In any case, there was no U-boat at our disposal.

Drag a stern anchor suspended from a float? The disproportion between the two masses would have been even greater than in the case of a U-boat. A stern anchor would not have had any effect at all on the *Bismarck*.

The answer to Junack's concluding question, "Who's to say what would have been possible with an unbroken fighting spirit?" lies in the above rebuttals to his proposals.

Not one of the options he indicates could have been carried out, either singly or in combination. Either they shatter on hard facts, such as the suction under the stern, the inaccessibility of the steering rooms, and the lack of a U-boat, or they are contradicted by logic, such as his ideas of stationing the officer of the watch in the engine-control station or the chief engineer on the bridge, towing the stern anchor, or blowing off the rudders without regard to other damage. I do not see that the ship's command or anyone else omitted anything that could have been done. And Junack has not proved, much less documented, his tacit reproaches. The fighting spirit in the *Bismarck* was not broken. The question should not be asked, even rhetorically.

Brennecke raises still other suggestions made by third parties as to how the *Bismarck*'s rudder damage might have been dealt with.* Among them is the idea that a hawser or heavy anchor chain put over the side might have stabilized the course of the ship before the following sea. According to this proposal, danger of the hawser or chain being drawn into the propellers might have been averted by suspending it from a spar projecting from one side of the ship aft. According to another proposal, the starboard side of the hull could have been "roughened up," so that it would have greater resistance to the flow of water. This might have been one way of offsetting at least to some degree the effect of having the rudders jammed in the port position.

The reservations already raised in regard to the U-boat and the stern anchor also apply to these retrospective theories. On one hand, the difference between the respective masses would have been much too great in regard to the anchor chain, hawser, or any material that might have been put over the side to increase the drag on the starboard side. And on the other, security, which required that the ship be darkened and her guns be ready to fire at any moment, would have argued against the illumination of the work place and the posting of working parties on the upper deck, as would have been necessary in these cases also.

*Jochen Brennecke, *Schlachtschiff Bismarck*, note 454.

The idea put forward in Brennecke's book that the *Bismarck*, by radio messages through the Seekriegsleitung, should have asked hydrodynamic experts at home what was the best way to counter the rudder damage has all the earmarks of being armchair strategy.

Retired Kapitän zur See Alfred Schulze-Hinrichs appears to me to have the most plausible ex post facto theories on what the *Bismarck* might have done.* This recognized expert in the field of seamanship wonders whether the *Bismarck* should not have tried, by contrarotating her three propellers, to reach St. Nazaire by backing.

This is not the place for a detailed examination of Schulze-Hinrichs's very interesting technical arguments. In retrospect, I think the explanation for not trying a maneuver such as he suggests must lie in the circumstances that existed that night, the presence of the enemy and the weather, as well as in our general experience of the *Bismarck*'s steering characteristics.

Given the pressure being put upon us by the enemy, it is readily understandable that the ship's command did not try such a maneuver, which would have required continuous, concentrated attention—and that for hours, over hundreds of nautical miles, on a pitch-black night with no horizon and not a single star by which to navigate. Finally, as we have seen, her earliest trials in the Baltic showed that the ship was extremely difficult to steer with her propellers alone. In backing she had a strong tendency, as do most ships, to turn her stern into the wind. In the Atlantic on 26 May this would have, in effect, put us on the same unwanted course to the northwest to which we were condemned in going ahead. Experience gained in her trials may have caused the ship's command to reject from the start the idea of attempting to reach St. Nazaire by backing through the Atlantic swells.† It is, however, possible that had such a maneuver been practiced more frequently and practiced in bad weather, it might have been tried.

---

*Alfred Schulze-Hinrichs, "Schlachtschiff *Bismarck* und Seemannschaft," pp. 6–7.

†In addition to the preceding reservations, it is doubtful if it would have been technically possible to back the ship all the way to the coast of France. The reverse turbines could only have exerted their—already greatly diminished—horsepower for brief periods, as the cooling system would not have sufficed for prolonged operation. The openings for the cool water intake were designed for forward motion. Because of this, the backing would have had to be periodically interrupted, and each time the ship would have swung off course, which would have been very difficult to regain, so from this viewpoint as well such a maneuver would have been an act of despair.

In view of the *Bismarck*'s actual situation that night, Schulze-Hinrichs's otherwise interesting line of thought is too theoretical.

The question whether the *Bismarck* did everything possible to remedy the rudder damage must, therefore, even taking into account the theories subsequently advanced by third parties, be answered affirmatively. Everything that could be responsibly undertaken, everything sensible, was tried. Brennecke is of the same opinion up to this point, but when he questions the presence of a will to win, he departs from my thinking.* What does "will to win" mean here?

As retired Admiral Erich Förste correctly states, Lütjens's aim could only have been to reach port and to continue the operation after undergoing repairs and refueling.† If, on the way to St. Nazaire, he had been forced to fight a doubly unwelcome action, he would have done so with the necessary vigor. That the fighting spirit was not broken was conclusively proved by the course of the battle on 27 May. If evidence as to the spirit of the crew after the rudder hit is needed, we have only to quote Maschinengefreiter Hermann Budich: "The ship's inability to maneuver did not even have a particularly negative effect on our morale. It is true that, because at the time we left Gotenhafen we were ordered by Korvettenkapitän Freytag to perform the duties of the main electric control station in our circuit room II without the benefit of extra help, we were totally exhausted. But we were full of hope and had great faith in our captain, whose personality was such that we were very devoted to him."

The reason why, in her inability to maneuver, the lonely ship was helpless in the Atlantic is not to be sought in conditions on board. The only thing that could have really helped during those hours was an attack on the enemy's forces by other German units, an attack that would have prevented or interrupted the operations of the heavy British ships against the *Bismarck*.

But no such help came. The battleships *Scharnhorst* and *Gneisenau*, then docked at Brest, were not able to go to sea. *Gneisenau* had sustained bomb and torpedo damage, while the *Scharnhorst* was having tubes replaced in her boilers. The destroyers there could not put

---

*Junack's words regarding morale on board after the Fleet Commander's address (*see* pp. 182–84 above) may have provoked Brennecke's question. Junack's actual words were: "The high fighting spirit that permeated the battleship on Saturday [24 May, the day of the battle off Iceland] was, however, irretrievably lost."

†Jochen Brennecke, note 299.

to sea because of the northwester. The weather was so bad that, even had they reached the battle area, they would not have been able to accomplish much—on the night of 26–27 May we saw what a difficult time the British destroyers had in the high seas. Of the eight U-boats in the Bay of Biscay that at the last moment were ordered to support the *Bismarck*—the *U-73*, *U-556*, *U-98*, *U-97*, *U-48*, *U-552*, *U-108*, and *U-74*—the *U-74* and *U-556* had expended all their torpedoes in earlier operations. The *U-74* had been damaged by depth charges and had only limited maneuverability. The intact boats were too far away when they received the order to assemble around the *Bismarck* to reach the scene of action in time. It was too late to send a fully equipped U-boat from a base on the west coast of France. There were still the supply ship *Ermland* and the oceangoing tugs, but it would take them between twenty and forty hours to reach us from the coast. They would have arrived too late even to rescue survivors.

Our naval headquarters ashore certainly mobilized every imaginable help for the *Bismarck*. But it was too little and too late.

The only other help we might have had was from our bomber squadrons stationed in France. But, of course, they needed notification and preparation. Apparently there was neither.

Inevitably, the questions raised earlier about the timing for Exercise Rhine and the best possible composition of Lütjens's task force come to mind. Even more important, however, is the question of how good were the arrangements for cooperation between the task force and the air and submarine arms, should that become necessary. But these are considerations that exceed the bounds of a survivor's story. So this line of thought must be abandoned with the recognition that, after the torpedo hit on 26 May, the *Bismarck* was consigned to a fate that she did not have the resources to avert.

E

Action between the *Rodney* and the *Bismarck* on the morning of Tuesday, 27 May 1941, as recorded by the battle observer in the *Rodney*

0844	Green 005 degs [starboard 5° from dead ahead]. Enemy in sight.
0847	*Rodney* fires first salvo.
0848	*King George* fires first salvo.
0849	Enemy replies, 1000 short of *Rodney*.
0852	Enemy shell 1000 over.
0853	Enemy shell just short starboard side.
0854	Enemy shell just over port side.
0856	Enemy salvoes over.
0857	Enemy salvoes over.
0858	*Rodney* straddled. Enemy, firing steadily, abeam on crossing *King George V* bow. *Rodney*'s secondary armament in action. Main and secondary armament engaging enemy port side.

0902	Hit on *Bismarck*'s upper deck.
	Enemy salvoes short.
0905	Enemy shell 1000 over.
0906	Enemy shell 300 over.
0910	Our salvoes falling well together astern of *Bismarck*.
	Enemy turning away firing at *King George V.* *
0913	Good straddle on *Bismarck*, which was completely obscured.
0914	*Rodney*'s shots falling well over.
0915	*Bismarck* passing down *Rodney*'s port side.
0916	*Rodney* turning hard to starboard, enemy ship passing under *Rodney*'s stern.
0917	Good straddles on *Bismarck*, one hit observed, enemy firing very intermittently and inaccurately.
0919	Salvo from *Bismarck*'s after turrets.
0921	Good straddle on *Bismarck*.
0922	*Bismarck* fires after turrets at *Rodney*. Near miss on *Rodney*'s starboard side.
0923	*Bismarck* hit.
0924	Enemy still firing after turrets.
0924	Enemy turning towards *Rodney*.
0926	*Bismarck* straddled.
0927	Salvo from enemy's forward guns.
0928	Enemy turning towards *Rodney*.
	Enemy hit abaft funnel.
0929	*Bismarck* on parallel course hit again.
0930	Another hit.
0931	Enemy fired after turrets.†
0932	Enemy still on parallel course to *Rodney*, range 2 miles.

*The expression *enemy turning* used in this and subsequent entries should not be understood to mean that the *Bismarck* was turning of her own volition. She was reacting to the combined influences of her jammed rudders, the seaway, and the wind. The salvos referred to in this entry are those directed by the author from the after station (*see* pp. 250–51 above).

†Parallel to this, Lieutenant Commander J. M. Wellings, USN, who was in the *Rodney*, reported: "at 0902 a hit was observed on *Bismarck*'s forecastle. *Bismarck* continued to fire regularly until between 0902 and 0908 when her firing became irregular and intermittent. *Bismarck*'s 'A' and 'B' turrets must have been damaged during this period as only one salvo was observed from the forward turrets after this period. This salvo was fired at 0927. From about 0919 to 0931 only 'X' turret of the *Bismarck* was in action, apparently in local control and very erratic. The last salvo was fired by *Bismarck* at 0931."

0937   Green 040 degs [starboard 40°]. Ship, probably *Dorsetshire* in sight opens fire.

0938   *Bismarck* passes astern and comes up on port side distance still 2 miles.

0940   Enemy on fire fore and aft.

0941   Enemy hit again forward turning towards *Rodney.*

0942   *Bismarck's* 'B' turret on fire.

0944   Enemy passes astern of *Rodney.* *Rodney* turning to starboard engages enemy starboard side.

0946   *Bismarck* hit at least four times during this run on starboard side and has not herself fired.

0949   *Rodney* turning hard to port. Enemy engaged port side.

0951   Engagement continuing port side.*

0955   Torpedo fired port side. No results observed.

0957   Torpedo fired port side and seen to leap out of the water two-thirds of the way across.

0958   Torpedo hit *Bismarck* amidships starboard side.†

0959   Enemy turning to starboard.

1000   Engagement on starboard side, enemy turning away.

1002   County Class cruiser, perhaps *Norfolk* on *Rodney's* starboard bow attacking enemy. *Dorsetshire* (?) on *Rodney's* port bow.‡

1003   Lull in action. *Bismarck* well alight, clouds of black smoke from fire aft.

1005   *Bismarck* has been slowly turning around and is now passing down *Rodney's* starboard side 1¹/₂ miles away smoking heavily.

*The word *engagement* used in this and subsequent entries should not be taken literally. Since the *Bismarck* was not able to fire after 0931, what was going on was a one-sided cannonade.

†Amid the din of the battle, I personally was not aware of any such torpedo hit. However, Donald C. Campbell observed the explosion of one of the *Rodney's* 60-centimeter torpedoes on our starboard side, near turret Bruno. Later he wrote: "I believe it was the first time in history that one battleship torpedoed another."

‡The *Dorsetshire* took part in the action from 0904 to 0913, from 0920 to 0924, from 0935 to 0938, and from 0954 to 1018. Altogether, she fired 254 shells. The interruptions were caused by her difficulty in identifying and evaluating the fall of her own shot amid the storm of shells hitting around the German battleship. During these interruptions she helped the *King George V* and *Rodney* observe their fire. In his after-action report the *Dorsetshire's* commanding officer, Captain B. C. S. Martin, did not claim any hits for his ship before 1002. It is doubtful that the *Dorsetshire's* gunnery inflicted significant damage on the *Bismarck.*

1006   Enemy hit starboard amidships.
       King George V, 5 miles astern, firing as opportunity offers.

1007   *Bismarck* passes astern. *Rodney* turns hard to port engagement continuing on port side. Much black smoke from the enemy.

1011   Salvo from *Rodney* blows pieces off stern of *Bismarck* and sets up a fire with greyish white smoke.

1012   *King George V* ahead of *Bismarck.*

1013   Salvo from *Rodney* explodes amidships enemy.

1014   Big flames for three seconds from enemy 'A' turret. Flash of exploding shell on enemy spotting top.

1016   *King George V* approaching *Rodney* on port bow, turns on parallel course and fires at *Bismarck* from 'Y' turret.

1019   Enemy smoking heavily. *Rodney's* guns will not bear.

1021   *Bismarck* dead astern of *Rodney.*

1023   Red 145 degs [port 145°]. Six aircraft.*
       Driving rain from port bow.
       Red 145. An unidentified ship firing at aircraft.†

1026   Green 130 degs [starboard 130°] County Class cruiser (*Dorsetshire*). *Bismarck* still smoking heavily passing to port well astern.

1027   Sudden red flash visible from enemy's stern.

1028   Enemy ship now about five miles astern.

1029   Enemy a smoking mass bows-on. *Dorsetshire* crossing her bows.

1038   *Bismarck* disappears in a cloud of smoke, sinking, bow or stern visible momentarily sticking out of the water.

1039   *Bismarck* sank.

---

*Swordfish from the *Ark Royal*, which did not carry out their intended attack.

†The ship was the *King George V.* According to Russell Grenfell, *The Bismarck Episode*, page 186, the Swordfish flew towards the British flagship to request that the firing cease so that they could make their attack. The *King George V* did not heed them, however; in fact, they were taken under fire. When her commanding officer, Captain W. R. Patterson, asked the antiaircraft battery commander if he did not see the flight crews waving, he replied that he took them for Germans "shaking their fists."

F

A Break in the Code?

I have often been asked whether the British success in
breaking the German naval code at the beginning of
the Second World War had anything to do with the pursuit and destruction of the *Bismarck*. Such questions have been inspired by recent publications describing this breakthrough, which was discreetly
handled for many years after the war, in a sometimes sensational
manner.* British experts did succeed in decoding some of the German operational radio transmissions so rapidly that the Admiralty
was able to take timely countermeasures and, at times, to frustrate
the intentions of the Seekriegsleitung. But by the end of Exercise
Rhine on 27 May the British were still not in a position to read the
secret radio traffic between the *Bismarck* and headquarters ashore—
even though they were only a single day away from gaining such a
capability. It is true that in the second week of May they were able to
decode the radio signals of German reconnaissance planes—which,
because of the limited cryptographic facilities of an aircraft, were not
very securely encoded—and through them to anticipate an imminent
German naval sortie into the Atlantic. Similarly, on 25 May they

*See, among others: F. W. Winterbotham, *The Ultra Secret* (London: Weidenfeld &
Nicolson, 1974); Anthony Cave-Brown, *Bodyguard of Lies* (London: W. H. Allen,
1976); David Kahn, *The Codebreakers* (New York: Macmillan, 1967); D. McLachlan,
Room 39 (London: Weidenfeld & Nicolson, 1968); F. H. Hinsley, et al., *British Intelligence in the Second World War* (London: H. M. Stationery Office, 1979); and, especially recommended, Patrick Beesly, *Very Special Intelligence* (London: Hamish Ham-
ilton, 1977).

learned of Lütjens's intention to head for the west coast of France from a German radio transmission, but this transmission did not originate from the *Bismarck* and only confirmed what they already knew from other sources. On that day Generaloberst* Hans Jeschonnek, the Chief of the General Staff of the Luftwaffe, was in Athens and from there out of some personal interest asked Berlin what the German fleet commander was planning to do at that moment. The answer, to proceed to Brest or St. Nazaire, was not long in coming; it was given in the simple Luftwaffe code and through this backdoor immediately came to the attention of British intelligence. Likewise, the British learned from easily decoded Luftwaffe transmissions of the preparations being made to provide the *Bismarck* with air cover from France on 26 May. On the whole, however, it was by using then-conventional means of reconnaissance that the British achieved their success against Exercise Rhine. These means reached their high-water mark in the operations against the *Bismarck*, as thereafter the increasingly valuable cryptanalysis of the German secret naval code made conventional means more and more superfluous.

*Colonel-General

Bibliography

I. Books

Ayerst, David, *Guardian, Biography of a Newspaper*, London 1971.
Ayerst, David, *The Guardian Omnibus 1821–1971*, London 1973.
Beck, Ludwig, *Studien*, Stuttgart 1955.
Beesly, Patrick, *Very Special Intelligence*, London 1977.
Bekker, Cajus, *Verdammte See*, Berlin 1974.
Brennecke, Jochen, *Schlachtschiff Bismarck*, Herford 1960 and ditto, 4th revised and enlarged edition, 1967.
Busch, Fritz Otto, *Das Geheimnis der Bismarck*, Hanover 1950.
Carell, Paul and Böddeker, Günter, *Die Gefangenen*, Berlin-Frankfurt/Main 1980.
Churchill, Winston, *The Second World War*, Vol. II, London 1967, and Vol. III, London 1968.
Demeter, Karl, *Das deutsche Offizierskorps in Gesellschaft und Staat 1650–1945*, Frankfurt/Main 1962.
Domarus, Max, *Hitler, Reden und Proklamationen 1932–1945*, Wiesbaden 1973.
Elfrath, Ulrich and Herzog, Bodo, *Schlachtschiff Bismarck, Ein Bericht in Bildern und Dokumenten*, Friedberg 1975.
Faulk, Henry, *Group Captives*, London 1977.
Feine, Hans Erich, *Deutsche Verfassungsgeschichte der Neuzeit*, 3rd edition, Tübingen 1943.
Fest, Joachim C., *Hitler, Eine Biographie*, Berlin-Frankfurt/Main 1973.
Garzke, William H., Jr., and Dulin, Robert O., Jr., *Battleships: Allied Battleships in World War II*, Annapolis, 1980.
Garzke, William H., Jr., and Dulin, Robert O., Jr., *Battleships: Axis and Neutral Battleships in World War II*, Annapolis, 1985.

Gilbert, Martin, *Sir Horace Rumbold, Portrait of a Diplomat 1869–1941*, London 1973.

Goebbels *Tagebücher aus den Jahren 1942–43*, edited by Louis P. Lochner, Zürich 1948.

Grenfell, Russell, *The Bismarck Episode*, London 1948.

Habermas, Jürgen, *Philosophisch-politische Profile*, Frankfort 1971.

Hampshire, A. Cecil, *The Phantom Fleet*, London 1977.

Hinsley, F. H., et al., *British Intelligence in the Second World War*, London, H.M. Stationery Office 1979.

Hitlers Machtergreifung, dtv Dokumente, Munich, 1983.

Höhn, Reinhard, et al., *Grundfragen der Rechtsauffassung*, Munich, 1938.

Jackson, Robert, *A Taste of Freedom, Stories of German and Italian Prisoners Who Escaped from Camps in Britain during World War II*, London 1964.

Jens, Walter, *Die alten Zeiten niemals zu verwinden* (Address on the occasion of the 50th anniversary of the book burning on 10 May 1933), Akademie der Künste, Anmerkungen zur *Zeit*, Nr. 20 (booklet), Berlin 1983.

Kennedy, Ludovic, *Pursuit*, London 1974.

Koellreuther, Otto, *Deutsches Verfassungsrecht – ein Grundriß*, Berlin 1935.

Lane, Arthur Bliss, *I Saw Poland Betrayed*, New York 1948.

McLachlan, Donald, *Room 39*, London 1968.

Maschke, Erich, *Die deutschen Kriegsgefangenen des II. Weltkrieges*, Munich 1974.

Maunz, Theodor, *Verwaltung*, Hamburg.

Maunz, Theodor, *Gestalt und Recht der Polizei*, Hamburg 1943.

Nesbit, Roy Conyers, *Failed to Return: Enquiries into Mysteries of the Air*, Wellingborough 1988.

Orwell, George, *The Collected Essays*, Journalism and Letters of, Vol. II, 1970, with reprint from the *New English Weekly* of 21 March 1940.

Poliakov, Leon and Wulf, Josef, *Das Dritte Reich und seine Denker*, Berlin 1959.

Putlitz, Wolfgang Gans Edler Herr zu, *Unterwegs nach Deutschland*, 2nd edition, 1956.

Raeder, Erich, *Mein Leben*, Vol. 1, Tübingen 1956, Vol. 2, Tübingen 1957.

Rauschning, Hermann, *Gespräche mit Hitler*, Zurich 1940.

Roskill, S. W., *The War at Sea*, Vol. 1, London, H.M. Stationery Office 1976.

Schmalenbach, Paul, *Die Geschichte der deutschen Schiffsartillerie*, Herford 1968.

Schmalenbach, Paul, *Kreuzer Prinz Eugen . . . unter 3 Flaggen*, Herford 1978.

Schmalenbach, Paul, *Warship Profile*, 18, Windsor, Berkshire.

Schnabel, Franz, *Deutsche Geschichte im Neunzehnten Jahrhundert*, Vol. II, Freiburg/Br. 1933.

Schofield, B. B., *Loss of the Bismarck*, London 1972.

Spörl, Johannes, ed., *Historisches Jahrbuch*, on commission for the Görres-Gesellschaft, 1955 (dedicated to Franz Schnabel).

Staatslexikon, Recht, Wirtschaft, Gesellschaft, edited by the Görres-Gesellschaft, Vol. XI, Freiburg 1970.

Stalmann, Reinhart, *Die Ausbrecherkönige von Kanada*, Hamburg 1958.

Steinmetz, Hans-Otto, *Bismarck und die deutsche Marine*, Herford.

Sulzbach, Herbert, *With the German Guns*, London 1973.

Toller, Ernst, *Eine Jugend in Deutschland*, Hamburg 1982 (original edition appeared in Amsterdam in 1933).

Tschirschky, Fritz, Günther von, *Erinnerungen eines Hochverräters*, Stuttgart 1972.

Wolff, Helmut, *Die deutschen Kriegsgefangenen in britischer Hand*, Munich 1974.

Wolff, Helmut, *Aufzeichnungen über die Kriegsgefangenen im Westen*, Bielefeld 1963.

II. Periodicals and Newspapers

Bidlingmaier, Gerhard, "Exploits and End of the Battleship *Bismarck*," *United States Naval Institute Proceedings*, July 1958.

Canadian Statesman, 11 November 1968.

Coler, Chr., "Bismarck und die See," *Wehrwissenschaftliche Rundschau*, Vol. 19 (1969).

Gribbohm, Günther, "Der Dolch des Mörders unter der Richterrobe," *Südschleswigsche Heimatzeitung*, 18 October 1969.

Schmalenbach, Paul, "Admiral Günther Lütjens," *Atlantische Welt* 1967.

Schmitt, Carl, "Der Führer schützt das Recht," on Adolf Hitler's address to the Reichstag on 13 July 1934, *Deutsche Juristen-Zeitung*, 1 August 1934, Munich and Berlin.

Schulze-Hinrichs, Alfred, "Schlachtschiff *Bismarck* und Seemannschaft," *Marine-Offizer-Verband Nachrichten*, Vol. 17, No. 1 (1968).

Flensburger Nachrichten, 28 August 1939.

Münchner Illustrierte, 1957: Original statements of *Bismarck* survivors.

The Review of Politics, (University of Notre Dame) Vol. XII (1950).

Voigt, F. A., "Yalta," *The Nineteenth Century and After*, No. DCCCXVII, March 1945.

Völkischer Beobachter, 18 December 1940.

III. Documents

A. Bundesarchiv-Militärchiv, Freiburg:

War Diary of the Battleship *Bismarck*, original and reconstructed.

War Diary of Naval Group Command North, May 1941.

War Diary of Naval Group Command West, May 1941.

Personal Notes of the Commander-in-Chief of the Navy, Grossadmiral Erich Raeder, January through June 1941.

Naval War Staff (Seekriegsleitung), preliminary instructions and operational orders, March 1941 through May 1941.

Naval War Staff, Situation Room Reports, 1941.

Naval War Staff, File "Rheinübung": *Bismarck* operation, after-action, and final reports.

Naval High Command (Oberkommando der Kriegsmarine), "Die Atlantikunternehmung der Kampfgruppe *Bismarck-Prinz Eugen,* Mai 1941," Berlin: *Marine-Dienst-Vorschrift* Nr. 601, October 1942.

Preliminary examination of Matrosengefreiter Herzog, Höntzsch, and Manthey on board the *U-74.*

Protocol of the statements by *Bismarck* survivors, recorded by Naval Group Command West, Paris, June 1941:

Matrosengefreiter Georg Herzog
Matrosengefreiter Otto Höntzsch
Matrosengefreiter Walter Lorenzen
Matrosengefreiter Herbert Manthey
Matrosengefreiter Otto Maus

War Diary of the *U-74,* 26–29 May 1941

War Diary of the *U-556,* 24–27 May 1941

Report on the operations of the battleship *Bismarck* by Weather Observation Ship 7 (*Sachsenwald*), Leutnant zur See (S) Wilhelm Schütte, 30 May 1941.

BA-MA Freiburg, III M 1005/7 KTB. 1 Skl Teil B V, extracts of various contents, January–June 1943, off-print from *Militärgeschichtliche Mitteilungen* 2/1973.

B. Other:

Reports of the German embassy in London, 1937–1939, and report of the German consulate in Glasgow, 1939. Archiv des Aüswärtigen Amtes, Bonn.

"Sinking of the German Battleship *Bismarck* on 27th May, 1941." Dispatch by Admiral Sir John Tovey, Supplement No. 3 to the *London Gazette,* 14 October 1947.

"Operations and Battle of German Battleship *Bismarck,* 23–27 May 1941." Narrative and enclosures (A) through (H), Intelligence Division, U.S. Navy Department.

Bock, Karl Heinrich, "Lebensabschnitte 1909–1950," unpublished.

"The Destruction of *U-202* by Ships of the Second Support Group on the 1st–2nd June 1943," Ref. ADM 199/1491, Anti U-Boat Division, Naval Staff, 5 July 1943.

Engel, Gerhard, edited and with commentary by Dr. Hildegard von Kotze, *Aufzeichnungen,* Stuttgart, 1974.

Second German Bundestag, 140th Session, 18 April 1956, Inquiry of the Social Democratic Party delegation regarding the speech of Kapitän zur See Zenker at Wilhelmshaven (Publication 2125).

Information on the *U-570* received by the author from the Naval Historical Branch, London, April 1971.

Institut für Zeitgeschichte, Munich, Zs 246 (Heye) and Zs 285 (Karl-Jesko von Puttkamer).

Kennedy, Ludovic, Script of BBC Television documentary "Rheinübung," March 1971.

People's Court (Volksgerichtshof), verdict in the case of Günther Paschen, 18 October 1943, 2 J 557/43, 1 L 132/43 and Paschen—FA 117/289, Führerinformation, Nuremberg Document NG-546 (Archive of the Institut für Zeitgeschichte).

Public Archives, Ottawa, Canada

RG 24 C1, C1, C 5407-7236-16-1		
RG 24 C1, vol. 2296, Oct. 1944–	Grande Ligne	
RG 24 C1, C 5416, May 1944–	Bowmanville	
RG 24 C	5396-7236-I-6-30	Bowmanville
RG 24 C	5370-7236-I-7-30	Bowmanville transfers
RG 24 C	5387-7236-46	Transfer of PoW, general
RG 24 C	5407-7236-85-I6-I	Anti-Nazis
RG 24 C	5416-94-6-30	Intelligence reports, Bowmanville
RG 24 C	5416-94-6-44	Intelligence reports, Grande Ligne
RG 24 C	5416-94-6-45	Intelligence reports, Sorel
RG 24 C	8249-31-1-30	PoW security Bowmanville
RG 24 C	8249-31-3-30	PoW security Bowmanville

Reichsgesetzblatt Part 1 No. 34 of 7 April 1933.

The Trial of the Major War Criminals before the International Military Tribunal, Nuremberg 1947, cited as IMT.

IMT XXXVII, pp. 546ff.

Schneider, Otto, "Letzte Begegnung," unpublished account.

Troubridge, Thomas, Captain, R.N., "Berlin Diary 1936–1939," unpublished.

West German Radio, "Stärker als Stacheldraht," transcript of a broadcast, 1963.

Woodward, E. L., ed., *Documents on British Foreign Policy 1919–1939*, Second Series, Vol. V, London, H.M. Stationery Office 1933.

C. Written and oral statements of *Bismarck* survivors.

IV. Correspondence

Dipl. Ing. Klemens Bartl, Augsburg, Federal Republic of Germany.

Captain Robert L. Bridges, USN (Ret), Castle Creek, New York.

Dr. Alfred Elsner, Hamburg, Federal Republic of Germany.

Herr Joachim Fensch, Weingarten, Federal Republic of Germany.

The Hon. James Galbraith, Jedburgh, Scotland.

Mr. William H. Garzke, Jr., Dumfries, Virginia.

Herr Franz Hahn, Mürwik, Federal Republic of Germany.

Mr. Daniel Gibson Harris, Ottawa, Canada.

Dr. Mathias Haupt, Bundesarchiv Koblenz, Federal Republic of Germany.

Lieutenant Commander B. J. Hennessy, R.N., Durban, South Africa.

Herr Bodo Herzog, Oberhausen, Federal Republic of Germany.

Herr Hans H. Hildebrand, Hamburg, Federal Republic of Germany.

Herr Konteradmiral a. D. Günther Horstmann, Basel, Switzerland.

Imperial War Museum, London.

Mr. Esmond Knight, London.

Mr. John Love, Newmarket, Suffolk, England.

Dr. Hansjoseph Maierhöfer, Chief Archivist, Bundesarchiv-Militärarchiv, Freiburg, Federal Republic of Germany.

Mr. Philip Mathias, Toronto, Canada.

Mrs. Mary Z. Pain, London.

Fregattenkapitän Dr. Werner Rahn, Mürwik, Federal Republic of Germany.

Professor Dr. Jürgen Rohwer, Stuttgart, Federal Republic of Germany.

Mr. James Rusbridger, St. Austell, England.

Dr. Hans Ulrich Sareyko, Auswärtiges Amt, Bonn, Federal Republic of Germany.

Franz Schad, UnivProf. em., MinDirigent a. D., Hattenhofen, Federal Republic of Germany.

Herr Rolf Schindler, Freiburg, Federal Republic of Germany.

Fregattenkapitän a. D. Paul Schmalenbach, Altenholz, Federal Republic of Germany.

Vice Admiral B. B. Schofield, Henley-on-Thames, England.

Kapitän zur See a. D. Hans-Henning von Schultz, Ramsau, Federal Republic of Germany.

Mr. George C. Seybolt, Dedham, Massachusetts.

Mr. S. W. Simpson, Shap Wells Hotel, England.

Herr Torsten Spiller, *Deutsche Dienststelle* (WASt), Berlin, Federal Republic of Germany.

Mr. Tom Wharam, Cardiff, Wales.

Kapitänleutnant a. D. Herbert Wohlfarth, VS-Villingen, Federal Republic of Germany.

Index

INDEX

Norfolk, HMS (crusier) *(cont.)*
  with the *Bismarck*, 27 May 1941,
  246–50, 447; fired at by the
  Bismarck, 131–32

Oberkommando der Kriegsmarine
  (OKM), 87, 116, 156, 192n, 221,
  449
Oberkommando der Wehrmacht
  (OKW), 361
Oberländer, Theodor, Professor, 379n
Oceana (barracks ship), 44
Oels, Hans, Fregattenkapitän, first
  officer of the *Bismarck*, 94–95, 98,
  144, 214; at commissioning
  ceremony, 30–31; in last battle, 254,
  265, 266, 269–71; last night on the
  Bismarck, 226; on possible
  differences with Lütjens and
  Lindemann, 149; responsibility for
  emergency drills, 57
Olga (corvette), 15n
Orwell, George (pseud.), 63

Paschen, Günther, Kapitän zur See
  a.D., 332–35
Passat (supply ship), 429
Patterson, W. R., Captain,
  commanding HMS *King George V*,
  242, 258, 275, 448n
Phillips, A.J.L., Captain, commanding
  HMS *Norfolk*, 244
Piorun (Polish destroyer), 215, 216,
  217, 220, 392
President, HMS (station ship), 328
Prince of Wales, HMS (battleship), 71,
  122, 123, 157, 166, 174, 176, 178,
  185, 201, 203, 289, 306; battle off
  Iceland, 137n, 139–40, 144, 147;
  after battle off Iceland, 149, 154,
  156, 158–60; damaged by the
  Bismarck, 145, 146; gunnery duels
  with the *Bismarck*, 164, 169;
  launched at Birkenhead, 19–20;
  sunk by Japanese, 348
Princess Royal, HMS (battlecruiser),
  333
Prinz Eugen (cruiser), 35, 70, 71, 72,
  98, 106, 107, 109, 112, 113, 116,
  117, 118, 119, 123, 127n, 128, 134,
  159, 160, 161, 163, 164, 165, 171,
  172, 176, 177, 178n, 182, 199, 228,

  255, 260, 302, 305, 306, 319; after
  battle off Iceland, 152, 153, 155; in
  battle off Iceland, 139, 142, 144,
  145, 149; cruiser warfare, 152, 160;
  damaged by mine, 85; deciphers
  Suffolk's contact signal, 130; orders
  for Exercise Rhine, 81–83, 85, 99,
  425, 431–34; picks up ship noises,
  135; in refueling exercise, 92–93;
  takes lead position in Denmark
  Strait, 132–33, 135
Prittie, Terence, 404n
Puttkamer, Karl Jesko von,
  Fregattenkapitän, 96, 98, 240

Queen Mary, HMS (battlecruiser), 144

Raeder, Erich, Grossadmiral,
  commander in chief of the
  Kriegsmarine, 49, 77, 78, 96, 127n,
  251, 300, 301, 302, 303, 334, 357,
  358, 430; birthday message to
  Lütjens, 185; confidence in Lütjens,
  239, 302; on German Navy, 323; on
  Hitler's waging of war, 323–24; on
  operational risks, 261, 302; on
  principles for surface warfare in the
  Atlantic, 85, 86; on resignation,
  400; reports to Hitler on Exercise
  Rhine, 97–98
Rahmlow, Hans, Kapitänleutnant,
  former commanding officer of
  U-570, 345–46, 348
Ramillies, HMS (battleship), 171–72,
  185, 201
Rangitiki, SS (passenger ship), 349,
  353
Rauschning, Hermann, 261–62
Ravenstein, Hans von,
  Generalleutnant, 378–79, 389,
  390–91
Rawalpindi, HMS (auxiliary cruiser),
  6, 172
Reichard, Kurt-Werner,
  Korvettenkapitän, chief of the fleet
  staff's B-Dienst team, 113, 114,
  116, 117
Reiner, Wolfgang, Leutnant zur See,
  adjutant to Lindemann, 59
Renown, HMS (battlecruiser), 118,
  137, 171, 173, 194, 198n, 201, 202,

About the Author

Burkard Baron von Müllenheim-Rechberg is a former naval officer, lawyer, and ambassador. Born in Spandau into a family where the profession of arms was an established tradition, he entered the navy of the Weimar Republic in 1929. During his naval career he served as an instructor at the Mürwik Naval School, as an assistant naval attaché at the German Embassy in London, and in cruisers and destroyers. He was assigned to the *Bismarck* in May 1940 and was the senior survivor at the time of her sinking on 27 May 1941.

In 1952 the Baron joined the diplomatic service of the Federal Republic of Germany and served in a variety of posts. At one time, he was Consul General in Toronto. He was also Ambassador to the West Indies, as well as to Zaire and Tanzania.

Baron von Müllenheim-Rechberg and his wife make their home near Munich, Bavaria.

THE NAVAL INSTITUTE PRESS

BATTLESHIP BISMARCK
A Survivor's Story
New and Expanded Edition

Designed by R. Dawn Sollars

Set in Trump and Benguiat
by BG Composition, Baltimore, Maryland

Printed on 60-lb. Glatfelter Offset B-16 regular finish
and bound in Holliston Roxite B
with Rainbow Natural Parchment endsheets
by The Maple-Vail Book Manufacturing Group,
York, Pennsylvania

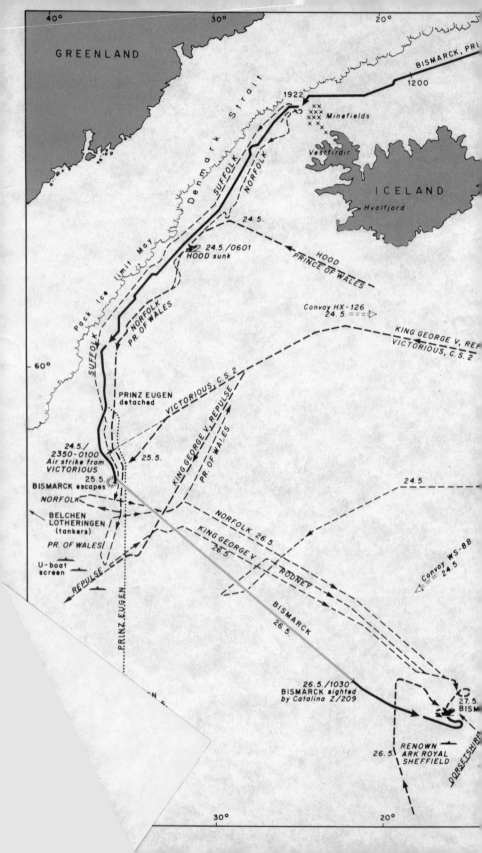

GREENLAND

ICELAND

Denmark Strait

Vestfirdir

Hvalfjord

BISMARCK, PRI

1200

1922

× ×
× × ×
× × × Minefields
× × ×
×

SUFFOLK

NORFOLK

24.5.

24.5./0601
HOOD sunk

HOOD
PRINCE OF WALES

Convoy HX-126
24.5.

KING GEORGE V, REP
VICTORIOUS, C.S.2

NORFOLK
PR. OF WALES

Pack Ice limit May

SUFFOLK

60°

PRINZ EUGEN
detached

VICTORIOUS C.S.2

24.5./
2350-0100
Air strike from
VICTORIOUS

25.5.

KING GEORGE V, REPULSE

PR. OF WALES

24.5.

25.5.
BISMARCK escapes

NORFOLK

BELCHEN
LOTHERINGEN
(tankers)

NORFOLK 26.5

PR. OF WALES

U-boat
screen

KING GEORGE V.
26.5.

RODNEY

REPULSE

Convoy WS-8B
24.5.

PRINZ EUGEN

BISMARCK
26.5

26.5./1030
BISMARCK sighted
by Catalina Z/209

27.5.
BISM

RENOWN
ARK ROYAL
SHEFFIELD

26.5.

DORSETSHIRE

40°   30°   20°

30°   20°